The Democrats

The Democrats

THE YEARS AFTER FDR

Herbert S. Parmet

Macmillan Publishing Co., Inc.

NEW YORK

Macmillan Publishing Co., Inc.
866 Third Avenue, New York, N.Y. 10022
Collier Macmillan Canada, Ltd.

Library of Congress Cataloging in Publication Data
Parmet, Herbert S
The Democrats
Bibliography: p.
Includes index.
1. Democratic Party. 2. United States—Politics
and government—1945–   I. Title.
JK2317.1976.P37   329.3   75-25990
ISBN 0-02-594770-2

First Printing 1976

Printed in the United States of America

For
Wendy Ellen Parmet

Contents

Preface

A venerable American cliché regards the two-party system as sacrosanct, as a fortuitous creation, the best guarantor of stability and political balance. Destroy it, the argument goes, sacrifice its utility for conformity, and the subsequent fragmentation will resemble ideological Balkanization. Liberals, conservatives, democratic socialists, Marxists, populists, reactionaries, and even regional sectarian interests, will inevitably dissipate themselves. The result will be chaos. Therefore, the price of the two-party system, with all its shortcomings, is much cheaper than any plausible alternatives, surely worth the inconvenience of having political organizations that must exist under a consensus so broad and with interests so diverse as to obviate the formulation of meaningful and constructive partisan programs.

After the death of Franklin D. Roosevelt, the Democratic Party was left without the cohesive influence of either a disastrous depression or a global war. Once again, the absence of a self-evident national emergency exposed partisan considerations to the vicissitudes of an umbrella organization, one that had to function somehow while placating a multitude of interests. For the majority, the forces that had become dominant, it was clear that there could be no return to the *status quo ante*. The necessity for a more carefully regulated society had been established; assumptions about economics and social welfare had become the ideology of the depression-born coalition, a legacy that could no more be undone than could Republicans deny their lineage with Lincoln and Emancipation simply to ingratiate themselves with the South. At the same time, however, keeping a working majority intact meant reconciling contradictory forces; such diverse figures as Harry Truman, Henry Wallace, Harry F. Byrd, Chester Bowles, Theodore Bilbo, and Hubert Humphrey all considered themselves Democrats. Could such an amalgam survive and respond with competence to a world of accelerating change?

The following account constitutes an examination of those forces that comprised the elements of the Democratic umbrella during the first three decades of the post-Roosevelt era, the years without either a Great Depression or a Pearl Harbor, decades that for all their turmoil may be regarded as a period of normality for the modern world. The experience, inevitably, questions the assumptions that have upheld the two-party system, raising doubts about the notion that accommodating diverse interests under a single umbrella is truly productive of the national interest, or whether it is really an anachronism retarding progress.

Once again, as with every major undertaking, the completion of the original goal requires the confidence of those willing to extend varied kinds of valuable assistance. To the State University of New York for its UAC/JAC Faculty Research Fellowship and Grant-in-Aid, I am particularly indebted for helping to support a portion of the research that went into the final product. Such individuals as my brother, Dr. Robert D. Parmet of York College of The City University of New York, and my talented long-time friend and former collaborator, Marie B. Hecht, were close to the project from its inception and contributed insights, encouragement, and advice until its fruition. As they have in the past, my wife and daughter mastered the art of coping with the chaotic existence and disruption of family life that "the book" makes inevitable.

Ultimately, every researcher must be indebted to the corps of men and women who provide the most basic prerequisites, access to the materials without which no serious book can ever be written. Both they and their institutions effectively constitute virtual field headquarters for traveling scholars, together with working facilities and other indispensable services. The congenial crew at the John F. Kennedy Library in Waltham, Massachusetts, took particular care to offer hospitality, thereby providing this researcher with edibles along with correspondence. Larry Hackman and Sylvie Turner, together with assistance from Donna Smerlas and Brenda Beasley, among others, helped to keep in sight the major objective of repeated trips to Waltham. Many thanks must also go to archivists in various other parts of the country, especially to Pamela Boll of the Earl Gregg Swem Library at the College of William and Mary; William Liebmann of the Herbert H. Lehman Papers at Columbia

University; Philip D. Lagerquist and Erwin Mueller at the Harry S Truman Library; Josephine L. Harper of the Historical Society of Wisconsin; Nancy Bressler for her invaluable organization of the Stevenson Papers at Princeton; H. G. Dulaney of the Sam Rayburn Library; Robert A. McCown of the University of Iowa; Mary Jo Pugh of the Bentley Historical Library at the University of Michigan; Father Thomas Blantz and Dr. Larry Bradley at Notre Dame; Michael F. Plunkett of the University of Virginia; and, at Yale, Diane Kaplan and the late Herman Kahn. Finally, appreciation is also due to such individuals as Harry Byrd, Jr., Virginius Dabney, Frank Mankiewicz, G. Fred Switzer, G. Mennen Williams, Hickman Price, and Paul H. Douglas, all of whom gave the author special access to collections, as well as to those who assisted through personal interviews and correspondence.

HERBERT S. PARMET
Bayside, New York
1975

PROLOGUE

★

A New Generation

They lined Constitution Avenue on that mild January afternoon to see a familiar scene: the four-wheeled caisson carrying the coffin; the riderless horse with boots placed backward in the stirrups; and the muffled drums of the Marine Corps Band. There was also the black limousine with the family of Lyndon Baines Johnson, followed by those carrying the president of the United States, Richard M. Nixon, and Vice President Spiro T. Agnew. Behind the spectators, on the grass just below the Senate Office Building, opposite the Capitol, stood a row of cannon prepared to fire a twenty-one-gun salute. Suddenly, as the procession reached Fourth Street, twenty-one Air Force fighter planes flew in formation overhead, a replica of the televised scene after the murder in Dallas in 1963. To spectators over forty, it also recalled memories of the death of Franklin D. Roosevelt, of the shock that had followed the news from Warm Springs, Georgia. But the procession that carried the body of Lyndon Johnson was an occasion that required more film than handkerchiefs.

For that afternoon, at least, the newly organized Ninety-third Congress suspended all other business to pay homage. Jake Pickle, the congressman from the district Johnson had once represented, said in his eulogy that his "presidency had changed America for the good and America will never be the same again." In the middle of Richard Nixon's Washington, there was a reminder of the recent past.

Events seemed to be moving swiftly that January, a month that had brought frigid weather to the capital city and finally, by the third week, a delightful thaw. Eager to see the new Congress organize itself, journalists were wandering from office to office attempting to assess the strength behind all the talk of challenges to the presidency. Some rambunctious freshmen seemed to offer hopes for change; but in early 1973, despite all the nasty stories circulating about Watergate, Richard Nixon was still clearly in control. Just the night before the procession down Constitution Avenue, he had announced that American boys had been relieved from the ground war in Vietnam. He had also used that occasion to note that his late predecessor had "endured the vilification of those who sought to portray him as a man of war, but there was nothing he cared about more deeply than achieving a lasting peace in the world."[1] In an extended press conference, Dr. Henry Kissinger was explaining the details of the negotiations.

"Bullshit," said one Democrat, talking back to a radio in his Rayburn House Office Building suite.

Along with many of his angry constituents, the congressman, a liberal Democrat from the Northeast, was more interested in explanations about the recent massive bombing of Vietnam and the audacity behind the continued sponsorship of President Thieu and his government. He was more liberal than most, highly respected, a veteran and established leader; and, despite Nixon's great electoral victory during the previous fall, he and his colleagues still retained the partisan dominance that had been interrupted only for brief periods since 1930. Still, Washington had become a Republican fortress. The White House was supreme. The executive branch and its powerful departments and agencies seemed omnipotent.

For all their paper strength, confidence was lacking in their ability to mount an effective partisan challenge. An extended tour of congressional and senatorial offices brought many platitudes about the party's past accomplishments: it was, of course, the party with "a heart," the party that "cared about people," the party for the little guy, the party of Roosevelt, the party of Truman, the party of the New Deal, Fair Deal, New Frontier, Great Society, the party that obviously stood in counterpoise to the big-business-dominated Republicans who cared only about stocks, dividends, and investments. Rare, however, was a specific word about what should be done now, except, of course, to challenge the president's usurpation of power. Endless references were made to the great diversity of the Democrats, to the fact that it was hardly a party at all in the European sense but an umbrella organization, one that had to cope with many factions. A former national chairman, Larry O'Brien, shared that lament as he observed, "The Democratic party today remains a fragmented national party, badly bruised by years of internal struggle."[2]

Only during two years of the otherwise unfortunate presidency of Lyndon Johnson had they, in recent times, resembled effective progressives. But unlike Nixon, who committed presidential suicide, the Johnson regime was aborted by his fellow Democrats. Nevertheless, before his fall, the Texan had demonstrated that the "fighting faiths" that had enabled the New Deal to reshape the party had not been entirely upset by time. On the day his body arrived in Washington to lie in state under the Capitol dome, the Washington *Post* appeared with a tribute by columnist Nicholas von Hoffman. "You were a big 'un, Lyndon," it said. "We're going to miss you, you old booger, and we're going to know, regardless of official proclamations, you deserve better than to be saluted, left at half-mast and forgotten."[3]

The death of the ex-president recalled an afternoon at the LBJ ranch nearly three years earlier. The man who had been so recently the most powerful individual in the world, defying his critics by insisting on both "guns and butter" and antagonizing old supporters almost daily, stepped out through a door that led to the front porch. He had been working in the fields under the hot late June sun of central Texas and appeared ruddy but tired, almost lethargic. He confirmed the success of his recovery after having been hospitalized only recently, but he was much more eager to comment about news reports that the communists had extended their domination to almost one-third of Cambodia. "When I left the White House," he said with satisfaction, "they didn't even have a fifth."

He had good things to say for just about everybody; almost nostalgic about his accomplishments as the party's Senate majority leader, he was eager to dispel his image as a "wheeler-dealer" who succeeded by "twisting arms." "I never tried to force anybody to do what he didn't want to do," he insisted. He merely gave advice and tried to show the way to do what was best for the country.

His only criticism was directed at Richard Nixon. He said he didn't like Nixon because the Republican had been "too partisan," a quality that Johnson admitted had been tempered somewhat since he had become president. As for himself, Johnson maintained that he had never considered partisanship very important or even desirable and, as majority leader, had rejected the concept that the duty of the opposition was, simply, to oppose. The responsibility, he insisted, was to the nation. The best interests meant supporting the president whenever possible and "trying to be constructive."

He wanted to be a progressive, he said, without being a radical.

He wanted to move ahead with advanced measures, but not so fast that the ultimate goals would be jeopardized. Progress had to be achieved with great care, a point very few seemed to understand. Nor did many seem to understand him, which did not keep them from writing anything they pleased. "One of my men," he recalled, "once brought me a stack of about a dozen books. All of them about me. Not one was written by anyone who came to see me. But they all wrote, anyway. I didn't give a damn about any of them and still haven't read a single one." All he really cared about, Johnson added, regardless of what anyone else may have thought, was to help people who needed help.

His face brightened considerably when his little grandson, Lyn Nugent, came out to join him and climbed on his lap. Their closeness was obvious.

"Tell the man what you call me," the former president said to the child.

"Poppy," said the boy.

"Now show the man what you'll do when you're running to be the president. What are you gonna do when all those people stand in front of the train waiting to see you?"

The child promptly waved to the imaginary electorate and then Grandfather looked pleased.

It was time to take Lyn for a walk. Holding the child's hand, Johnson strolled across the front lawn, facing the nearby Pedernales River. "You know," he suddenly said, without having been asked, "I want Lyn to be able to say that his grandfather gave the people medical care and civil rights and tried to wipe out poverty—or at least as much as they'd let me do. Someday he'll finish the job."[4]

Johnson had tried. Within two years after taking over from John F. Kennedy, he had secured passage of the most ambitious social program since the New Deal; and in the area of human rights had affected housing, voting, travel, employment, and the basic prerogatives of equality.

Such measures had been pushed by the man whose selection as Kennedy's running-mate had drawn cries of outrage from liberal northern delegations. Of all the potential candidates for the party's nomination that year, he had been the most unacceptable among the party's liberals, even more suspect than the oldest son of Ambassador Joseph P. Kennedy. Hadn't he come out of the conservative politics of Texas? And hadn't his crowd represented the conservative faction? Certainly, he was anathema to the state's lonely liberals, such as

Ralph Yarborough; and he had fronted for the oilmen, coddled the tycoons, and tarried with the bigots. One muckraker wrote that "where Johnson is concerned, what at first appears to be unction will usually turn out to be pure petroleum."[5] Consistently, he had opposed efforts to pass civil rights legislation; and before the first modern law for racial justice finally cleared the Senate in 1957, he assured its impotence. As the opposition leader to the conservative Eisenhower administration, he often appeared as a more faithful ally than numerous Republicans. As president, he waged a war complete with relentless bombing that outraged virtually the entire liberal establishment and provoked a revolt of the nation's youth and all the "nervous Nellies."

And yet he had also been a staunch New Dealer. Franklin D. Roosevelt had been his mentor and hero; loyally, he had stood up for the president during the Court-packing controversy, when even such faithful disciples as New York's Herbert Lehman came out in opposition. Cabinet officers who served under both Kennedy and Johnson considered Johnson as the one with the greater degree of sensitivity for the nation's deprived, both black and white.[6] The personality of Lyndon Johnson became as closely identified with the Great Society as FDR's with the New Deal.

As with Harry Truman before him, and later Richard Nixon, he had been effectively driven from office. The elements of support had been shattered, both in the streets and in Congress. From the captaincy of the Great Society, his leadership had deteriorated and provoked passionate divisions. The rift was tripartite: whites versus blacks; the North against the South; the intellectuals versus what Nixon would later call "the silent majority." Diverse classes of Caucasians were belligerently aligned; but standing apart were those less enchanted with the American faith in inevitable progress within the sanctified "system." It nourished Republicans and decimated the Democrats. The party over which Lyndon Johnson had presided both from Capitol Hill and from Pennsylvania Avenue had fractured once more, resembling the condition of political movements in early America, the concentration of coteries around dominant personalities. By the time Johnson surprised the nation with his statement withdrawing from the 1968 campaign, the Democratic Party was an impotent anachronism. Unable to preserve its consensus under the Johnson leadership, it was unable to govern.

Its only remaining base was common aversion to the GOP. Beyond that, there were as many differences from left to right as among the French deputies after the fall of the Bastille: the New Left, a movement that included Marxists, Maoists, democratic socialists, and assorted radicals who shared an alienation from the consensus that was justifying capitalism; the antiwar "children's crusade" behind the perplexing Eugene McCarthy, a hero of the Vietnamese War doves; the workers, blacks, and Chicanos who turned to Robert F. Kennedy for help; the middle-class-oriented workers, especially those of organized labor, and the children of the New Deal who still regarded Hubert Humphrey as FDR's legitimate successor; and the uneducated and unsophisticated and just desperate workers and little people who knew that something was wrong and who saw in George Wallace deliverance from the intellectuals, social planners, and capitalists who simply failed to understand that they, too, had dreams, needs, and frustrations. Their common distrust of Republicanism devolved on to what degree Democrats should share the basic assumptions that characterized what had become the party of Barry Goldwater, Richard Nixon, and Ronald Reagan. Their loose association under the umbrella recalled a much-quoted Will Rogers observation, "I'm not a member of any organized political party. I'm a Democrat."

During the Nixon years, Rogers' jest gained new currency. After LBJ, the party found itself unable to use the latent support it still commanded to make repairs and return to power behind new leadership supported by a revived coalition. Hopeful as it then seemed, as enthusiastic as the youngsters had been in New Hampshire in 1968, when they sacrificed beards to solicit votes by being "clean for Gene," they never had a credible chance to get their man into power. McCarthy himself seemed to have a coy aversion to leadership, and Bobby (everybody seemed to call him that) had been killed in a Los Angeles hotel kitchen, just as his primary election campaign was getting more hopeful. Ed Muskie, everybody's second choice, had become a victim of Nixon dirty tricks. His tears in defense of Mrs. Muskie had been impolitic, upsetting to the American concept of masculinity and leadership. George McGovern and his band of idealists and tacticians filled the vacuum in July but disintegrated by November, another in a series of comparisons with the Goldwater campaign of 1964. Meanwhile, large numbers of Humphrey people, the very ones who had complained about defections on the left four years earlier, decided that Nixon was the lesser of two evils and contributed their votes to the greatest of all landslides. Still, what was left of the Roosevelt legacy was sufficiently large to retain control of both houses of Congress.

But, as the Ninety-third Congress convened, and the death of Johnson provided a brief reminder of the last years of Democratic control of the White House, the outlook was uncertain for those who remained convinced that the Democratic Party was still the best, if not the only, force left to improve society and replenish the political system. Rarely in the nation's history, even during the years of the Great Depression, had so many found so much to criticize. From among the ranks of those once counted as instinctive Democrats was a strident anti-Americanism that implicitly accepted the American dream but gave it a radical twist. If meaningful change could be achieved through constitutional devices, at least given that assumption, it could only come from those who spoke for the discontented, displaced, and disfranchised. So it was with confidence that democratic socialist Michael Harrington, in organizing a new force to work within the existing party, declared: "We believe that the left wing of realism is found today in the Democratic Party. It is there that the mass forces for social change are assembled; it is there that the possibility exists for creating a new first party in America."[7]

PART ONE

★

Disintegration

CHAPTER I

★

A New Era

1

Franklin D. Roosevelt's death on April 12, 1945, left a Democratic Party that had been realigned and given substantial ideological focus. Its various interest groups had formed a majority coalition that sought to ameliorate past grievances. More clearly than before, personal income and partisanship were related as, for many, past allegiances to the party of Lincoln and Theodore Roosevelt had been severed by economic policies that signaled the federal government's acceptance of responsibility for public welfare.

A new assumption, then, had instituted the new liberalism: that a civilized state could not remain indifferent toward those at the mercy of the economic system. Ample evidence had demonstrated that laissez-faire capitalism had never existed in any pure sense and that it was a myth perpetrated by those who proclaimed its virtues and profited from its selective acceptance. In the very nature of things, indifference—granting even true neutrality toward financial interests—encouraged the extension of power at the expense of the powerless. The self-destructive contradiction of that force had finally led to the great crash and the subsequent Great Depression.

The economic chaos had produced the New Deal, an expedient combination of pragmatism and ideology that, for all its shortcomings, nevertheless offered hope not only to the businesses that would thus be saved from themselves but to the underprivileged as well. The old Democracy was redefined and realigned. Republicans had dominated American politics since 1860, had pursued the policies of economic disaster during the 1920s, and had fatalistically supported Herbert Hoover for a second time amid the almost total collapse of 1932. But their vital sources of strength had been sapped, and the Democrats had become a majority force. Black Americans who could vote were forsaking Lincoln for FDR. Older-generation Jews, mostly of German origin, also moved away from Republicanism in large numbers and joined the political affiliation of their eastern European co-religionists. Irish Catholics, largely urbanized and already deeply committed to the party of Tammany Hall paternalism and Al Smith, were augmented by additional ethnic groups that entered the cities. Most belonged to the working class. Many farmers, particularly the smaller, independent growers, also followed the trend. Additional support came from progressives whose Republican loyalties had become increasingly tenuous since the William Howard Taft/ Theodore Roosevelt split of 1912. All added to the solid base of support already contributed by the South. By the end of the Depression and World War II, America's two major parties looked less like the Tweedledum and Tweedledee twins that Lord James Bryce had written about.

But even before the passing of Roosevelt and the nuclear finale to the global conflict, disharmony was clearly evident. Southern bourbons, traditionally Democratic, were recoiling at northern domination. Not only had it meant economic policies repugnant to nascent industrial interests, but the marriage between the Democratic Party and organized labor was offensive. Conservative businessmen had long since fallen out from under the New Deal and had begun to rebel against the leadership that had fostered stronger unions, higher taxes, governmental bureaucracy, and interference with the prerogatives of management. Many had become supporters of the dissenting American Liberty League. On January 8, 1938, Secretary of Interior Harold Ickes noted in his diary, "It is clear that the war is on fiercer than ever between the reactionaries and the liberals within the Democratic Party. What the result will be, God alone knows."[1] The consequences of the president's attempted purge of anti-New Dealers after the attack against a "horse-and-buggy" Supreme Court widened the rift.

There were, in addition, signs of cracks in the impressive support that had been given to the party by Roman Catholics, particularly the Irish Democrats. Al Smith's hostility to Roosevelt, even leading to his prominence as a Liberty Leaguer, had been significant. The open and vitriolic rebellion by the noted "radio priest" and ex-Roosevelt supporter, Father Charles Coughlin, and his publication, *Social Justice*, influenced a considerable following to whom the New Deal was both dangerously liberal, Jewish, and close to Great Britain. They recoiled when dedicated Roosevelt partisans devoted themselves to the support of the Spanish republican government against Generalissimo Francisco Franco. Ironically, then, despite the administration's use of the Neutrality Act that helped seal the death of the republic, Catholics had found new reasons to equate liberalism with anticlericalism. During the 1940 campaign, many Irish Catholics joined Coughlin behind Wendell Willkie, although the Republican candidate emphatically repudiated the priest's support.[2] In New York City, substantial inroads were made into normally solid Democratic majorities; several Irish Republicans in Brooklyn won seats in the state legislature after local leaders had worked to sabotage the Roosevelt campaign.[3] After FDR won his fourth term, *The Catholic World* declared that his election may be "a mortal blow to democracy. The political party which until recent years advocated decentralization, home-rule, local self-government, division of power between the states and the nation, distribution of authority among the three branches of the Federal Government, was designated as 'Democratic.' Since 1932 that party has been in decline. . . . Democracy in America is more nearly dead than it ever was before."[4]

It was a critique that was seconded by a significant number of southerners as well. Eliminating the two-thirds rule for selecting presidential candidates, a landmark change that occurred during the 1936 Democratic national convention, had virtually deprived the South of its power to veto nominees. Described by one scholar as a "giant, nation-wide cornucopia from which federal aid poured into the desperately Depression-ridden South," the New Deal nevertheless precipitated revolts from conservatives in the very region that had gotten most assistance.[5] A variety of developments, then, were combining to weaken the future loyalty of the solid South: its declining influence within the party, economic policies that threatened its competitive advantages over northern industry, worry about the enhanced status of subservient black labor, the creation of a new urban middle class, and the Supreme Court's rejection of the white primary. More and more, southerners were echoing John Calhoun's protests about northern exploitation. Liberal politician Ellis Arnall, who had been Georgia's governor since 1943, argued that "the most immediate question for America to decide is whether this country is to be one nation, or whether it shall permit an empire-within-the-nation, to turn the great part of our common country into colonial appendages and make the people of the South and West inmates of gigantic almshouses."[6] Battles over the right of labor to strike during wartime and over the legality of having soldiers able to vote without paying poll taxes portended further cleavages between North and South.[7]

So the war itself had not entirely soothed the sources of rebellion. There had been such setbacks to the Roosevelt leadership as the overriding of his veto of the Smith-Connally Act. But, for the most part, the coalition had managed to come through intact. Conservative businessmen found ample influence in wartime Washington, a prominence, in fact, that had not been had since the earliest days of the New Deal.[8] Despite the bitterness that had already appeared, Roman Catholics were still overwhelmingly Democratic and intended to remain that way; and despite southern grievances, Dixie seemed unalterably Democratic. Republicanism still connoted Black Reconstruction and high tariffs for Yankee industrialists. So it was laughter and applause that greeted Mrs. Lennard Thomas, the national committeewoman from Alabama, when she told the Democratic National Committee's meeting in 1944, "I assure you that next November down South, it's going to rain and probably snow, but it won't be Dewey."[9] Further, most Americans, despite their traditional hostility toward communism and fear of the Soviet Union, shared aspirations for a peaceful postwar world.

"It makes me feel a little better to know that the *whole* world is not going reactionary and that there are still some people willing to speak out vigorously for the principles of the New Deal," wrote Chester Bowles to Vice President Henry Wallace, "and for the kind of international understanding and collaboration on which our future will depend."[10] Just one week after his fourth election, the president spoke at Soldiers Field in Chicago and promised a future that included an "Economic Bill of Rights" and sixty million jobs.

2

On March 1, 1945, only thirty-six hours after he had returned from Yalta, Franklin D. Roosevelt sat under the spotlights in the well of the House. Few knew that he was dying; but he was noticeably grayer and thinner and some thought he had aged considerably since his last appearance before Congress some two years earlier. The applause that had greeted his arrival in the chamber was not for any ordinary president of the United States: it was for "Dr. Win the War," for the man who, having provided resuscitation from the throes of the Great Depression, was completing his final monumental mission.

He began by ignoring the prepared text. Apologizing for the "unusual posture of sitting down during the presentation of what I want to say," he explained that it would be much easier "not having to carry about ten pounds of steel around on the bottom of my legs." So the tone was set. The delivery was unlike a speech. It resembled an earnest talk, a professor describing his findings before his seminar. As he spoke, there was little applause, but his audience was attentive. When he finished, nearly an hour later, Americans had reasons for hope about avoiding a future war, if everything would go as the conferees had planned.

Roosevelt explained that military realities had influenced diplomacy; he had done his best and so had the big three powers, the United States, England, and Russia. Areas that appeared to be falling within national "spheres of influence," a concept that was "incompatible with the basic principles of international collaboration," had been the focus of the most intensive negotiations. Germany and eastern Europe were of particular significance. Poland had necessitated special arrangements. With Churchill and Stalin, however, compromises had been made that involved boundary adjustments and agreements to secure a broad-based coalition government that would function independently of Moscow. Efforts to establish a United Nations and find a "common ground for peace," the president told the Congress, warranted their approval despite the many doubts. He acknowledged that he, too, had reservations about what had been accomplished.[11]

That same day, news was made by another event. Like the circumstances that surrounded the president's message, the development was a product of the past and raised questions about the future. It was the confirmation, at last, of the former vice president, Henry Wallace, to become the new secretary of commerce, in a rather perfunctory vote to install a successor to Jesse Jones. It was accomplished by a fairly secure fifty-six to thirty-two roll-call. Finally successful in getting a cabinet seat, Wallace was one of the symbols of the New Deal, a man whose influence could be expected to mold the direction of postwar liberalism. The event seemed to at least compensate for his having been deprived of a second term as vice president and replaced by the uncertain liberalism of Senator Harry S Truman of Missouri. "This is written to let you know that many of us 'New Deal' Democrats resent the pushing of Mr. Henry A.

Wallace out of the Vice Presidency," wrote two loyalists to the president, "and now we want him put in a position where he can do the most for the majority of the people."[12]

So it seemed to have been a good day for supporters of the administration. Dissent had been minimal; there was hope for peace and progressivism. Not far below the surface, however, despite the general satisfaction, lay growing divisions that would widen and have profound consequences for the Democratic Party.

For one, the initial reaction to the Yalta speech revealed little of the hostility that ultimately equated that conference with the prewar session at Munich that gave appeasement a sordid connotation. Most of those who heard the president's report wanted to believe that he had indeed accomplished his mission, that unlike Woodrow Wilson's predicament after World War I, solid gains had been achieved. Lessons had been learned. At last there had been acceptance of the need to stop aggressors by bold, swift responses; parochial national interests had to yield to broad global cooperation for the preservation of a stable international order.

Less hopeful that the president had returned with anything of merit was Senator Burton K. Wheeler. The progressive New Dealer, who had later become prominent in opposition to American involvement in World War II, reacted to Roosevelt's speech by pointing out that "unfortunately, the actions of Great Britain and particularly of Russia do not inspire in thinking people the hopes the President seeks to have."[13] Two months earlier, Wheeler had delivered a radio broadcast denouncing the Allied policy of "unconditional surrender" as a brutal means of enabling the Soviet Union to dominate eastern Europe. "Certainly," he warned, "we are not fighting this war to transfer the control of Europe from Hitler to Stalin or to Stalin and Churchill."[14]

Resolving the Wallace matter also exposed party strains. To describe the final settlement as routine suggests a contrast with the bitter and deep-seated divisions that had preceded the vote, but the reality was that his confirmation had become possible only after his post was stripped of significant monetary powers. It was a southern Democrat, Senator Walter George of Georgia, who introduced a bill to remove all lending agencies from the control of the Commerce Department. Majority leader Alben Barkley of Kentucky carefully assured the president that the matter involved merely the principle of whether the agencies should remain within Commerce or should be independent.[15] Still, the tactics employed over the George bill nevertheless gave sufficient evidence that, for conservatives, the real principle involved whether so fervent a New Dealer should control the money. The vice president of the F. W. Woolworth Company, in a letter to a Virginia industrialist, expressed pleasure that Senator Harry F. Byrd had taken the lead in opposition to the nomination. "I don't know of any appointment that has been made in Washington that stands out as being quite as ridiculous and dangerous," he wrote.[16] When the final vote came, it was after all the safeguarding of financial powers from the clutches of the "irresponsible" Mr. Wallace had been achieved. Even then, his confirmation brought nays from such key Democrats as Kenneth McKellar of Tennessee and Byrd of Virginia, as well as Wilbert Lee ("Pappy") O'Daniel of Texas and Tom Stewart of Tennessee. They had been unmoved by the argument of fellow southerner Lister Hill of Alabama that the "malignance and hysteria" that had opposed Wallace should be put aside so that the "base of support" for the government could be strengthened during the critical years.[17] Nor was *The Tablet* pacified. The organ of the Archdiocese of Brooklyn, a paper that reached one of the country's most significant concentrations of Catholic Democrats, warned that replacing Jesse Jones with Wallace would be tantamount to having CIO president Sidney Hillman supplant General Dwight D. Eisenhower.[18]

The issue had been obvious. "Make no mistake about it," warned the liberal *New Republic,* for "this is a fight against Roosevelt and the New Deal."[19] Wallace had come to represent the continuity of all Roosevelt symbolized to the new coalition. Letters from the public expressed a common theme: diluting Wallace's authority represented a betrayal of New Deal liberalism and a surrender to vested interests. A Pasadena, California, woman pleaded to the president: "I, and undoubtedly many others who worked just as hard or harder than I, shall feel that we have been let down if the conservative Jesse Jones is given preference over Mr. Wallace during the next four years."[20] From Orlando, Florida, came a telegram urging the consideration of the "little man" as against "Jones whom I personally have known for years as a hardbitten Texas banker who wouldn't give me or any other little fellow consideration because I am just too darn little."[21]

On April 12, Roosevelt died. A stunned nation could not believe he was gone. He had stood for hope, humanity, freedom, and democracy; and for millions who preferred to forget the past, he had become the personification of the Democratic Party.

3

    The combative little man with glasses was sworn in somberly, quickly. With virtually no preparation, he had risen to the top because FDR had considered him less harmful politically than any other potential candidate for the vice presidency. He was from a border state, his ancestry included Confederates, and he seemed to augur some relief from the hostility coming from Dixie. At the very least, the most rabid anti-Roosevelt elements of the party could suspend judgments for awhile, and even former Vice President John Nance Garner was hopeful. "I was particularly pleased to note that you all were going to get behind Truman and help him all you can," Garner wrote to Sam Rayburn on April 18. "That is the proper spirit. Truman is honest and patriotic and has a head full of good horse sense. Besides, he had guts. All of this can be made into a good President."[22]

CHAPTER II

In the Name of Jefferson

1

John Nance Garner stood with many from below the Mason-Dixon line who were hopeful about Truman. After all, southern pressure had been instrumental in persuading Roosevelt to dump Wallace, a determination compounded by the growing suspicion that FDR could not possibly survive a fourth term. Further, although Truman's voting record had supported the New Deal, the South generally saw him as a safe national leader, one who did not symbolize the more leftist impulses of the Roosevelt era. Truman's much-praised congressional investigation of the defense program had brought him national respectability. His best publicized ideological view was hardly anathema to most Americans: the hope that the Nazis and the Russians would destroy each other, a point of view expressed before Pearl Harbor. Moreover, and vital to the Roosevelt interest, he had provoked less opposition than had any of the other potential running-mates; so while he could not have been rated as the South's first choice, neither did he threaten their interests.

A Truman presidency might even be second best to getting Harry Byrd into the White House. Byrd himself was assured, within days of the new chief executive's inaugural, that the rather nondescript politician was a "man of unimpeachable integrity, energetic and courageous and able."[1] Similar expectations were consistent with Garner's confidence, expectations that, as it turned out, were without much knowledge of the man.

Truman's elevation also coincided with the liquidation of the European war and the final push toward victory in the Pacific. He had been vice president for less than three months and had served the traditionally innocuous role. He knew only the bare outlines of the Allied diplomacy that worked to mold the postwar world and, upon his subsequent accidental rise to the White House, found him-

self an outsider who had been ignorant about the secret of the
atomic bomb. For a politician of limited stature, the situation was
indeed awesome, fully justifying the humility with which he approached his new burdens. To further complicate matters, he inherited the intraparty rift.

In the South, even the most ardent conservatives continued to
regard the Democratic Party as the only tolerable political force.
Republicanism was synonymous with the Civil War and Radical
Reconstruction, as well as high tariffs, discriminatory railroad
freight rates, and isolationism. Members of the GOP were among
those favoring the extension of equal rights to Negroes and their
party's 1944 platform had actually endorsed equality in employment. Moreover, Republicans continued to stand for everything
repugnant to the commercial interests of the South. They were the
chief exploiters of Dixie, the ones most likely to keep the region a
virtual colonial appendage of Yankee capitalism, perpetuating the
"conquered province" that was stripped of constitutional safeguards.
So while the South would ultimately spawn converts to the old
enemy and would be seduced twice by Eisenhower, consumed by
Goldwater, and romanced by Nixon, substantial resistance remained
before there could be serious desertions to the party of Lincoln,
Thaddeus Stevens, and Calvin Coolidge. Instead of embracing the
GOP, southerners accepted the need to recapture the machinery of
their own party.

To Byrd it was axiomatic that northerners were the ones who
needed to change, for it was they who were ensnared by alien elements and had to be freed from such concepts. In their disregard of
the South, they were traducing the party's most basic and loyal region, the region that provided the fundamental bloc of electoral
votes needed to carry presidential elections. The South contributed
solid congressional delegations that continued to save the legislature
from Republican rule and, in its attempts to preserve the principles
of Jeffersonian democracy, asked only for social, political, and economic independence. To those who noted that Byrd's Senate voting
record was consistent with the Republicans instead of his own party
and that he had opposed the New Deal almost from the start, he
liked to explain that he still supported FDR—that is, the 1932 presidential candidate who had extolled the virtues of balanced budgets.
Byrd's Virginia colleague, A. Willis Robertson, viewed himself as a
force within the party working for the preservation of states' rights
and American constitutional freedom.[2]

For a region with intramural, one-party politics, the situation had become desperate. Without substantial political and ideological competition, with an electorate well restricted by poll taxes that deprived the poor of both races from credible citizenship, with a largely rural base that offered the lowest level of education in the nation, power was in the hands of the few. They owned the farms and plantations, the large tracts of land still worked by sharecroppers or leased to industry; they were also the industrialists, the realtors, bankers, lawyers, and communications leaders. Allied with them, and usually their agents, were the politicians. Every now and then, through the force of personality and the creation of successful independent factions, there were independents who often expressed progressive or populist positions. But the conventional professional derived his power from the feudal-commercial establishment.

To such leaders, the idea of a "new" South had special significance, the growth of an industrial base that would provide much-needed economic momentum. Gallup pollsters demonstrated in 1943 that this vision was not confined to a chosen few but was shared, in fact, by seven out of ten southerners.[3] It had become an article of faith, among both diehards and moderates, that ending dependence upon the North meant freeing Dixie of her "colonial" status. Given such advances, left to her own devices and resources, the region would ultimately solve the most pressing problems, including the fulfillment of its paternalistic responsibility toward the large black population.

Southerners, of course, had no trouble supporting the administration's conduct of the war. Few had forgotten the loyal backing they had given Wilson during World War I. Fighting back was the traditional Dixie way. Incidental to such patriotic responses, of course, were the wartime economic benefits and, from Secretary of State Cordell Hull and General of the Army George C. Marshall on down, southern representation was significant at the most vital levels of military and domestic mobilization. So the war at least provided partial relief from the smoldering resentments. But the national emergency nevertheless failed to resolve basic differences.

In fact, there is ample evidence that the discord only widened because of changes brought by the war; and since the term "solid South" was synonymous with Democratic Party dominance, the rift was bound to have broader implications. Hardly ignored was the fact that the decision in the case of *Smith v. Allwright* of 1944, which declared as unconstitutional the white primary elections of Texas, had been handed down by the "Roosevelt Court." Further, the activities of the CIO's Political Action Committee (CIO-PAC) among wartime industrial workers in southern towns and cities were suspected of being closely tied to the administration, as was the soldiers' voting act of 1942, a measure that exempted GIs from paying poll taxes.[4] In the midst of the war, even the general principle behind the taxes had come under direct attack. Besieged, southern leadership hoped that Truman would bring relief.

2

Richard M. Dalfiume has pointed out that "The democratic ideology and rhetoric with which the war was fought stimulated a sense of hope and certainty in black Americans that the old race structure was destroyed forever."[5] Even in the South, resistance to Jim Crow was becoming evident as regional population shifts, principally from farm to city, were helping to speed the process. Black preachers and newspaper editors had begun to demolish the complacent delusion that Negroes were happy to live with the traditional system. Such spokesmen cited the nation's wartime democratic pronouncements that contradicted the realities of life in Dixie. Sympathetic reactions did follow, with the loudest contempt reserved for those moderates who advised continued accommodation with the sociopolitical mores.

"The issue of segregation seems now to be paramount in the thinking of all the Negro leaders," wrote Virginius Dabney. "Three or four years ago they never admitted that they wanted to get rid of segregation, and in fact frequently denied that they had such an objective."[6]

Dabney himself exemplified the southerners caught up in the crossfire between the new awareness and the status quo. The influential editor of the Richmond *Times Dispatch* and author of books and articles that attempted to emphasize the positive side of southern enlightenment agreed that segregation was often harsh and unjust. He considered some of its aspects hypocritical and detrimental to the system it supposedly served. Such hints of liberalism, however, were leavened with the belief that more humane standards could be achieved even while tolerating continued segregation on the theory that legislation would be no more effective than had been the attempt to outlaw liquor.[7] Extravagant steps, measures that would satisfy the militant reformers, also contained the threat of violence that could bring bloodshed instead of progress. Consequently, Dabney intellectualized his opposition to any permanent Fair Employment Practices Commission (FEPC), such as the one introduced in 1945 by Representative Mary Norton of New Jersey, that would impose fines and even jail sentences for offending employers. In 1942 and 1943, his editorial admonitions of the black press for "extremism" and for "demanding an overnight revolution in race relations" that threatened to produce "interracial hate" brought swift denunciations from many Negro papers.[8]

In late 1943, however, Dabney exposed himself to the other side of the question. He urged the city of Richmond to desegregate its buses. It was a suggestion that contained nothing radical, merely simple recognition of what was logical and sensible in view of what was actually happening. The transit lines, he pointed out, were so crowded anyway that attempts to separate the races were futile. Dabney's position won surprising support from liberal organizations, especially the Southern Conference for Human Welfare, the most determined force operating within Dixie to aid the politically and economically disadvantaged.

The essential conflict that frustrated the Dabney moderates was duplicated elsewhere, within an organization usually credited with working toward racial equality, the Southern Regional Council (SRC). Organized in 1944, it was an elite group that aimed at analyzing and working for the betterment of conditions. Dabney was a member along with fellow editors of both races, and the membership included clergymen, labor leaders, businessmen, educators, and other professionals.

Still, by no means did the organization take a clearly affirmative stand. As some members pressed for clearer commitments behind the cause of racial justice, others became more resistant. Dabney helped to provoke the dichotomy at the organization's session of late 1944 by calling on the SRC to go on record accepting segregation as "the law of the land" while expressing nevertheless a willingness to work within that framework to improve conditions for Negroes. One black newspaper publisher from Houston led the fight for Dabney's resolution; but the other Negro members opposed it firmly and the tactic was rejected by about two to one.[9] Dr. Guy Johnson, the SRC's executive director, reacted to the conflict by despairing that the organization was becoming a "race relations" lobby rather than a force for simple "broad progress in the South." If they cared to condemn segregation fully, he suggested, the SRC might just as well be turned over "to somebody like Lillian Smith," the Georgia novelist who had recently published *Strange Fruit*.[10] Johnson's position had the support of the organization's businessmen, not one of whom, Dabney confided to a friend, "has been willing to take a leading role."[11]

Even while the war was ending, the growing resistance to increased demands for action was becoming more obvious. What Dabney had proposed with surprisingly little opposition in 1943 stood less and less chance of acceptance by 1945. The detachment of the moderates and the SRC's reluctance to take a firm stand left the fight to others, principally to those who could get financial assistance from the more aggressive CIO-PAC, the very group that was so feared by the southern white establishment. At the same time, sympathetic observers were becoming worried by the "growing emotional attitude on the part of vocal Negroes," who had "no confidence in any of us with them in their program of action."[12] Dabney felt compelled to admonish a banker friend for suggesting that the Negroes were getting "uppity."[13] Virginia's Governor Colgate Darden, underestimating the hardened attitude, proposed to the General Assembly that Piedmont Sanatorium should be staffed with Negro doctors and nurses to attend to *black* tuberculosis patients, only to be astonished by their bitter rejection of what had seemed far more compassionate than revolutionary. In reporting such developments, a black publisher from Norfolk lamented that "I am certain that the outlook for minority groups in the South is much darker now than it has ever been."[14] By then, Dabney, too, had come to recognize the futility of his own mild reforms.

3

Clearly, the ambitions of the federal government were unlimited. Sacred areas of local control were being threatened. The party, now dominated by urban interests, was pushing ideological prescriptions to the danger point. Interference in one area could easily lead to a whole array of obnoxious measures detrimental to state prerogatives. And there was no lack of evidence to demonstrate the trend.

One area of contention, a factor that would remain an issue in southern politics until 1952, was the question of tidelands oil. Oil was a particularly sensitive matter, one that involved some of the region's most powerful interests, especially in Texas and Louisiana. And few controversies become more explosive than the merging of corporate needs with constitutional questions. Both were present in generous quantities, each feeding the other.

As early as 1937, Secretary of the Interior Harold Ickes termed as vital for national defense the deposits of oil that were offshore, between the low-tide mark and the three-mile limit. Finally, in 1947, the Supreme Court agreed that the federal government had "paramount rights" to such deposits, while simultaneously stating that Congress alone could decide the legal title. The reaction came quickly.

Already, the National Association of Attorneys General, which represented almost every state in the union, had gone on record several times in opposition to federal jurisdiction. At a conference of the southern governors held in Asheville, North Carolina, the fight was led by Beauford Jester of Texas. Specifically, the governor tried to wage the battle on ideological grounds, warning against the kind of campaign that would betray getting heavy support from the oil industry "whether we were or not." The states that had no such claims fell behind his leadership anyway, explaining that they concurred in opposing federal attempts to transfer such property to the national domain.[15]

But the administration in Washington continued to buy the liberal solution, that offshore oil rights were to remain under federal jurisdiction. Truman continued to cite the "national defense" rationale, while more doctrinaire liberals viewed the controversy as part of the larger question involving federal versus state responsibility and suggested other public uses for the revenue. One such beneficiary, proposed by Senator Lister Hill of Alabama, could have been aid to education.

While southern conservatives were joined in a happy union with congenial Republicans, the prospects of confining the war to a single front gradually dimmed with Truman's moves toward civil rights legislation. Less than two months after taking over, the president sent an open letter to the chairman of the House Rules Committee, Adolph Sabath of Illinois, advocating support for an FEPC. Southerners, angered, responded by dispatching a delegation to the White House; but the president had "no time" to see them. Thereupon, Congressman Joe Ervin of North Carolina (a younger brother of Sam Ervin) urged every member of the House to rally opposition to FEPC. He urged that the protests not be confined to the South.

Newspaper publishers throughout the country must be enlisted in the fight, and the opposition, he cautioned, had best be expressed not on the basis of race but, rather, as a protest against the specter of an FEPC that would become "an overall employment agency with power and authority to select employees for practically everybody."[16] The victory of Clement Attlee's British Labour Party also confirmed to Ervin his fear that "nationalization" could be the wave of the future. After digesting the returns from overseas that summer, he warned that an FEPC could bring economic havoc and pointed out that everybody with any "knowledge of the South fully realizes that every manufacturing plant would close its doors and that there would be no employment for anybody and that there would be much hunger, suffering and distress."[17]

While Ervin's fears were still not, at the time, representative of the entire South, they were also not the alarms of an isolated point of view. Similarly disturbing to FEPC's opponents, and confirming the immediacy of the danger, were the pockets of support for such legislation among certain progressive white southerners. Working out of Atlanta, one integrated group actively circulated pro-FEPC petitions.[18] Senator Theodore Bilbo of Mississippi denounced them as "Quislings of the white race, and other racial minorities, [who] hail from the city of Atlanta, the hotbed of Southern Negro intelligentsia, Communists, pinks, Reds, and other off-brands of American citizenship in the South."[19] Truman, after endorsing such equality in a comprehensive message to the Congress, then backed off and remained silent even as the FEPC was being crushed under a Senate filibuster.

The need to keep the electorate small and docile also appealed to the entrenched powers. The combined effect of poll taxes and the Byrd machine minimized Virginia's voting population. Although the state had about three million people in 1945, only 138,788 (5 percent of the total) voted in that year's gubernatorial primary, which was the only meaningful contest.[20] It was not merely the actual fee of $1.50 that reduced the size of the electorate, but the imposition of other obstacles. The payments, for example, had to be kept up to date for at least three consecutive years, which meant handing over the money before either the issues or the candidates had become known. Further, the process discouraged active efforts to enroll the disinterested, so it was a matter of making an effort to qualify or not voting. The objective of the requirement was hardly subtle as it effectively disfranchised the poor of both races. Francis

Pickens Miller, the Virginia liberal, tried to present the case for its abolition and was told by one large landowner, "I do not want my white tenants to vote."[21]

Anti-Byrd mavericks had been attacking the restriction. Moss Plunkett, an attorney from Roanoke and a member of the liberal Union for Democratic Action, had begun to lead the fight by challenging not only the state's districting laws but the tax itself. On July 12, 1945, he charged that the poll tax and democracy "cannot live in the same State," and observed, "We either have one or the other, and we certainly have not had democracy in Virginia during the reign of the poll-tax machine."[22]

Opponents claimed that limiting the electorate was not unique, that poll taxes did for Virginia what was done elsewhere, even in the North, by such devices as literacy tests, mandatory annual registrations, and residence requirements.[23] Congressman A. Willis Robertson, then about to succeed to the Senate with the death of Carter Glass, was somewhat more paternalistic than most defenders of the system. Writing to his Virginia colleague, Howard Smith, Robertson agreed that they did not accept the idea of an unrestricted electorate and pointed out that experiences with mass voting elsewhere had demonstrated the complications of democracy along with demagogic candidates and high campaign costs. Nevertheless, Robertson added, it was hard for an organization candidate to successfully maintain the position that the people of Virginia should not be given the right of a direct vote on the subject of the poll tax.[24]

4

The idea of a monolithic South was, of course, an old piece of fiction. Actually, as V. O. Key's *Southern Politics* demonstrated, its political structure was comprised of varying personalities and forms. There were the highly institutionalized machines under Harry Byrd in Virginia and Ed Crump in Tennessee. There were the business-dominated factions that characterized Texas, where so-called regulars had long since rebelled against liberalism and the national party. Elsewhere, local fiefdoms centered around commanding personalities, more often than not conditioned by the physical, demographic, and economic character of the area.

Nor was the South "solid" in other ways. Winston County, in northern Alabama, had been rock-ribbed Republican since the Civil

War. Substantial GOP support also came from all along the Appalachian highlands, from Virginia's Shenandoah Valley, the hills of North Carolina, and eastern Tennessee. There were the mining regions of southwestern Virginia, Kentucky, and northern Alabama, where industrial unionism was incongruous with romantic views of the Old South. All through the black belt (named for the soil, not the population) and the Delta as in Virginia's southside, where slavery had been most prominent and where the Negro population still dominated many counties, racial attitudes were most traditionally repressive. There the whites were most determined to keep political, social, and economic power in their own hands. Politics in Alabama, to cite but one example, cannot be understood without reference to the two major regions that split the state geographically.[25]

During and after the congressional debates over FEPC and poll taxes, race became more acceptable as a political issue. It was used in an attempt against the gubernatorial candidacy of Jim Folsom in Alabama. Portraying that populist as a tool of the CIO-PAC, Handy Ellis warned that Folsom's election would bring the complete destruction of the tranquillity that had existed under segregation.[26] The inability to stop Folsom by exacerbating racial fears, however, did not deter the passage of devices to restrict the electorate more than was being done under Alabama's 1901 constitution, which was sold to the electorate on the basis of race in order to restrict black voting. When presented in the form of an amendment in November of 1946, the Jim Crow appeal was the most potent means of getting it accepted. But its real objective was never obscure: fear that successful efforts to repeal poll taxes would produce undesirable poor white voters in the state's northern counties. As one conservative politician explained, it would "keep the white electorate small and more easily within control."[27]

The conflicts within the state of Virginia and the experiences of the Byrd machine provide a good example of what was happening. In that state, black veterans, exempted by federal law from paying poll taxes, were returning to the tidewater cities of Norfolk and Newport News. Voting registration was going up in the urban districts; an additional boost came from the absence of the white primaries following the *Smith v. Allwright* decision. There were also the white industrial workers and miners in the Piedmont and the Alleghenies, as well as in the northeastern counties along the Potomac River that housed the thousands who commuted daily to Washington, D.C. Well educated and middle class, they were often concerned about such things as good government and social justice. For them, enlightened Republicanism was preferable to anachronistic Harry Byrd Democrats. They were closer to the liberalism of a Francis Pickens Miller, who had been a Presbyterian minister, had seen the world, and believed in equal rights and the principles of the New Deal.

A Richmond lawyer, Martin Hutchinson, enlisted much of their support in 1946 when he entered the primary against Byrd. It was the senator's first primary opposition, and the machine began to feel the threat. Hutchinson's fight was vigorous and was supported by the CIO-PAC, which claimed a southern membership of 400,000 and worked to have its so-called "Operation Dixie" enroll an additional million members.[28] Alerted to the dangers, Byrd informed the chairman of the Rockingham County Committee that there were "evidences of activity on the part of Republicans and others in the coming campaign. There has been quite a registration, I am told, in some of the cities."[29] Even more alarming was the large number of black veterans qualifying to cast ballots in such cities as Richmond and Norfolk. Byrd heard that they were registering at the rate of about one hundred a day.[30]

Once the senator had managed to dispose of Hutchinson, he faced the prospect of a Republican challenger. Interest in the GOP as an opposing force had been stirred in part by a pre-election speaking tour conducted in the area by Harold Stassen, the former Minnesota governor and a candidate for his party's nomination in 1948. No longer was there room for the usual complacency. Byrd received warnings that substantial Republican activity was arousing interest among Virginians with the potential for considerable harm.[31]

The outcome of both the primaries and the regular election left the machine intact, although Hutchinson had managed to carry both the coal counties and the area adjacent to Washington as well as Norfolk.[32] A. Willis Robertson, running for the Senate in a special election to succeed the late Carter Glass, came in two percentage points ahead of the machine's boss. E. R. ("Ebby") Combs, the clerk of Virginia's state senate and the real guardian of Byrd's power within the state, explained to the boss, "If you, like the many other Democratic Senators had gone along with the New Deal program it is altogether possible that you . . . might have suffered the same defeat . . . suffered in other states."[33]

But the real significance was the response to what had been feared as formidable threats. Hutchinson had contributed to the acrimony with sharp attacks against Byrd himself and, moreover, Republicans were suspected of easing the way for their own candidates by having voted in the Democratic primary to defeat the stronger machine choices. On the defensive, then, the machine fought back. Combs advised that "our campaign should emphasize the importance of getting as many new voters registered as possible" and noted that even some Democratic workers had not bothered to qualify to vote.[34] Accordingly, poll-tax lists were checked to make sure "friends" were included. Intensive drives were also launched in districts where Republican voting had been particularly low. But the most effective means of luring nonparticipants to the polls was by sounding alarms.

That summer, all possible appeals to fear were unfurled. Threats were waved before the electorate: the menace of the CIO, communism, and the loss of white supremacy. As elsewhere in the nation during that 1946 midterm election, Virginians were warned that the communist menace was behind all the designs for change. The weapon, simply, was too tempting to be overlooked by the unscrupulous. One campaign letter in behalf of the Byrd and Robertson drives promised that both men would hold some of the radical and communistic trend in check if only the voters would go to the polls and vote and take along ten others and tell each of them to take ten.[35] The CIO, which did have substantial numbers of communists and was actively trying to organize industrial workers, therefore became a handy target. Along with the popular hostility toward militant unionism, a mood further provoked by the serious inflationary trend and strike wave, the CIO was additionally on the defensive against the rival American Federation of Labor (AFL). In various areas of the South, including Boss Crump's Shelby County, Tennessee, the AFL was not averse to securing its position by working with the establishment to defeat the CIO.[36] What happened in Virginia, then, was entirely predictable. Even an anti-Byrd paper, the Portsmouth *Star*, endorsed the senator because of Hutchinson's CIO-PAC support.[37]

In other areas of the South, the Virginia experience was duplicated. A contributing element was a Supreme Court decision that June in the case of *Morgan v. Virginia*, in which a statute requiring segregation on public buses moving along interstate routes was invalidated. It was, interestingly enough, a decision that was denounced by few newspaper editorials, but the implications were not lost. Virginius Dabney surmised that it could herald the "abolition of all segregation on public transportation lines, whether interstate or intrastate."[38] In the Georgia gubernatorial race, Eugene Talmadge seized the issue for his own purposes. Since there were 110,000 newly registered Negroes in the state as a consequence of the abolition of the white primaries, he faced a rising challenge. Accordingly, Talmadge promised to restore the white primary and to counter the "Communist doctrines from outside the state" that were disrupting racial harmony and even added that he would, if necessary, abolish interstate buses.[39] The opponent of Congressman Brooks Hays of Arkansas began his campaign by denouncing the "radical principles as advocated by the national leaders of the CIO."[40] Senator Bilbo called for working together to "defeat the plans and schemes of this communistic CIO-PAC crowd." He also had some advice for dealing with the new black electorate: "Mississippi's good white people should go to any means justifiable to maintain white supremacy at the polls. . . . And if you don't know what I mean you're just plain dumb. The time to see the nigger is the night before election."[41]

Other forces were also at work. Returning veterans organized themselves to overthrow the political machine of Leo P. McLaughlin in Garland County, Arkansas, where a former Marine Corps lieutenant colonel, Sid McMath, began his career by leading other GIs and became a formidable threat in the primaries. McMath captured the nomination as prosecuting attorney and, while his running-mates were not equally successful, he nevertheless launched a threat that could not be ignored by Governor Ben Laney. Even in Tennessee, the domain of Boss Crump that centered around Memphis was jeopardized by a CIO-backed campaign against the machine's representative in Washington, Senator Kenneth McKellar. But the incumbent had little trouble resisting the challenge, as he received help from the AFL in his successful effort to link his opponent with both radical unionism and communism.[42] West Virginia's Harley Kilgore was placed on the defensive against a Republican candidate who tried to associate the liberal Democrat with communism. "I have constantly asked people to define a communist," Kilgore responded during a debate with his opponent. "Never yet have I heard one give a proper definition."[43] Eugene Cox of Georgia, a ranking member of the House Rules Committee, made a campaign charge that the CIO-PAC, as the "hand of Stalin," was manipulating the black vote.[44]

States' rights, racism, and protection for business were all fused in a unified resistance to change. The specter of communism was the handiest repellent. The intensity of the opposition was increased by two positions taken by the president that year. Neither involved civil rights. One was his veto of the Case bill, which he cited for its use of antitrust provisions and injunctions as setbacks to labor's right to strike, measures that had the support of most Republicans and the great majority of southern Democrats. Also, to stem the record inflationary direction of the economy, he called for an immediate extension of the Price Control Act. An additional development was the Wallace opposition to the administration. To many southern leaders, the Commerce secretary represented an instrument of radicals who were waiting in the wings to deliver the final coup de grace to whatever was left of the party's freedom from left-wingers. All together, they comprised an imposing array of grievances.

Behind the conservative drive, giving vital prestige and financial support, was the Southern States Industrial Council. With headquarters in Nashville, Tennessee, and a membership list that included some six thousand leading industrialists in chapters throughout Dixie, the organization was headed by Remmie L. Arnold, a Petersburg, Virginia, pen manufacturer. Arnold, writing in behalf of this group, reacted to the price control proposal with a long letter to Truman that charged government abandonment of its "true constitutional role of arbiter" in order to become "an active participant in behalf of favored groups." Arnold also objected to depriving the farmer of being able to merchandise his commodities in a free market while, at the same time, he was being compensated for losses through subsidy payments. "The most dangerous ideology ever advanced is the suggestion that the government owes its citizens a life of financial security," declared the manufacturer.[45] Two weeks later, Arnold asked Byrd about the possible danger of "any comeback so far as Mr. Wallace is concerned, which might affect me personally. . . . Frankly, Senator," he added, "it seems to me that somebody has got to take a definite stand regarding Communist sympathizers and Socialists endorsed for any candidate who is suppose [sic] to come to Washington to look after our country's interests."[46] On March 12, the Southern States Industrial Council circulated "A Statement to the Businessmen and Industrialists of the South." Beginning with "We, the People," it attempted to rally southern businessmen to protest that "the people of the South are not satisfied with the way things are going and that something must be done about it."[47]

Arnold's group was already fighting back against local enemies as well. The activities of the Southern Conference for Human Welfare, which was led by the president of Black Mountain College, North Carolina, were regarded as subversive. They were promoting FEPC, desegregation, poll tax abolition, and were being financed by northern money. Word had been passed by an informant that two of their Washington meetings were "comprised of about one-third Negroes, one-third Jews, and one-third Gentiles," and that "all were extreme Left-Wing New Dealers."[48]

Nor was Arnold's fear simply that of a negligible sectarian organization. "Truman's veto of the Case Bill seems to be universally unpopular," reported a Little Rock automobile dealer.[49] Letters from constituents supported the same observation. When the party's publication, *The Democratic Digest*, asked for a show of support to uphold the president's opposition to unrestricted unionism, the southern response was vociferous. *The Nation* suspected a Dixie attempt to force a showdown on their status within the party as opposed to the CIO-PAC.[50] Then, despite Senate Majority Leader Alben Barkley's hints of a forthcoming veto by the president, the only southern senators who voted against the antilabor measure were Claude Pepper and Lister Hill. The South then joined en masse with the Republicans in a futile attempt to override the veto.

Clearly, southern progressives were becoming a lonely group. They also watched the simultaneous resurgence of the Ku Klux Klan (KKK), which was festering on the assortment of grievances. Friends of Henry Wallace reported that the Klan was being used by certain Texas businessmen to defeat liberal opposition to Governor Beauford Jester. Dr. Homer P. Rainey, Jester's opponent, was an ordained Baptist minister. He had also been removed from the presidency of the University of Texas at Austin after harassment by reactionary members of the Board of Regents. Rainey's campaign, supported by the state's progressives, had suddenly drawn a barrage of direct-mail circulars that accused him of atheism and being a "nigger-lover." A whispering campaign also spread the word that he was a sexual degenerate. With Du Pont, Mellon, oil, and insurance-company sponsorship suspected, Wallace was advised that the hope of the liberals rested on "proving that the fundamental KK [sic] strength" was working as "the instrument of big oil, big utility, big bank combines who hope to 'hold down taxes' and have 'a safe Governor' to carry on in 'normalcy.'" In October, the first cross since Pearl Harbor was burned on Stone Mountain, outside Atlanta,

Georgia. In that state, also, Gene Talmadge had welcomed the Klan, which dedicated itself to attacking organized labor and to cleansing the state of its "alien" influences.[51] W. B. Twitty, an Allsboro, Alabama, lumber merchant, warned Eleanor Roosevelt that "we are faced with blood shed and violence throughout the South, and something must be done and quick."[52]

"You have no conception of the situation existing in the Senate of Virginia today," wrote a dissident legislator. "There is hardly a whisper of liberalism in the whole membership, because they are bound to the chariot wheels of Senator Byrd and his crowd of buccaneers. They very much prefer a Republican in the White House to a Democrat with the slightest liberal learnings."[53]

5

Southern moderates and liberals were clearly on the defensive. The private ponderings of A. Willis Robertson often seemed as troubled by the sectional schism as by radicalism, and he was far from alone. To them, the signals were clear. With little confidence in the Truman administration, with rebels getting louder and the KKK getting bolder, their one hope lay with the Congress. After the GOP decimated the strength of the northern liberals in the fall elections of 1946, that became even more obvious. Their vital interests had also become more dependent upon the personal prestige of Congressman Sam Rayburn of Bonham, Texas.

Rayburn, the man who had been serving the Democratic majority as Speaker of the House, had decided soon after the elections not to become minority leader in the Eightieth Congress; but, immediately, he found himself in a dilemma. The leading candidate to replace him was both a northern New Dealer and an Irish Catholic, Democratic Whip John McCormack of Massachusetts. Installing the New Englander threatened to widen the regional gap. A fierce fight against his election by the new Congress would be even more damaging, especially if the cause were to attract the more rabid "fire-eaters," which was precisely what the southern loyalists wanted to avoid. So there was intense pressure for Rayburn to reconsider. One fellow Texan, Wright Patman, reasoned that without the Rayburn candidacy, the post would be denied to McCormack because of the southern strength that could be exerted after the defeat of so many northern Democrats in the recent elections and that the designation would, therefore, go to somebody from below the Mason-Dixon line. That, Patman feared, would create a situation that "will further divide our party ranks during these next two years when unity will be so essential."[54] Louisiana's F. Edward Hébert issued a similar warning about scarring the party's unity because of the inevitability of a bitter fight with the same militant southerners who would destroy the party.[55] Similar warnings stressed the need to appease all factions. Even driving out the party's liberals was viewed with alarm by those in the South who emphasized the importance of keeping the party as a truly national organization.[56] Finally, Rayburn, who had already expressed his support for McCormack, capitulated and accepted the Bostonian's offer to nominate him. In agreeing to become minority leader, Rayburn was recognizing the party's dilemma. While plugging the dike would not be that simple, its foundations would be maintained by the moderates and conservative loyalists.

★

CHAPTER III

The Rebellion
of "Rum and Romanism"

1

Don't forget the minorities, especially Catholics, Agnes Meyer once warned Adlai Stevenson. "Now I can hear you shudder at the thought of intimate, heart-to-heart talks with such varied groups," she added. The wife of the publisher of the Washington *Post*, aggressive, well connected with religious and political leaders, was writing one of her long and often persuasive letters to the man who, by then, had become every liberal's favorite moderate.

Most liberals had largely either ignored or failed to appreciate her point. The situation in eastern Europe, of course, had contributed in a major way to cold-war tensions. Since routing the Nazis, the Soviet Union had become entrenched in the region. All the attempted negotiations, appeals, propaganda, and the subsequent military build-up by the West had merely helped to strengthen the Russian grip. Only indigenous forces offered any hope of working toward autonomy. Demands for "free" elections, territorial integrity for ethnic groups, and relinquishment of their status as political satellites had brought niggardly results. Soviet power remained a fact; its presence uncontestable, except via the unacceptable alternative of waging World War III. Therefore, anyone raising the cry about freedom for the "captive nations" was merely engaging in the most obvious form of political rhetoric. As much as such appeals might raise the expectations of Americans whose origins had been in eastern Europe, cold-war animosities would only be exacerbated without any positive results. Taking up the cause with sufficient passion to satisfy the frustrated Slavic Americans, who were overwhelmingly Catholic, would make liberals sound uncomfortably like the hated "red-baiters."

Still, Mrs. Meyer had a point. Such ethnic groups were bitter.

Many had remained sufficiently close to their native lands to retain family ties and, for others, the attachments were emotional and cultural. Of major importance, too, was the survival of the church, an institution that was inseparable from national existence. In short, realistic or not, "red-baiting" or moral righteousness, their aversion to the Soviet Union represented a cause that, for millions of Americans, was more than another chapter of jingoism. Moreover, the bulk of those involved were Democrats; many were among the party's staunchest supporters; and their co-religionists who had long since battled against communism had been stalwarts long before the New Deal had created the modern coalition. Not only was it a moral issue, then, one consistent with the principles of democracy and self-determination that had twice justified sending American troops to Europe, but it was also, on the most practicable level, absurd to alienate so many voters.

Mrs. Meyer also had a plan. She advised Stevenson to begin by meeting with Polish groups in Chicago, while she attempted to use her personal contacts to gain additional assistance. Cardinal Stritch, she confided, planned to tell the November meeting of the Catholic bishops that he "has you in his pocket and that the Catholic Church had better back you up at the next election." Stritch would thereby score a point in his rivalry with Cardinal Spellman of New York, whose support for Senator Joseph R. McCarthy had inevitably thrown him in with the Republicans.

Pointedly, she advised that endorsement by the prelate was two-edged. It will "do no harm, except among the liberals who will hear about it at once," she wrote. "But I can make contact with my liberal friends and reassure them by telling them how difficult it is to pocket a good Unitarian."[1]

Stevenson was not unique. He was but one of many who needed a gentle reminder. Nowhere was there greater tension than between the old-line Catholic Democrats and the party's liberals. The New Dealers, intent on forwarding social and economic goals after the end of the war, increasingly receptive to the long-neglected plight of American blacks, united with other progressives in agreeing that Jewish survivors of the recent horrors deserved fulfillment of their goals in Palestine, were nevertheless strangely insensitive to the grievances of Roman Catholics. Not surprisingly, the old Irish Catholic and Polish Catholic affinity for the Democrats was in jeopardy.

Indeed, something had happened to American Catholics. Desertions from the party of their parents, the party with which they had made their earliest identification in the New World, had begun to occur even among those to whom the New Deal had been a happy development. The rejection of old ties that was occurring virtually paralleled the defections among southern Democrats. And it could not be entirely explained by their economic success as a group, even if such "upward mobility" necessarily did lead to Republicanism (which studies have shown was not at all certain), because they continued to lag behind the Jews. And Jewish voters were remaining far more loyal. Negroes, even where they were gaining economically, were actually moving more emphatically into the Democratic Party. And while such commentators as Vermont Royster have pointed to a general decline in the party's support since the high point of 1936, outside the South Roman Catholics led the shift. Their conservatism gained additional emphasis by prominence in the John Birch Society, a development that was taking place even while the first Irish Democratic president was in the White House. In 1974, Irish Americans in South Boston gave an enthusiastic reception to the national director of the Knights of the Ku Klux Klan.[2] It was an incident that, ironically, linked them with the hated southern Democrats, the bigots who had attacked Al Smith and then deserted en masse when John F. Kennedy headed the party's ticket. Therefore, it was clear that however much the New Deal had realigned the electorate along income lines and was, in fact, charged by the gentry with promoting "class warfare," Americans continued to retain the human habit of surrendering to other distractions. At all income levels, white Protestants remained predominantly Republican; and at any given place along the class spectrum, Catholics had begun to vote Democratic less often than either blacks or Jews.

2

With few exceptions, the Irish had been loyal Democrats. From the earliest days of their arrival in America, they had become identified with the anti-British party. It was also the political outlet for the urban workers, and the Irish were destitute and settled largely in the cities of the eastern seaboard, most notably in Boston and New York. A small minority found jobs in the interior as laborers and some were instrumental in helping to build the early canals and railroads. While touring the ante-bellum South for the old New York *Times*, Frederick Law Olmsted found foremen preferring to risk the lives of free Irish workers at hazardous jobs rather than valuable slave property. In the growing urban centers, with their heavy immigrant population, they soon became skilled at politics. In a century when anti-Catholic hostility was pervasive and often expressed, nationally, through such groups as the Know-Nothings and the American Protective Association, the Irish found security and advancement within their new society through the structure of the political machine.

Their relationship with Tammany Hall-style organizations was reciprocal: they supplied the votes and the organization provided jobs and other humane services that government ignored. Not surprisingly, politics became a handy means of moving upward for the children of Irish immigrants. Even during the Civil War, when their opposition to slavery was minimal and when they constituted the bulk of the antidraft rioters in New York City, they remained true Democrats.

Their constant enemy was the hostility from an overwhelmingly Protestant society. Their defense centered around protecting their heritage and the Catholic Church, which they came to dominate. Irish reactions to the Reverend Samuel Dickinson Burchard's charge that the Democrats were the party of "rum, Romanism, and rebellion" helped to confirm their vote for Grover Cleveland despite misgivings about pro-British attitudes of the party's presidential candidate. Four years later, when the English minister to the United States permitted himself to be duped into advising that a vote for Cleveland would also help the cause of John Bull, he found himself the embarrassed victim of a ploy for Irish votes. New York, despite Cleveland's hasty dismissal of the envoy, that year went Republican by fourteen thousand votes. Irish defections from the ticket in 1920 constituted a rejection of the party that had drawn the nation into a war alongside those guilty of the bloodshed during the Easter Rebellion of 1916.

They remained hostile to all threats to Ireland and the Church. Their enemies were often anarchists, socialists, communists, and progressives, a cultural heritage that has led a recent student of ethnicism to point out that such political concepts as "reform" and "morality" are uncomfortably close to being traditional code words for anti-Catholic. "Compaigns to 'reform' city machines and to end 'corruption' in city governments have for generations borne an anti-Catholic, anti-immigrant edge," noted Michael Novak.[3] Another writer, Father Andrew Greeley, has been even more outspoken. "I am not suggesting that the majority or even a large majority of left-wing Democrats are semi-conscious anti-Catholics," he declared, "but I am suggesting that anti-Catholicism is by no means absent in the left-wing Democratic circles."[4] Liberalism was regarded as a materialistic creed, one that emanated from the Middle Ages in opposition to the spiritualism of the Church; and liberals, in the complaining words of Currin Shields, have looked on the "Catholic as an enemy of progress," which has, in turn, led the Catholic to regard the liberal as "a wrongheaded heretic. The tradition still exists today," he observed in 1958.[5]

Such sensitivities had already been provoked well before the death of Roosevelt. The hostility to Governor Alfred E. Smith's presidential candidacy of 1928, whether directed toward his religion, his championing of a good drink, or toward the shape of his hat, caused widespread defections in the South. Not since Reconstruction had the solid South failed to be solidly Democratic. And the blatant bigotry bore the direct responsibility of the most traditional Democrats; for Roman Catholics it served as a reminder about the lack of true acceptance in America. Such a shock does not die very easily; and it lingered, fanned in part by the myth that Al Smith could otherwise have become president. A second jolt came in 1932. Smith's loss of the party's nomination to Franklin D. Roosevelt, the patrician from the Hudson Valley, proved to be bitter for both the governor and his admirers. Throughout the 1936 presidential campaign, Smith did his best to sever their Democratic connections with his frequent warnings about the New Deal's communistic tendencies. Speaking before a Liberty League dinner early that year, he denounced the collection of far-left intellectuals around the president. "It's all right if they want to disguise themselves as Norman Thomas, or Karl Marx, or Lenin, or any of the rest of that bunch," he said. "But what I won't stand for is allowing them to march under the banner of Jefferson, Jackson, or Cleveland."[6] Many of the Irish Catholics who agreed with Smith but did not accept the Republican candidate in 1936 expressed themselves by supporting Congressman William Lemke of the Union Party. Although the minor party's main strength was in the Midwest, where it drew strength from German Catholics, Irish wards throughout Massachusetts gave Lemke anywhere from 15 to 25 percent of their votes.[7]

The Smith alarm was shared by many who were dismayed by what was happening to their party, particularly the coming of new competition for power and prestige. Many of them were WASPs and had been Republicans disillusioned with the post-Theodore Roosevelt GOP. Some, like Henry A. Wallace and Harold Ickes, were even in the president's cabinet. There were also the Jews who could be found in large numbers among the academicians and reformist lawyers who were attracted to Washington. Gradually, too, despite the president's reluctance to provoke a showdown on the race issue, blacks were joining the coalition, a development that would inevitably become a vital force as the war industries accelerated northward movements of Negroes. Particularly uncongenial to most Irish Catholics was the association being established with left-wing and even radical labor unions. A special target was the Political Action Committee of the Congress of Industrial Organizations. Having been organized in 1943 to mobilize the labor vote in response to the Smith-Connally Act, the CIO-PAC accommodated the liberals, democratic socialists, and communists, the leftist "popular front." Accordingly, it became the victim of steady barrages from the ultra-conservative *Tablet*, the paper of the Brooklyn Archdiocese. A progressive publication, the Jesuit journal *America*, preceded the 1944 elections by noting the widespread condemnations of alleged communism within the PAC that was being fanned by the Hearst and Patterson-McCormick segments of the press and warned against playing into communist hands "by firing blindly every time someone yells that he sees a red flag." But when the election was over, and the CIO-PAC's influence had been exerted in support of the Roosevelt-Truman ticket, *America* expressed its own concern: "One may speculate on the effect which the resounding success of CIO-PAC may have on the President and the Democrats. Will it now attempt to dictate?"[8] The PAC, which was chaired by Sidney Hillman, thus joined the American Labor Party of New York State in being condemned as radical allies of the New Deal.

Liberals were also openly hostile to Generalissimo Franco's overthrow of the Spanish republic. While the American left was alarmed at the specter of a democracy being overthrown by Hitler-assisted fascists, Catholics rushed to Franco's defense. In their view, he was saving Spain from communism and simultaneously protecting the Church, arguments they thought validated when the Soviet Union came to the republic's defense. Many years later, Samuel Lubell observed that "the heritage of antagonism left over from the Spanish Civil War . . . although it ended in 1938, remains one of the more important political dividers in the country."[9]

At the same time, many of the Irish Catholic workers had fallen under the spell of Father Charles Coughlin. The "radio priest" from Royal Oak, Michigan, voiced their frustrations in a torrent of nihilistic accusations that filled numerous broadcasts and his publication *Social Justice*. He championed the cause of the Church in Spain and complained about liberal indifference to its plight while the predicament of Jews on the Continent seemed to have captured so much attention. When the administration became more open in its sympathies with England in the face of the Nazi threat, the intensity of his accusations increased. Jews were portrayed as behind the international interests that were trying to drag America into a war against Hitler. His followers responded to his blend of populism, Anglophobia, and anti-Semitism. After Wendell Willkie repudiated the priest's support during the 1940 campaign, the Republican candidate's mail was flooded with letters from outraged Coughlinites. "Not only did you take a slam at Fr. Coughlin, but at the whole Catholic church, for Fr. Coughlin takes his orders from his bishop, who in turn answers to the Pope, and I am sure if Fr. Coughlin showed any traces of race prejudice his supporters would not have stood for it," wrote a Queens, New York, man. From Kansas City, Missouri, came the "hope" that "Hitler does not stop until every Englishman and Jew have their snouts kicked out of continental Europe." In New York City, sidewalk battles broke out among the priest's followers and Jewish supporters of the president's bid for a third term.[10]

That election also produced, in the minds of many Irish American Democrats, a second Al Smith. Again, one of their own had lost out in competition with FDR. This time it was Jim Farley, a loyal old Democrat, the political architect, postmaster general, and chairman of the Democratic National Committee, the man who had dispensed much of the political gravy of the New Deal. Farley, for his own ambitions more than for any ideological reasons, had to go one way or the other: either by moving upward to a high elective office or by rescuing his distressed personal finances by rejecting government for private business. He had convinced himself that he could become an exception to the popular aversion against electing political bosses. With the assumption that he had received assurances that the president would not run for a third term, he had begun to prepare for his future.

That included moving closer to the southern Democrats. Some of his allies, such as Harry Flood Byrd and Carter Glass, the two Virginia senators, had long since broken with the New Deal. Their

support of a place for Farley on the 1940 ticket included an arrangement to nominate Secretary of State Cordell Hull for the presidency.
That would enable the South to have a prominent Tennesseean on
the ticket while keeping things in balance with the presence of an
Irish Catholic from the town of Grassy Point, New York. The party
would be kept intact, and so would conservative congressional interests. At the convention itself, Glass prepared to deliver on the strategy by nominating Farley for the presidency. But Roosevelt's
determination to run again, made obvious just as the delegates gathered at Chicago, caused Farley and the whole concept of a Hull-
Farley ticket to lose out to the president.[11]

Farley's subsequent tepid support of the Democratic national
candidates, an endorsement out of loyalty to the party, did little if
anything to arrest the Irish anti-administration drift. Moreover, the
prospects that the administration would actually commit America in
a war on the side of Britain intensified such anxieties. In opposition
to the Interventionist Committee to Defend America by Aiding the
Allies that had been formed by William Allen White, an American
Irish Defense Association was organized. Irish Democrats joined
with pacifists and German sympathizers in supporting the America
First ideals. Distressed by the course of events, Bishop James Hugh
Ryan of Omaha lamented that, as for himself, "I am ashamed of the
Irish. They are shortsighted, selfish, dominated by old hatreds, with
little or no conception of their duty toward Western Civilization."[12]

That was the climate when Roosevelt, facing a predominantly
Gaelic audience in Boston and with Willkie giving him a tougher
fight than he had ever had before, made one of his more unfortunate
public promises: that he would not send American boys overseas.
International developments were clearly exacerbating a growing
trend. The Smith and Farley rebellions, the condemnation of Franco
by liberals, opposition of reformers to machine politicians, the
party's association with left-wing labor unions, and growing liberal-
conservative tensions of the post-New Deal period inevitably colored
the election returns. Roosevelt's greatest losses were among the Irish.

And yet the trend was only a precursor. Irish American voters,
just as the newer Catholic groups, were still mainly Democratic.
Their defections did not constitute a realignment but merely a little
rebellion, much as had their support for Harding in 1920. They
gave Roosevelt thirteen percentage points less than in 1936, but that
still left him with a comfortable 68 percent of their vote. For not
only were they traditional Democrats, but the New Deal had been

consistent with their class interests and had also given them generous representation in the power structure. Moreover, the machines that functioned so efficiently in urban centers—Ed Kelly in Chicago, Dan O'Connell in Albany, Tammany in New York City, Frank Hague in Jersey City, Jim Curley in Boston—continued to mobilize their votes behind the party's leadership.

So Irish power within the Democratic Party remained viable, although it stood as a more conservative force in opposition to the reformers, the democratic socialists, and to the whole generation of intellectuals who stressed issues over organization. Throughout the Northeast and in key midwestern states, Gaelic names continued to dominate the precincts, wards, and statehouses. Even in New York City, where there was a much-publicized Episcopalian Italian-Jewish reform mayor, Fiorello La Guardia, leadership rolls contained Buckleys, Rowes, Kennedys, and Sullivans; and the battle to pick a new Tammany sachem in 1944 came down to a fight between a Loughlin and a Mahon. At the top of the national committee, it had become almost obligatory to maintain the kind of succession that went from a Jim Farley to a Frank Walker to a Bob Hannegan to a J. Howard McGrath.

3

At least the Irish were part of the Democratic establishment, which served to minimize the alienation between ideology and institution, a factor that hardly applied with some of the other groups that had been brought into the coalition. It was certainly not true, for example, of the German Americans. Especially in the upper Midwest, large numbers of them were hostile not only to Roosevelt's foreign policy for its closeness to England but also to the process that led a Democratic president to take the nation into a war against their native land for the second time in less than half a century. What Samuel Lubell has called the "politics of revenge" thereby helped to disaffect other supporters of the New Deal's economic programs.[13]

So domestic events continued to play midwife to American foreign policy. For the well-integrated liberals and the wide majority of Americans, the choice was clear. Global objectives hinged on liquidating the war promptly and moving to create a structure strong enough to keep the peace. The world organization would avoid the blunders of the defunct and discredited League of Nations. With the Axis powers out of the way, and particularly with the Nazis surrendering unconditionally, it seemed entirely realistic to expect a stable world order. The greatest likelihood of a future threat would in all probability be from revived power of the chronic aggressors. But Treasury Secretary Henry Morgenthau, Jr., determined to short-circuit that possibility, promoted a plan to destroy German military-industrial capability once and for all by converting that nation into an impotent pastoral state. As it turned out, it was the plan that was ultimately buried. But keeping Germany divided during rehabilitation was thoroughly acceptable.

Liberal concern with Germany and permanent peace was, to growing numbers of worried Catholics, a means for completing the destruction of the Church that the war had begun. Liberals could cheer the swiftness of the westward Russian advance as it went back across the Polish plains and drove the Nazis from the Slavic states, but they largely overlooked the fears of their fellow Democrats. Russian military hegemony was tightening over eastern Europe. Old grievances could be used to justify new travesties. Once Russian positions had been secured, how could the Red Army be dislodged?

American troops were fighting to penetrate Hitler's west wall and were nowhere near the region. Even if they were, they hardly contemplated risking war with Moscow. The British, of course, had their old imperial interests in the east, but largely in the Mediterranean; besides, they could command little more trust from many Americans than could the Russians. Steadily, the outlook for the Slavic groups, for the safety of the Church and freedom for all Catholic institutions, became increasingly ominous.

Polish Americans, despite their own ideological and nationalistic divisions, had long feared for Polish freedom. The war itself had begun with an invasion of their homeland by both Germany and Russia, and the country had been divided between the two powers. Only those very few who were concerned about fascism were apathetic about Poland becoming a pawn of the Soviets. Numerous petitions were sent to Washington pressing the issue of territorial integrity. Congressmen with large Polish constituencies pushed the matter with particular vigor. In the Senate, Arthur Vandenberg undoubtedly found that nearly a half million Slavs among his Michigan constituents expedited the abandonment of his prewar isolationism.[14] In 1943, having received information from their underground, Poles were convinced of Russian responsibility for the murder of ten thousand Polish officers whose bodies were uncovered in a mass grave in Katyn Forest. Then, shortly after Soviet troops had entered Poland, Moscow insisted that there was no possibility of dealing with the government that had gone into exile in London, which was probably a valid judgment. But they followed that with an announcement that a more "sympathetic" regime would have to be established in Poland itself. Creating additional consternation were the pointed intentions of maintaining permanent Soviet possession of land as far west as the Curzon line, a frontier that had been disputed after World War I and that embraced territory claimed by Stalin as a historic extension of White Russia and the Ukraine. And so, by 1944, Polish American fears had mounted. Evidence of their determination to do something about the grim situation was the merger of various groups behind the cause into a single umbrella organization called the Polish American Congress.

As much as they were mainly Catholic, they were also predominantly working-class Democrats. They had, in fact, become staunch partisans. To one Democratic president, Woodrow Wilson, they were grateful for Polish national independence. To another, Roosevelt, they gave enthusiastic support for anti-German-American intervention. Further, to the New Deal they attributed policies favorable to those who labored for a living.

For the party itself, they constituted a vital component of the old New Deal coalition. While only a minority within both the Church and the Democratic establishment, their strength was substantial. They constituted the largest Slavic ethnic group in the country, and the 1940 census showed that Poles comprised 8.4 percent of first-generation Americans. Much of their political significance, however, came from their concentration in a wide belt of industrial states from New England through Wisconsin. They could easily provide the winning margins in New York, Pennsylvania, Michigan, and Illinois, all of which had a substantial number of electoral votes. After the Polish American Congress became a reality, the Roosevelt administration, becoming conscious of their political significance, was warned about the "terrific resentment" among leading Polish Americans that will "eventually crystallize in some unfriendly form"; and, as early as October 6, 1944, Henry Wallace's diary noted the "great deal of unrest now in the United States, especially on the part of congressmen who have Polish constituents because of the way in which the Polish patriots had died at Warsaw."[15] The following months brought continued pressure on politicians to go on record, even if only by symbolic gestures, in behalf of Polish freedom. All that was long before Roosevelt met with Stalin and Churchill at Yalta.

The Poles were not alone. Their anti-Russian campaign coincided rather conveniently with the warnings long since sounded by the traditional anticommunists. Throughout the fall of 1944 and the following winter, the betrayal of Poland became the leading international concern of most Catholic periodicals in America, particularly many of the diocesan papers. An outstanding example was *The Tablet*.

The Brooklyn paper had no doubt about who was the enemy. Its strident tone, however, made it easy to disregard the repeated warnings. On October 14, 1944, for example, it declared that "all fair-minded people know that between brown and red Fascism there is little difference, and Catholics particularly know it." The following week, repeating the theme, *The Tablet* added that both "destroy liberty, peace, and religion."[16] While it is easy to understand the paper's repugnance to liberals and enlightened laymen, particularly as many of its overtones seemed to reflect what one would have expected to find in *Social Justice*, it nevertheless was read by a large and politically potent Roman Catholic community and expressed the anxieties of a mass audience. Further, those most concerned about "international communism" were later able to cite such alarms as prophetic.

That same fall, in the days immediately before Roosevelt ran for a fourth term and was opposed by New York's Republican governor, Thomas E. Dewey, *The Tablet*'s position was far from unique. Other organs of American Catholicism, less insular and more respectable, were also becoming apprehensive. The Jesuit periodical, *America*, much less hysterical and hardly in the same league with *Social Justice* and anti-Semitic publications, had also begun to worry about the postwar world. The only real issue, *America* declared, was peace—and that meant a "just social order at home and abroad."[17] *The Catholic World* ran a lead editorial predicting that Moscow's treatment of Poland and the Baltic states would be duplicated and "perhaps worse will happen to Hungary, Yugoslavia, all the Balkan States, Austria and Italy."[18] While the publications were sounding such warnings, thousands of pre-election-day appeals flooded the White House urging opposition to a "fourth partition of Poland." On Polish Constitution Day, some 140 congressmen filled *The Congressional Record* with their sympathy for the cause.

The issue, in fact, became only a minor threat to Roosevelt's re-election. In addition to the requirements of wartime bipartisanship, Dewey was also reluctant to risk renewing the isolationist-interventionist schism that was dormant among his fellow Republicans.[19] When the governor did broach the matter, it was with caution and not much force. Further, he did little with it until late in the campaign and then mainly as a domestic issue.[20]

But there is sufficient evidence of administration fear about the Catholic vote. John Lewis Gaddis has noted that it was a preoccupation that actually diverted attention from the diplomatic question. Joseph Davies, the American ambassador in Moscow, sent a warning to Stalin advising that any statements made by him that appeared to be in accord with Roosevelt's view could provoke domestic disruption in the United States that would have unfavorable diplomatic ramifications.[21] *America* noted rather dryly that there was very little talk about the Catholic vote, but "both parties have made obvious bids for it just in case."[22]

Roosevelt's own optimism was tinged with reality. The military deployment was hardly conducive to a demonstration of Western might in eastern Europe. In September, the Quebec conference had anticipated postwar territorial demarcation along the probable military fronts. Russian westward advances, moreover, were more rapid after that settlement, especially when last-ditch German resistance at Bastogne in late December slowed the Allied advance. When the president left for Yalta in early February, it was amid denunciations of "unconditional surrender," the kind of conclusion to the war that could easily give the Soviets an opportunity for aggrandizement over central Europe. That provoked some major demonstrations of support for Polish liberty. "The President and the Prime Minister [Churchill] are faced with a dilemma," warned *The Tablet*: "either they put up a joint stand and tell Stalin, for the first time, 'No!', or become parties to a compromise with violence."[23] Roosevelt himself agreed that the prospects were limited. Before leaving, he told Ed Flynn that permanent peace would be impossible without religious freedom for the large Slavic Catholic populace.[24] He also warned Cardinal Spellman about being too optimistic.[25] When he faced the joint session of Congress shortly after returning, his report was a sober account of where reality had necessitated compromise and hope.

But while the immediate public reaction was relatively mild, the reports of the conference, issued before the message to Congress, had already foreshadowed the postwar dispute. Agreement with the Russians on the Curzon boundary and continuing the pro-Russian Polish government at Lublin were both flatly unacceptable. On February 19, Vandenberg sent his "deep disappointment" to Undersecretary of State Joseph Grew.[26] *America* proclaimed the settlement a "Stalin victory" and claimed that it had been done without "the slightest evidence that anyone tried to find out the wishes of the millions of people transferred by this settlement from Poland to Russia."[27] The Polish American Congress promptly demanded congressional rejection and, in mid-April, branded the pro-Stalin Polish leaders as a "handful of Communist fanatics and dishonest adventurers." Some 350 Polish American priests appealed to Washington for the implementation of Russian promises of Polish freedom.[28] At a rally sponsored by the Congress, Robert A. Taft, the Republican senator from Ohio, said that Russian policies in eastern Europe justified discontinuing lend-lease assistance.[29] Truman, meeting with Stalin at Potsdam, reminded the Soviet leader that a free election in Poland, reported in the American press, would make it much easier to deal with the six million Poles in the United States.[30]

Most critics agreed that the only hope of salvation lay with the forthcoming establishment of the United Nations. Persistent demands were expressed for the fulfillment of the hope that had been sparked by the preliminary agreements for international cooperation that had already been reached at conferences at Bretton Woods and Dumbarton Oaks. A secret report by the Organization of Strategic Services, the American wartime intelligence unit, showed the Polish groups comprising by far the strongest lobby at the opening of the charter meeting of the United Nations in San Francisco.[31] Faith in the possible accomplishments of a cooperative world organization also came in the form of support from the Irish clergy. Father Robert C. Hartnett, for example, while acknowledging the limitations of the sessions at Dumbarton Oaks, wrote that backing for the United Nations had "a strong claim on us as Catholics and as Americans."[32] Even *The Tablet*, while challenging both Britain and the Soviet Union to "collaborate dramatically," supported the concept.[33] Bishop Bernard Sheil warned that jettisoning plans for an international order would bring the "risk of a bad peace."[34] There is, in fact, little doubt that American support for the birth of the United Nations that came from groups with isolationist histories was motivated by anxiety to have the international organization become an agency for coping with the Russians. But the court-of-last-resort route faced inevitable frustration as Russian control only tightened while American diplomacy both blundered and stiffened. The veto power that American insistence had contributed to the charter became a handy device for Soviet obstructionism. Whatever relaxations Stalin may have intended were thus obviated by cold-war exigencies.

That Roosevelt's policy had failed was no longer the exclusive obsession of hysterical anticommunists. Most charitably, he could be viewed by liberal Catholics as an idealist who had had great confidence in his ability to cajole Stalin into sweet reasonableness. His efforts could also be seen as a characteristic example of the much-publicized pragmatism. Had he remained alive, his tactics might well have changed. His final communication certainly pointed in that direction. Nevertheless, those who had begun to resist President Truman's firm and bellicose stance, most notably Henry Wallace in a Madison Square Garden speech on September 12, 1946, called for a return to FDR's foreign policies. Such critics were now charged with misunderstanding Roosevelt's tactics, with being either too naïve or too gullible. To worried Catholics, the demands of the Democratic left were sounding suspiciously like appeasement. The strains upon the popular front that had contributed so much to the New Deal coalition were becoming more burdensome. By November of 1946, *Commonweal*, the most influential publication of progressive Catholics, noted editorially that "It is disturbing the extent to which certain leftist political groups have apparently succeeded in creating a legend about Mr. Roosevelt. . . . 'Back to the Roosevelt foreign policy' is a slogan without legitimate current application."[35]

Such developments only seemed to widen the Catholic-liberal schism, enforcing mutual suspicions. Catholic association of liberals with hostile, anticlerical Reds seemed substantiated by the insensitivity toward their co-religionists by the same groups that offered such ready sympathy for other victims of oppression. Mortimer Hays, who headed the foreign policy committee of the liberal Union for Democratic Action, observed to an associate that "There is still agitation for free elections in Poland," and then added: "Why not for Greece also?"[36] Earlier, the organization had issued a foreign policy statement that viewed future Soviet behavior in Poland as a "test" of Russian cooperation but approved the decision to adopt the Curzon line "because it corresponds generally with the ethnographic factors."[37] At the very time when reliance was still on diplomatic rectification of grievances, Henry Wallace pointed to a "small group in the Catholic hierarchy" that was together with "the American big-business hierarchy" and military interests in demanding war with Russia.[38] Subsequent attempts by historians to blame the cold war principally on Truman-Acheson diplomacy have conveniently minimized the distress felt by millions of ethnic Americans, whose grievances were as real to them as those emphasized by the liberals. The most studious account of the controversey over Yalta even insists that such passions were held by just a few "extremists" and "certain prominent Polish-Americans."[39]

4

The anticommunist drive of the Church in America had also been inspired by the revival of old tensions. With the end of the war, the Catholic hierarchy was hearing the return of familiar themes. If they were not precisely on the sordid level that had marked the hostility of the 1830s or the thinking of the later American Protective Association, they nevertheless were jarring, perhaps even more upsetting because they came from more literate, more influential sources; in short, they were voiced by responsible spokesmen of the Protestant establishment. By 1945, Bishop G. Bromley Oxnam, the Methodist bane of the Catholic hierarchy, was declaring that there was serious tension "developing between Roman Catholics and Protestants in the United States."[40] Two years later, the public observation by Cardinal Spellman was emphatic: "Bigotry once again is eating its way into the vital organs of the greatest nation on the face of the earth, our beloved America," said the cardinal. "Once again a crusade is being preached against the Catholic Church in the United States."[41]

The conflict was serious, furnishing an important element in helping to understand the rhetoric that mounted in the years before the din matured into a new wave of anti-Red hysteria. Standing in the line of fire, with its New Deal popular front, was, of course, the Democratic Party. Its Catholic supporters, caught between deteriorating international conditions and the return of nativism at home, responded by vigorously reasserting their perceptions about the threats to God and country. Those years were, consequently, crucial to the formulation of both domestic and diplomatic policies. They were responses that not only exceeded by far the passions evoked within any major Western ally but also seemed, from the distance of later years, to have been contrived by rather artful forces.

The New Republic's editorial of June 7, 1943, expressed "shock" that a recent article could have evoked such incriminations as were filling the magazine's mail and the pages of the Catholic press. "It is discouraging to print such truthful and friendly discussion of Catholic problems as the one by George West," the periodical declared, "and then see the comment come in from Catholic papers—long, badly written diatribes against Mr. West and *The New Republic* on the simple but wholly false assumption that any public discussion must grow out of mortal enmity."

Mr. West was George P. West, a California newspaperman, a writer not generally known as a bigot. No less an authority than Father John Ryan himself expressed surprise that he was its author. West was the "last person" from whom such charges could have been expected, wrote a disappointed Father Ryan. If *The New Republic*'s editors really believed that the article would be received as an objective scholarly treatise, they were being naïve. It was nothing of the sort.

The Catholic Church, West argued, had reached a high point during the 1928 campaign for Al Smith. Even such Protestant luminaries as John Dewey had pledged him their support. That election, for all the bitter anti-Catholicism in many parts of the country, had actually marked what West called the "high tide of liberal friendliness toward the Church." Clearly, many progressive Protestant intellectuals had been drawn to the governor's side.

But the consequences of that experience, with its unhappy conclusion, had left Catholics "disillusioned and embittered and it ended their policy of appeasement and conciliation." So, following the examples offered by such well-organized groups as the Anti-Saloon League and the American Legion, the Church began a campaign of "organized assertion and aggression." It graduated from the grass-roots wards, where it had largely controlled the Catholic Tammany-type organizations that influenced the Democratic Party, and extended upward into the very chambers of the White House itself.

"What first aroused and alarmed us," West explained, "was the part played by Catholics in perverting our foreign policy after the outbreak of the Nazi-Fascist inspired revolt against the government of Spain." Catholic influence on the Roosevelt administration had been obvious. And the subsequent arms embargo hastened the fall of the Spanish republic. Further, claimed West, the rightward shift of Catholic policies "approached affinity and alliance with the reactionary business community," a power that "heretofore has maintained a historic affiliation with Protestantism." Today, West continued, "the threat looms as a conscious coalition between parafascism and reactionary clericalism, joining hands in their fear of democracy and socialism."

Mr. West suggested solutions. A dialogue should, of course, be opened with such enlightened pillars of the hierarchy as Father Ryan. But Protestants and liberals must also "organize an open, fighting opposition to the reactionary Catholic pressure on officeholders, the press, the stage, the movies, to organized Catholic attempts to use a fanatically loyal and largely ignorant following to boycott and blackmail and coerce." Finally, West concluded his alarm by announcing that "the time has come for the majority to assert itself against those who would take advantage of our tolerance and generosity."[42]

The liberal journal's own defense of West's article, protesting that it was not anti-Catholic, explained that its target was but a minority within the Church. That minority "insists on importing into this country ideas *alien* to the democratic tradition and to the dignity of their fellow Catholics."[43]

Throughout the rest of the year, the controversy appeared in subsequent exchanges, which included a rejection by Father Ryan of the burden of West's arguments and an additional defense by the independent Protestant theologian, John Haynes Holmes. Holmes, in fact, tried to calm things down by contending that the Catholic Church was a pressure group no more significant than organized labor, big business, political parties, or any other interest that had the right to compete for attention.

But the Holmes type of ecumenicism was not very popular. Clearly, the key word was *alien*. Catholics and their Church were not so dangerous when they constituted an impotent minority that had to operate within the constraints of Protestant society. All that was changing, however. Their numbers were gaining rapidly. Projections of the Catholic birthrate revealed that it would soon reach alarming proportions. All told, in every possible way, their presence was far more obvious than it had ever been in the past; and, most emphatically, it was already stronger than any single Protestant denomination.

In fact, warned Harold E. Fey in the pages of *The Christian Century*, they were not at all like legitimate Americans. These "millions of Americans are subject to the spiritual direction of an Italian pon-

tiff who represents a culture historically *alien** to American institutions." They function not as a democratic group but as a monolithic
force controlled by the Pope through his power to appoint the
bishops and archbishops. The ultimate threat was the one to American culture, which was molded by Protestantism "before the great
masses of immigration swept across the continent." Then came Fey's
rhetorical coup de grace: "Is this Protestant nation destined to pass
into another and different cultural phase under the religious and
social preponderance of the Roman Catholic Church?"

Fey's article was but the lead piece of an eight-part series called
"Can Catholicism Win America?" Subsequent essays were devoted to
proving the growth of Catholic influences in every aspect of American life, from the Lynds' "Middletown" to the press, Negroes, workers, and even the Protestant preserves of rural America. Another
ominous bit of evidence used to support the thesis was the successful
fight to censor movies, which actually resulted in a spate of bucolic
films featuring Bing Crosby and Spencer Tracy as singing and congenial priests. Further, Catholic groups were leading the fight
against birth control and were struggling to win public funds for
parochial schools. At the same time, the Church was making sure
that the United States would accept the idea of having an official and
permanent ambassador at the Vatican.

The sixth article of the Fey series showed that the Catholic fight
against communism was largely aimed at winning Church control
over American workers. "Against Marxism," he wrote, "particularly
in its American form, the Roman Church therefore wages an open
and unrelenting war." The formation of an Association of Catholic
Trade Unionists and the appointment by the Vatican of Archbishop
Francis J. Spellman as a military "vicar of army and navy chaplains"
in America's armed forces were, to Fey, examples of Catholicism
being "extended among industrial workers and military personnel."[44]

At about the same time, other developments provoked Catholic
sensitivities. The sectarian press gave much prominence to accounts
of the large crowd that had gathered in New York City's Madison
Square Garden on the evening of January 2, 1945, to demand that
the United States sever relations with Franco Spain. *The Tablet*
reported that "belligerent phrases" and "hatred" had come from
many of the speakers, several having "appeared to swing the flag of

---

* Author's emphasis.

Red Fascism." Moreover, the event proved that it was not simply in opposition to the dictatorship in Madrid, because Bishop Oxnam, "one of the many non-Communists deceived by the Communist bait of anti-Catholic hatred in 1936–1939," had used the occasion to deliver a bitter attack against the Church.[45]

The predicament was clear. Old hostilities were being replenished. Suffused with large doses of pro-Red sympathies, the left was attacking the Church and all true opponents of communism. Liberal Protestants and Jews, inadequately appreciative of Moscow's real designs, were being misled into vehement anticlericalism. A warning by pollster Elmo Roper of the pending "great revival and renewed virulence of some form or another of Ku Klux Klanism" confirmed such fears. After ten years of depression and five more of terrible war, with anti-Semitism passé and concern finally being shown for the plight of blacks, *America*'s analysis concluded that "they find a ready virulence by renewing their attack on the Catholic Church." Both right and left had joined the crusade against Rome.

In the view of the Catholic hierarchy, such critics had failed to understand that the real alien force, the one that was an actual tool of a foreign power, was international communism. Its dangers had been compounded by postwar European conditions, with the communization of the East and burgeoning Marxism threatening to dominate such countries as Greece, Italy, and even France. In America, anticlerical radicalism, encouraged by the New Dealers, had already reached alarming proportions.

The agitation, then, had to be turned away from its current target and directed toward the dangers of communism, the real threat to all American institutions. And, if many Protestants were willing to ignore the risks, the function of Catholics was to educate and alert. It was, therefore, with great satisfaction that the Catholic press greeted the act of the Seventy-ninth Congress in accomplishing, as one of its first tasks and on a motion introduced by John Rankin of Mississippi, the establishment of the Committee on Un-American Activities on a permanent basis. Its life guaranteed in early January of 1945 by a 207 to 186 vote, it immediately resumed the old Dies Committee's hunt for "un-American activities."[46] Whatever revelations followed, whether from that committee or the findings of the House Military Affairs Committee, which warned that summer about the determination of American communists to subvert the armed forces, they were immediately reported—often in sensational detail—by the molders of Catholic opinion. The task was accomplished by more than just the limited powers of the more elite national publications. Brooklyn's *Tablet* had its counterparts in diocesan papers throughout the country and such clerics as Cardinal Spellman contributed their support. *The Tablet* chose that moment to recall to its readers that "Communist influence" had become a "powerful factor in government, labor, education and even in religion" since the early days of Roosevelt's administration.[47]

The drive was on. "One Munich is enough in one lifetime," proclaimed *America*.[48] Additional publicity was given to a series of articles by Republican Congresswoman Clare Boothe Luce. Carried in the Hearst papers, they accused prewar opponents of appeasement with suddenly changing their tunes now that the Soviets had become the threat to civilization. All liberals, "particularly befuddled liberals like Senator Pepper," were urged to read Brooks Atkinson's articles in the New York *Times* about his recent trip to Russia. They demonstrated the impossibility of any "one world" coexistence with the USSR.[49] When Henry Wallace made his dramatic charge that the Truman administration was responsible for provocative policies, the "fellow-traveler" indictment of his kind of liberalism was confirmed.

Cardinal Spellman entered the battle openly in 1946 with a magazine article called "Communism Is Un-American." Printed in the *American*, it abandoned any considerations of restraint by declaring:

It *can* happen here and everywhere that Communism, with its riot of rash promises, takes root. In America the seeds of confusion and disunion are spawning and spreading, and Communism is growing. . . . Their subtle, sinister schemings sway and mislead Americans who, in ignorance or weakness, yield to Communism their loyalty to God, to country and to their fellow man.[50]

Fanned by simultaneous events at home and abroad, the communist issue had become a major preoccupation that was gaining the attention of more than the traditionally anticommunist Roman Catholics and Protestant fundamentalists. Sensational disclosures about Soviet spies were hard to ignore. Two former communists, Whittaker Chambers and Elizabeth Bentley, went to the FBI with stories of espionage and subversion. Allegations undermined the reliability of anybody with a responsible post in Washington. A code clerk working in the Soviet Embassy in Canada created new headlines by turning over information to his government that helped lead to the arrest of Dr. Klaus Fuchs, a British physicist, and that disclosure was followed by the arrest of several Americans, including Julius and Ethel Rosenberg.

Meanwhile, however much the diplomacy of Truman and Secretary of State James F. Byrnes dismayed the Wallace liberals, to Catholics trying to alert the public their hard line was too mild. Only some six weeks before Wallace called for more understanding of the Russian position, *America* complained that "our concern for the realization of really free elections in Poland has not been publicly expressed by" Mr. Truman.[51] Senator Vandenberg of Michigan, with his large Polish constituency, was finding greater difficulty justifying the rejection of demands for harsher anti-Soviet moves.[52] In that climate, fueled by several determined congressional leaders, the administration laid plans for capitulating to the pressure by establishing a commission to formulate procedures for dealing with an alleged "fifth column."[53]

The response, no doubt, was prompted in large measure by the widening charges of "softness toward communism" being made against the very administration that would later be condemned by a future generation as cold-war provocateurs. Further, it coincided with the anxieties about the forthcoming elections. The communist issue, fed by the general rebellion of anti-New Deal conservatives in possession of a potent weapon to use against the liberals, promised to further complicate the already dim outlook for November 1946. Postwar revival of anticommunism had, in fact, already become evident in some local elections. Lurid stories about the "Russian rape of Poland" and attempts to portray the Democratic candidate (who was also a labor union official) as a puppet of Stalin appeared during the Detroit mayoralty campaign in 1945. Polish working-class districts were flooded with special bilingual editions of hate propaganda that proved effective in defeating the liberal candidate.[54]

It had become obvious that 1946 would bring a record number of Catholic defections against the party's liberal leadership. Such Democrats had "sold out" at Yalta and Truman's foreign policy was not exerting enough muscle to rectify the damage. Only the Wallace critique, which came less than two months before the votes were cast, seemed to offer some hope that the trend could be reversed. Sam Rayburn suggested to John McCormack that it might become an advantage "in those industrial districts where there are a great many Poles."[55]

But that was wishful thinking. Catholics were ready to punish the Democrats. A macro-study of "Paper City" (Holyoke, Massachusetts) showed that its large Catholic population was being torn "between traditional Democratic party loyalties based on domestic economic interests and the mounting criticism of Democratic foreign policy."[56] In Wisconsin's Fourth District, the primary election had left the party with a candidate who was accused by his political opponents of being a communist. Edmund Bobrowicz, an international representative of the CIO-affiliated Fur and Leather Workers Union, merely retorted that communism "was not an issue."[57] But the state's three leading Democratic politicians promptly repudiated his candidacy, obviously ignoring his legitimate victory in their party's primary. When a Polish Catholic and old-line Democratic conservative, Thad Wasielewski, the man defeated by Bobrowicz in the primary, entered the November election as an independent, the divided vote produced a Republican victory. Wasielewski received at least tacit support from the Wisconsin regulars but failed in his attempt to get the party's national leadership openly to oppose the legitimate nominee.[58]

In New York, the position of the church was clear. As much as Governor Dewey had wanted the GOP to put up a Catholic for the Senate against former governor Herbert Lehman, political obligations invariably forced him to back Irving Ives. Fearing criticism for the absence of any Roman Catholic from the statewide Republican ticket, Dewey telephoned Cardinal Spellman to apologize for the omission. The response flustered the governor.

"There is a Catholic on the ticket," Spellman insisted to Dewey.

"There is?" said the governor. "Who?"

The cardinal promptly mentioned the name of a relatively insignificant judicial candidate. His message was simple: the Church did not need an ethnic attraction to support Republicans that fall.[59] With subsequent clerical opposition to Lehman, and with many Catholics simply staying at home, Ives won handily and the GOP also gained six congressional seats from New York.

In Minnesota, the Democratic-Farmer-Labor Party (D-F-L), the result of a merger between that state's progressives and the moribund affiliate of the national party, was denounced by the Catholic hierarchy as a communist front.[60] In addition to picking up a seat in the House, Minnesota Republicans also retained the governorship and handily elected Ed Thye to the Senate. Hubert H. Humphrey, the energetic mayor of Minneapolis who had helped forge the D-F-L merger, would subsequently move to correct that situation before 1948.

For the Democrats, the national loss was fifty-five House seats and twelve in the Senate. They also lost control over three state capitols. Not since the 1920s had the Republicans done as well; their sweep was easily sufficient to enable them to organize the Eightieth Congress. Catholic defections had not been the only cause of the tide, but there was little doubt that a point had been made.

CHAPTER IV

The Crisis of the New Order

1

The election of the Eightieth Congress was a Democratic disaster. The Republicans took comfortable control of both houses, and, by teaming up with conservative southerners, they could be unbeatable. Although more than half of the votes for congressional candidates did go to the Democrats, despite the GOP's success, the party had not done as poorly since the 1930s.

For the old coalition, most disturbing was the repudiation of liberalism. The major victims were the friends of labor, especially those openly supported by the CIO-PAC. In Pennsylvania, Senator Joe Guffey, a mainstay of unionism, was crushed under a plurality of more than 600,000. Illinois Congresswoman Emily Taft Douglas, the wife of Paul H. Douglas, was defeated by William G. Stratton. Stratton had campaigned with the promise to oppose "any program sponsored by the Congress of Industrial Organizations," while Mrs. Douglas had loyally supported the administration's foreign and domestic policies. Senator David Walsh of Massachusetts, the state's most powerful politician, lost his seat to Henry Cabot Lodge, Jr. Moreover, over and over again, throughout the country, the pattern was similar: friends of Truman, friends of labor, were defeated by conservative antiunionists. As a result, the liberal labor bloc in the House was decimated.

And the results were equally devastating just about everywhere. The key states of New York, Pennsylvania, Michigan, Illinois, and California—all industrial and vital for Democratic victories— together sent twenty-seven additional Republicans to Congress. The border states of Delaware, Kentucky, Maryland, Missouri, and West Virginia, still considered hostile territory for the GOP, nevertheless replaced ten Democrats with Republicans, the start of a significant southward penetration.

Another measure of the tide was the number of conservative Republicans who entered the Senate: Joe McCarthy of Wisconsin, John Williams of Delaware, John Bricker of Ohio, James Kem of Missouri, Zales Ecton of Montana, George Malone of Nevada, Arthur Watkins of Utah, William Jenner of Indiana, Edward Martin of Pennsylvania, and Harry Cain of Washington. The so-called Class of '46 was virtually a revolutionary repudiation of the preceding sixteen years. At the same time, California sent to the House Richard M. Nixon, who defeated a respected progressive, Jerry Voorhis, after charging the incumbent with being a "tool of the PAC." Collectively, they would do much to shape American postwar conservatism and also to determine the future of the Republican Party.

The rebuke to the administration was inescapable. William J. Fulbright, a young senator from Arkansas, offered what he called a "suggestion." Since the Republicans had taken over both houses, said the Democrat, "President Truman should appoint a Republican secretary of state and resign from office." With the succession law then in effect and with the absence of a vice president, that senior cabinet post was next in line for the presidency. Fulbright, who thought the designation should go to Arthur Vandenberg, hoped thereby to avoid the crisis of a deadlock between the chief executive and the Congress. Alabama's Luther Patrick, miffed because his endorsement by the CIO-PAC had prevented his renomination to the House, quickly agreed. The Atlanta *Constitution*, the South's most respected newspaper, advised the Democratic Party to give the plan serious consideration, and Marshall Field's Chicago *Sun*, which had complained about the administration's conservatism, ran a front-page open letter to Truman calling for his resignation.[1] Henry Wallace, however, less than two months after the president had capitulated to pressure by forcing him out of the cabinet, disagreed. "I still say," Wallace wrote in confidence, "that Truman is better than Byrnes or Vandenberg."[2]

In effect, the party that had overseen the Depression and the war had been given a vote of no-confidence for the responsibility of continuing the reconversion to peacetime. Tested at the polls for the first time without Roosevelt, it had collapsed. In many ways, the outcome was more significant than the result of many presidential elections. Only later would its importance to the course of postwar American politics become fully evident.

Few elections provide a clear referendum on any single issue, but the 1946 vote was not the result of intangible factors. Inevitably, keeping the New Deal coalition intact without serious defections was an inherently futile task. What had been shaped during years of national emergency, a crisis sufficiently serious to obscure secondary interests, simply could not guarantee the permanence of what was essentially a tenuous alliance, regionally, ethnically, economically, and ideologically. Within the context of a pluralistic society, virtually every association that fused the coalition was the potential creator of a countervailing force. The absence of both economic disaster and wartime conditions, plus the cumulative grievances under Democrats too long in power, had created a centrifugal reaction.

A multitude of frustrations and fears had helped to mold the change. East-West tensions rather than peaceful tranquillity had begun to characterize the postwar international order. At home, serious inflation, "catch-up" strikes, shortages of essential commodities—especially beef, gasoline, and housing—and a president whose leadership was so uncertain, so vacillating and uninspiring that the Gallup polls were showing less than one-third popular approval, all prepared the scenario for a political rebellion. Not least of the incentives for change was the desperation of Republicans for returning to power.

So it was, in that context, natural to find that Roman Catholics and insecure southern politicians were not alone in helping to foment the "Red" issue. For the first time since the early 1920s, it had been used so freely that, even without centralized orchestration, it became a national theme. Practically everything that was troublesome, especially labor agitation and the CIO-PAC, was linked to the same culprit. "Bring on your New Deal, Communistic and subversive groups," challenged senatorial candidate John Bricker. "If we can't lick them in Ohio, America is lost anyway."[3] The ads in California's Twelfth District, just outside Los Angeles, included the advice that "A vote for Nixon is a vote against the Communist-dominated PAC with its gigantic slush fund." Voorhis fell while trying to dodge the CIO-PAC label. The accusations that he had been "consistently voting the Moscow-PAC-Henry Wallace line in Congress" helped to make his challenger invincible.[4] Similar themes enabled Republican Red-hunter Fred Busbey to unseat Congressman Edward A. Kelley in Illinois. The rising tide of anticommunism was reported by the New York *Times* to have secured Governor Thomas E. Dewey's re-election by a margin of over 675,000 votes. So aware of the potency of the Red issue was Bronx Boss Ed Flynn that he ordered his local Democratic candidates to reject the endorsement of the communist-led American Labor Party. A pre-election visit to Brooklyn by Henry Wallace embarrassed and angered Borough President John Cashmore. Meanwhile, New York State's Democratic leaders began to reassess the price of their association with the American Labor Party (ALP) and contemplated establishing relations with the anticommunist Liberal Party of David Dubinsky and Alex Rose. In Massachusetts, defections in heavily Roman Catholic areas contributed to Lodge's victory and to the upset triumph of Robert Fiske Bradford over the incumbent governor, Maurice J. Tobin.[5] All over the country, newspapers and political challengers picked up the theme. Espionage stories and Winston Churchill's "Iron Curtain" speech at Fulton, Missouri, provided helpful nutrients. Nevertheless, the major focus was on domestic rather than international communism.

There was also evidence of some racial movement away from the Democrats. Of the country's six largest black communities, four showed substantial defections. St. Louis, Detroit, Philadelphia, and New York City all revealed Negro shifts toward the GOP that were in excess of the citywide trends. In Harlem, Adam Clayton Powell, Jr., who had run without opposition in 1944, lost 38 percent of his constituents to a Republican opponent.

The reasons were not hard to find. Not only were the economic reverses more serious there than elsewhere, but some of the most publicized political activities and violence of that year (especially in Georgia, where the only black man who dared to vote in Taylor County was murdered) involved the white-supremacy campaigns of the southern Democrats. Negroes, like the rest of America, were tuned in to the incredibly obscene campaign of Theodore Bilbo, a performance that contained such blatant appeals to racism and even violence that it could not be easily divorced from the party as a whole and even seemed to restore the Republicans as the legitimate heirs of Lincoln.[6] Then, too, along with the Catholic shifts, Samuel Lubell has described the pro-GOP trend among German Americans in the Midwest. Similar patterns were evident in New York City's Queens County. Defections among Polish Americans rose above ten percentage points in Chicago and gave Republicans much more than their usual meager share of the vote in Hamtramck, the largely Polish enclave adjacent to Detroit.[7]

The true importance of that election, however, was its influence on the political relationships of the remaining Truman years. Men, as always, tended to make interpretations through highly individualized perceptions. Thus, Oscar Chapman wrote to defeated senatorial candidate Herbert Lehman, "While dark days may be ahead for liberal causes in this country, I believe the Democratic Party, if it takes advantage of its mistakes and its present opportunity to rebuild, will soon again be given the support of the majority of the voters of this country."[8] Lehman, much gloomier, responded that the cause of progressivism and liberal government would probably "now be under serious threat."[9] Wallace was certain things would have been different if only Truman had not allowed himself to be swayed by the more militant anti-Russians.[10] Most telling, however, were the dynamics of the conservative reaction and its ability to strangle the postwar Democrats. How much of the coalition could survive was almost a moot point.

2

There is a strong temptation to exonerate Truman from personal responsibility for the election. He refrained from any direct participation, not even campaigning for selected candidates. A retrospective glance at the American scene during those early postwar days encourages the conclusion that Democratic Party vulnerability was the inescapable problem. They had been in power too long; the coalition was composed of too many quasi-independent elements; the transition to a peacetime economy and the problems of a postwar world order were irrelevant to the circumstances that had created the New Deal. No single man, it may be argued, could have withstood the impending reaction. His confusion was hardly less than the dilemma being experienced by the party's theological components. Still, there is no way of avoiding the reality of the inept leadership that had compounded the problem.

It was, in fact, logical to give the president his share of the blame. He had fumbled badly, gradually managing to antagonize conservatives, liberals, and the democratic left, the entire popular front that had supported the New Deal. Initially appearing to press for an FEPC, he later stepped aside and watched the filibuster do its job; asked about taking a stand on abolishing poll taxes, he simply referred to past statements of disapproval, thereby further vitiating his public ardor for civil rights. During the nationwide railroad strike in the spring of 1946, he shocked just about every progressive in the country (as well as civil libertarian conservatives) by asking for power to draft the strikers into the army. Yet, only a few weeks later, he denounced and vetoed the antiunion Case bill, outraging the would-be capitalizers of the antilabor climate but gaining little gratitude from the liberals. In the face of what was supposed to have been a "full" employment bill, he seemed hapless as the legislation was being emasculated by the conservatives. The resulting Employment Act of 1946 hardly fulfilled FDR's vision of governmental responsibility for helping to provide jobs. Instead of postwar affluence, the release of consumer dollars that had been pent up during the war touched off a serious inflationary spiral, which became far more serious after Truman capitulated to conservative pressure by removing price controls. Then, denouncing as inadequate a weaker controls law, he used his veto power and became responsible for a new and more explosive round of increases. A series of major strikes and shortages of commodities added to the economic distress. After the last two New Deal stalwarts—Harold Ickes (with a loud protest over Truman's appointment of oil millionaire Ed Pauley as undersecretary of the navy) and Henry Wallace—had left his cabinet, liberals and progressives had little stake in the administration. Lost, too, was the promise of Truman's twenty-one-point program. Delivered to Congress in September 1945, it had requested a full range of domestic legislation in addition to an FEPC. About all it accomplished, aside from foreshadowing his subsequent Fair Deal program, was to convince conservatives that the little man from Missouri was as untrustworthy as FDR. Additionally, Truman's speech delivery was a disastrous contrast with FDR's fireside chats. Virtually nothing remained of the initial confidence that had fortified his start. Instead, the new joke was, "To err is Truman."

As the time neared for the selection of a new congress, conservatives at least knew they had the upper hand and were confident that the future would bring more congeniality from Capitol Hill. But the popular-fronters had no faith in either end of Pennsylvania Avenue. Their disenchantment combined with conservative opposition to reduce the president's rating of approval, by October of 1946, to just 32 percent of the electorate. That fall, *America* summarized the condition rather succinctly: "To those who follow the Henry Wallace-Senator Pepper line [Truman] is a man who has shed too much of the New Deal; to conservatives, both Democrats and Republicans, he is a man who has kept too much of it."[11]

3

For the left, then, the Democratic party itself was retreating from progressive ideals. Those goals were encapsulated in a broad body of agreement, embracing the liberals who sought ways of perfecting the means of developing a more responsible system of private enterprise and the advocates of democratic socialism who visualized placing more of the nation's goods and services in the control of the public rather than the private domain. At the extreme end were the radicals with more revolutionary solutions. Among this group were the American communists, many of whom had followed Earl Browder's lead by joining with the popular front and taking up the cause, albeit more actively, of the advanced progressives.

Their collective portrait of postwar America, their American dream, was an ideal worth fighting for. While their tactics differed in certain essentials, they had reached a general consensus; it assumed a peaceful world that kept alive the wartime Soviet-American cooperation, with a United Nations standing by to promote international harmony and justice. At home, their goals called for racial equality that would reject notions of white supremacy just as the idea of Aryan superiority had been destroyed. The federal government would take measures to free workers from the precarious fluctuations of the business cycle. Full employment would become a humane as well as an economic goal, and its accomplishment would not require war. Workers and farmers deserved to get their full share of what labor produced. Logically, too, the prewar goals should now be extended into such areas as guaranteed employment, medical protection for all, and satisfactory housing. Underdeveloped areas of the country could blossom through defiance of the mammoth power interests and by duplicating the achievements of an outstanding example of New Deal progress, the Tennessee Valley Authority. Thus were joined the aspirations of social democracy at home with Wendell Willkie's concept of "one world" abroad. They were incorporated as the objectives of such groups as the American Federation of Labor; the National Farmers Union; the Union for Democratic Action; the CIO-PAC and its affiliate, the National Citizens Political Action Committee; the Independent Citizens Committee of the Arts, Sciences, and Professions; the American Communist Party; and local political groups that functioned in various states.[12]

Freda Kirchwey, writing in *The Nation* in 1944, predicted that a new progressive party would inevitably become the umbrella for all forces. Reactionary Democrats would join with Republican brethren and that would leave the New Dealers "weakened by endless concessions, now all but homeless," free to join the lonely followers of Wendell Willkie. The existence of such strength was obvious from the popular support for Henry Wallace. Although he had been dumped by the Democratic convention, there was still confidence in his ultimate restoration. James Loeb, Jr., the director of the Union for Democratic Action, and James G. Patton, the president of the National Farmers Union, jointly advanced such hopes by pointing out that Wallace had almost defied the conservative opposition by winning a plurality of the delegates' votes on the first ballot.[13]

From the outset, then, the Truman presidency was, to progressives, a Babylonian captivity of the New Deal. Wallace himself was uncertain about both its future course and his personal role. Shortly after his displacement by Truman on the 1944 ticket, he had noted in his diary that the man from Missouri "is a small man of limited background who wants to do the right thing."[14] The fundamental question was whether progressives would do as Mrs. Kirchwey had suggested or attempt to reverse the malaise that had overtaken the Democrats.

4

Discouraged New Dealers faced a basic decision. Truman was obviously unreliable and his reputation as a conservative was being enhanced with each new appointment. Wallace, as early as the summer of 1945, informed Frances Perkins that with her departure from government "the Roosevelt flavor has completely gone out of the Cabinet," to which she replied, "I find myself wondering profoundly about the future political future [sic] as well as moral future."[15] Jim Patton and Jim Loeb had already speculated about whether the postwar Democratic Party was necessarily the best hope for liberalism, whether advances could not be achieved through the Republican Party. The GOP, they pointed out, was "not encumbered by the reactionary Southerners with their almost unbreakable seniority in Congress or by big city machines as strongly entrenched or as indispensable as existed in the Democratic Party."[16] The Truman policies were increasing cold-war tensions, with administration spokesmen taking an increasingly harder line. In such places as New York

State, for example, party loyalists were interpreting the election results as a signal to spurn the left.

One exception within the administration, about the only man
through whom the liberals felt they could operate, was Robert
Hannegan. The postmaster general and the party's national chairman at least seemed conscious of keeping the ties with the left. He
had even managed to get the president to accept a corps of talented
liberals as advisers. But Hannegan's pragmatic enlightenment had
also come under fire: Southerners resented his defense of the Office
of Price Administration and the right wing was offended when he
gave Wallace equal billing with Truman as speakers at the Jefferson-
Jackson Day dinner. One southern Democrat, Tom Stewart of
Tennessee, introduced a bill aimed at making Hannegan yield either his party chairmanship or his cabinet post. Could the remnants
of the popular front, then, remain within the coalition, or should it
pursue an independent course? The temptations to do the latter
were great.

Forming a third party would, of course, involve severe risks. The
history of such movements in America offered virtually no encouragement and, moreover, there was no evidence that the public
would now be more receptive. They were even opposed to suggestions that the existing parties be realigned ideologically.[17] Eleanor
Roosevelt, the most durable New Deal symbol, cautioned against
attempting to make such a force potent "when things need to be
done quickly."[18] Henry Wallace agreed that the built-in difficulties
posed by the problem of getting such a party on the ballot in the
various states made the idea highly unsatisfactory.[19] Even a mass
meeting of the popular front that took place in Chicago in late
September—the Conference of Progressives—produced more sentiment for working to control the Democratic Party's machinery as the
best backing for a progressive candidate in 1948.

The popular coalition attracted a variety of liberals, progressives,
and communists. Organizational support was supplied by the CIO-
PAC through the National Citizens Political Action Committee
(NC-PAC), and the independent Citizens Committee of the Arts,
Sciences, and Professions (ICCASP). Not until the end of the year
was there the realization of the merger of the NC-PAC and the
ICCASP to create the Progressive Citizens of America. Addressing
their charter session in New York City late that December was the
featured speaker, Henry Wallace. His conclusion, after prescribing a

more sensitive attitude toward the needs of the Soviet Union as the best route toward both world peace and the promotion of American capitalism, consisted of the objective of making the "Democratic party out-and-out progressive."[20]

Whether they would remain with the Democrats was the major question, much more so than the question of leadership. Even before Roosevelt's death, popular support for Wallace was firm and his attractions increased with each new assault from the conservatives. Also, his battle to succeed Jesse Jones undoubtedly helped to enhance his reputation as a defender of the nation's smaller producers against the industrial giants. "Wallace is feared and fought by several groups because of what he might do, or refuse to do, with the government's war plants," advised the *Harland Allen Economic Letter* of Chicago. "Some acknowledged monopolies are backing this fight because Wallace is known to favor the allocation of war plants as far as possible to the smaller business units, even to the point of 'subdividing' vast plant 'acreage' on long term leases from the government."[21] One prominent industrialist also warned Wallace that "the longer the dislocation or the harder the scramble for available raw materials, the more certain it is that this Administration in particular will be open to continued and continuous attack."[22] Wallace himself, on July 23, sent the president a long analysis of the international situation. Its theme was simple: mutual understanding between the United States and the Soviets would "arrest the new trend toward isolationism and a disastrous world war," and, at the same time, would promote the international economic needs of both nations. The president's answer was a polite acknowledgment that failed to notice Wallace's argument.[23] The secretary then used the same theme in his Madison Square Garden speech on September 12, an occasion that determined both the inevitable course of his dissent and the character of the Democratic Party.

When questioned by the press as soon as the text was released to the papers on the morning of the twelfth, Truman saw no problem. He readily acknowledged having approved the speech, but then qualified his initial statement at a subsequent news conference. He explained, in his second reaction, that he had agreed with Wallace's right to make the speech but not necessarily with its contents, which had not received unhurried attention. Only fifteen minutes had been spent with Wallace, said Truman, and most of that time had been devoted to other matters. On the other hand, Wallace's position was supported by friends who had been told about the president's response right after the conference, and his personal diary for that day also showed that he had the more convincing story.

As soon as he became embarrassed, Truman began to backtrack. The Wallace speech appeared to be a bold repudiation of the administration's own policy, especially a vigorous "get tough with Russia" address that Secretary of State Byrnes had delivered in Stuttgart only a few days before. The protests to the president from within the administration included a resignation threat from Byrnes. Finally, Truman summoned Wallace and asked him to quit.[24]

Readers of the press accounts of Wallace's speech and witnesses of its delivery in the Garden were actually reacting to two different versions. The full text was almost impossible to find in the press; reportage chose to emphasize the more conciliatory passages. In actual delivery, however, it had been far more balanced. Wallace had been sharply critical of Soviet misuse of power, both in Russia and in eastern Europe. In fact, the largely pro-Soviet audience had a very mixed reaction to his words, at times booing and hissing, forcing Wallace to retreat at some points from the harsher criticism of his prepared text. After jeers greeted his statement that the Russians would be "forced to grant more and more of the personal freedom," he extemporized: "Put it any way you want. That's the course of history just the same."[25]

His message had simply warned that "getting tough" with the Russians would merely provoke reciprocal belligerence and that the United States had no more business interfering within the Soviet sphere of interest than did they in such places as Latin America. As in his July 23 letter to Truman, he had also stressed the importance of markets and trade. American commercial interests, he had suggested, would be advanced more successfully in a peaceful international setting that featured greater cooperation between the two major powers. That argument led to criticism of Wallace from the left as an advocate of the administration's brand of "imperialism" through a different route from that being developed by Truman and Byrnes.[26]

Of additional importance was what the episode hinted about contemporary popular attitudes. Less than two months before the midterm elections, when fear of communism was being exploited so brazenly, the reaction to even the published version of the speech was surprisingly favorable. Within the first six days, the communications received at the Commerce Department were in agreement with

Wallace by a margin of about five to one.[27] *The Commonweal* failed to see that he had said anything "particularly pro-Russian," only an attitude based on a "misconception of the world in which we live." After some additional reflection, the magazine declared that he had not offered "anything basically different" from Byrnes' position.[28] Other reactions also evaded ideological lines, with the left continuing to find the same faults as had the Garden audience and New York's right-wing *Daily News* observing that Wallace had defended the policies that were undermining FDR's ideals.[29] A conservative Democrat wrote to the secretary at length to agree that American foreign policy was as prone as the Russian to "truculence and intransigence" and as likely to lead to war.[30] The Gallup survey made soon afterward confirmed that the public did favor Wallace's position by the remarkable margin of 78 percent to 16 percent.[31] The same public that was susceptible to anticommunist explanations of what was going wrong at home was evidently not ready to go to war against communism abroad.

Democratic Whip John McCormack, barely managing to type a legible letter to Sam Rayburn, found more fault with the president than with the secretary of commerce. The speech, McCormack wrote to the Speaker, would not have been made if the president had told him not to do so. "Furthermore, frankly speaking, Sam," he added, "my state of mind is such that I do not think some persons like one to tell them the truth, or what their honest views are, if telling them something is not good news."[32]

Wallace, however, was out of the administration. Accepting an offer from publisher Michael Straight to become editor of *The New Republic*, he became a private citizen until circumstances moved him toward the Progressive Citizens of America (PCA).

Meanwhile, fear about the stigma of association with the communists was so intense among the liberals and social democrats of the Union for Democratic Action (UDA) that a splintering of the popular front was set into motion. Two weeks after the midterm elections, letters went out to about fifty prominent anticommunist liberals inviting them to a meeting in Washington on January 4 for a session that would make "a real effort to rechart a desperately-needed path for American progressives for the months and years ahead."[33] So in January the UDA became the Americans for Democratic Action. Convening only a few days after the PCA's charter meeting in New York, the new organization barred members or followers of "any totalitarian organization" or subscribers to "totalitarian political beliefs." The policy defied warnings that hysterical Red-baiters would conveniently ignore the exclusion, anyway. By pushing the more idealistic left toward greater dependence on the PCA as the one group receptive to all progressives, the process of fragmenting the popular front was being promoted.

CHAPTER V

★

The Reprieve

1

Liberals, progressives, and democratic socialists gathered on January 4, 1947, to convert the Union for Democratic Action into the Americans for Democratic Action. From that start, there was acceptance of the proposition that the Democratic Party constituted, as Arthur Schlesinger, Jr., told the charter session, "the most likely medium for the progressives in this country." After a discussion about whether they should be known as "liberals" or "progressives," Jerry Voorhis, who had just lost his seat to Richard Nixon, pointed out that " 'Liberal' cannot be applied to economic progressiveness" because its meaning had changed in recent years; but the majority nevertheless agreed that "liberal" would be the more apt description. The word "progressive" had become too imprecise.[1] The point was a moot one because the other group of dissident Democrats, the Progressive Citizens of America, had been established in New York City only a few days earlier.

Schlesinger reminded the group about Harold Ickes' comment that the PCA should have excluded the communists. That, of course, would now be the criteria of the ADA: a liberal organization devoted to civil liberties and progressive programs at home, international responsibility abroad, and minus the stigma of associations with communists and "fellow travelers." Reinhold Niebuhr told them that a progressive movement could not be "tainted by a suspicion of another loyalty," a point that was made very clear in Chester Bowles' opening statement of principles.

From the outset, it was obvious that keeping their distance from the Democratic Party would be difficult, if not impossible. They planned to demonstrate their independence by endorsing any worthy Republicans or Socialists. The daily operations of the ADA, however, soon established the group as a liberal lobby for the Democrats. They organized rapidly and worked through friendly unionists such as Walter Reuther of the United Auto Workers, who was present at the founding session. While attempting discretion about official connections with the Democrats, both organizations exchanged mutual assistance and financial aid. Within ADA, their closeness to the party did continue to bother the purists and was the subject of numerous deliberations.[2]

An important incentive for ADA's anticommunist goals was the need to compete with the PCA, which had the advantage of having Henry Wallace as its main attraction. Getting rid of Wallaceites became part of the drive to counter leftist influence in a multitude of places, particularly within the ranks of industrial unionism. Consequently, there was much activity in Michigan where they co-operated with Reuther's union as well as with the AFL. In Massachusetts, a statewide United Labor Committee combined ADA, CIO, and AFL operations. Where firm noncommunist control of local chapters was needed, as in Chicago, they were not shy about using the kind of ethics normally attributed to their competitors. Left-wing control of the independent Voters of Illinois, which had become the local ADA organization, was destroyed by maneuvering to concentrate their own minority votes in a manner that defeated a proportional-representation voting system. The radicals suddenly found themselves without delegates. "The commies screamed to high heaven," reported ADA Field Director Richard Bolling, and "with some justice."[3] But their more dramatic significant success was in Minnesota, where Mayor Hubert H. Humphrey used the new organization to further his own power and then, with its support, rose to national prominence.

Humphrey, before winning the mayoralty in 1945, had successfully worked to merge his state's Democrats with the Farmer-Labor Party. The more potent product was the Democratic-Farmer-Labor Party, which became the foundation for Humphrey's successful campaign to win the Minneapolis city hall. Assorted left-wingers, including communists, remained an influential but small minority under the spiritual and intellectual leadership of former governor Elmer A. Benson. Humphrey and Benson came to represent the liberal versus Wallaceite forces within the state. With an appeal that was not above using such cries as, "If I have to choose between being called a Red-baiter and a traitor, I'll be a Red-baiter," Humphrey went to work. Getting substantial ADA support, the liberals forced the progressives out of the D-F-L. Excluded and defeated, the left-wingers were reduced to a rump session that formed a feeble and short-lived Minnesota Progressive Party.[4]

Meanwhile, the national ADA, despite the announcement that Truman would definitely seek re-election on his own, refused to endorse the president. Within their ranks, there was much sentiment for Supreme Court Justice William O. Douglas, a Roosevelt appointee and a liberal celebrity, and Harvard students had already organized a campaign to have the Justice replace the incumbent.[5] The Massachusetts ADA circulated an open letter in opposition to Truman. While it urged the consideration of Douglas, it also included the name of General Dwight D. Eisenhower.[6] A survey of the organization's chapters showed a similar ambivalence between the two men, with sixteen endorsing Douglas, fourteen preferring Eisenhower, two standing by Truman, and the fifteen other units taking no position.[7] Humphrey also declared himself for either Douglas or the general, and the early April meeting of the ADA's national board produced a call to the Democratic convention for consideration of both men. Only the presence of Truman supporters prevented an outright endorsement. Nevertheless it was Eisenhower who offered the greatest promise of political success, with a Gallup Poll confirming his obvious vote-getting advantages over Douglas and placing him first among all potential candidates.

The Eisenhower boom was symptomatic of the abyss into which Democratic liberals had fallen. Ideologically, of course, they could agree that Douglas was the more attractive man and that his candidacy would constitute a credible revival of New Deal appeal. But there were problems about the breadth of his support and whether he would also be acceptable to the South. Unfortunately, however, having so many liberals turn to the popular general—Jake Arvey of Illinois, Franklin D. Roosevelt, Jr., of New York, and labor leaders James B. Carey of the CIO and Emil Rieve of the Textile Workers Union—meant little more than their conviction that he could carry even their decimated party to victory. A poll by Elmo Roper quickly confirmed that much.[8]

They were ready to install as their presidential candidate a general with the most obscure political principles; indeed, had they known much about either his sentiments or his background, they would have had no trouble discovering his conservative sentiments toward both the economy and organized labor, let alone his spiritual attachment to the Republican Party. The ADA's own investigations of the general's past should have been able to provide the clue. Yet they could come up with no better substantiation of his latent "liberalism" than an eloquent tribute to Western civilization in his London Guild Hall speech of 1945, some paeans to democracy in an address before the CIO the next year (after which Phil Murray told him that "Every man and woman in this hall is a friend of yours"), and a laudatory evaluation of the man by Schlesinger in a review of Harry Butcher's *My Three Years with Eisenhower* in *The Nation*. Even the general's testimony before the Senate Armed Forces Committee on integrating the military services was culled for its more enlightened responses, as when he told Senator Richard Russell that "a Negro can improve his standing and his social standing and his respect for certain of the standards that we observe, just as well as we can." Downplayed in a research report that was working hard to find what it wanted to see was Eisenhower's dim view of the prospects for integrating the armed forces.[9]

Chester Bowles received a first-hand view of the general's fitness for the presidency. Bowles had been out of government since having resigned from the Office of Price Administration (OPA) and had decided to fight for the governorship of Connecticut. His fear was that he, along with such other liberals as Adlai Stevenson and Paul Douglas in Illinois and G. Mennen Williams in Michigan, would suffer with Truman at the head of the ticket. So Bowles took his case directly to Eisenhower. He found the general, then president of Columbia University, ignorant about domestic issues and so naïve about partisan politics that he contemplated the possibility of being nominated by both parties. "I came away badly shaken," Bowles later wrote in his memoirs, but still he wanted Ike.[10]

However much such liberals who were fond of "realism" wanted to fool themselves, the general simply was not available. Without much choice, then, the anticommunist left moved toward acceptance of the only available man who truly expressed their own views. That was Harry S Truman. Instead of being able to name a foil for Wallace, they were forced to settle for a much more modest goal, a liberal platform at the party's convention. At Philadelphia, they were also encouraged by the highly effective keynote address delivered by Senator Alben Barkley, who then became the vice presidential candidate.

The ADA, having discredited itself intellectually by romancing a conservative general, went on to provide much of the ideological and organizational substance that did much to help salvage a Truman victory from what appeared to be certain defeat. Where a strong pro-civil rights stand could attract wavering blacks in the northern cities, the ADA worked to force the issue against adminis- tration hopes of placating rebellious southerners. It was the intro- duction of an advanced statement for racial equality by Humphrey and his ADA supporters, in the face of last-minute administration efforts to temporize on the issue, that created the crisis: southerners walked out and civil rights promoters were pleased. In a climate of rising anticommunism, the ADA worked to convince liberals that not only was the Wallace position contrary to the way most Ameri- cans believed the cold war should be handled but that it also rested on naïve assumptions. It was the ADA that promoted awareness of the administration's domestic boldness against the business-linked Republicans who had put over antilabor legislation. In the face of revolts from the far right and the far left, it became clearer that the ADA's search for a congenial candidate should have stopped at the White House. Even one of the organization's two choices to head the ticket, Justice Douglas, became Truman's first preference as a running-mate. But Douglas, believing with everybody else that the Democrats were doomed in 1948, chose to resist and wait until 1952. Then, he reasoned, he could step in and become the liberal candi- date for whom a revitalized and desperate coalition would be looking.[11] Thus, the result was a Truman-Barkley ticket in 1948.

2

At the Democratic convention, the battle had been rewarding for the liberals. Despite White House attempts to placate the South by retreating from the advanced civil rights position that had been enumerated back on February 2, Humphrey and his backers defied the anticipated states' righters walkout by fighting for the strongest civil rights plank that had ever been adopted. Their victory yielded a statement that committed the party to work for the eradication of "all racial, religious and economic discrimination" and verbalized such sentiments by endorsing "the right to live, the right to work, the right to vote, the full and equal protection of the laws, on a basis of equality with all citizens as guaranteed by the Constitution."[12] The platform also called for repealing the Taft-Hartley Act, for almost doubling the forty-cent-per-hour minimim wage, for federal aid to education, and for the admission to the country of at least four hundred thousand displaced persons. The GOP was charged with passing an inadequate "and bigoted bill for this purpose" that imposed "un-American restrictions on race and religion upon such admissions," phraseology that was viewed as an open appeal for the Catholic vote.[13]

Having entered the convention hall still hopeful of getting rid of Truman, the liberals emerged with a surprising amount of euphoria. Victory itself hardly seemed as vital as the paramount issues. Liberals had, after all, put together a program that constituted a progressive statement of what postwar America needed, one that left little to be added by impotent Wallaceites while still remaining forthright in opposition to totalitarianism. Roosevelt himself would have been pleased. "I came away from Philadelphia," wrote Chester Bowles, "feeling immensely encouraged about the future of the Democratic Party." To Bowles, inability to remove Truman was less important than proving "that we had the makings of a strong liberal organization; and as the elderly gentlemen who occupied the platform gradually step aside, we should be able to accomplish a great deal."[14]

Truman and the other Democratic candidates made the subsequent campaign a battle for a revived New Deal. Sitting as a perfect target was the Republican-dominated Eightieth Congress, its bipartisan support for the administration's foreign policies as overlooked as the obstructionists within the president's own party. The scapegoat Congress was depicted as the "tool" of antilabor and big-business interests; it was accused of blocking progress at all levels, from public power to housing, medical care, and civil rights. Truman's own veto of the Taft-Hartley Act, which became law anyway and was attacked by unions as a "slave-labor" bill, became the focal point for blasts at what he called the "do-nothing" Eightieth Congress.

The president supplied a major stroke of postconvention liberalism by issuing Executive Order 9981, which mandated racial equality in the armed forces. It had been promised in his February message. Cautiously delayed until after the convention, in the face of the impending southern revolt, the regulation was a strong antidote to take care of substantial administration concern about the direction of the black vote. In mid-April, a report had circulated in the White House that projected as much as 75 percent of the Harlem vote moving toward Wallace and other candidates on New York's American Labor Party ticket. There was, in fact, no single domestic issue articulated by the Progressives with more ardor than the need for racial equality. It was, after all, easy to denounce the Democrats as the party of Bilbo and Talmadge. Dissolving military segregation became a top priority item.[15]

The articulation of a liberal program on all fronts, behind a leader awakening to fight a spirited grass-roots campaign, offered new hope for progress whatever the outcome in November. Louis Bean was virtually alone among the political analysts to believe that the persuasive evidence being compiled by the pollsters could be wrong. As Truman relished the battle more and more, while presidential positions enhanced his strengthened image, his audiences became more responsive and larger, undoubtedly pleased by his slashing style. Cooler observers of such reactions, particularly newsmen, noted the many past discrepancies between such receptions and the actual flow of ballots on election day. So the late campaign surge was ignored; only in retrospect would the little signals be recognized.

The ADA's efforts complemented the Democrats. While working harder to defeat Wallace than to promote the president, they supplemented the campaigns of a number of liberals—Bowles, Humphrey, Paul Douglas, Adlai Stevenson, Henry Jackson, and the congressional race of Richard Bolling in Kansas City, Missouri. Their accomplishment was impressive. Seventy-nine congressmen, five senators, and four governors were elected with ADA help. In Detroit, they succeeded with thirty out of a slate of thirty-five candidates, ten of whom belonged to the local ADA chapter.[16]

3

Fortunately for Truman and the Democrats, the candidacies of Dewey, Thurmond, and Wallace did little to hurt their cause. There is even the possibility that their peculiar combination of challenges balanced various impulses within the electorate and helped to make the outcome possible. In Dewey's case, it was relatively simple. He was the obvious beneficiary of any Truman disaster, so few disagreed with his strategy of avoiding any risk to Republican harmony and his own position when he was a sure winner. Overly cautious, then, eschewing bold stands, the New York governor did nothing that distinguished him from the burden carried by the party that continued to symbolize hard times.

Consequently, when grain prices dropped throughout the wheat belt that summer and fall, Dewey became vulnerable to the scare

tactics and demagogic campaigning of Truman and Agriculture Secretary Charles Brannan, both of whom painted images of Republican eagerness to pull out the bottom from farm price supports. On
election day, there was the fruition of a trend that was missed by
most pollsters. The states of the Middle West, usually predominantly
Republican, gave Truman 101 electoral votes. That included three
that had been Dewey's in 1944.[17] Probably more than anything else,
Republicans were hurt by their inability to escape from the op-
probrium of Hooverian economics. While their loss in the farm belt
was Truman's salvation, the significance of his electoral majority
must consider what happened to the serious challenges that came
from the fringe candidates of the right and the left.

Once the administration had spelled out its civil rights program in
early February, the making of some type of revolt was ensured. A
series of meetings among southerners then followed. Led by such
activist governors as Ben Laney of Arkansas, J. Strom Thurmond of
South Carolina, and Fielding Wright of Mississippi, they remon-
strated against the usurpation of federal power and included references to all of the major issues in contention, from railroad freight
rates and tidelands oil to the FEPC and the southern hopes of restoring the two-thirds rule at the party's national conventions. Thurmond addressed a Conference of States' Rights Democrats in Jackson,
Mississippi, on May 10 and pictured the dissidents as the true upholders of the constitution as well as the ones with the most genuine
concern for the welfare and progress of Negroes. The nearly four
thousand gathered in the city's Civic Auditorium also passed a resolution reminding the Democrats that the "national party organization is merely an association of the various state party organizations."[18] Before adjourning, they prepared themselves for defeat at
Philadelphia by planning to reconvene afterward, if necessary, at
Birmingham. What happened at the national convention was virtually a self-fulfilling prophecy in the form of a gamble that left them
disjointed and exposed to defeat.

That they lacked the votes was obvious. They found that out over
the fight to restore the two-thirds rule. Uncompromisingly, however,
they moved ahead to win their objectives: eliminating from the platform any endorsement of the president's February 2 civil rights
proposals and replacing him at the head of the ticket. They rejected
an offer to kill any mention of Truman's call for federal control of
the tidelands oil if they would accept the racial equality plan. They
were even dissatisfied with a deadlocked platform committee move

to restate the tepid, almost invisible, civil rights language of 1944. They wanted, instead, a clear reaffirmation of states' rights. Consequently, they were defying not only the heavy numerical disadvantage of an outvoted South, but also the impressive loyalist sentiment within their own region.

The convention later adopted the strong Humphrey-ADA civil rights plank and even added a commendation for the president's personal role. Ben Laney, who had appeared ready to become the states' rights candidate, suddenly backed off. He explained that he could not stand even momentarily on the party's new platform. Other respected southerners who could have become credible candidates, such as Senators Richard Russell of Georgia and John Sparkman of Alabama, would have nothing to do with the rebels. Laney himself added to the confusion by declaring that their purpose was not to bolt but to bring the party more nearly under southern direction. At the Dixie caucus, Governor Thurmond, whose own reputation had been as a moderate until he became involved in the movement, shouted, "We have been betrayed, and the guilty shall not go unpunished!" Still, among those at the center of the rebellion, such political leaders as Judge Leander Perez of Louisiana, Gessner McCorvey of Alabama, and Governors Fielding and Thurmond, there was little doubt that the plans for a postconvention session at Birmingham were much more than a mere hedge against failure at Philadelphia.

That evening, after the adoption of the civil rights plank, convention chairman Rayburn began the roll-call for the nomination. Handy Ellis, the head of Alabama's delegation, had failed to gain recognition to speak earlier. Now he had his chance. Rising on a point of personal privilege, he began by recalling that half of his state's delegation had already pledged their readiness to walk out. Then he added that "the delegation from Mississippi would not be true to the people of that great state if they did not join in this walk-out and therefore they join with us, and we bid you good-bye." With the Mississippians in the lead, followed by half of the Alabama contingent waving their state flag in defiance, thirty-four rebels walked straight down the center aisle under boos and jeers from the galleries and numerous delegates. They left the sweltering hall and went directly outside into a heavy rainstorm. Eager to gauge the newsworthiness of their protest, they rushed to the few TV sets that were then available.

The remaining southerners made the symbolic gesture of nominating Russell. In placing the senator's name in nomination, Charles Bloch of Georgia recalled an eloquent speech at a Democratic convention fifty-two years earlier. "The south is no longer going to be the whipping boy of the Democratic party," he said, "and you know, or if you don't know you can learn here and now, that without the votes of the south you cannot elect a President of the United States. I do not mean to suggest, even, secession from the Democratic Party, but I do mean to say to you Democrats of the north and west and the east, paraphrasing the language of the great commoner of a generation ago, 'You shall not crucify the south on this cross of civil rights.' "[19] The cheers were loud and the band played "Dixie"; but Russell could get no more than 263 votes to Truman's 947½, so the president was renominated on the first ballot.

The bolters then reconvened at Birmingham. Significantly, and much to their distress, the newspapers began to call them "Dixiecrats," which certainly belied their attempts to suggest national representation. Officially, they called themselves the States' Rights Democrats (SRD). But weakness and disorganization became their chief characteristics and there was much enthusiasm but little clarity at Birmingham. Would they make a serious attempt to field presidential candidates or would they merely withhold electoral votes through unpledged electors and try to throw the decision into the House of Representatives? Finally, Thurmond and Wright became their presidential and vice presidential candidates.

Even in the South, a number of factors worked to limit their appeal. There were very substantial fears that they could only serve the cause of a Republican victory. Expressing a theme that was heard with increasing frequency after the Birmingham meeting, the Arkansas *Democrat* called the strategy of the States' Rights Democrats "futile and bad." Republicans were behind a civil rights program hardly different from Truman's, so their victory would be just as harmful and would leave the South less influential than if they remained within the Democratic Party. The wise strategy, cautioned the paper, would be to strive to check obnoxious measures the Republicans might pass.[20]

That theme had endless variations. What the South really feared was overturning its economic order through racial equality. And the biggest threat to that was the FEPC, which could best be blocked by preserving southern strength in Congress and not by handing power over to the GOP. A. Willis Robertson, who announced his support of the Truman-Barkley ticket, explained that the "only hope that

Virginia and other Southern States have from being utterly crushed by Northern Republicans as well as Northern Democrats is to keep States' Rights Democrats in Congress."[21] It had even become possible to suspect the GOP as a subrosa ally of the States' Rights Democrats. The Democratic National Committee claimed it had evidence of Republican promises to help southerners kill civil rights legislation in the Senate in exchange for bolting the Truman ticket, and wide circulation was given to a story about how Indiana Republicans had aided the efforts of a Mississippian to get the SRD ticket on their state's ballot.[22]

Furthermore, an impressive list of southern leaders either remained aloof from the bolters or stated their outright opposition. That number included Sam Rayburn and extended all the way to such people as John Sparkman, Lister Hill, and Richard Russell. Indeed, the ingredients that made for loyalty were becoming clear: those dependent upon the federal government for offices and jobs; states with firm, secure leadership such as Virginia, where Byrd and his followers sympathized with the dissenters but, except for a brief move to withhold electors from Truman, nevertheless stopped short of outright rebellion; and those places that had the greatest fear of potential Republican competition. North Carolina, Tennessee, and Virginia were most concerned by that possibility.

In May, the North Carolina state convention rejected a move to instruct their delegates to Philadelphia not to vote for Truman or any other civil rights advocate. Former governor Cameron Morrison cautioned them to "step under the Democratic flag and help elect him. Then, we'll let our Congressmen and Senators beat him down when he needs beating."[23] Later that summer, a Texas loyalist received enthusiastic applause from delegates in Austin for warning that "If we fight among ourselves over Negroes' rights this fall and permit the election of Dewey—with his moustache—before the end of his Administration we will wonder what became of white people's rights."[24]

Within the ranks of those desiring to remain loyal, for one reason or another (a desire not necessarily related to the intensity of their ideological differences with the administration), the prospect of getting General Eisenhower to head the ticket was as appealing as to the ADA liberals. As early as March, Robertson confided to Dr. Douglas Southall Freeman, the Virginia newspaper editor and biographer, that Eisenhower was the one man who could unite the country. He could, Robertson reasoned, bring the American people together and, at the same time, talk to the Russians in a "way that will be friendly and yet firm. General Eisenhower has a big heart and the people of America love him. . . . If we stand at a distance and cuss Russia and Russia cusses us it is inevitable that when at last we reach striking distance of each other we will fight. In that fight, we all will suffer and there will be no victor."[25]

Robertson went to see the general and told him he could aid the country as had George Washington after the Revolutionary War. He gave his assurances of support from other senators. During the hour's conversation, the general explained that he belonged to no political party and that he had only two loves, his family and his country. He did not believe a military man should become president. Only the interests of international cooperation could get him to change his mind. Robertson came away from that meeting with the conviction that the general would succumb to a draft, and he urged southern colleagues to accompany him to the White House to persuade Truman to step aside in favor of the general. "But they did not have the guts to make that move," the senator recalled three weeks later. When the dissident threats within the ranks of their colleagues began to undermine their own positions, Robertson was asked to reconsider his earlier plan to visit Eisenhower. It had once been possible, he explained, but the convention was too near and events had moved too quickly to get rid of Truman.[26] Still, before they convened at Philadelphia, delegates from Georgia and Virginia were officially instructed to work for an Eisenhower nomination.

The most determined of the southerners were suspicious of the general, considering him a potential "front man" for the "crowd of New Dealers."[27] The intensity of their struggle against such heavy odds did frustrate attempts to confine their protest to rational constitutional arguments and attracted extremist personalities and rhetoric. The presence of embarrassing demagogues like Gerald L. K. Smith, who was ignored by Thurmond, was given exaggerated prominence in the movement. So were the old anti-Catholic elements who had fought against Al Smith. Thurmond's own unfortunate lapses into wild hyperbole also helped to create an aura of extremism. A careful study of the Georgia situation has demonstrated that the establishment of that state tended to reject the SRD as unsophisticated populists who could jeopardize the state's economic growth. Both of their senators, Russell and Walter George, announced for Truman. In Tennessee, Ed Crump gambled on the Dixiecrats and lost. His candidates were defeated by Estes Kefauver, who was elected to the Senate, and by Gordon Browning, who unseated Governor James N. McCord, even though the latter had indicated his own opposition to the movement.[28] Senator McKellar then startled just about everyone by coming out for Truman, which was taken as a sure sign of SRD weakness. Sid McMath in Arkansas won the governorship while supporting the national ticket. Not insignificant was the work of key newspaper editors. The three most influential in the South, Virginius Dabney in Virginia, Ralph McGill in Georgia, and Jonathan Daniels in North Carolina all strongly opposed the Thurmond-Wright ticket.[29]

As the SRD campaign progressed, it also became apparent that its assumptions were supported by those most opposed to the economic concepts of the New Deal. It had little appeal to organized labor; frustrated at not being able to sway workers after addressing them in Woodland, Florida, in September, Thurmond descended to the kind of demagoguery that was characteristic of the more rabid firebrands. As one student of the movement has concluded, his "rebellion had attracted ardent white supremacists, rabidly anti-union industrialists, wealthy oil men who would have preferred return of the tidelands to the states, and sincere constitutional conservatives who harbored deep fears of an enlarging federal government."[30] Thirty-eight of his thirty-nine electors came from the four states that were central to the movement and 1,169,000 popular votes were not unimpressive for a regional candidacy.

Failing to make a significant impact, they inadvertently placed a halo around Truman and the national party. Back in 1947, Clark Clifford's long memorandum had advised the president to seek the liberal vote because the largest electoral prize lay with the urban coalition. Clifford had erred in assuming that the South had no place to go and would remain loyal; but the margin of his miscalculation may have been given dividends by the enhanced position the president had won among Negroes and liberals. Aided by the kind of opposition emanating from the Dixiecrats, Truman had an easier time making the transition from a liberal goat to a liberal hero. In October, he went to Harlem and delivered a vigorous speech for equality. There was nothing more fortuitous, then, than the Dixiecrat revolt in helping the president compete for the black vote among the Republicans and the threatening Wallaceites. As the incumbent and the candidate of the regulars, he obviously carried the additional authority as a more credible choice. There is also reason to believe that the SRD revolt helped to influence those Catholics who perceived the president as the victim of the same forces that had opposed Al Smith.[31] For Catholics, labor, and liberals, he had become the only choice. Considering that Truman had managed to hold most of the South, his loss of thirty-nine electoral votes may have been more than adequately compensated for by the hairline victories in California, Illinois, and Ohio, which were worth seventy-eight. Those three states cast a total of 10,942,000 popular votes, but the president's *combined* plurality was only 66,000.

The Wallace crusade paid similar dividends. Two days before the end of 1947, the former vice president bowed to the PCA's request that he seek a third-party nomination. To progressives convinced that Democrats and Republicans offered no choice, that both were controlled by "militarists" and "big business interests," there was finally a chance to turn America away from reaction and the inevitability of war. At least, wrote a lady from Boston to Eleanor Roosevelt, "If the Republicans win, we shall have a better chance in 1952. . . . We won't have this stupid Truman on our necks."[32] Such exuberance got a considerable boost on February 17 from the results of a special congressional election in New York City.

A Wallaceite candidate, Leo Isacson, scored an impressive victory against a Democrat who had the blessings of Mrs. Roosevelt and Mayor William O'Dwyer. Philosophically, there was no substantive difference between Isacson and the man about to become the presidential candidate of the Progressive Party. He won by calling for greater understanding of the Soviet Union, strong civil rights legislation, and, in his heavily urban and Jewish area, he also stressed the need for rent controls as well as support for Zionist objectives in Palestine, all positions endorsed by the Progressives.[33] Isacson's dramatic victory inflated left-wing expectations almost as though all of the United States had the outlook of New York's Twenty-fourth Congressional District. Projections of national expectations for a Wallace ticket zoomed upward, with Gallup forecasting a possible four million votes. Partisan expectations ranged far higher.[34]

Only gradually did the self-delusions become obvious. The Wallace following was actually declining and had been going downhill since its peak in June. The New York election proved little except that the American Labor Party had strong local strength, which included ethnic support for censuring the administration's confused and wavering policy toward the Palestine question, an area where the president was trying to maneuver between the conflicting demands of the State and Defense departments and political expediency. The Progressives and Wallace supported the Zionist principle

with enthusiasm. Similarly, they attacked the administration's position as inadequate in the areas of civil rights, inflation, and for
pushing the cause of universal military training.

Throughout 1948, however, it was the cold war that undermined
Wallace's campaign. Already, most Americans supported the granting of military assistance to Greece and Turkey and economic aid
under the Marshall Plan to rehabilitate western Europe as appropriate responses to Soviet power. ADA liberals and others backed them,
differing mainly over whether to emphasize economic rather than
arms aid, and joining such conservatives as Harry Byrd in question-
ing whether the programs did not violate the United Nations Charter. But few agreed with the Wallace contention that Russian threats
were in response to the administration's belligerence. As arguments
about the initial responsibility for having begun the cold war became more academic, the Progressive point of view became more
isolated, vulnerable to charges of fronting for international communism. The development of a bipartisan approach to American
diplomacy, a position endorsed by Republican candidate Tom
Dewey, further helped to place debate outside the acceptable
boundaries of criticism. The Progressives, then, found themselves
beyond the pale.

What was left of the credibility of Wallace's foreign policy was
then shattered by Russian moves in the half year before the November elections. A series of shocks, the communist coup in Czechoslovakia in February and then the Berlin blockade, underlined what
appeared to be the wisdom of Truman's policies. They sharpened
the contrast between the administration and the Wallace appeal.
The former vice president, instead of condemning what had happened in Czechoslavakia, attributed the putsch to a legitimate
response to plans for a right-wing coup involving the American
ambassador. He also accepted the Russian version of Jan Masaryk's
death, claiming that cancer had caused the Czech foreign minister to
commit suicide. Truman, meanwhile, ordered a dramatic around-
the-clock airlift to save West Berlin. Oddly enough, that autumn it
was the president who tinkered with the idea of sending Chief Justice Fred Vinson to Moscow on a mission that might, hopefully,
break the impasse with the Russians. Dissuaded by Secretary of
State George Marshall from following through with the plan, Truman's sincerity as a peacemaker was nevertheless enhanced.[35] Most
Americans considered his approach rather than Wallace's the more
likely way to avoid war.

The president further undercut an area of Wallace strength by making a late campaign promise of federal aid and *de jure* recognition for the new state of Israel being created by the United Nations. At a Madison Square Garden rally in late October, his pro-Israel position became even firmer. Together with a foray into Harlem, where he mentioned civil rights for the only time during the campaign, it was effective in helping to move New York's voters toward the Democratic ticket during the final days before November 5.[36]

The essential weakness of the Wallace campaign, however, and the great gain for Truman's effort, was the vulnerability of the Progressives to what they called "Red-baiting." Without any inhibitions, the Democrats, who had been the victims of that kind of appeal in 1946, now did their share. The director of publicity for the Democratic National Committee candidly admitted that "through every avenue we were pointing out that Wallace and his third party were following the Kremlin line slavishly."[37]

From the December 1947 start of the third party's effort, the Progressives were in a joint venture with the American Communist Party. A decision had been made to work under the cover of the Wallace group as the most expedient tactic for implementing both domestic and cold-war goals.[38] While the communists thought they could use Wallace for their purposes, he accepted their assistance and remained confident he could control them. At the Progressive convention, the delegates rejected a resolution that merely intended to disown any move to give "blanket endorsement to the foreign policy of any nation," meaning, of course, the Soviet Union. Rejection of that, the so-called Vermont Resolution, furthered the growing number of defectors. The press also did its share to emphasize how the "commies" had run the convention. The legislative representative of the New York State Communist Party was given prominent space for his announcement that his group intended to work for the first phase of communism through the Progressives.[39] In August, the Communist Party's convention announced that, instead of nominating their own candidate, they would "join with millions of other Americans to support the Progressive Party ticket to help win the peace."[40] Meanwhile, their followers worked at taking over the operation at each local level.

On the matter of communist support, Wallace remained silent. He held that they had as much right to their views as any other group and refused to descend to "Red-baiting." The closest he came to a rejection of such support was at Center Sandwich, New Hampshire. Speaking before the Progressives had held their convention, he promised not to engage in "Red-baiting" but admitted that "If the Communists would have a ticket of their own, the New Party would lose 100,000 votes but gain four million."[41] He then spurned appeals to repeat that remark, a decision he later said he regretted. Yet, curiously enough, after all that was so obvious about the kind of sponsorship he was getting, Wallace explained to a correspondent on July 12 that the Center Sandwich comment was made only with the thought "of the political necessity of broadening our base as much as possible and assuring the faint-hearted that the New Party is not communist dominated."[42] As his campaign progressed, the return movement of the noncommunist left to the Democratic Party accelerated. Their pique at Wallace was also increased because the Progressives were running candidates against several liberal Democrats in various parts of the country, a tactic that was judiciously dropped in October.[43]

The greatest political gain for the Democrats was the freedom to use the communist issue against the Progressives, an opportunity they exploited to the fullest. It was a device employed from Truman on down. Their attacks complicated making distinctions between blatant "Red-baiting" and legitimate political charges, which were at least as valid as calling Republicans "tools of big business."[44] Winning not a single state, Wallace finished with twelve thousand votes less than Thurmond's far more sectional ticket. Drawing from forty-six states, the Progressive candidate totaled 1,157,172, far short of the most modest earlier projections. The only damage to the Democrats was inflicted in New York, where half a million Wallace votes (44 percent of his national total) easily deprived Truman of that state's forty-seven electors.

Just as the States' Rights attack had enhanced the administration's liberal image, the Wallace campaign saved the Democrats from being tagged with the communist issue. The administration's foreign policy, especially its handling of the Berlin crisis, strengthened that advantage.[45]

Both Truman and his party, consequently, did surprisingly well. Strong races by Democrats in various states—Ed Johnson in Colorado, Guy Gillette in Iowa, Hubert Humphrey in Minnesota, Jim Murray in Montana, Estes Kefauver in Tennessee, and Lester Hunt in Wyoming—had undoubtedly extended coattails upward to the top of the ticket. The national percentages also showed that the president had trailed his party's congressional candidates. But outside the South, where Truman lost so many votes to Thurmond, the figures show that the president ran ahead of the Democratic congressional candidates. He was 2 percent behind in the Northeast, where Wallace drew 4.5 percent of the presidential vote, but totaled 5.5 percent better in the West and the Middle West combined.[46] He also won six states that elected Republican governors. The Truman campaign, with the aid of the ADA and organized labor, and capitalizing rather than suffering from the extremist defections, resulted in what contemporary observers quickly called the most astonishing upset in American history.

4

It is tempting to argue that the election was a tribute to the persistence of the New Deal appeal. Instead, there is every reason to believe that there had been merely a reprieve from the great conservative conquest of 1946.

The peculiar circumstances of the Democratic victory, in fact, offered little solace to liberals eager to interpret the results as a mandate from the old coalition. Over a million southerners had seen fit to deny their political heritage. The farm vote was hardly more than the reaction of a self-interested group, much as labor found it was more expedient to support the man who stood for getting rid of the Taft-Hartley Act. The mass return of Catholics to the ticket, which in some cases exceeded Al Smith's showing and even FDR's margins, included old supporters of Lemke's 1936 Union Party and Father Coughlin, a group attracted by Truman's vigorous foreign policy and further brought into line by the administration's purification from the Wallace taint.[47] It would have been foolhardy to believe that they and the liberals could work together for the simultaneous promotion of strident anticommunism and progressivism. With the aid of the newly formed Nationalities Division of the Democratic National Committee, the party kept the Polish vote intact. The most liberal segment of the Jewish vote, an ardent New Deal following, became highly susceptible to the Wallace appeal, their defection paralleling the return of the conservative Catholics. Only among black Americans was the gain not built on sand. Even with the attractions of the Wallace candidacy, which was strongest in Harlem and went well above 10 percent in several places, Negroes turned in some encouraging reversals of the downturn of two years earlier. In Illinois, where the Progressive candidate was not on the ballot, black districts gave Truman 78.8 percent.[48] A coalition composed of loyalists limited to blacks, intellectuals, labor leaders, and ethnic groups fearful of spreading international communism would inevitably become vulnerable before the mounting stresses of the cold war.

Encouraged by victory, however, Truman unveiled his ambitious Fair Deal program in early 1949, the most far-reaching list of social legislation since Roosevelt's era. But the Eighty-first Congress, controlled by the Democrats, was hardly more cooperative than the famous Eightieth. With an effective conservative coalition of Republicans and southern Democrats, such items as a national health care program, a vast new public power project, repeal of the Taft-Hartley Act, aid to public education, civil rights legislation, and a revised farm plan were turned back. Only when conservatives consented, as in the case of the National Housing Act of 1949, was success possible.

Such efforts by Truman were marred by other distractions. Far greater interest was captured by the announcement in the fall of 1949 that the Russians had entered the nuclear age and, soon after that, by the complete collapse of Chiang Kai-shek from the Chinese mainland. At home, the names of Alger Hiss, Julius and Ethel Rosenberg, and Judith Coplon became better known than the substance of the president's legislative program. In February of 1950, Senator Joseph R. McCarthy, a freshman Republican from Wisconsin, joined the cold war by announcing that the State Department was harboring 205 communists. Four months later, Truman swiftly sent American troops to repel an invasion of South Korea, and a seesaw, inconclusive, and oddly "limited" war was under way. Not only did the Republicans do well in the midterm elections of 1950, but more significant was the conservative character that marked the shift, largely nullifying whatever congressional gains had been made in 1948. Five months after a disastrous Chinese Communist onslaught against advancing American troops, the president abruptly fired General Douglas MacArthur. Again, Truman's popularity plumeted.

It was indicative of their despair, a level of despondency that began even before the MacArthur incident, that several Democrats again looked toward General Eisenhower to salvage the situation. Joining them was Senator Robert Kerr of Oklahoma, who was advised by Willis Robertson in March to approach Truman through Senator Clinton P. Anderson. "What Eisenhower is willing to do will of course depend on what Mr. Truman is willing to do," Robertson pointed out. "Eisenhower was willing to accept the nomination in 1948 if Truman had asked him to do so but not on any other terms. My personal belief is that his attitude will be the same in 1952."[49]

Robertson's personal campaign had begun. He viewed Eisenhower as an internationalist who had the additional virtue of sharing southern attitudes toward civil rights, and pointed out that Eisenhower's sympathy for the working man would nevertheless not permit him to let labor unions take charge of the White House.[50] On October 2, 1951, the Virginian sent a confidential telegram to Bernard Baruch asking the financier to help promote the general for the Republican nomination.[51]

That fall, John Cogley, the liberal editor of *The Commonweal*, endorsed Eisenhower with a glowing "We Like Ike" editorial. Cogley did not care much which party adopted him. "The typical American in the ideal sense," he wrote, "should be neither Republican nor Democrat. . . . A certain amount of vagueness is essential to the role. . . . Dwight Eisenhower as President may prove to be what the doctor ordered."[52]

A few days later, in early November, the general visited Truman at the White House. He was on a brief stay in Washington from his NATO headquarters in France. During that session, he was told that the earlier offer to head the Democratic ticket still held good. According to the way Truman told the story later that same day, the soldier protested that his attitude on a number of issues, especially toward organized labor, could not be reconciled with Democratic policy. One of those who heard Truman's version leaked the story to Arthur Krock, the respected Washington correspondent of the New York *Times*.

The informer was Justice William O. Douglas.[53] His revelation could have only served the interests of damaging Eisenhower with the considerable number of Republicans who already considered him too close to the Democrats and result in having him frozen out of either party's nomination. The story was gleefully publicized by the GOP's Taft supporters and vehemently denied by Eisenhower partisans. Douglas apparently still hoped that the Democrats could win behind the candidacy of a certified liberal. He failed to realize how far the New Deal coalition had disintegrated.

PART TWO

"A Spell in
the Wilderness"

★

CHAPTER VI

Adlai and Lyndon

1

Adlai Ewing Stevenson, after much cajoling and hesitation, finally came out of the Middle West in the summer of 1952 to run against Dwight Eisenhower. The Illinois governor's career and background were both distinguished, his grandfather having been vice president of the United States under Grover Cleveland and his own career having included service as a counsel to the Agricultural Adjustment Administration in the early days of the New Deal and with the American delegation to the United Nations. Liberal in temperament more than in dogma, and an effective governor of a key state, he had been regarded by Harry Truman as the ideal choice to fight for continued Democratic control of the White House.

There had been a formidable slew of hopefuls, undoubtedly inspired by confidence in the continuing strength of the Democratic majority. The most ambitious, Senator Estes Kefauver, the Tennessee progressive, had capitalized on his sensational crime committee hearings that had given television its first real boost in the field of public events reportage. But Kefauver was anathema to not only his southern colleagues but to party bosses generally and had competition from three others who were decidedly more acceptable to those eager to avoid either a repetition of the 1948 fracture or outright capitulation to liberal interests. With three great issues dominating southern concerns, civil rights, retention of the Taft-Hartley Act, and securing the tidelands oil deposits for the states, those reluctant to see the party defeated by Eisenhower turned to more congenial candidates. Perhaps the most respected of the group, and the most formidable possibility, was Senator Russell of Georgia, but he carried the burden of the traditional regional disadvantage. Robert Kerr, the Senate's oil millionaire from Oklahoma, had key friends in the White House, including the president himself. Kerr, however, was much too vulnerable to being labeled as a special interest candidate. Even Alben Barkley, although seventy-five years old, had been tantalized by the thought of running. Stevenson added to the confusion with his reluctance about accepting, and the hopefuls received additional encouragement in late March when Truman announced that he would retire at the end of his term.

But it was Stevenson who was finally presented with the nomination, the result of a genuine draft, one that has been recounted in considerable detail in many different sources.[1] Virtually unknown to the rest of the nation, the governor became an overnight sensation with his eloquent acceptance address, which helped to launch what became his extraordinary appeal to intellectuals and idealists. The man who would inspire a generation of what came to be known as "eggheads" to participate in politics was a leader of extraordinary sensitivity. Criticized throughout his career for indecisiveness, he was inhibited by the conviction that he did not have godlike powers to resolve the world's complexities.

Stevenson found it hard to understand how others could speak in conclusive terms about issues involving a myriad of considerations and end up with bold statements. Nevertheless, he had been an effective governor of a major state, one whose substantial accomplishments did not prevent him from insisting that "the difficulties are beyond my limited capacity, and moreover, I have become so preoccupied with this job, which seems to me of worthy magnitude, that I am loathe to leave to go to sea without a chart"; or from writing to James P. Warburg, some two months later, that he wished he "knew the right and wrong of all these things. If I did I might have found the direction of the 'finger of destiny' more agreeable. As it is, the more I think of this horrible mess the more I want to be President less." Later that spring, watching Kefauver fight through one primary after another in a struggle to make hostile party leaders accept his candidacy, Stevenson was puzzled. "Perhaps," he responded to one of Warburg's many letters, "I sense the horrors of the next few years more clearly than he and some of the other gentlemen who seem so eager to assume burdens and decisions that dwarf the imagination."[2] At the end of July, after he had been nominated, he told Dean Acheson: "The road is hard and very unfamiliar and I know only too well how limited the rewards. But I have loved the stars too fondly to be fearful of the night."[3]

Stevenson's eloquence could neither retrieve the party's standing nor gain confidence from a public whose economic insecurity had been largely replaced by fear of communist expansionism. Although the governor tried to separate his campaign from Truman's record, his efforts failed to dispel the widespread recognition that, for a divided America, torn by paranoia and unable to understand what had disrupted the anticipated tranquillity of the postwar world, the time for change had really arrived. Neither Stevenson nor anyone else could have dissuaded the electorate from its desire to repudiate "Trumanism."

Time had passed for arguing about how many angels could dance on the head of a pin. More than anything else, that reality, the momentum of frustration that had been generated, had destroyed Truman's standing and ensured a Republican victory. That conclusion had become compounded the moment when Eisenhower, speaking in Detroit on October 24, promised that his election would be followed by a personal inspection trip to the battlefront in Korea.

About all the Democrats could salvage from that campaign was the semblance of unity, not a minor matter to those who compared it with the superficial success of 1948. All the possible fractures had been avoided—self-consciously and with considerable dexterity, to be sure, but avoided just the same. While there was disappointment over some of Stevenson's positions, first from the left and then from the right, the organizational defections were more limited than they had been four years earlier. Nevertheless, the defeat had its serious portents of the future. Southern losses were actually greater than they had been in 1948 and the vital Catholic segment of the coalition had turned against the party in greater numbers than in any presidential election since 1920.

As hard as they had worked, giving special attention to ethnic groups who were distraught over foreign policy, Democrats simply could not mount an adequate defense against Republicans waging an all-out fight for the ethnic Catholic vote. Inspired, perhaps, by the success of John Foster Dulles in appealing to the Polish vote in Buffalo, even while losing the statewide senatorial election to Herbert Lehman in 1949, the GOP's platform promised that the "captive peoples" would be "liberated" and called for the "repudiation" of the Yalta agreements. The Slavic defections were neither as great as the Republicans had expected nor as extensive as among the Irish, but nevertheless helped to contribute to a conservative movement toward Eisenhower, which, in the North, was heavily middle class and Catholic. Arthur Bliss Lane, the former American ambassador to Poland and a powerful critic of the communist regime in that country, estimated that some three million Democratic voters of ethnic origins had gone over to Eisenhower. In New York City, the general's thirteen best assembly districts were all heavily Catholic.[4] Later, contemplating his defeat, Adlai Stevenson agreed that the "communism in government" issue had compounded the problem.[5] A political writer in the *Reporter* declared that the coalition that had been expected to win for Stevenson "no longer exists. A phase in American political history has come to an end."[6]

2

If a computer were to evaluate the work done by Lyndon Johnson for the Stevenson candidacy a printout would undoubtedly feature such conclusions as "perfunctory," "halfhearted," or "virtually nonexistent." Johnson did introduce the candidate at Fort Worth and spoke for him at other times, but without much enthusiasm and late in the campaign. About the fairest conclusion is to state that, unlike what happened elsewhere in the South, the senator did not actively sabotage the party's nominee.

A much more vigorous contribution was made by Sam Rayburn. The congressman from the sparsely populated district at the northern part of Texas, above Dallas, left no doubt about the dangers of a Republican victory and his loyalty to the candidates chosen by the Democrats at Chicago. The minority leader, who celebrated his seventy-first birthday two weeks before Eisenhower's inauguration, was emerging from the loss as a major unifying force.

That fact could also be stated in another way: Rayburn was the most powerful individual left in the Democratic organization. After twenty years, the White House had been lost; moreover, for the first time since the dismal Hoover year of 1930, each end of Pennsylvania Avenue was in Republican hands. That meant the loss of federal power and patronage. Rayburn's mission, then, was twofold: to steer the Democrats toward regaining control while defending New Deal accomplishments from the conservative administration that had moved into power behind the general. Meanwhile, the party's leader in the House had to protect his own flanks from the dangers posed by the Byzantine political structure in his own state.

The anomaly was that Texas, after the election of Lyndon Johnson as Senate minority leader at the start of the new congressional session, was the home of the country's two most powerful Democratic legislators. The names of Johnson and Rayburn seemed to flow in tandem, as though both constituted an independent force that comprised what was left of the party in Congress. Yet they came from a state that had gone for Eisenhower by better than 53 percent, thus contradicting traditional loyalties. An additional factor was Texas' domination by powerful business interests, particularly the oil and natural gas industries. They bore little similarity to constituents that strengthened Democrats elsewhere, and left little political power to the state's numerous poor whites, blacks, and Mexican Americans.

The complexities of the one-party state were enormous. Power factionalized around dominant personalities and interests. Much of the conservative pattern evident elsewhere in the South had also become important there, as when anti-New Deal and so-called "Regulars" took over the state delegation at the 1944 national convention. Loyalists had fought back and held their own and the party's adherence to Truman in 1948, but the continuing trend within Texas was toward more conservatism. Its major cities had lured thousands of newcomers from the North, many of them business executives and white-collar workers, adding greatly to an increasingly urban middle-class Republican constituency. Conservative pressures, aided by dominant newspapers, successfully amassed a vote that was enough to overwhelm Stevenson.

Texans reacted against the national party's continued liberalism, against a candidate who not only favored an FEPC and stated that the Taft-Hartley Act needed to be changed and possibly even repealed but who had also taken a clear stand for giving the offshore oil rights to the federal government. It was the latter point that was crucial in making Johnson's support so difficult. Unquestionably, it also helped to provoke similar hostility throughout the rest of the South, especially since Eisenhower took the opposite position. "I am beset by pressure on the tidelands oil issue," Stevenson informed Rayburn during the campaign. To the candidate, torn between loyal southerners who feared a return to reactionary Republicanism and the hostility of oil money, the situation was mortifying.[7]

Oil had made a heavy contribution not only to the loss of Texas but to the party's general predicament in the South. States not about to benefit from such rights viewed the matter as essential for the principle of states' rights; not necessarily, as has been often pointed out, to deprive themselves of largesse from Washington, but to deter interference with sacred local interests. But it was far more than just oil. Above all, it was Truman and what he represented. Nowhere else in the country was the president so detested. Southern opposition to his civil rights requests had been whipped to a high pitch by the ambitions of key politicians. The Fair Deal program, even while largely destroyed, convinced southern conservatives that "Harry the Haberdasher"—border-state politician and all—was trying to emulate Roosevelt. His reluctance to bomb the hell out of China and to give General MacArthur whatever he needed for "victory" over communism in Asia were less acceptable in the South than elsewhere. The additional issue of "Reds in government" helped to dislodge traditional voting loyalties.

In substantive ways, the revolt was more serious than in 1948. Even though Governor John Battle supported the candidate, the Virginia organization under Harry Byrd took its cue from the boss and remained "neutral." Jimmy Byrnes, then governor of South Carolina, went with Eisenhower. And the oil governors, Robert Kennon of Louisiana and Allan Shivers of Texas, became "Eisencrats." In all, the electoral vote loss was greater than in 1948: fifty-seven went to the Republican candidate from four states. Stevenson also lost such border states as Oklahoma and Missouri, both of which had been for Truman, in addition to Delaware and Maryland. Kentucky was won by a thousand votes out of 993,000. Louisiana and South Carolina were also taken by uncharacteristically thin majorities. Even without the competition of a States' Right ticket, Stevenson's southern performance, then, was poor. In a two-way fight, he got just one percentage point more of the popular vote from the eleven ex-Confederate states than had Truman, 51.4 percent to 50.5 percent, marking a gain of just 1 percent despite the absence of a ticket that had taken nearly 20 percent of the total vote. There was little doubt that the old Dixiecrats had led the movement toward Eisenhower.

And that had come after a relatively harmonious convention, one that had seen contention and near revolt but, finally, compromise by both sides. A fight had broken out over the issue of a loyalty oath that required delegates to promise their support to the party's nominees. After its introduction by Senator Blair Moody of Michigan, it was modified to free delegates from having to make pledges that were in conflict with either the laws or instructions from conventions held in their own states. But, for the South, a matter of principle was involved. Several states refused to sign, and another walkout was near. Only a switch by the Illinois delegation, which was boosting Stevenson's candidacy, salvaged the situation by accepting Virginia's contention that being asked to sign was an insult, especially since their own state law mandated compliance with the party's choices. While there was insufficient national support to nominate Richard Russell at the head of the ticket, a gesture to placate the South was made by naming John Sparkman as Stevenson's running-mate. The civil rights portion of the platform was tempered. The previous call for "enforceable" federal action was smudged over by the statement that "we favor Federal legislation effectively to secure these rights to everyone," rendering it slightly more palatable.

The congressional loss of the Democrats had also helped to restore the legislature to southern control. But, nevertheless, the Congress was also reflecting the national condition and mood. The urban coalition had taken a beating and was in poor shape even to make much noise about the survival of the power that had shaped the party since the Depression. It all meant a movement away from the politics of the past. The New Deal was dead. So was the Fair Deal, if it had ever existed except as a reminder of the old order. Both Rayburn and Johnson, products of the 1930s and admirers of Roosevelt, signaled the change by abandoning previous liberal positions. Thus, the party's congressional leadership became dedicated not to vigorous opposition but to "responsible cooperation," which often meant giving Eisenhower more support than his own party was willing to give, especially for foreign assistance programs and domestic causes that commanded the support of moderates.

At the most, the Democrats waged a holding action in behalf of established programs and differed with the administration mainly in a greater willingness to spend money for the limited social programs that were introduced. Democrats, generally, tended toward more stress on additional legislation for public power; but even there they found themselves in retreat, merely resisting administration attempts to reduce established and widely accepted achievements, such as the Tennessee Valley Authority. Such issues as aid to education and urban assistance became bogged down, to the delight of conservatives, over whether they should contain antidiscrimination provisions. Pet insertions by New York Congressman Adam Clayton Powell, Jr., they were also resisted by liberals who argued that they were merely redundant as well as destructive of the programs they intended to democratize. To Republican economic programs that were blatantly pro-business and attractive to the enlarged middle class, Democrats simply lacked adequate responses. Their arguments remained wedded to the traditional anti-big-business, anti-Hoover appeals. Over foreign policy, the congressional leadership argued mainly for the continuation of bipartisanship and was reduced to pointing out that each Eisenhower-Dulles move merely continued the Truman-Acheson containment policy. At the same time, they charged that the administration was both pursuing reckless cold-war militarism by "unleashing Chiang Kai-shek," advocating "massive retaliation," and engaging in "brinksmanship" by expressing a willingness to go "to the brink" to avoid war.

Out of all the administration's moves, ranging from the defense of Formosa and the offshore islands of Quemoy and Matsu to the establishment of a European Union to include a West German army, the Middle East, disarmament, the recognition of Communist China, and rapprochement with the Soviet Union, there emerged but one line of opposition that came closest to representing the collective voice of the Democratic Party. And that was the politically feasible line that penuriousness had weakened the nation's defenses. Out of power, the Democrats were mostly groping, counting on economic setbacks for their own recovery. They did regain control of the Congress with a comfortable victory in the 1954 midterm elections, but that failed to overcome the party's submission to the conservative coalition. It did, however, restore Sam Rayburn as Speaker and made Lyndon Johnson the majority leader.

Left unresolved, however, was the question of whether the congressional Democrats should constitute themselves as a party of the opposition, perhaps in the European manner. The plight of the handful of liberals illustrated the loneliness of their cause during those years in the "wilderness."

3

Stevenson's stature impressed just about everybody but a majority of the electorate. Still, he tended to attract to politics those with hopes of finding leaders who eschewed dubious expediency and empty rhetoric for reason and intelligence. While he had made his own concessions, mainly by ultimately advocating an FEPC and the repeal of Taft-Hartley (to the annoyance of southerners to whom he had indicated he would do otherwise), such accommodations were in sharp contrast to Eisenhower's appeasement of the Republican right. It was a loss, therefore, that many thought could become the source of future strength.

The Democratic leader of Michigan, Neil Staebler, advised him that the next four years would provide time to heal the party's problems.[8] In much the same vein, one of the governor's many academic admirers was hopeful that the foundation for future success had already been established; now there was need to develop the party as an effective opposition.[9] Adolph Berle, Jr., the old FDR "brain-truster" and diplomat, was closer to Stevenson's own mood. Berle speculated that the Democrats might even find that "a spell in the wilderness will be good for its soul, though I hope," he added, "unlike the case of the children of Israel, the spell will not last for forty years."[10]

Disappointment in defeat is hard enough, even when expected. Stevenson, never ebullient about his personal role, was fully aware that however well the party had managed to retain its structural integrity, much remained to be done. Almost immediately, his own position as the Democratic titular leader would be tested. He wondered how that responsibility, if he chose to exercise it, could be discharged despite the diverse elements gathered under the umbrella, especially in the absence of a cornucopia in Washington. "As for party 'leadership'," he wrote just before New Year's Day, "the path is thorny and filled with pitfalls, ambushes and similar unpleasantnesses."[11] Chester Bowles, who had been defeated for a second term as Connecticut's governor after an administration that had been too ambitious in seeking early reforms, was similarly pessimistic. "The Democratic party is uncertain and frustrated," he complained to Stevenson. "Practically no one is speaking out on anything."[12]

The little band of liberals left in the Senate tried. They worked to push legislation for social programs and public power and, above all, to modify Rule XXII, which effectively protected filibusters that killed all civil rights bills. But even when the party returned to dominance with the Eighty-fourth Congress, conservatives were in control of the key committees; six of the ten most important were in the hands of southern chairmen. Outspoken members such as Herbert Lehman, whose liberalism seemed to increase with old age, found themselves isolated and with little power. Lehman's criticisms of Joe McCarthy and pleas for racial equality were little more than solitary campaigns. For such efforts, he found himself deprived of committee assignments to which he was entitled by the normal process of the seniority system, by a succession of majority leaders, first Ernest McFarland and then Lyndon Johnson. In successive attempts to join the Foreign Relations and the Judiciary committees, Lehman found himself blocked; finally, his ostracization from power and advancing age encouraged his retirement at the end of his term.[13] Paul Douglas of Illinois, also a vigorous battler for civil rights as well as a harsh critic of the nation's inequitable tax structure, encountered similar experiences. Douglas, also conscious of left-wing associations in the past and having been placed on the defensive about his proximity to radicals, not only became a charter member of the Committee of One Million that was dedicated to the prevention of recognition for the Peking government of China, but also voted for the McCarran Act that compelled the registration of communist groups. Together with Hubert Humphrey, he had decided that opposition would be construed as procommunism.[14] Nothing demonstrates Douglas' perpetual insecurity over the "Red issue" better than the assiduous compilation, in two thick scrapbooks, of anticommunist positions that he had taken since 1927.[15] Hubert Humphrey, suspected as a radical for his civil rights fights and unappreciated by conservatives despite his anticommunist efforts within the D-F-L, tried to get the best of all worlds by pushing through the Communist Control Act of 1954. Of dubious constitutionality, it was opposed by such stalwart Red-fighters as J. Edgar Hoover and Attorney General Herbert Brownell. Fellow liberals were aghast, and the ADA dissociated itself from it. One of the organization's chief fund-raisers was relieved that letters soliciting contributions were sent out just *before* Humphrey's move. "Had I waited a week, I would not have sent them out," he informed the senator.[16] Eleanor Roosevelt advised, "If the Democratic liberals do many more things like outlawing the Communist Party, I'm not sure I'll consider them liberals."[17] Even Lehman, who had been one of the seven senators to stand up against the McCarran Act, capitulated and joined the unanimous vote. Humphrey, moreover, unlike either Lehman or Douglas, preserved his own future by gradually moving into a working alliance with Johnson, a relationship that the majority leader viewed as useful for a link to the northern and liberal elements of the party.[18]

The party's subservience to the prevailing political mood, especially the tyranny of Senator Joe McCarthy, was illustrated by the reception given to a Stevenson speech at Miami, Florida. The occasion was a fund-raising dinner of the Southeastern Democratic

Conference. Stevenson's words were, in effect, an extension of re-marks made three days earlier by the party's national chairman, Stephen A. Mitchell, a Stevenson ally and appointee. Mitchell, de-viating from the current trepidation about attacking the popular president directly, had said that the time had come for making the general in the White House responsible for the actions of all Re-publicans. Picking up that theme, Stevenson went still further, into territory that had become forbidden. He charged Eisenhower with accepting McCarthyism as the Republican Party's "best formula for political success." As the audience sat in restrained silence inter-rupting the long speech with applause only six times, the 1952 can-didate ventured into the kind of attack that was rare even on the Senate floor. Ignoring his own party's acquiescence in helping to empower the demagogue, he warned that GOP acceptance of that strategy could only end in "a malign and fatal totalitarianism." As the influential diners sat there impassively, Stevenson added, "A political party divided against itself, half McCarthy and half Eisen-hower, cannot produce national unity—cannot govern with confi-dence and power."[19]

For the man from Illinois, it was a perfect evocation of Lincoln as well as an incisive barb at the dilemma of the modern Republican Party. Yet the reaction was guarded. Few permitted themselves to be quoted in approval. Immediately after the speech, only Senator Mike Mansfield of Montana was quoted by the New York *Times.* Stevenson, he said, had "laid it on the line."[20] Most of the others questioned the willingness to expose the party to risks at the polls the following November by such direct criticism of Eisenhower's role and thought the entire matter should be left to the Republi-cans. Almost one month after that dinner, Hubert Humphrey, who had said nothing for publication right after the address, met Steven-son and attempted to placate him by saying he had revised his initial negative reaction. But, added Humphrey, he could give no assur-ances that others on Capitol Hill had substantially changed their sentiments.[21]

It went that way all down the line; in fact, it had become far easier to avoid the controversy. Instead of functioning as a party of the opposition and checking the excesses that were doing irreparable harm to the nation, Democrats had accepted the thesis that their fortunes were most secure by severing even the most tenuous links with "radicalism."

Ironically, a victim of that atmosphere was the ADA itself, the

same organization that had been denounced by Progressives for join
ing the "Red-baiters." Since 1949, increasing efforts had been made
to portray the group not as a liberal lobby but, more ominously, as a
"leftist" claque bent upon steering the Democrats toward "collec-
tivism," which was a code word for communism. Where the ADA
was not directly charged with being inheritors of the Wallace movement, it was a handy substitute for the CIO-PAC as a target of
conservatives. That perception came almost as much from the Democratic right, particularly in the South, as from Republicans. ADA's
self-consciously vigorous anticommunist position meant little to
those who disliked liberal opposition to the Internal Security Act of
1950, Joe McCarthy, and unrestricted private enterprise. Having
been valuable and effective allies of the Democrats, certain segments
of the party had begun to become embarrassed by the association.
Republican critics and the conservative press exacerbated such feelings by using every possible means of condemning the ADA. In late
1953, it was the Stevensonian national chairman, Steve Mitchell,
who tried to scuttle what had become a counterproductive relationship.

Twice, in Philadelphia and later in Chicago, Mitchell appeared
on television and responded to questions about recent criticism of
the ADA that had come from a Democrat, Foster Furcolo of Massachusetts. In his first response, made to the chairman of the organization's Philadelphia chapter, Mitchell clumsily attempted to
minimize ADA's significance. He said he had never seen a "live"
member and would be glad to meet one "in the flesh." Two weeks
later, asked whether he thought an endorsement by ADA would
help or hurt candidates, Mitchell responded that "we can get along
without it all right." He elaborated his critical attitude soon afterward in an interview with Carlton Kent of the Chicago *Sun Times*,
which published the account on the first day of 1954. Less awk-
wardly, the national chairman explained that ADA was injuring the
party because of inevitable organizational conflicts. Both groups
were being forced to compete for the same dollars from wealthy
liberals. Instead of working outside Democratic auspices, Mitchell
suggested, those interested in the same programs should abandon
independent efforts.[22]

Bloodshed among the liberals was hardly an antidote for Democratic problems. Sam Smith, the man who had started the whole
thing by raising the first question to Mitchell in Philadelphia, complained that the chairman was suggesting that the labor and liberal

supporters were not welcome by the professional Democrats. "I would want to see its umbrella broad enough to cover all such decent forces," Smith wrote to Mitchell shortly after the telecast, "and controlled by none. The Party must obviously be run in the interests of all those who make it up and not any one group."[23] The liberal New York *Post*, edited by ADAer James Wechsler, defended the organization as "a lively political gadfly" that was keeping the Democrats from unholy accommodations with right-wingers.[24]

ADA officials squelched all temptations to retaliate publicly, even when placed on the spot by newsmen eager to fan the story. They preferred to interpret Mitchell's views as personal and not reflective of the party's position. Their desires to retaliate were tempered by the consideration that attacking Mitchell would have been embarrassing to Stevenson; both men were too closely associated in the public mind.[25]

Operating from behind the scenes, Stevenson dissociated himself from the controversial remarks and, after a conference, dispatched Arthur Schlesinger, Jr., to confer with Mitchell. The chairman agreed to modify his position at the first possible opportunity, which he finally did by voicing his hospitality to all independent liberal groups, including the ADA.[26] Mitchell had compromised with the reality of the liberal lobby's influence, but doubts that his view had really changed were completely valid. Regardless of what kind of truce had been achieved, the fact was that ADA had become a hindrance to those anxious about keeping conservatives Democratic. During the subsequent congressional election campaign, Republicans verified such apprehensions by exploiting the theme that the ADA was virtually a Red arm of the Democrats, a line pursued most vigorously by Vice President Richard Nixon.[27] Ironically, there was no evidence that it made any difference.

Still, the matter was not really resolved. When Paul Butler advanced from being the Indiana state chairman to taking over from Mitchell in early December, he, too, found it expedient to keep his distance from the ADA. Although he had been on record as having paid dues to the organization in 1948, Butler denied the fact of his membership. He told the press that there had been a "friendly relationship because the chapter had been started by some friends of his at Notre Dame," which was a not too subtle way of dispelling suspicions of communist contamination.[28] During that same period, Averell Harriman, who had received strong backing from liberals at the 1952 convention and whose high hopes for the presidency had increased since becoming governor of New York, got into a squabble with ADA co-director Joe Rauh, Jr., because he had refused an invitation to address the organization.[29]

To the liberals, such conflicts were ominous. They indicated that Democratic leaders, Stevenson included, were willing to jettison them for conservative support. Tours of the South by both Mitchell and the titular leader, with Stevenson pausing to address the Georgia legislature after having been welcomed by Governor Herman Talmadge, were disturbing signs. Having little faith in any future formulated by the congressional wing of the party, they feared the imminence of a "sell-out" for temporary party unity. Any compromises that may be necessary to keep the South happy, warned Eleanor Roosevelt, would backfire throughout the North and the West.[30] Meanwhile, Stevenson was not only monitoring the South as a whole but especially the state of Texas, where some interesting differences were beginning to emerge between Sam Rayburn and Lyndon Johnson.

4

Jim Rowe was an adviser to Lyndon Johnson whose intimacy with Democratic politics on Capitol Hill went back to early New Deal days. On January 27, 1954, Rowe dropped a tactful suggestion to Adlai Stevenson. He reported that the governor's strongest supporter in Washington was Sam Rayburn, which was also a fact of some anxiety to the "Congressional king-makers group," a category that, of course, included Johnson. Stevenson, Rowe suggested, could further his own cause and encourage Rayburn's position by exerting some gentle flattery toward the aging House leader. Since Johnson was chagrined about Stevenson and wounded by opposition from the liberals, he could also use some attention. The Senate leader "bleeds rather easily" and, at the moment, his "heart belongs elsewhere," Rowe advised.[31]

It was, of course, of great consequence that the party's congressional leadership was under the control of the two Texans. Both had been suppressing past progressive reputations and Johnson, in particular, had become loathesome to Lone Star liberals. Rayburn, too, twenty-six years older and a member of the House since his first election back in 1912, had been replacing his image of New Deal regularity with zeal for expeditious party harmony. Together, they upheld the best interests of Texas oil producers and opposed both an FEPC and repeal of the Taft-Hartley Act.

The state's Democratic Party was under the control of Governor Allan Shivers, a close ally of the oil industry and the strongest supporter of ceding tidelands rights to the states. Shivers had, in fact, led Texas into the Eisenhower camp in 1952 and there was no reason to doubt that he was planning to repeat that success.[32] That move had made him anathema to the loyal Democrats. Many such opponents, mostly liberals brought together by labor leaders and ADAers, formed a Democratic Organizing Committee to counter what they regarded as the reactionary alliance of "Shivercrats" and Dixiecrats. They fought against any attempt by the national party to recognize the legitimacy of the governor's leadership. There was particularly indignant defiance to the news that Democratic National Chairman Paul Butler had held a tête-à-tête in the kitchen pantry of a Washington hotel with Shivers himself. The quickly dubbed "Pantry Conference" had featured an agreement to dump Wright Morrow as the Texas national committeeman for his pro-Eisenhower position in 1952 and to remove the tidelands issue from the party's next platform, which provoked astonishment from some Texas liberals. One of them said, "It may be that the National Chairman's so busy trying to get the Benedict Arnolds back in the Party that he don't [sic] have time to pay attention to the Nathan Hales any more. Wonder what he expects to do—beat the Republicans next year with Judas Iscariot leading the troops?"[33]

The state's ADA leaders, seeking to sabotage any rapprochement between the national party and the Shivercrats, then went to work. To embarrass the governor, they publicized the details of his concessions, especially his agreement to drop Morrow. Friendly contacts also helped to place the adverse publicity in an influential newsletter, the *Austin Report*. They also began to praise Butler as a "great liberal," thus helping to achieve a rift between the embarrassed Shivers and his Dixiecrat allies, which forced the governor to boycott a statewide tour that Butler made that June.[34]

The liberals had made an important gain in their attempt to destroy Shivers. The governor's control of the party's regular apparatus had assuredly tended to inhibit both Johnson and Rayburn. Johnson's first election to the Senate had been by a primary vote plurality of just eighty-seven ballots, and he now felt under the threat of a Shivers move to oppose his re-election in 1954. There were also such considerations as the conservative backing he was getting within the state and the politically expedient rationale that it was best to avoid direct criticisms of Eisenhower. Rayburn also had good reasons for caution. More thoroughly involved in statewide politics than Johnson, he had agreed to Steve Mitchell's plan to set up a Democratic Advisory Council to service the national party in Texas. At the same time, pursuing a careful balancing act, he did everything possible to thwart the liberal Democratic Organizing Committee from coming into existence.[35] In a state where the party was fragmented by industrial conservatives, Dixiecrats, party loyalists, ADA and AFL and CIO liberals, and minority-group New Dealers, Rayburn was working to establish the broadest possible centrist coalition. He needed financial support from the party's Washington headquarters. Also a threat, one that could have ended his national career, was the frequently mentioned possibility that Shivers might undertake some deft and justifiable redistricting. Both the interests of equitable representation and Rayburn's demise could have been promoted by joining the Speaker's constituents with the much more populous and heavily conservative suburbs of Dallas. A few months before his death in 1954, Maury Maverick, the San Antonio Democrat whose independence had kept faith with the word his grandfather's spirit had contributed to the English language, suggested that Rayburn "would sell out his grandmother if he thought that would again make him Speaker of the House."[36]

The Shivers power, however, had weakened by 1955, so much so that his early retirement was widely assumed. Publicity about the "Pantry Conference" had not helped, of course; and Butler's five-day tour of the state had attracted crowds that were openly hostile to the governor. But the most significant shock to Shivers had occurred in 1954 when Ralph Yarborough, a liberal attorney from Austin, had forced the primary election into a run-off. So there was considerable reason for believing that both Rayburn and Johnson were beyond the governor's reach.

Johnson was starting to build his own position with the national party. As majority leader, after the election of the Eighty-fourth Congress, he had far more resources of his own. Assisted by his alliances with senators who quickly became indebted to him, he gradually began to work at dispelling notions that he was just another southern politician. At an Advisory Council fund-raising dinner in Whitney, Texas, he announced a thirteen-point program of Democratic priorities for the next congressional session. Billed as a "program with a heart," it included obligatory support for the Natural

Gas Bill exempting independent producers from federal utility-rate control, a measure as valid for him to promote, he explained to reporters, as Humphrey's efforts for Minnesota's dairy farmers.[37] But his other items were all attractive to northern liberals, including opposition to poll taxes, which his own state continued to retain. Hubert Humphrey joyfully said that Johnson had made twelve hits in thirteen times at bat.[38] Even before his announced program, which was moderately liberal at best, *The New Republic* had begun to say nice things about his work as majority leader.[39] Others, including Johnson, were entertaining thoughts about his possible run for the presidency.

Rayburn had different ideas. For one, he regarded the Stevenson nomination as preordained, so there was little point in Johnson's expending himself in a futile attempt to prevent the re-election of the popular Eisenhower. As much as he was loyal to his friend and would work to promote his interests, the Democratic Party's "Mr. Sam" had his own hopes. He would be seventy-four in 1956 and wanted one more honor. That was the vice presidency.[40]

To Rayburn, Stevenson was in many ways the best bet to keep the party together. The governor's positions had not been extreme. Even when taking a pro-FEPC position, he had done so with obvious reluctance and had been forced into the position by the exigencies of the campaign. Since 1952, he had made visits to several southern states and, along with Mitchell, had worked at persuading leaders who knew that there was no reasonable chance to get Richard Russell. The senator from Georgia had made his own early prediction of Stevenson's nomination and ultimate victory. Further, he was far more acceptable than liberals who were deemed hostile to business. While Stevenson had engaged in some standard Democratic rhetoric, the barbs had been aimed at the business-domination of the Eisenhower administration. Jibes at General Motors had become standard fare, but Stevenson was plainly not an anti-business New Dealer. In 1954, he had written confidentially that he hated to see the party "go in the direction already apparent, of separating the respectable and privileged from the Democrats!"[41] During the 1952 campaign, he had discounted the logic of tension between business and the Democrats, adding, "We are for private, and profitable, business."[42] After providing similar assurances in a *Fortune* article, Stevenson informed an approving correspondent that "the hostility of businessmen to Democrats and the New Deal is one of the absurdities of our time." His fear was that business rejection of liberalism would drive the party more to the left. Business, he explained, was no more of a liability than labor, farmers, "or any of the other smaller special interest groups." The only real danger was *"dominance."*[43] To conservative Democrats, then, especially those in the South, Stevenson was far more acceptable than the other major contenders, Averell Harriman and Estes Kefauver.

While all that was quite obvious to Stevenson's advisers, they were discovering that one of their most frustrating tasks was getting the potential candidate, the man who had been fulfilling his responsibility as the party's titular leader, to make some decisive early moves toward the nomination. The right steps could enable him to coordinate the active leadership necessary to mount an effective opposition to the administration, something Congress was hardly prepared to do. It would also be a way of quietly convincing the pros that he had to be taken seriously. Above all, he was urged, was the necessity of "avoiding indications of vacillation, indecisiveness, reluctance or doubt on the question of your possible candidacy."[44] Finally, in June 1955 the sought-after preliminary step was taken with the organization of a Stevenson Steering Committee with an account set up on the books of Steve Mitchell's Chicago law firm. Among the committee's employees were John Brademas, who later became a highly regarded congressman from Indiana; speechwriter John Bartlow Martin; Sam Wilhite, a former assistant to the governor of Mississippi; and D. B. Hardeman, a future confidential assistant to Sam Rayburn.[45]

Within three months, two heart attacks changed the political situation. In early July, Johnson was stricken and confined to Bethesda Naval Hospital. The second attack, on September 24, left President Eisenhower critically ill near Denver. Prospects for a Democratic victory in 1956 brightened and the convention prize seemed much more valuable. Almost overnight, Harriman switched from lauding Stevenson's possible candidacy to declaring that he had no obligation to support his rival. A conference between Paul Butler and "Mr. Sam" revealed that Rayburn's friends were attempting to organize a serious presidential drive on his behalf. A committee of one hundred Texans was being formed to raise $200,000 for a pre-presidential campaign. Oil and gas interests, disappointed with Eisenhower, were turning to the Speaker.[46] At a Dallas dinner in November, Rayburn was lauded by the personal attorney of oil millionaire Clint Murchison, who said that no one in America had done more than "Mr. Sam" to make oil men rich by preserving the 27½ percent tax depletion allowance and by fighting for other reforms of tax preference for the industry.[47] With Johnson out of the way, support for a Rayburn presidential candidacy, however short of its goal, could well result in the second spot on the ticket for a Texan who had worked to keep the party regulars together.

While Johnson recovered at his ranch on the Pedernales, the ambitious hastened to stroke his vanity, so the hill country of central Texas received a generous flow of visitors. They included Stevenson, who arrived in late September after delivering a speech at the University of Texas in Austin. At the ranch, the two men were joined by Rayburn. Stevenson then made plain his plan to announce for the presidency, probably in November, while Johnson advised that he enter the key primary contests and, while carefully avoiding any endorsement, the convalescing senator promised that, if Stevenson were nominated, he would support him as "enthusiastically" as in 1952.[48] As soon as he left the ranch, Stevenson wrote to tell Rayburn that his visit had given him "a better perspective and at least some little understanding of the intricacies of the political life in Texas."[49]

But Stevenson's Texas problems were far from over. Alarmed liberals were beginning to fear that Shivers was insinuating himself into an alliance with Johnson, probably to use the majority leader for returning to party respectability. At a conference of southern governors in Mobile, Alabama, Shivers predicted that Stevenson would not get the nomination.[50] Two days later, while the governors were still at the site, suspicions of a Johnson-Shivers ploy were confirmed with the publication in the New York *Times* of a story by William S. White. White was known to be particularly close to Johnson, and the story was obviously based on an interview with the majority leader himself and timed to coincide with the conference. It revealed that the senator was working to create a "powerful centrist coalition within the party." Its purpose would be to force an "open convention" that would have to accept a platform compatible with the moderate congressional leadership under Johnson and Rayburn. With control of the big bloc of Texas delegate votes, additional support from border and western states would bring their total well above the 294 obtained by Russell in 1952. Also crucial to the strategy was the control of the forty-eight votes from Texas by pledging them to Johnson as the "favorite son" candidate.[51] Confirming perceptions of increasing rivalry between southern senators and southern governors, there was a notable lack of enthusiasm for the plan among those gathered at Mobile.[52]

The Johnson move, which failure soon led him to disavow, had momentarily succeeded in creating a dilemma for Rayburn. The Speaker had been far from reticent, at least in private, about stating his preference for Stevenson. Some of his own lieutenants were working with the Democratic Organizing Committee of Texas in a drive that had labor unions, the ADA, and the NAACP allied in an effort to enlarge the voting rolls by getting liberals to pay poll taxes.[53] Rayburn, then, was in a bind. A friend of Johnson, he could now hardly go through with plans for a public declaration for Stevenson, as the candidate's people were urging him to do. Any forthcoming Johnson declaration of his own ambitions for the convention would have to be followed by Rayburn's open support. He could do no less. Such efforts would not only undermine Stevenson's nomination, and whatever hope existed for the Speaker becoming his running-mate, but would also endanger Johnson's Senate leadership. Rayburn warmed up to pleas that he work to "head Lyndon off." Congressman Hale Boggs of Louisiana, much agitated by the contretemps, feared that Johnson's activities would "snafu" the whole South and advised that Stevenson and Rayburn were the "most effective agents" to stop him and "they should do what is necessary."[54]

But Rayburn did not need to work too hard. Johnson's trial balloon sank quickly. On October 25, the majority leader told Willis Robertson that White's story was "considerably exaggerated" and suggested that "nothing would hamper our chances of obtaining the objectives which you and I agree are so desirable quite so much as the formation of any kind of coalition or block with a regional flavor."[55] Two weeks later, Johnson sent Stevenson a picture of themselves with Rayburn that had been taken during the September visit to the ranch. With a self-conscious touch of irony, he noted that "this must have been the occasion upon which the so-called 'Southern coalition' was formed. Sam Rayburn is a Southerner and I understand your farm is south of Chicago." Then he added: "It has been rather interesting to watch the stories in the press about what I am doing and what I am thinking and I am wondering just when some of the writers are going to get around to what appears to be the unusual expedient of asking me."[56] On November 21, Johnson appeared at Whitney, Texas, for his first major speech since the heart attack. It was at that occasion the delighted liberals not only heard him deliver his thirteen-point legislative program with its call for abolishing poll taxes but also a powerful plea for a delegation pledged in advance of the election to support the party's nominees and to work for their victory in Texas. One observer in the hall reported that his statements were "received with even more incredulous amazement by the liberals and loyal Democrats in the State than had been Rayburn's similar announcement in October."[57]

After several weeks of prodding, Stevenson flattered the sensitive Johnson with a friendly telephone call. They spoke for forty-five minutes, a time span that led Jim Rowe to conclude that the governor may have been able to get in five minutes' worth. But the call had helped. Afterward, word began to circulate that Johnson was telling intimates that he was for Stevenson and could not support either Harriman or Kefauver. Still, the ties were precarious; Stevenson had not been sufficiently attentive. Rowe advised that "those who lived by the side of the Perdanales [sic] River in central Texas made it unmistakably clear to me that they were most unhappy about the Governor's silence on Lyndon Johnson's 13 Point Program. . . ." Public approval from Harriman and Kefauver had already been noted. Johnson, Rowe reminded Stevenson, "is a man who requires constant cultivation and who . . . is over-sensitive to its lack." With a little effort, real assistance from Johnson was possible. Already, Rowe noted, "Stevenson has Rayburn lock, stock and barrel."[58]

CHAPTER VII

★

All for Unity

1

In 1956, there were good reasons for greater concern with the party's future direction than with regaining control over the White House. The brief optimism that had followed Eisenhower's heart attack had vanished with his decision to run again. The president's illness and his earlier hope of serving but one term had been subordinated to the interests of Republican harmony and victory in November. Unless the voters doubted his physical condition enough to worry about elevating Vice President Nixon, it was obvious that any Democratic challenger would face great odds.

By regaining control of the Congress in the midterm elections of 1954, the Democrats had again demonstrated that, on a district-by-district basis, they could still command safe majorities. Being able to coalesce around a single national leader, and behind issues sufficiently compelling to overturn Eisenhower, was the crucial dilemma. Willis Robertson analyzed the outlook in the South by claiming that now, regardless of the nominee, Eisenhower would carry Virginia and Florida and perhaps some other Southern States, while the electoral votes received by the Democratic candidate would be small enough to rattle around in the shell of a Jumbo peanut.[1]

The recession of 1953 and 1954 had been relieved and the subsequent months had brought remarkable recovery; numerous corporate and individual income records were broken in 1955. In the midst of a boom, liberals faced the task of trying to persuade the electorate that the popular incumbent was neglecting intrinsic weaknesses. Even among many labor union members, old New Deal themes seemed out of tune, however, and arguments that Ike was merely fronting for big business made little difference. In a Gallup survey taken while the economy was still sluggish, two out of every three voters rejected the notion that President Eisenhower favored any single group.[2]

Much had changed since the New Deal. The American public had recovered with a vengeance from its distrust of big business. As suburban homes and automobiles proliferated, and the Dow Jones averages reached new heights and disposable income was above anything seen before, old goats were forgotten. If there was a bogeyman, he would more likely be identified as a union leader or as a big-city politician. Reform was akin to "socialism," which, in turn, was suspiciously as alien as communism. Harvard professor John Kenneth Galbraith's ideas about countervailing power and the need for public versus private spending was fine for stimulating intellectuals about the future of American capitalism, but arguing about the need to redeploy resources was tantamount to asking the middle class to share incomes with the less fortunate. The liberal critique, while still acceptable to a substantial segment of the populace, was nevertheless woefully inadequate for convincing a majority of Americans that a Democrat should replace Eisenhower.

Despite all the critical barbs, denunciations of "massive retaliation" and scorn at such "changes" in policy as the "unleashing" of Chiang Kai-shek, the Republican administration had gained wide confidence with its handling of foreign policy. "It is easy for John Q. Public to relax back into the comfortable belief that Ike after all knows best," Chester Bowles wrote to Thomas K. Finletter. But when Bowles expressed the conventional liberal complaint by arguing, "It doesn't seem to me that we are even beginning to break through this barrier as we must if we are going to win," he was asking Americans to deny what they regarded as self-evident.[3]

The predicament was stated simply but accurately in a memorandum that resulted from a meeting of Adlai Stevenson's friends. "I believe," it began, "that as things now stand a large part of the independent vote believes that they are more apt to avoid war with the Republican Party than they are with the Democrats."[4] Thus, how to regain the "peace" issue from the Republicans was a major problem.

Eisenhower had taken charge of the Korean War, a war that the Truman administration had entered but had been unable to end; and the fighting had stopped less than six months after the inauguration of the new president. Elsewhere, crises in Asia, in Indo-China and the Formosa Strait, had been managed without overt American military involvement. Fighting had stopped; American boys were not dying. Despite Republican votes to "liberate" the "captive peoples," responses to such uprisings as the East Berlin riots of 1953 were prudently nonprovocative. Indeed, with the signing of regional defense pacts in the Middle and Far East, coupled with the Formosa Resolution that the administration won from a cooperative Congress, it appeared that the Eisenhower-Dulles policy, for all its promises of cold-war militance, was hardly more than an extension of Truman-Acheson containment. While the administration kept its own fragile intraparty harmony with a judicious mixture of bluster and caution, public confidence remained high. Ike's trip to Geneva in 1955 to meet with the Soviet leadership at the "summit" provided additional confirmation of his desire for peace. If he appeared casual about overseeing the executive branch of the government, he was at least trustworthy with power. It had become routine for pollsters to discover that the public had more confidence not only in Ike's judgment but in Republican handling of diplomacy. Half a year before the hopeful "spirit of Geneva" resulted from the summit, Gallup studies of opinion reported that Americans were less fearful about the imminence of war than at any time during the past seven years.[5] Liberal Democrats were hard-pressed whenever they tried to argue that the peace was not real. One ADA leader betrayed his frustration when he wrote, "It is politically impossible and unnecessary to argue the merits of the Korean War and the Korean truce in this campaign."[6]

The tendency of such liberals was to blame the Johnson-Rayburn leadership, as well as Senate Foreign Relations Committee Chairman Walter George, for failing to articulate a sufficiently identifiable partisan alternative to administration policies. But that also had its risks, particularly with the continuing confidence in Eisenhower's diplomatic wisdom and the vulnerability of criticism to charges of "softness" toward communism. At the same time, Democrats felt that their behind-the-scenes achievements had been substantial, that the sort of quiet persuasion exerted by Senator George had helped to move the administration toward an exploration of the hints of possible détente that began to come from Moscow in the spring of 1953. Eisenhower's decision to go to Geneva was, in that analysis, a logical outcome. Still, Chester Bowles feared, "The word will go out from Republican headquarters to bill the Republicans as the 'Peace Party,' and the Democrats as the 'War Party.' Republican orators will go around the country explaining that for forty years we've had a war every time we've elected a Democratic president." At least, he speculated, the peace issue could be neutralized by Republican willingness to invite Democratic assistance at the policymaking level in exchange for greater cooperation.[7] More realistically, in a long memorandum called "The Foreign Policy Issue and the Democratic Party" that he sent to all significant formulators of policy, in and out of the Congress, Bowles pushed hard for the wisdom of charging that the internationalist-isolationist schism had debilitated Republicans since 1916 and was continuing to cripple their ability to conduct foreign policy.[8]

Further defeat in 1956, despite the public's willingness to keep Democratic control of the legislature, widened the differences between the issue-oriented liberals and the congressional leadership. Critics of the Johnson-Rayburn type of opposition held that the failure to move ahead with new policies and new programs that were consistent with American needs at midcentury deprived the party's presidential nominee of a substantial platform. "Let's face up to it," Hubert Humphrey had written in confidence one year before Stevenson's second loss to Eisenhower, "the leadership of the Democratic Party must represent more than the Congressional Democratic forces and more than a previous administration."[9]

2

Paul Butler was one of those who tried to do something about the situation. In 1953, while still a national committeeman from Indiana, he presented a proposal for holding a midterm Democratic conference. Outside of platform-writing at the quadrennial meetings to nominate the national candidates, neither party had ever convened to formulate a comprehensive program representing a unified partisan statement of principles.

The Butler plan, presented on behalf of the Indiana committee, implied that Democrats had to go beyond the level of mere fund-raisers and caretakers who were overseeing the distribution of congressional power. Instead, the party should become an effective author of national policy, an advocate expressing the collective voices of the country's 435 congressional districts. Its role would begin to approximate the function of parties in European parliamentary systems. Even in America, although nothing like it had ever been tried before, the idea was not new. Butler cited the 1950 recommendation of the American Political Science Association in behalf of holding biennial national conventions. The plan had won the approval of such individuals as President Truman, Senator Humphrey, and former national chairman Frank McKinney. Others had discussed it, agreed that it had merits, but nothing had been done.

At the time Butler formally introduced his proposal, before a meeting of the Democratic Executive Committee in Chicago in the spring of 1953, the party had neither congressional nor presidential control. The Eisenhower administration had been seated only recently, and whatever hopes for a comeback rested with the upcoming 1954 congressional elections. Finding themselves with less national power than at any time since 1930—and unaccustomed to being in the minority—it seemed appropriate for new proposals to receive serious attention.

Butler's idea was to make such a convention "a gigantic national Democratic rally," one that would enable a minority party to "captivate the eyes and ears and hearts and minds of American voters in 1954." It would serve the psychological function of personifying ideas and issues in the absence of a "presidential candidate as a factor in mobilizing votes." As a prelude to the campaign, it was conceived as capable of promoting the party's ability to provide the "single, clear voice" that would be lacking without the quadrennial platform. To make the body more representative of the party, Butler proposed granting official status in the meeting to congressmen, senators, governors, candidates for federal offices, and state chairmen and vice chairmen. Speaking for the party, they would assume responsibility for the conduct of the legislative branch. An important by-product would assuredly be "a closer working alliance between the Democratic members of Congress in both the House and the Senate and the Democratic National Committee." Thus, in Butler's view, the Democratic "umbrella" would become a true party.

The heart of the plan related to the longer view, beyond 1954 and toward resolving in advance the probable divisions that were bound to trouble the next presidential nominating convention. The midterm conference, Butler advised, would scout out the major areas of disagreement. He warned that any expectations of victory "cannot afford to approach that election year with these conflicts unresolved."[10]

Butler's plan, however, was twenty years ahead of its time. In an address before the Lexington Democratic Club in New York City on January 18, 1957, Herbert Lehman proposed a similar scheme. But, meanwhile, nothing happened, its still-birth probably due to the persistence of what Paul Butler had hoped to avoid. As Jim Rowe recalled not long after Butler had introduced his plan, "Every professional politician I know shuddered at the idea because once the Democrats start talking policy the North-South cleavages appear."[11] The ability of the Democrats to function responsibly and to help mold domestic and international policies was, in other words, dependent upon getting themselves together.

3

Advocates of either position could agree that Stevenson was the most likely man to keep the party from fracturing once again. Yet the governor's own attitude toward his personal assumption of power and toward the leading questions of the day provoked frustration and some despair. The man whose reluctance had already necessitated a draft was not any more ready to agree that he had all the answers, that the future of both the party and the nation required his personal leadership.

That came out during a talk he had with Mrs. Roosevelt in London in the summer of 1953. He explained his hesitation about becoming an active titular leader. Mending the fragmented party seemed to him intellectually unrewarding; working with diverse and frequently recalcitrant politicians, leading efforts to rebuild local organizations in state after state, and cultivating unattractive individuals were simply not very tasteful enterprises. If that was the meaning of political leadership, he was not sure he was the man for the job. Moreover, he told her, he was willing to step aside for others who were perhaps more capable or better equipped to play that role. It was something that could be done by such people as Lyndon Johnson or Stuart Symington, neither of whom was a hopelessly regional figure.

Mrs. Roosevelt rebuked him for that kind of talk. Winning was hard enough, she said, even when one had the will and drive; without it, impossible.[12]

Nor did Stevenson's sentiments modify very much. After the televised portion of his address before the national committee at New Orleans at the end of 1954, he gave his immediate audience a postscript to his public remarks. For the past two years, he explained, he had devoted himself to the responsibility of being a titular leader. Much of that time had been at the expense of his private law practice while he had been repairing the party's financial situation. "So if henceforth I cannot participate in public and party affairs as vigorously as in the past," he added, "I hope you will understand and forgive me, and I assure you that it reflects no lesser interest in our party's welfare and no ingratitude for the inspiration and encouragement you have given me in such abundance."[13] Although the self-imposed exile lasted just four months and by the spring Stevenson's course was clearly headed toward declaring his candidacy, Agnes Meyer was compelled to deliver the kind of lecture that Mrs. Roosevelt had given two years earlier. His weakness, she advised, was in "not wanting" the nomination sufficiently, to which he replied: "To know the proper measure of this task precludes everybody but the lightheaded or ruthless from 'wanting it,' it seems to me."[14]

Neither did he change very much once he had become an active candidate with his announcement of November 15. He still seemed to prefer the Hamlet role. Max Ascoli, the editor and publisher of the six-year-old liberal journal of opinion, *Reporter*, had been one of the intellectuals drawn to him. Ascoli had made several offers for Stevenson's services as a contributing editor. But he, too, was perplexed by the apparent distaste for power. A month after Stevenson's declaration of his candidacy, Ascoli wrote an editorial called "Dear Governor Stevenson" in which he urged, "Will you show that you are ready not only to talk but to act as President? If you do it, Governor, you will become one."[15]

Still, it was Stevenson who had the clearest perception of himself. Pulling the party together required extraordinary confidence, and even a generous touch of arrogance about his organizational and administrative competence. He was no more prepared to command that area than he was to offer what he believed were the simple solutions to conflicts that evoked passion and a multitude of panaceas from others. He was reluctant to give the electorate the impression that only he was qualified to lead the way. The most momentous matters were the most complex; yet, millions wanted to hear simple solutions from the mouth of a political leader. Instead, Stevenson viewed them with academic objectivity, as problems that needed careful analyses and consideration of all relevant elements.

Thus he was impatient with the compulsions to take a forthright, unequivocal stand on a matter of importance to a vital group of loyal Democrats, namely, Israel and the status of that new nation vis-à-vis the Arab states. Distraught that his followers wanted him to tell them what they would like to hear, he unburdened himself to Hubert Humphrey. "I have been hopeful that we could help to temper the passions in this country," he wrote. "It is a most intricate problem, with deep currents of emotion in Islam as well as Western Jewry.... Competitive inflammation in this country seems to me neither wise nor constructive. Peace between Israel and her neighbors is the only ultimate solution, and I am not sure that it draws nearer from unilateral exhortations and bicep-flexing."[16]

Publicly, his attitude was visible and the political price was becoming apparent. Both in their financial contributions and in their willingness to vote and to work for Democratic candidates, especially those congenial to liberal causes, American Jews constituted an influence far in excess of their limited numbers. Although the vice president's character was thoroughly suspected by them, Eisenhower was regarded as a man of goodwill, an impression that grew after the president's delayed but inevitable open conflict with Senator McCarthy. If Jews had to choose between the Eisenhower-Dulles brand of leadership, with all their attempts to placate the Arab states, and a potential leader with mixed thoughts about the wisdom of firm assistance for Israel, they were tempted to be swayed toward the former. At least there was no question about his military acumen which, in the final showdown, could be the most crucial element. Half a year before the Egyptian seizure of the Suez Canal, Stevenson's advisers were hearing about threatened defections among traditional contributors who were able to write sizable checks. Noting the situation in Massachusetts, Arthur Schlesinger, Jr., reported that he had been advised of the importance of Stevenson's attitude in stopping that kind of disenchantment.[17] The situation was analogous to the candidate's inadequate sensitivity (as Agnes Meyer had reminded him in October) toward the feelings of Polish Americans regarding the communist domination of eastern Europe.

Nor was he any more helpful on the matter of civil rights, an issue that was rapidly becoming more heated than ever in the wake of the Supreme Court decision. On that, too, Stevenson had his doubts. History, culture, and economics had, to him, made the attitudes impervious to the simple remedies liberals were advocating. Most of the reformers, he believed, were unwilling to recognize the concomitants of change. Their zeal ignored the realities of the South, which had such moderates as Francis Pickens Miller, Virginius Dabney, and Brooks Hays, not to mention the better known band of progressives. The "Young Turks" in Virginia's assembly had already introduced bills to repeal that state's segregation laws and had advocated the establishment of a Virginia civil rights commission to study race relations as well as the bases for remedial legislation. The year before the Brown decision, Old Dominion Republicans, fighting to defeat the Byrd machine, had also called for abolishing poll taxes.[18] Elsewhere in that region, especially in North Carolina and parts of Tennessee and Florida, attitudes were even more enlightened.

"I get a little amused by the Northern liberals," Stevenson confided, "who damn us for making friends with the Southerners whom they seem to consider all conservatives," while simultaneously having to contend with southerners who were complaining that their indigenous liberals were being neglected.[19] He was equally impatient with the NAACP lobbying for the Powell Amendment to link compliance with desegregation to whatever aid-to-education bill might emerge from Capitol Hill. Desegregation and improved relations, he contended, "are going to gain more from advancing education than from stubbornness and perhaps even reaction," and then added with resignation, "but it won't be the last time that we have scratched our own backs with our own daggers."[20]

While campaigning in California during his primary contest against Estes Kefauver, he encountered the hostility of youthful liberals. To Mrs. Meyer, he wrote, "Evidently what they want to hear about is civil rights, minorities, Israel, and little else, and certainly no 'vague futures.' "[21] But not only young liberals were concerned. His use of the words "gradualism" and "education" during that California campaign to describe his civil rights aspirations drew considerable opposition. A sadly disappointed Herbert Lehman lamented that the cause of equality had been hindered by acceptance of terminology that had been "used by apologists for discrimination and injustice for many years."[22] Perplexed by the dilemma, Stevenson complained to Eugene Meyer that "the intensity, cultivated by ministers, labor leaders, and politicians, is all directed to the South, and as intemperately as any place I have ever visited, I fear."[23] At the same time, Chester Bowles forwarded for Stevenson's consumption the following appraisal from a Negro woman:

I don't think Stevenson's education on the country and civil rights is complete enough. I do not doubt him but he has no sensitivity to the words that must not be used. He seems to be speaking to an audience which no longer exists. I do not think that his advisers are deliberately misleading him—only that they, too, are not current in their knowledge or analysis. . . . Stevenson's approach to this question is similar to the approach a college professor would use in a classroom. It's not merely an attitude of moderation; he wants to get all the facts before him to weigh them carefully, and then to proceed in a gradual manner. . . . Stevenson should simply realize that a moral issue is involved which is not susceptible to the usual approaches.[24]

Stevenson was plainly more congenial to the counsel of such aides as Harry Ashmore, the Arkansas *Gazette* editor, who advised that southerners were ready to stage a bigger bolt than in 1948 because of the steadily deteriorating racial situation. Ashmore feared that legislation in the form of Powell amendments or laws to enforce the Brown decision "will not promote the integration of a single school district in the South, but on the contrary will probably only serve to stiffen resistance." Stevenson would be the conciliator, the man who had not become wedded to the "irreconcilables on either side of the issue, and who has the respect and confidence of all parties to the dispute."[25] As much as that view was consistent with the governor's conservative temperament, it was also in line with the thinking of virtually every southerner other than the leaders of the growing massive resistance movement. It was, in short, an outlook that both moderates and traditional segregationists could live with, and essentially not much different from President Eisenhower's.

4

Given Stevenson's views on such issues as civil rights and business, it was almost paradoxical that his symbolic leadership of the party had attracted a loyal band of theorists willing to pool their energies and talents. They had no official capacity; their funding was entirely independent; and not all were equally ardent about advancing the governor's interests. But with the Democrats impotent and almost voiceless but for the titular leader, there were good reasons for sorting out the issues and articulating liberal objectives. Essentially, what came to be known as the "Finletter Group" functioned as a Stevensonian "brain-trust."

It began during the late summer and early fall of 1953, when a number of the governor's discouraged friends and followers had concluded that something needed to be done about advancing a liberal program for the coming years. As an informal group, they had no need to make their membership representative of the geographic and ideological interests within the party. They could concentrate on synthesizing mid-twentieth-century liberal values. John Kenneth Galbraith posed their basic question: "How can we do the most to keep the Democratic Party intellectually alert and positive during these years in the wilderness?" The need was to salvage the rhetoric from its 1930s moorings. For too long, Democrats had been trading on New Deal appeals and, as Galbraith put it, that "capital is running thin." The lack of ideals would encourage far greater disunity.[26] Their output would provide material for use by various Democrats, although there was little doubt that Stevenson was the man they most had in mind.

The idea intrigued the governor. In early October, he asked Tom Finletter to contribute his organizational talents to the formation of such a group.[27] Finletter, whose own interest was in foreign affairs and who had also served President Truman as secretary of the Air Force, immediately began to enlist a varied number of specialists. Largely concentrated in such centers of talent as New York, Chicago, and Cambridge, the group's composition was fluid, with different individuals called upon to contribute at various times. At the start, its activists included Wilson Wyatt, Galbraith, Schlesinger, Charlie Murphy, John Sharon, Paul Nitze, Jim Warburg, Clayton Fritchey, and Adam Yarmolinsky, as well as such old New Dealers as Ben Cohen, Chester Bowles, Sam Rosenman, and Averell Harriman with his friend George Backer. Meetings with Stevenson himself were infrequent after an initial launching session at the governor's Libertyville farm in October.

Their enthusiasm and diligence led to a quick enumeration of topics, namely, Secretary Ezra Taft Benson's farm policy, the Bricker Amendment, the Taft-Hartley Act, budgets and taxation, the McCarran-Walter Immigration Act, and public power. Having begun their work well before the Brown decision, there is no evidence of prolonged concentration on civil rights; more thought went to economic and diplomatic matters. Chester Bowles called for restoring the aborted word "full" to the Employment Act of 1946. He and Harriman, however, were primarily interested in foreign policy, with Bowles emphasizing the containment of communism through economic and political reforms and the former ambassador to the Soviet Union eager to counter John Foster Dulles' more dramatic positions.[28] It was also the "Finletter Group" that labored to counter the impact of Attorney General Herbert Brownell's charge that President Truman had promoted Harry Dexter White despite FBI reports that he had spied for the Soviet Union.[29] One member, Professor Schlesinger, contributed the eloquent anti-McCarthy speech that Stevenson delivered at Miami. Ultimately, the group became only one of several crews that funneled ideas to Stevenson.

Always sensitive to charges that they were merely a Stevensonian front, they encouraged more extensive sharing of their output with other Democrats, including Harry Truman. Meanwhile, they continued to mail Stevenson accounts of their proceedings and texts of position papers. Exasperation and discouragement began to seep in with the growing realization that the governor was not all that interested in their production and becoming somewhat indifferent about the papers they were turning out. His aloofness and resistance to some of their ideas nevertheless failed to encourage mass defections, probably because they wanted to remain close to the seat of power, a consideration that, in Stevenson's case, held the possibility of becoming more valuable in the future. That, however, fails to explain why they preferred him to Kefauver.

The Tennesseean had many assets. He had not been defeated in a national election; his performance in the 1952 primaries, in fact, had been unmatched. There was no evidence that his vote-getting ability had declined. A fighter for society's victims, he was far less conservative than Stevenson and more compatible with the New Deal tradition, especially in his willingness to criticize business and to champion consumer interests. Never a rabid segregationist, always well ahead of the racial attitudes of his constituents, he further isolated himself from the white supremacists by spurning the "Southern Manifesto" that they wrote in March of 1956 to defy the Brown decision.

Yet few of the urbane liberals took him seriously as a presidential contender. Despite his evident intelligence and Yale Law School-background, folksy campaigning in Tennessee while wearing a coonskin cap had bequeathed him a reputation as a self-publicist who would not be a credible candidate. Nor could his qualifications for leadership in the all-important field of international relations compare with Stevenson's, whose background and continuing articulation of the issues had made him the administration's most formidable critic. Although Kefauver's labor record was good, especially for a southerner, union leaders seemed to prefer either Stevenson or Harriman. George Meany was heard telling friends, "Kefauver isn't fit to tie Stevenson's shoe-strings but he has the popular appeal."[30] Others were put off by his drinking. After a telephone conversation with Kefauver, Agnes Meyer reported, "I hung up on him—I suspect he is cracking up. Jim Carey was right when he thought K is drinking too much."[31] Intellectuals also found that, in contrast with Stevenson, he seemed uncomfortable with them and difficult to penetrate.

It was Stevenson, then, who was much preferred by those most concerned with the principles for which the party should stand. He was witty and graceful, striking his companions as an eminently civilized man whose intellect would permit his ultimate acceptance of liberal ideas.[32]

5

Sam Rayburn's advocacy of Stevenson hinged not at all on his urbanity and intellect. Above all else, party unity was the most persuasive point for the Speaker, and that had convinced him that the governor would be the ideal man. At the same time, it was a preference that Rayburn knew might have to be abandoned at any time. For all Stevenson's attractions to many southerners, resistance remained. Some still smarted from his stand against state control of tidelands oil and his comments about repealing the Taft-Hartley Act. Senator Robertson could hardly mention the 1952 campaign without a bitter reference to having been let down on what he had interpreted as a pledge not to attack the labor law or to back an FEPC. While gaining additional acceptance from within the region, Stevenson's support was still too tenuous to withstand going on record in support of the possible use of federal troops to force compliance with the court's desegregation decision. Meanwhile, "Mr. Sam," who had been considering backing Stuart Symington of Missouri, was still for Stevenson.

During the fall of 1955, the party's titular leader awaited an endorsement from the Speaker of his still unofficial candidacy. But there had been a delay. At the end of October, the governor informed Senator John F. Kennedy that any statement was dependent on an important prerequisite, the resolution of "some Texas problems which I think you can surmise."[33] That was a direct reference to the confusion induced by Lyndon Johnson's "centrist coalition" plan and its attempt to form a conservative bloc in the path of northern liberal control of the national convention.

Upset by the latest development, Rayburn worked to bury the idea. His efforts were assisted by the cool response to the Johnson-Shivers ploy. Rayburn's fears centered on his own need to wrest control of the Texas delegation from the renegade Shivers, whose readmission to party respectability would be considered sacrilegious by the loyalists. Having cooperated with Steve Mitchell to establish the state's Democratic Advisory Committee (DAC), Rayburn was eager to dethrone Shivers.[34]

Rayburn's strategy called for Texas to offer Johnson as its "favorite son" at the national convention, not at the head of a Shivers-trained "centrist coalition" but as a device for controlling the state's delegation. The plan required backing from Texas liberals, who were well represented on the advisory committee. That meant overcoming the resistance of Texans who regarded the majority leader as only slightly more palatable than Shivers and considerably more undesirable than Rayburn. Without clearing his step with the DAC, and very possibly without getting final approval from Johnson himself, Rayburn released a statement to the press that presented the senator as the solution to the Texas political situation. It could be solved, it said, by making him the state's "favorite son." Implying the scheme's anti-Shivers motives, he added that "it would well follow that he should be chairman of the Texas delegation to the Chicago convention. Under his demonstrated leadership, I think Texas would have a real voice. . . ."[35]

The Texas liberals, feeling their strength, were no more willing to accept dictation from a Rayburn-Johnson combination than to acquiesce to Shivercrat control. In an agitated response to the Speaker's move, the DAC's steering committee acted to assert its independence from the man who had sponsored its birth. By a vote of nine to two, the members rejected Rayburn's "dictation." They deplored giving Johnson a blank check that he could use as chairman of the state's delegation at Chicago in August. Although fearing the possibility that Johnson might still choose to join with Shivers and his renegades, they nevertheless countered with demands that were calculated to preserve their prerogatives within the context of Rayburn's anti-Shivers objectives. They even demanded that any agreement to back Johnson's favorite-son candidacy be restricted to the first ballot and that the delegation have the right to make its own decisions on all other matters without dictation from the chairman of the delegation. The independence of Democrats in faction-riddled Texas was still out of hand.

What had begun as a Rayburn-led revolt against the state's right-wing Democrats, a revolt that required a coalition of loyalist liberals and moderates, had become a two-stage rebellion. The dissent, of course, was of only limited consequence; the Johnson-Rayburn

liberal-moderate coalition had no trouble controlling the state convention that spring, commanding nearly 1,800 of the 1,900 votes at
Dallas on May 22 and eliminating Shivercrat power. But the liberals
were able to stop the Rayburn-Johnson forces from electing Mrs.
Lloyd Bentsen, Jr., as national committeewoman by persisting until
the triumph of Mrs. Frank Randolph. Fearful of the potential consequences of what had been unleashed by the unseating of Shivers,
Johnson wrote to Stevenson in September expressing apprehension
that "harsh and bitter words" produced in another liberal-conservative split could throw the state into the Republican column once
again. "The point, of course," wrote the majority leader, "is to pit
Democrat against Republican rather than Democrat against Democrat. There are not enough Republican votes in Texas to win an
election, but there may be enough Democratic factions to lose an
election."[36] Eighteen years later, recalling Johnson's attempts to
placate the liberals, Allan Shivers said, "I told Johnson, several
times, that he couldn't trust those people because they'd take it away
from him."[37]

6

By all odds the clear front-runner, Stevenson soon found himself
in a two-way battle. The first, the one that drew most attention,
involved primary clashes with Kefauver in states from New Hampshire to Oregon and California. On a secondary level was the competition from New York's Averell Harriman, the same man who had
only recently expressed public support for Stevenson's possible candidacy. Stevenson, finding the situation much to his distaste, wrote
privately, "Averell *is* intent and determined. I am a little disappointed, and I hope we can avoid any conflict." There were also, he
had heard, rumors that the governor of New York was ready to offer
financial support to Kefauver, "in order to try to damage me on the
off chance that Harriman would benefit ultimately."[38]
    Harriman was ready to display his credentials as the most faithful
heir to the New Deal. The appeal, of course, would be to the basic
core of northern liberal, labor, and big-city votes, the urban coalition that had not quite abandoned the search for another Roosevelt.
With that as a foundation, and a potentially potent one considering
its large concentration of electoral votes at stake, Harriman's strategy
was simple. It called for letting Kefauver check Stevenson in a series

of primaries. Meanwhile, with confidence in the Tennesseean's continued popularity, he would remain on the sidelines promoting his assets with party leaders, most of whom would surely accept him in preference to Kefauver. With Carmine De Sapio of Tammany Hall and the large New York delegation already sure bets, he had hopes that other big-city bosses would ultimately join him. Even Pittsburgh's Mayor David Lawrence, a Stevenson supporter, would have little choice if it boiled down to a question of Harriman or Kefauver.[39]

The Stevenson-Kefauver-Harriman competition created a considerable dilemma for Democratic liberals. Kefauver's southern origins almost seemed to purify his progressive image, which was then strengthened by his rejection of the "Southern Manifesto." An additional sweetener was the type of opposition that had built up against the senator in his own part of the country. So strong was the hostility (which also came from Senate colleagues who complained about his frequent absenteeism and failure to "pull his share of the oars") that only massive popular support offered any hope for his nomination. While Harriman had a firm New Deal reputation and was certainly the second choice of most ADAers, he had not demonstrated much popular appeal. In his only political campaign, he had seemed uncomfortable and awkward and had been elected New York's governor by a very thin margin. Still, when it came to such vital issues as civil rights, he was by far the most liberal of the three men. But Stevenson had the strongest hold among the small but influential group of intellectuals, many of whom he had inadvertently drawn into political activity for the first time. Realists also regarded him as the voice of reason who offered the best chance of unifying the party and, even if he lost, of articulating issues and programs for the future.

Harriman thought his diplomatic background would bring recognition as the man most familiar with Slavic American anxieties over eastern Europe. One month before the opening of the convention, he exploited that theme by declaring that he was the only candidate who could not be accused of "softness" toward communism.[40] At age sixty-five, he was by nine years the senior Democratic contender. He also had the most extensive background in national and international affairs. By far the wealthiest candidate, Harriman shared in one of America's great family fortunes.

But conservatives regarded their stake in the national ticket as nil. Without being particularly enamored of Eisenhower, especially since the Brown decision by—as Vice President Nixon remarked—a "Republican court," they felt confronted by a situation that made the president's likely re-election more palatable than most of the possibilities being offered by their own party. With all his assets, Harriman was still unacceptable. Many of his associations were repugnant: organized labor, civil rights legislation, deficit spending, big-city bosses. He was also favored by Jim Patton of the left-wing National Farmers Union, even if, as Patton agreed, Harriman was only "warmed over New Deal."[41] Of the three candidates, only Stevenson could get even their tentative backing.

The bulk of Stevenson's conservative strength came from the South, the same region that had virtually deserted him in 1952 and the source of continuing uncertainty. Failure to implement the loyalty oath at the convention left doubt about the placement of the national ticket on the ballots of dissenting states in future elections. The matter, then, was unresolved and threatened to create another brouhaha. Another possible impediment was the touchy question of how to write a civil rights plank, especially after the Brown verdict, that could manage to satisfy both the North and the South. There were indeed good reasons for believing that the identity of the presidential candidate was a relatively minor matter among many leaders in Dixie.

Stevenson lost little time making his own détente with the region. It was noteworthy that when Richard Russell addressed a Jefferson-Jackson Day dinner in Raleigh, North Carolina, only four months after the election of 1952 and denounced the "self-styled liberals" who were trying to mold the party "to their own image," he nevertheless praised Stevenson and John Sparkman as "great Americans." There was little doubt among his listeners that accusations of a northern "conspiracy to drive the South out of the party" were aimed at the "extremists" who had caused the candidate's downfall rather than at Stevenson himself. They were the ones who failed to appreciate, Russell said, that the Democratic umbrella was large enough to cover all who wanted to crowd under it.[42] Since his defeat, Stevenson had moved quickly to gain the confidence of such leaders as Russell and Lyndon Johnson, in addition to cementing his ties with Sam Rayburn.[43] He established a relationship with the segregationist governor of Georgia, Herman Talmadge. In Atlanta, addressing the state legislature on November 24, 1953, he referred to civil rights merely by saying that he joined "with the great majority of thoughtful white people of the South that his [black] improvement must and will continue, particularly in enlarged opportunities for Negro employment in the South's expanding industries." He also gave assurances about his attitude toward loyalty oaths when he said that "it isn't in the nature of a party structure that covers a nation to have total discipline and total conformity of views."[44] At the University of Virginia, in commemoration of the one hundredth anniversary of Woodrow Wilson's birth, Stevenson talked about the "new international spirit without which Wilson knew that neither institutions nor material programs could succeed," but said nothing about the intensifying civil rights controversy.[45] He also used his visit to confer with several of Virginia's political leaders and left hopeful about Democratic chances of carrying the state in 1956. Representative Howard W. Smith, a staunch conservative, emerged from the conversation believing that Stevenson was probably the best of the poor "pickings" available to the party. To William Colmer of Mississippi, Smith wrote, "The whole trend of his conversation was that of a moderate middle-of-the-roader."[46]

Steve Mitchell, Stevenson's choice as the party's national chairman and an amateur in politics, spent virtually full-time healing the wounds in Dixie. It was Mitchell who strengthened Stevenson's connections with Rayburn and Russell, arranged for the governor's visit to Georgia, and worked at establishing bonds with Virginia Democrats. Ralph McGill noted in the Atlanta *Constitution* that "the architects and the necessarily slow, patient, tedious work of binding up wounds and of restoring confidence and enthusiasm were the contribution of Adlai Stevenson and Stephen A. Mitchell."[47] "Those who want to keep Stevenson as a candidate for 1956 would do well to keep Mitchell also," one news bureau advised the press. "For without Mitchell, there possibly will be no Stevenson in 1956."[48]

Mitchell was also the man who led the way to a formula for preventing a second loyalty oath dispute. Once granted authority by the national committee to work toward that goal, he set up a Special Advisory Committee on Rules. Its tenor was cleared in advance with Russell as the spokesman for the party's southern wing, a procedure that made ADA liberals sure that ideology would thus be sacrificed for unity. Russell himself helped such suspicions by making the prediction that any real contention would be resolved before the convention.[49]

Actually, the ideological composition of the special committee was less important than the political standing of its personnel. They were elected officials, all professionals—all, in other words, men imbued with the self-interest that was implicit in finding a solution to thwart dissension. Its chairman was a thorough "practical" politician, Mayor David Lawrence; and the membership included such proponents of harmony as Rayburn and Congressman Brooks Hays of Arkansas. But perhaps its most crucial members were two men who understood how to blend ideology with expediency: Hubert Humphrey and Governor John S. Battle, the Virginian who had been persuasive at the 1952 convention with his antiloyalty-oath speech. Shrewdly, they agreed to the following statement:

Resolved, That it is the understanding that a State Democratic Party, in selecting and certifying delegates to the Democratic National Convention, thereby undertakes to assure that voters in the State will have the opportunity to cast their election ballots for the Presidential and Vice-Presidential nominees selected by said Convention, and for electors pledged formally or in good conscience to the election of these Presidential and Vice-Presidential nominees, under the Democratic Party label and designation.[50]

Promising far more than it was designed to enforce, it did the job of placating all sides. Few were surprised, then, by the unanimous acceptance of the rule by the 1956 national convention. From liberals, however, came another reaction, a suspicion that Hubert Humphrey had permitted his personal ambitions to dictate a revised relationship with the South, a maneuver he later confirmed by reassuring friends that his "error" would not be repeated.[51]

Overcoming the touchy loyalty-oath issue did not, by that one stroke, end the potential for chaos at the convention. Senator Robertson, for example, while in complete approval of that compromise, had warned back in 1954: "I don't hesitate to tell you that if we have the same platform and same candidate two years from now that we had two years ago, I will not be in a position to do any campaigning for any one."[52] Of course, that also reflected the same spirit as Mayor Lawrence's reference to the loyalty-oath matter as "darn rot," a view that was shared by many others.[53] Just having the names on a ballot in a given state with but perfunctory local endorsement and campaign effort spent on alternate candidates would give it little value. The pros were clearly far more interested in the platform and the candidates. As the convention neared, it became obvious that there would be a particularly significant relationship between the two.

The fragile southern support for Stevenson, the kind of backing that constantly carried with it rumors of shifts to Symington or Johnson, hinged on the governor's hewing to a moderate course, meaning one deemed inoffensive to the South. Any sanctioning of federal force to get compliance with desegregation decisions or even explicit endorsement of the Supreme Court could topple the alliance. One way to effectuate a rupture was by fighting for a strong civil rights plank at the convention. Forcing the candidate to take an unequivocal stand, one blatantly nonconciliatory, could cost him a major share of his support. The drive to win the South was provoking fear, even within Stevenson's camp, that the black vote was being taken for granted at the very moment Republicans were getting credit for desegregation and Eisenhower's personal popularity among Negroes was rising.[54] Nor was Stevenson happy when cornered by a labor union delegation, led by Walter Reuther, who let him have "both barrels" for the party's failure to fulfill its commitments toward desegregation and the protection of organized labor in the South. "But," reported Stevenson after the encounter, "I can't believe they are going to go Republican!"[55]

The winter of 1955 and 1956 had been a period of growing civil rights tensions. The White Citizens Councils were making progress with their program of massive resistance, even infiltrating southern unions and influencing the membership away from the national leadership.[56] The shooting of a black voter registration worker on the lawn of the Lincoln County courthouse in Mississippi had been followed by the murder of a fourteen-year-old Negro visitor from Chicago, Emmett Till, for having whistled at a white woman. The Till incident provoked much national indignation, but no act of antiblack violence resulted in any convictions. In Alabama, a boycott against the segregated city buses of Montgomery soon brought the Reverend Dr. Martin Luther King to national prominence. Miss Autherine Lucy's attempt to enroll at the all-white state university was resisted by rioters and officials in defiance of a court order. Meanwhile, a civil rights bill offered by Attorney General Brownell was fulfilling its calculated purpose by dividing congressional Democrats among resisting southerners and a small band of diehard liberals who fought as though its merits were the only thing that mattered. "The Civil Rights legislation at this point is so completely transparent," Senator Johnson was advised by an aide, "that practically no one has been deceived except Senator Douglas and a few others. . . ."[57]

Fearing that losing because of the civil rights issue would be intolerable, Jim Loeb reminded the ADA's leadership that most of the organization's members had "no genuine exciting alternative to Stevenson." He worried that Harriman's forces were preparing for a showdown on the issue as a way of stopping him, and that could leave the party without any pretense of liberalism, its policies removed from the influence of the urban coalition. Most of all, he warned, the governor must not become a candidate who had been put over by the South.[58]

7

The crux of the matter, it had become abundantly clear, related to unity versus ideology. For the small band of ardent liberals most committed to the cause of civil rights there was a temptation to disregard party harmony. To what end? What had unity brought? Recalcitrant segregationists, many of them veterans of the Dixiecrat movement, had been readmitted to the party in good standing. Their numbers had provided the foundation for Democratic domination in Congress; living with that situation had demonstrated the futility of progress simply through majorities. The risks of alienating that bloc, of even inducing them to start a new third party, seemed to offer the possibility not of political disaster but of gains. Chester Bowles voiced the dilemma that many others were wondering about when he asked Stevenson in late March, "How can we explain Eastland's election as chairman of the Judiciary Committee to a Negro group?"[59]

But he had no answer to the dilemma. He was committed to his friend. Stevenson, moreover, was the outstanding critic of the administration's foreign policies and he and the liberal from Connecticut, despite occasional differences in emphasis, viewed the world in much the same way. His civil rights inadequacies were a mere cultural gap that would ultimately be overcome.[60] Others pondered the willingness of the South to go along with Stevenson regardless of all the concessions that might be made.[61] After having shed their principles, what would victory mean? The prospect of making such sacrifices only to almost certainly lose another election to Eisenhower rendered the bargain especially unappetizing.

Few southerners would agree that their solution lay with embracing Eisenhower. Anger over the court's decision was strong, much of it directed at the president and his party. Some even suspected that

Attorney General Brownell's visit with Earl Warren before the announcement of his nomination to the Supreme Court had been undertaken to get advance confirmation that he was in favor of the NAACP's position in the pending case of *Brown v. the School Board of Topeka.*[62] Still, there was the realization among conservatives, especially in the South, that their economic interests were more secure with the current administration than under any government dominated by northern liberals. Senator Robertson predicted to Lyndon Johnson that "there will be a number of businessmen in Virginia and in other Southern States who will vote for Eisenhower, as they did four years ago, on the assumption that he will be better equipped than Stevenson to keep us out of war and that his Cabinet, including George Humphrey, would be more conservative in fiscal matters than the one that would be picked by Stevenson."[63]

It made perfect sense, then, for southerners to try to get the best that could be achieved, to make indignant noises about "ultra-liberalism" for hometown consumption, and to regard Stevenson as their most congenial candidate, without dividing the party by staging another walkout. The special committee established by Steve Mitchell to deal with the loyalty-oath question had, fortunately, put that matter out of the way. Their own preconvention planning served more to frustrate the few who were ready to stage a new open rebellion than to commit themselves to an obviously suicidal course.

Governor George Bell Timmerman of South Carolina had tried. His state party had passed a resolution to present the convention with a program for those interested in "constitutional government"; and, in terms reminiscent of 1948, for the convening of special state conventions that would not adjourn before the party's big meeting at Chicago but would merely recess and be prepared to reconvene later.[64] However, a follow-up session of seven southern state chairmen that met in Atlanta spurned Timmerman's efforts and especially opposed "any bolts, walkouts or third parties" and settled simply for a preconvention caucus that would give them "solidarity" before the national Democrats.[65] To clinch the matter, a subsequent session that brought together thirty-seven delegates from eleven southern states had a decidedly moderate cast. Stevenson supporters were dominant.[66]

Close observers of that session, while agreeing that there was no responsible third-party movement, detected elements that could still force a revolt. The breaking point, Stevenson was advised, could come if the party's platform contained specific provisions for enforcing compliance with the Court's decision. A simple endorsement of the *principle* of the decision would bring protests "for the record," but most were resigned to swallowing at least that much.[67]

By the eve of the convention, there seemed to be little doubt about Stevenson's eventual nomination. Kefauver's official entry into the race, which had been announced one month after Stevenson's, had forced a series of primary elections between the two men. The Tennesseean had done well for awhile. New Hampshire had been easy, largely uncontested; he upset Stevenson in Minnesota, despite the work that was done by Humphrey and Governor Orville Freeman. The result was attributed to Kefauver's folksy style, a strong appeal to farmers, a voter rebellion against what was generally regarded as the state's Democratic-Farmer-Labor Party's arbitrary commitment behind Stevenson, and to crossover voting by Republicans.[68] A clean victory in Oregon and a fine two-to-one sweep in California, managed to salvage the situation for Stevenson. At the end of July, Kefauver announced his withdrawal and threw his support to his recent opponent.

But even victory, with its apparent clear road to the nomination, had further damaged Stevenson's credentials with many liberals. While campaigning in Florida, he had remained silent when former governor Millard Caldwell introduced him as the "most moderate man the South can elect" and denounced Kefauver as a far left "integrationist" who was a "sycophant of the Negro vote."[69] His California remarks about the wisdom of "gradual" racial progress and the need for education in preparation for change had forced Eleanor Roosevelt into the state on a rescue mission. She, too, had accepted the possibility of constructive gains through moderation. In response to her encouragement, Stevenson wrote, "I would gladly withdraw from this political contest if it would serve in any manner to save the party from breaking up and enthroning the white extremists in the South or losing the Northern cities and thus the election."[70]

As the convention approached, with the members of the platform committee already convened in Chicago, Stevenson came under mounting pressure to modify his moderate views. Joe Rauh, Jr., urged him to use some public forum for a clear statement of support for the Supreme Court's decision.[71] ADAers conferred with senators Lehman, Humphrey, Wayne Morse, and others and decided that the party's plank could do no less than offer a clear endorsement of the Brown verdict as morally correct together with calling for its implementation by all branches of government.[72] Finally, on August 7, one week before the convention opened, Stevenson appeared on John Daley's ABC television program. "I have had a very strong feeling that the platform should express unequivocal approval of the Court's decision," he said; and then added, in typical Stevensonian fashion, "although it seems odd that you should have to express your approval of the Constitution and its institutions."[73]

With knowledge of the southern coolness toward another bolt, Stevenson's statement was designed to please liberals without permanently alienating his Dixie supporters. Public protests were made, of course. The Democratic chairman of Georgia's delegation, John Sammons Bell, was particularly vocal, promising not to vote for the candidate at the convention. Robertson professed to having expected it all along, coming from the man who had "reneged" on his FEPC "pledge" four years earlier. But he, too, agreed that there would be no walkout.

It was, then, Steve Mitchell who worked quickly against that possibility, however remote. He arranged, first, a telephone conversation between Stevenson and Governor James P. Coleman of Mississippi. Indications are that the candidate gave assurances that he had not suddenly become intransigent. Coleman then met with all southern members of the platform committee. Their caucus yielded the following conclusions that were given to Mitchell:

1. It would be unwise for Stevenson to try to back away from his statement on the Supreme Court decision, because by doing so he might lose as much in the North as he has already lost in the South.
2. Stevenson should be urged to give all hope and help to keep from the platform a specific approval of the Supreme Court opinion.
3. The whole group from the South—except Bell, who already made a statement—have agreed to withhold any statement and to hope that the platform will provide the solution. They are going to meet again in 48 hours.
4. If the platform endorses the Supreme Court decision, or the use of force in the implementation of the decision, the moderates in the South are washed up and they cannot help Stevenson in the nomination nor in the general election.[74]

Mitchell then met with the northern group, explained the seriousness of the matter, and they agreed to work out a solution. Their efforts produced a report that was acceptable to all but the outnumbered extreme liberals, Harriman, and his New York State delegation. The small northern bloc then produced a minority report. The difference between the two versions was the difference between platitudinous obeisance toward antidiscrimination and the readiness to use federal legislation to enforce the Court's decisions.

For Harriman, who had declared his candidacy official shortly after Stevenson's California victory, the only hope left depended upon the efficacy of Truman's coming endorsement and a blow-up over the civil rights plank before the full convention.

8

The Truman efforts for Harriman had been under way at least since the fall of 1955. Watching the ex-president carefully, the Stevenson people guessed that he was participating in a strategy that required the organization of a large bloc of unpledged and favorite-son delegates that could effectively impede the front-runner. Truman, however, later denied that the New Yorker had been his first choice and claimed that he had wanted Stevenson to run again. He had gone to the titular leader, he explained in confidence, but had found him unable to decide about making another race. That threw Truman behind Harriman as the man most likely to fight for the principles of the Democratic Party.

Other elements of the Truman-Stevenson relationship, however, seem equally persuasive. There was still much resentment over the governor's 1952 efforts to dissociate his campaign from the Truman administration. Truman had been particularly stung, as he told Mrs. Meyer as late as 1958, by Stevenson's campaign acknowledgment that there indeed had been a "mess" in Washington, which led Agnes to admonish Adlai by writing, "From no point of view was that a smart thing to say."[75] There was also speculation that Truman doubted Stevenson's liberalism and thought him contemptuous of politicians.[76] All such strains must have exacerbated the inherent differences between the patrician whose sensitivity and concern for taste and style seemed to minimize the importance of "good horse sense" and the earthy ex-machine politician from Missouri. That kind of gap enabled Truman to recall Stevenson as being "too busy making up his mind whether he had to go to the bathroom or not" and to contrast him with Vice President Adlai Ewing Stevenson by saying that the grandfather "wasn't any reluctant debutante."[77]

The Truman announcement for Harriman came in Chicago on the Saturday before the convention opened. Virtually all it did was to inspire a little flurry of activity about stopping Stevenson. At that time, there was still an outside chance that a "dark horse," someone like Stu Symington or even conservative Governor Frank Lausche of Ohio (who was the favorite of Harry Byrd's Virginia delegation), could emerge as a compromise choice. A more pronounced reaction to the Truman move came from Lyndon Johnson, who suddenly dropped assertions of "neutrality" and proclaimed himself as a "serious" candidate. To prepare himself for business, the Texan had installed a forty-line switchboard in his hotel room.[78]

The Truman announcement notwithstanding, it was obvious all along that the platform issue would decide matters. The question reached the floor during the evening session on Wednesday the fifteenth of August. It was after midnight when John McCormack, chairman of the platform committee, read aloud the majority civil rights plank. Then came the minority report, which had gathered just enough signatures to win the right to a hearing. Arguments in behalf of each then followed.

The procedure soon yielded to a surprise witness, one who was not even a delegate, but whose stature clearly merited the courtesy of a hearing, the party's only living ex-president. Reminding the gathering that he "had done more for civil rights than any other President," Truman praised the majority platform, not the one favored by Harriman and the liberals, and called it the "best platform this convention has ever had put before it."[79]

Then Rayburn called for a voice vote on the dissidents' plank. Loud howls of rejection came from the floor, easily drowning out the shouts of approval. Several attempts to gain recognition to force a roll-call vote, one that would make rejection of the minority report extremely difficult for delegates with liberal and Negro districts, were overlooked by Rayburn as he banged his gavel and declared, "In the opinion of the chair, the noes have it, and the minority report is rejected." One on-the-spot observer reported that Rayburn had thus saved the South for Stevenson.[80]

It was 1:41 A.M. and the Texan at the rostrum declared the convention adjourned until the next day. Willis Robertson, not one of Mr. Truman's admirers, told a colleague that the former president was imbued with far more political sagacity than any of the party's present leaders. Truman, Robertson pointed out, was well aware that neither Stevenson nor any other Democratic candidate could win the presidency without the South.[81]

CHAPTER VIII

★

Architects of a "New America"

1

Having made all the necessary compromises, having deterred moves among southerners to choose unpledged electors, Stevenson did go on to win the region—but just barely, losing to his opponent almost half the states of the Old Confederacy and trailing by 1 percent in the popular-vote column. Further, his majorities fell almost everywhere, as even such reliable Democratic strongholds as Kentucky and West Virginia went for Ike. In Virginia, where Harry Byrd maintained his "golden silence" for the second straight presidential election, Stevenson's share of the popular vote slipped to the incredibly low figure of 38.4 percent. Only in Georgia did the party majority resemble the old solid South. The losses came despite persistent reports, including from Virginia, that sincere efforts were being made on the part of many who had resisted the party's national ticket in 1948 and 1952 to organize support for Stevenson and his running-mate, Estes Kefauver.[1]

There were, then, neither gains in the South nor the compensation of additional votes from northern blacks. Paradoxically, the Negro electorate showed a reversal of the trend that had been established since the New Deal, as it shifted to Eisenhower by even a greater percentage than the white vote. The Harlem district of Congressman Adam Clayton Powell, Jr., who had announced his support for the president early, increased Eisenhower's total by a full 16.5 percent. It was a shift that was general throughout the nation, including among southern Negroes, who defected from Stevenson in large numbers.[2] Overall, blacks still voted heavily Democratic, but the decline in a presidential election marked the only trend toward the GOP since Roosevelt's time.

Moreover, Eisenhower cut deeply into the labor vote. Republican majorities were common among skilled and well-paid organized workers, most of whom thought of themselves as part of the middle class. Each of the major Catholic ethnic groups also gave the Republican candidate a record-high percentage. The president's success among urban workers had come despite the fact that Jimmy Hoffa and Dave Beck of the Teamsters were alone among major labor leaders in support of the Republican ticket.[3]

Adding to the Democratic dilemma was the party's congressional success. For the first time since Zachary Taylor's election in 1848, both houses had been swept without a simultaneous capture of the White House by the same party. Holding their two-seat margin in the Senate, the Democrats actually enlarged their advantage in the lower chamber. While just under 57 percent of the presidential ballots went to Eisenhower, virtually the same share went to Democratic congressional candidates. It was as though the decisions had been made by different electorates.

In effect, then, there had been two elections. It had become obvious that securing the Democratic congressional majority was quite another matter from being able to convince Americans that Ike, for all his Republicanism, should be replaced. Right from the start of the general's political career, a nonpolitician image had been a key strength; and the four years in office had not diminished that appeal. Of course, critics of Democratic congressional behavior felt that that was precisely what had been aided by the Johnson-Rayburn leadership, excessive cooperation that often surpassed what the president could get from his own party, furthering the process of enabling Ike to appear as a national nonpartisan chief executive.

And there seemed to be few compelling reasons for dissuading the public from that secure perception. Although Democrats continued to insist that the Korean situation was uncertain, that the armistice was tentative, that the administration had merely turned its back on the government of Syngman Rhee, the war had ended. No Americans were dying on that remote peninsula. Anything else was academic. Eisenhower's reputation as a man of peace, who knew how to end fighting without undertaking other reckless involvements, was enhanced by his much-publicized sessions at the "summit" with Khrushchev and Bulganin; and, whatever it had meant, the "spirit of Geneva" was far better than battlefield communiqués. Even the domestic scene had become quiet. Joe McCarthy had finally been rebuked by the Senate and was being ignored by the media. Moreover, once the 1953–1954 recession had been relieved, the economy had moved into a substantial boom. The enormous proliferation of material goods left few Americans conscious of the persistence of poverty and hardship in the land of plenty.

From the start of his campaign, Stevenson's emphasis was on convincing the voters that the well-being was only superficial, that the administration and the nation were ignoring intrinsic problems, that security meant more than just keeping a military balance of power against the Russians. Fearing their candidate's inability to pierce the general's reputation as an expert on international affairs, Stevenson had accepted the advice to pursue domestic issues. Further, every survey reaffirmed the fact that voters were still more apt to trust the Democrats on how to cope with problems at home. While there had been some lessening of hostility toward the party for having acquiesced to communist expansionism, Republicans were still experiencing considerable success with their "party of war" charges. Staging a national debate against an Eisenhower on how to handle the world seemed foolhardy to all but a handful of those close to Stevenson.

So the Democratic candidate's acceptance speech expressed his vision of a "New America." "Indeed, it is a central issue in this election," he said to a campaign audience at Harrisburg, Pennsylvania, in mid-September, "whether America wants to stay on dead center, mired in complacency and cynicism; or whether it wants once more now to move forward—to meet our human needs, to make our abundance serve all of us and to make the world safer—in short to Build a New America."[4] To elaborate upon the suggestions contained in his speeches, with the help of brain-trusters drawn from the "Finletter Group," he issued position papers on such subjects as medical care, civil liberties and civil rights, problems of the elderly, public power, education, the economy, agriculture, and what to do about depressed areas. "The difference between the two parties can be stated very simply. When the Republican leaders think of economic problems, they see a ledger and a cashbook. When Democrats think of economic problems, they see men, women and children," was a typical conclusion.[5] As in the past, his conception of the role of business was as a partnership with the government for their mutual benefit. Toward the close of the campaign, he said, "For government and business will continue to be mixed up together in the common task of keeping the American economy strong and growing." Having already spelled out how past Democratic programs had helped to make businesses more secure, he added, "Indeed, the whole history of American progress has been a history of constant government-business interaction—at its best, a creative interaction which has advanced the welfare of the whole nation."[6]

From the start, the campaign went poorly. Countless speeches made during the long primary contests against Kefauver had exhausted the candidate's ability to remain enthusiastic over words that had become stale. They read better than they sounded. The complaints of the pros that he was addressing only the "eggheads" reached a new high; in district after district, local leaders concentrated on getting their own candidates elected and ignored the national ticket. Many also resented the new flock of amateurs and "enthusiasts" that Stevenson had attracted to politics. In some places, such as in Manhattan where Tammany was being challenged by a new corps of reformers, there was evidence of what Mrs. Roosevelt called "deliberate" sabotage.[7]

Meanwhile, such individuals as W. Willard Wirtz, Jim Warburg, and Chester Bowles were convinced that Stevenson's weakness stemmed from his failure to explicate a substantial foreign policy. They thought it somewhat ironic that the candidate whose appeal was often attributed to his saner view of the international order should have been devoting himself to issues that the American public were regarding as less important than matters of war and peace. Dean Acheson, calling for such a switch in campaign tactics, indulged in a characteristic complaint when he wrote to Stevenson, "I just don't believe the professionals who know how to elect mayors and governors have any competence to judge what moves people when they are choosing the man in whose hands, more than any other, will be their destinies. . . . There is such a thing as galloppolling [sic] ourselves into a frustrating paralysis." Reacting to Stevenson's suggestion that a professional army might be wiser than continuing the draft, a possibility that he had contemplated long before the campaign had begun, Acheson added: "I am for making foreign policy—analysis and therapy, not disconnected 'original' ideas—a main theme for the rest of the campaign."[8]

But Stevenson's further elaboration of the thesis that conscription might be the less effective means of providing for national security was still vulnerable to the kind of refutation that had the authority of the general in the White House. So was his suggestion to mitigate the hazards of nuclear fallout and nuclear proliferation by having the United States take the lead in halting further tests of such bombs. No amount of "expert" testimony in its behalf could nullify Eisenhower's judgment that it was a "design for disaster." Nor did it

seem to jibe with either his or his party's charges that the Republicans were permitting American defensive capacity to fall behind the
extension of military commitments. On October 29, Senator Robertson informed Senator J. W. Fulbright that Eisenhower had a good
chance of carrying Virginia. Stevenson had incurred severe popular
opposition by trying to make the testing of nuclear weapons and the
ending of the draft major issues in the campaign.[9]

In October, there was violence abroad with the uprising of the
Hungarian "freedom-fighters" and the Anglo-French and Israeli
invasion of Egypt. With Eisenhower taking the initiative to stop the
Middle East war, Stevenson was reduced to desperate warnings that a
Republican victory would bring Nixon to within a "heart-beat" of
the presidency. The futility of his struggle was realized when, in
addition to losing badly in Virginia and the failure to win in forty
other states, his efforts were criticized by supporters for permitting
concesssions to the pros to lower the tone he had set four years
earlier. What was needed, it was easy to conclude, was the careful
development of programs that would restore the attractions of both
the Democratic Party and its candidates in national campaigns.

2

Soon after Truman's surprise victory of 1948 and considerably
before the futility of the Fair Deal program had become evident, a
group of New Yorkers who resided in Manhattan's "silk-stocking"
Ninth Assembly District came together to oppose the area's regular
Democratic organization by forming the Lexington Democratic
Club. The local party was described as "run by a small group of
insiders" and as "both ineffective and undemocratic. It had no specific program. It did nothing to encourage young people to participate in politics. It failed to campaign aggressively for the Democratic
Party in the District. It was completely dominated by the New York
County Democratic organization, popularly known as 'Tammany
Hall.' "[10] In other words, it lived off its patronage, controlled the
judgeships, took care of its supporters, and feasted upon the usual
political boodles. The first objective of the Lexington people was to
elect a district leader who was not a candidate of Tammany.[11] In
1953, they finally achieved that goal and two years later, after continuous prodding by the reformers, Tammany Boss Carmine De
Sapio instituted the direct elections of district leaders.

The Lexington Club had thus preceded by more than three years the national rise of Adlai Stevenson, the man who would become the natural hero of such genteel reformers. His two campaigns, especially the first, were notable for accelerating that process, the drawing to the Democratic Party of the most important infusion of new activists since the formation of the old Roosevelt coalition. The newcomers were well educated; they were not the types who usually frequented local political clubs; their substantial upper-middle-class means freed them from the common concern with patronage. Largely issue-oriented, they were far more preoccupied with ideology than with tactics. Some, like Lexington Club member Tom Finletter, had had conservative backgrounds. Finletter, in fact, had been closely associated with the air-power lobby.[12]

But it was Stevenson who had imbued them with confidence that reason and compassion could alter the tone of American politics and doubtless lead to a saner world. Most of the reformers were convinced that it was the Democratic Party, with all its contradictions and embarrassments, that offered the best hope for that ultimate achievement. The second Stevenson defeat, coming in the face of what they were convinced was the obvious contrast of their candidate with the mediocrity in the White House who seemed more concerned with ledger-books than with society, had left them certain of the futility of compromise, of the shabbiness of politics without principles, of the suicidal consequences of expediency, of the wisdom of never again making the kind of compromises their own man had attempted in 1956. Thus, their earliest intuitions, which predated their political involvement, were reinforced. Having "sold their souls" and failed anyway, the lesson they had learned was one to which a whole new generation of idealists would be particularly receptive.

Inevitably, the dichotomy between the party's entrenched leadership, especially those in control of its congressional delegation, and the new-generation liberals led to a struggle over its direction. Lyndon Johnson, as the Democratic Senate majority leader, therefore, found himself as early as the mid-1950s on the defensive against the forebearers of the people who would one day drive him from the top. With Sam Rayburn, he attempted to continue the politics of conciliation by molding the kind of consensus designed to prevent further Democratic fractures. But the congressional leadership was merely fortifying against inevitable changes.

While Stevenson's first national chairman, Steve Mitchell, had been a political novice and resembled the newer breed, he had gone along with the assumptions of the pre-1956 liberal intellectuals by accepting the need to compromise and maintain an expansive Democratic umbrella. His labors to soothe regional and ideological differences were, in most ways, largely successful. Despite complaints that he was not politically adroit, Mitchell did hold the center. When he indicated his desire to return to private law practice, Jim Rowe warned that by letting Mitchell resign, the Stevensonians would lose control of the party's national committee.[13] It was also Mitchell who saw to it that his successor would be a man in his own image.

The leading contenders were such political veterans as Mike Di Salle of Ohio; Jim Finnegan, the president of Philadelphia's city council; and the national committeeman from Indiana, Paul Butler. Di Salle, who had served in the Truman administration and was well thought of by most liberals, had the support of the former president. Finnegan had the backing of Mayor Lawrence and such other big-city bosses as De Sapio and Richard Daley of Chicago.[14] About the only prerequisite that Stevenson saw in making a decision among the contenders was, as he put it, "an increasing feeling that it [the national chairmanship] should continue Catholic for the present." When contemplating Butler, the party's titular leader wrote, "I have unqualified respect for Butler, whom I am coming to know well. He is definitely the 'new look' type, gentler than Mitchell, but physically not strong, and there are some difficulties in the Indiana organization."[15] Butler's conflict with the Hoosier Democratic machine run by Frank McHale and Frank McKinney, who had served as Truman's last national chairman, was viewed as a formidable obstacle.

Nevertheless, when the election to choose Mitchell's successor was held in New Orleans on December 4, 1954, Butler emerged with a better than two-to-one victory over the combined vote for his successors. He had drawn almost unanimous support from the national committeemen representing the Far West, Mountain, and Midwest states, the opponents of domination by the heavily urbanized East and North.[16] That his victory did not come at the party's national nominating convention, with the all-influential support of the presidential nominee, made it that much more surprising. Further, about all that was known of Butler was his attempt to organize a midterm conference for 1954 and his identification as an activist in the draft-Stevenson movement. When introducing the new chairman, a congresswoman-elect from Georgia said, "Mr. Paul . . . what is your name?"

Butler's inauspicious start failed to stop him from continuing for an extraordinarily long time as the party's national chairman. By the time he stepped down, when the Kennedy machine replaced him nearly six years later, the emaciated-looking diabetic from South Bend who looked more like a Wall Street lawyer than a party boss had made his mark as the antithesis of the Jim Farley-type Democratic leader. Butler was not one to concentrate on fund-raising and the pacification of national committeemen. More and more, he subscribed to the concept that ideology should not be subordinated to unity, that the party out of power had the duty to formulate programs and positions. His controversial reign was inaugurated early when he declared at a press conference that President Eisenhower had been demonstrating his "incapacity to lead the American people." Continuing in a vein that was virtually heretical to the Rayburn-Johnson policy of accommodation with the administration, he added that Ike's "military background does not qualify Eisenhower as a political leader."[17] Moreover, he went on to express his own personality at the expense of winning friends, and traditionalists charged him with over-eager partisanship and excessive emotionalism. Still, he retained his support as one less likely than any possible replacement to rip the party apart. Facing the national committeemen in the grand ballroom of the Sheraton-Blackstone Hotel at the Chicago convention, Butler received a standing ovation for his services. Again he betrayed emotionalism by wiping away tears, after which he said, "I'm sure you do not realize you are writing my political epitaph. In a moment, I shall submit my resignation and I urge you to accept it."[18]

But Butler's greatest controversies were yet to come. Disturbed by the pending change, unwilling as usual to upset the status quo by altering the direction of the national committee, it was Sam Rayburn who urged Stevenson to tell the committeemen to retain him. So a compromise was struck as suggested by the Speaker: Finnegan would manage the Stevenson campaign, a function normally given to the national chairman, while Butler would be permitted to keep his title.[19] Butler then went on to assume the leadership of the newer breed versus the congressional delegation. He took the initiative in urging the national committee to renew its 1956 convention rule to guarantee that the official ticket would at least appear on the ballots of each state, a move directly opposed to an unpledged-elector campaign that had begun to spread throughout the South in 1959. Unlike the equivocation of the past, he took a firm position in behalf of a strong civil rights stand and, in what was regarded as one of his more impolitic statements, even suggested that southerners who were unhappy ought to join the Republicans.[20] Nor did Butler spare the party's congressional leadership for its lack of a forthright opposition program. Harry Truman, suspicious of what he later deprecated as "self-appointed" liberals, wrote to Sam Rayburn, "I noticed that Paul Butler is 'firing from the hip,' without any consultation with Democrats that count."[21] A Newport News attorney complained to his friend Senator Byrd, "It is my humble belief the Democratic Party no longer exists as a national party except as a label to elect certain people at election time. The Democratic Party nationally has been in a continuous process of deterioration since the advent of Franklin Roosevelt."[22] Still, when the national committee met in September of 1959, amid much talk of replacing Butler—including the possibility of making Truman the national chairman—Butler remained in command.[23]

But the philosophical clash between the issue-oriented liberals behind Butler and the position of the traditionalists was too deep. At a one-hundred-dollar-a-plate dinner to honor Mrs. Roosevelt on her seventy-fifth birthday, the controversy received public airing via the CBS radio network. Truman, speaking first, denounced the "self-appointed guardians of liberal thinking who have become rather vocal lately" and wondered who had given them their mandate. "We know that a vigorous and united Democratic party," he explained, "is the only decisive force for liberalism, and there is no other choice." Mrs. Roosevelt, like Jackson responding to Calhoun at a Jefferson Day dinner over a century earlier, took up the challenge in her talk by declaring that she welcomed every kind of liberal. "I want unity," she added, "but above everything else, I want a party that will fight for the things that we know to be right at home and abroad."[24]

For the liberals, the split was truly intramural rather than a clean party division along ideological lines. The Johnson-Rayburn leadership was not lacking congressional support from those members of the legislature who were left of center. Such liberals were with the conservatives in following the traditional belief that party policy should be made by those who had been elected to their offices rather than by theorists without portfolio. Even more accurate would be the statement that they were skeptical of any attempt at formulating specific policies for adherence by all members of so diverse a national party. Such attitudes later shaped their hostility to Paul Butler's most significant contribution as national chairman, his leadership of a unique affiliate called the Democratic Advisory Council.

3

There was nothing coincidental about the birth of the Democratic Advisory Council (DAC) so soon after the 1956 elections. The ability of the party's congressional candidates to retain numerical supremacy despite Eisenhower's impressive re-election was interpreted by many leaders, especially those from big cities and the West, as evidence of popular endorsement of liberalism. Even if Sam Lubell were correct in his observation that the public seemed to prefer divided government to one-party dominance, it was a problem that could, in their view, be overcome by offering Americans real alternatives to Republicanism. A vigorous forward-looking program, they believed, could rally support in sufficient numbers to defeat any future potential GOP candidate.

All the earlier calls for a more coordinated formulation of party policy, including Butler's own plan for a midterm conference, were finally gaining some credence. It was a conclusion that won the support of a number of other powerful Democrats, particularly Jake Arvey of Chicago, California's national committeeman Paul Ziffren, David Lawrence, and Adlai Stevenson. Stevenson visualized its potential for generating the kind of opposition publicity that Charlie Michelson had helped to create during the Roosevelt years.[25] Hubert Humphrey, enjoying a reputation as perhaps the most important liberal on Capitol Hill, explained to national committeewoman Margaret Price of Michigan that "some of us in the Senate feel it is wrong to let the impression exist that we Democrats do not have a legislative program, and must wait to see what President Eisenhower asks.... As a result, a group of us in the Senate are publicly proposing ... what we regard as a minimum Democratic program for action at the coming Congress. We hope the DNC Executive Committee will consider that program at its meeting, and express its support if it concurs with our objectives."[26]

Ten days later, the committee showed its basic agreement with Humphrey's point by authorizing the establishment of the Advisory

Council, which later stated its objective in a resolution that said: "We can win in 1960 only if we begin now to hammer out a forceful, coherent policy and to keep communicating it to the public."[27] The group's chairman, Paul Butler, moved quickly to get the kind of support that the council needed from the party's congressional leadership. Invitations went out to twenty Democrats, but the most vital assurance of its success as a political force was dependent upon the membership of both Sam Rayburn and Lyndon Johnson.

Rayburn, however, was distinctly cool from the very start, and Johnson's reaction may have been hardened by the Speaker's influence.[28] Several long-distance telephone conversations took place between Butler and the majority leader, who was then in Texas. Finally, on December 3, after giving much attention to the implications of the plan, Johnson sent his own thoughts to "Mr. Sam." Explaining that having the council would open "a real hornet's nest," he provided the following analysis:

If the committee becomes operative along the lines conceived by its sponsors, it can result only in defeating all Democratic legislation in the Congress and assuring Democratic defeat at the polls in 1958 and 1960. . . . the American people will bitterly resent the idea that a group of appointive professional politicians are supervising the work of the men they have elected to Congress. . . . the existence of such a committee will make it virtually impossible for any Republican to vote for Democratic legislation. . . . Republicans who will normally vote for certain types of Democratic legislation because they consider it good for the country are highly unlikely to vote for that legislation when they are told that it was advanced by a committee whose sole objective is to sponsor a Democratic program that will elect a Democratic Congress in 1958 and a Democratic President in 1960. *In other words, the Democrats would be doomed to suffer a string of DEFEATS—hardly a recommendation for campaigning purposes in 1958 and 1960.* . . . the existence of the committee will do nothing to compensate for the losses by keeping the narrow Democratic majorities in line. It is completely powerless to produce any votes. But it is capable of deepening divisions in the Democratic Party. Since no Democrat agrees with every line in the Democratic platform, the only result of such a committee will be *to label individual Democrats as party deserters on almost every vote that is of any importance.* It will keep the spotlight of publicity on every Democratic division and take the spotlight off the Republican divisions.[29]

Johnson's points deserve recognition as more than convenient rationales. Despite sizable numerical superiority, the large number of potential defectors in any presidential competition had kept the

Democrats continually dependent upon support from Republicans and independents. Therefore, both the majority as well as the minority party, as was later demonstrated more emphatically in 1964 and again in 1972, had ample grounds to refute arguments that preached partisan ideological orthodoxy. Moreover, the differences between the presidential and congressional wings were also significant. Undoubtedly, the poor response to the council that came from Democrats on Capitol Hill (only Humphrey and Estes Kefauver accepted, and Congresswoman Edith Green of Oregon rescinded her initial approval) was influenced to a considerable degree by the Johnson-Rayburn opposition. But, even without that factor, the distinctions between the two wings were apparent among those who would have had nothing to do with it in any event. After all, the Democrats already were in control of both houses. Like Louisiana's Overton Brooks, who informed Butler that "We are having enough trouble already in the Deep South," they attributed whatever success they were enjoying to the leadership of the Speaker and the majority leader and were hardly ready to entertain competitive power from a ban on nonelective liberals.[30] Accordingly, not a single southern Democratic congressman or senator agreed to serve.

With only two of the ten congressional invitations accepted, by mid-December it looked as if the council were doomed. Butler, upset by a New York *Times* story that he was being forced to retreat on the plan, wrote to Managing Editor Turner Catledge: "I am sorry that Senator Johnson and Speaker Rayburn do not wish to be members of the Committee, but I believe that we can accomplish our purposes by cooperation and consultation with these two Democratic leaders whether they are on the Committee or not on the Committee."[31] Butler's determination to press on was fortified by the consolation that, even while refusing actual membership, Johnson and Rayburn had expressed willingness to listen to the recommendations of a group that was, after all, sanctioned by the national committee.

The council had another source of strength, and that was its battery of luminaries who had an appeal to large numbers of liberals. In addition to Humphrey and Kefauver, among its appointed members were Stevenson, Truman, Harriman, Lehman, and Governor G. Mennen Williams. Mrs. Eleanor Roosevelt was listed as a consultant who sat with the council. Charles S. Murphy, the former special counsel to President Truman, also served the group. Tom Finletter, a member of the DAC's administrative committee, became an active fund-raiser. Lehman was the first wealthy liberal to respond, with a check for $10,000. By the summer of 1957, $54,750 had been received in cash or solid commitments.[32] All in all, the Democratic Advisory Council, having been established with the stipulation that it pay its own way, finally received between $300,000 and $400,000 in contributions.[33]

Further, its advisory committees that were established to turn out policy positions, some thirteen working groups, were dominated by intellectuals whose reputations gave them status as leading opponents of Eisenhower-Dulles-Republican policies. The committee on economic policy was chaired by Professor John Kenneth Galbraith and included such other academic figures as Seymour Harris, Walter Heller, Arthur Schlesinger, Jr., and Richard Lester, as well as such influential individuals as John Snyder, Henry Fowler, Leon Keyserling, and Wilson Wyatt. Foreign policy was the function of a committee that was headed by the prestigious Dean Acheson. But that group had the additional advantage of such names as Chester Bowles, Paul Nitze, Ben Cohen, Herbert Lehman, and Professor Hans Morgenthau.

So the DAC operated as virtually an institutionalized version of the old "Finletter Group." They went to work in rented quarters at 1028 Connecticut Avenue, N.W., Washington, where formal meetings took place in the elegant and airy corner room of a suite that had once belonged to Senator Tom Connally of Texas. Charles Tyroler II, a New Yorker who had acquired considerable experience in Washington, was hired as its executive director because of his acceptibility by the council's basic groups, especially those led by Stevenson and Truman.[34]

For all its subsequent reputation as an extra-legal liberal cabal strong enough to be labeled (although somewhat excessively) as a "shadow government,"[35] the council had trouble spelling out those positions that progressives had hoped would inspire policies capable of providing relief from domestic economic inequities and the continuation of the cold war. There were some positions that were considered rather bold; one was the declaration that Arkansas Governor Orval Faubus' prevention of the integration of Little Rock High School "does not represent the position or policy of the Democratic Party."[36] Another, which brought dissent from the three southern members of its executive committee, denounced efforts to enact federal right-to-work legislation.[37] Liberals could also applaud the council's advocacy of rules to thwart Senate filibusters, to increase minimum wages to $1.25 per hour, and to make possible long-term

commitments to the Development Loan Fund.[38] Still, there remained strange inadequacies for a group with such liberal credentials, shortcomings that seemed to make the council a virtual
microcosm of the national debate between the party's congressional
leadership and its left-wing.

While the council hoped to influence the course of the Democratic
Party, Johnson and Rayburn had not, by their boycott, intended to
remain totally detached from the proceedings. In 1958, the Speaker
wrote to Paul Butler, "I trust your group does not go into too much
specifics on legislation."[39] Further steps were perceived in efforts
being made by Johnson, whose stature as the party's political leader
had increased greatly since 1956, to overturn Butler. He tried to
employ his power to line up congressional opposition to the national
chairman. "Every senator and member of congress," advised an aide
to Herbert Lehman, "has been subject to consummate pressure,
brought by Johnson and Rayburn and their allies, to stand up and
be counted. . . . Every senator or member of congress who wants or
might want anything from the Leadership, has been told, in one way
or another, that he had better line up."[40] But Butler, drawing support from the national committee rather than from Capitol Hill, was
relatively immune, surviving even a number of public statements
that outraged fellow Democrats. Within the council itself, however,
Johnson and Rayburn had friends.

Humphrey, of course, was close to the majority leader, but he had
to be cautious about preserving his reputation as a liberal. Those
who observed him at first-hand could not doubt the depth of his
presidential ambitions.[41]

A more likely candidate for being able to bridge the two groups
was Harry S Truman. His standing having actually increased since
his controversial White House years, there was little question about
the former president's continuing prestige. He had not been able to
do much for Harriman at the 1956 convention, but numerous circumstances had foreclosed that possibility. As a member of the DAC,
he rarely undertook the long train ride from Missouri to attend its
session; his connection was mostly confined to letterheads. Still,
the fact that he was a member gave the council great caché among
hostile Democrats and drew much publicity from the press. Truman's hand was further strengthened by fear that congressional
pressure might induce him to quit. If anything could compel him to
take that step, it would have been the arguments that he was lending
himself to furthering the Democratic schism. But Truman was in a

dilemma between his concern with party unity and his sympathy with the more liberal attitudes toward economics and labor that were held by the great majority of the DAC's members. In terms of domestic programs, for example, his position was well in advance of Stevenson's. Those on the council who knew him best have maintained that his efforts, therefore, were directed toward getting his friends on Capitol Hill to accept the council.[42]

Insofar as the council was concerned, one essential way to keep Truman happy was to retain Dean Acheson as chairman of the Advisory Committee for Foreign Relations.[43] Especially after the breakdown of bipartisanship following the collapse of Chiang Kai-shek and the frustrations of the Korean War, Acheson had been pilloried by the Republican opposition. The vehemence of right-wing attacks charging him with pursuing "no-win" policies and with responsibility for communist gains would imbue with more than just a touch of irony the later writings of revisionists who charged the secretary of state with having been a supreme cold warrior. Watching the subsequent Republican administration attempt to cope with the international situation could not have failed to enhance Acheson's usual self-righteousness. But more than that: the evidence that Eisenhower and Dulles were merely continuing the same policies, with added embellishments for the satisfaction of the Republican right-wing, enabled both Acheson and Truman to justify their policies. For the ex-secretary, it was a marvelous opportunity for vindication. Writing to Chester Bowles, he declared, "I do not believe that there is 'no political mileage' in sensible discussion of foreign policy, and that the American people are incapable of adult thought. I don't believe either that a sound policy position can be based on attempts to get the votes of national groups, protectionists, isolationists, atomic pacifists, those who want to pay no taxes, and mothers of sons in their twenties." And then, directing his thoughts toward the council, he added, "My idea of the Committee's function is to tell the Advisory Council what we think is the best foreign policy for the United States."[44]

Against such determination, such self-confidence—and such arrogance—the Chester Bowleses of the committee had no chance. Further supported by Paul Nitze, Acheson dominated the foreign policy statements. Far from de-emphasizing military responses to the cold war, far from concentrating on what Bowles and his fellow liberals considered the more pressing menaces—destitution and hunger and corruption that compelled turning toward communism for relief from the known exploitations—Acheson's hard-line cold-war papers colored the Advisory Council's responses to Eisenhower-Dulles policies.

Thus, instead of calls for rapprochement in the face of nuclear proliferation, instead of recognition that the forces of nationalism were stronger than the power of "international communism," the Acheson papers turned out in the name of the liberal Democratic Advisory Council charged that the Eisenhower administration was permitting, even encouraging, communist expansion. It was the Republicans, in other words, who were now betraying the folly and weakness that, in the early 1950s, the spokesmen of the GOP had attributed to Acheson's own State Department. The cold-war argument at home had come full circle. The concept of massive retaliation, Acheson and Nitze wrote in a paper dated September 18, 1957, "has opened the way for the communists to subvert, to surround, to pinch off exposed positions of the free world, now that in fact they run little risk of incurring the awful sanction of an all-out nuclear war. . . . There is no cheap or easy road to military security in a nuclear age. All of us should be made fully conscious of the threat presented by developing Russian capabilities."[45] Paper after paper spelled out the same theme: the American military position relative to the Russian was being weakened; isolation from our allies was increasing physical vulnerability; administration preoccupation with balanced budgets was leading to virtual unilateral disarmament, thus weakening deterrence, and "we can be sure that others will probe and challenge our every action knowing that we are unprepared to support our political actions."[46]

At a meeting of the committee in Washington on Saturday, September 28, 1957, Acheson was particularly emphatic. Returning to the theme of the fallacies of making concessions to popular opinion, he argued for massive dedication toward winning the battle against Russia. The well-informed should demand more sacrifices from the public. If the Russians advance into western Europe, he warned, America will become a minority in the free world. Therefore, we must continue to expand. "Automobiles block the road, the TV bemuses the mind," he was noted as having said. We should build up our military power and dispense with futile efforts at disarmament. It is madness, he warned, to follow the administration's desire to further reduce the size of our armed forces. "People are being deluded. Our people would make minor sacrifices to maintain and expand our armed services if they understood."[47] "As long as

Dean Acheson is its mouthpiece on foreign policy," wrote Jim Warburg, whose friendship with the secretary had been ruptured by their differences over foreign policy, "its utterances on that subject are practically indistinguishable from those of the calamitous Mr. Dulles."[48]

The irony of Truman's impact on DAC's ideological position, then, was that it succeeded in prevailing where its influence was the more traditional, as on foreign policy, but failed when it attempted to formulate more progressive economic views. As Acheson had led the writing of diplomatic position papers, Leon H. Keyserling and Galbraith, who headed the Advisory Committee on Economy Policy, dealt with the key questions relating to domestic programs. Keyserling was an old New Deal economist and lawyer who had worked on the staff of Senator Robert Wagner and later served during the Truman years as the second chairman of the Council of Economic Advisers. Despite Galbraith's nominal title as chairman of the committee, Keyserling had an important influence in the formulation of major statements.[49]

Galbraith had long condemned the Eisenhower administration for fostering both economic inertia and the stagnation of social programs by favoring the private over the public sectors of the economy, an argument that he explained in his popular book, *The Affluent Society*. In a position paper subtitled "The Next New Deal," he argued for the society of abundance to stop regarding "public needs as inferior to private needs" and charged that vital welfare programs were suffering under Republican neglect.[50]

Keyserling argued for the importance of economic growth. Expanding the productivity of American capitalism would best provide the resources for the essential services that, as Galbraith agreed, could only be furnished by the government. In a 1957 booklet called *Consumption—Key to Full Prosperity*, Keyserling held that "there is something even more wrong with our human and moral values, when we measure prosperity by the increase in luxury items, but neglect the schools which serve our young, the social security systems which protect our old, and the other programs designed to fortify economic strength with economic justice."[51] In Keyserling's view, Galbraith was neglecting the means to accomplish his ends, that economic growth "automatically did more for the public sector than low economic growth, that it enabled us to do more for the public sector than a lower rate of growth, and above all, that doing more for the public sector was absolutely indispensable to maintaining the economic balance which was essential to economic growth itself."[52] In a magazine article published in 1959, Sidney Hyman observed that Galbraith's committee had fallen under the domination of Keyserling and his Truman-backed supporters by making "the Council an early leader in stressing the need for, and the implications of, sustained economic growth."[53]

Strangely missing from that position, however, was the concommitant call for the kind of spending that such growth would make possible. If Keyserling and the Trumanites on the committee had indeed prevailed, something vital had been lost on the way. The Keyserling view of the ability of economic growth to generate greater public spending was detailed at length in 1960 in a position paper called "Toward a National Purpose in Our Economic Life: Specific Goals and How to Achieve Them." But the projected figures of how much could become available for such outlays led the Kennedy partisans on the committee, headed by Galbraith, to prevent its publication through fear that the Democratic Party and its probable presidential candidate would be labeled the "big spenders."[54] By that time, Senator John F. Kennedy had thought it appropriate to join the Democratic Advisory Council.

Nor did the council's activities achieve much distinction in the handling of what had become the sine qua non of liberals in the late 1950s, the civil rights movement. Justifiably, the DAC took credit for having made a well-publicized response that both repudiated the moral standards of some fellow Democrats and had been interpreted as virtually the official position of the party. When the Civil Rights Act of 1957 was enacted, the council prodded the administration to implement the first piece of federal legislation since Reconstruction by moving swiftly to establish the Civil Rights Commission. Yet, within the DAC itself, there was disappointment with its failure to deal more energetically with the problem, to become truly the body that would subordinate considerations of political strategy to moral imperatives. Lehman and Paul Butler fought with astonishingly little support for firmness against "gradualism" and regional appeasement. Lehman, in particular, became singlemindedly devoted to the subject, even appearing to bring up the topic "every five minutes," as one witness later recalled.[55] Mrs. Roosevelt, too, was disappointed to find that, in addition to persisting with a hard-line cold-war position, the supposed spokesmen for Democratic Party liberalism were strangely reticent when dealing with the generation's most significant domestic problem. Not until 1960, during the final months of the DAC's life, was a committee on civil rights established, and Eleanor Roosevelt was made its chairlady.

Ironically, then, it was on Capitol Hill where the greatest gains were made. With the passage of the acts of 1957 and 1960 to protect civil rights and the freedom to vote, a significant change had occurred; not through the contribution of the DAC, where the northern liberal membership had split over the problem of what to do about the South, but through the twin forces of popular demand and political ambition. Leading Capitol Hill Republicans was Senate Minority Leader William Knowland, whose conservatism was at variance with his new efforts to achieve civil rights legislation. George Reedy, advising Lyndon Johnson, noted, "There is a definite cynicism in [the] attitude toward Knowland's sincerity about civil rights. . . . They believe he is acting for political motives and their only speculation is whether he is running for Governor . . . or for President."[56] Johnson himself, attempting to rehabilitate his reputation by becoming known as something other than a southerner while at the same time identifying himself with civil rights legislation that could avoid splitting the party, made the issue a vital ingredient for his future.[57]

In 1957, Johnson marshaled all his resources to supply the votes for something acceptable on both sides of the Mason-Dixon line. Fortified by the legal expertise of such people as Abe Fortas and Dean Acheson, and pacifying the South by providing for jury trials in cases of criminal contempt and rejecting a provision that could have exacerbated the school integration dispute, he was able to shape a bill that had the protection of voting rights as its major goal. Giving assurances to a Fort Worth constituent, Johnson explained, "It is a mistake to designate the legislation which was passed by Congress as a Civil Rights bill. As a result of the long debate in the Senate, all of the objectionable features which would have permitted the Federal government to intervene in every segregation problem were eliminated. The proper designation for the bill . . . is a 'right-to-vote' bill. . . . I cannot see how any Texan can refuse to vote to guarantee the same rights to every citizen of the United States as those presently enjoyed by the citizens of Texas. This would appear to me to be a repudiation of my entire Texas heritage."[58] As feeble and as full of compromises as the law was, it nevertheless prepared the way for the more effective measure that came three years later and, more significantly, for the landmark advances that would later embellish Johnson's own presidency.

Neither the shortcomings nor the achievements of both the congressional Democrats and the Advisory Council, however, can account for the party's great election victory in 1958. Already plagued by the embarrassment of the Russian Sputnik coup and the Sherman Adams-Bernard Goldfine scandal, the Republican burden was intensified by the combination of recession and inflation. The absence of a popular president heading the ticket also meant that all GOP candidates had to stand alone. So the Democrats increased their control over each house to nearly two to one, drawing over 62 percent of the votes for Congress.

While, by 1958, neither the party's congressional nor presidential wings, with the DAC identified almost entirely with the latter, can be said to have constituted a negative force, the voters had nonetheless reacted to actual conditions rather than to political formulas. Yet, what would possibly become the best justification for its existence during the years in the wilderness was the influence the DAC continued to exert long after it had been permitted to expire. Almost one-third of the 275 people who had served on the council and its committees were appointed to positions in the next Democratic administration.

CHAPTER IX

Reconstituting the Coalition

1

Before the Democratic national convention of 1960 produced the surprising ticket of John F. Kennedy and Lyndon Baines Johnson, Jim Warburg was among those who, until the very last minute, continued to hope for a Stevenson candidacy. But the two-time loser, despite the pleas of supporters eager to see a modification of cold-war policies and the arrival of the "liberal hours," seemed coy, unwilling to remove himself unequivocally by yielding to the pressure to come out for Kennedy or to make the kind of overt moves that would have heartened his followers. Along with many other liberals, Warburg, financier, philanthropist, and pamphleteer-critic of America's role in the cold war, would have preferred a Stevenson-Kennedy combination. He explained to a friend that that, at last, we may have enabled the party "to break away from the sterile Truman-Acheson influence."[1]

Kennedy undoubtedly was an attractive man. His intelligence, wealth, and the aura of dynamic glamour overshadowed his inexperience and projected him as a refreshing contrast with the past. He had been sufficiently bold to take the Senate floor for a speech critical of French determination to perpetuate the fiction that Algeria was an integral part of Metropolitan France, a stroke that was particularly appealing to Stevenson intellectuals. Emulating the best traditions of aristocratic devotion to public service, Kennedy had also graduated from Harvard and had even turned out a senior honors paper that was published as a book called *Why England Slept*. He also contributed articles to *Foreign Affairs* and had managed to produce a Pulitzer Prize-winning book, *Profiles in Courage*.

Long before the Democrats convened at Los Angeles to, in effect, ratify the pre-ordained choice of the youthful politician to head the ticket, he had won the loyalty of a considerable segment of the old

Stevenson brain-trust. Once again, much as they had done for the "Finletter Group" and the Democratic Advisory Council, intellectuals from academia had committed themselves. Sixteen of them, including Schlesinger and Galbraith, and supported by such other attractive luminaries as James MacGregor Burns, Henry Steele Commager, and Allan Nevins, had issued a public statement in June declaring that, in Kennedy, they had found a man who "has expounded with force and clarity the great issues of the 1960s and has given overwhelming evidence of his deep commitment to liberalism on the widest possible range of issues." Moreover, they were convinced that "Kennedy's adherence to the progressive principles which we hold is strong and irrevocable."[2]

Meanwhile, Stevenson had come under increasing two-way pressure: from the Kennedy people eager to get his much-prized endorsement and from his own dedicated loyalists whose distrust for the ambitious senator made them all the more eager to urge him to announce his own availability. In early June, Stevenson reminded Mrs. Thomas Finletter that to do so would be a violation of a long-standing decision and it was not something that could be broken. "That I will accept a draft—yes—who wouldn't or couldn't!" he added. "But to actively seek the nomination for a third time is quite inconsistent with the position I have taken for so long, and it would make me feel also quite out of character."[3] After Eleanor Roosevelt had abandoned an earlier vow to remain neutral by coming out for a Stevenson-Kennedy ticket, he replied to her in much the same vein.[4] Agnes Meyer, weary of her long efforts to induce Stevenson to work in his own behalf, finally wrote in despair, "I have a feeling that our young friend may get enough delegates lined up to make it on the first ballot." Then she added: "I really don't know and find strength in the fact that I don't seem to care. I am afraid this will make you angry."[5] No less unhappy over the party's obviously predetermined course, Harry Truman wired Sam Rayburn and reminded the Speaker of their year-old agreement that the nomination of either Lyndon Johnson or Stuart Symington of Missouri would be more desirable. Now, however, Truman concluded, "It looks as if this Convention has been packed against both of them and it is almost impossible for me to stand a situation like this."[6]

There was little doubt that, to the two old Democratic warriors, having a Roman Catholic as the party's presidential candidate would be both a personal and a political disaster. Neither was personally immune to the prejudices and fears of those Americans with old aversions toward Catholicism and apprehensions about the power of the Church at Rome. The so-called "religious factor" was dominant in large areas of the South, where reports indicated that it constituted the sole serious source of opposition to a candidate who, after all, had not cloaked himself with excessive liberalism. But by no means was it confined to either southerners or white Protestants. The gradual awareness of Kennedy's faith, which began to develop as 1960 neared, was disturbing to many blacks as well. The frequently repeated incident concerning Kennedy's bemused reaction to hearing that Martin Luther King's father had opposed him because of his faith, which led him to say, "Well, we all have fathers, don't we?" did not arise from an isolated example of Negro resistance. Among Jews, too, especially those with live memories of the Coughlin era, it was especially easy to link the senator's religion with the alleged anti-Semitism and pre-World War II insensitivity toward Hitlerian aggression on the part of Ambassador Joseph P. Kennedy. To the many liberals whose suspicions of the Roman Catholic Church had been inflamed by Paul Blanshard's writings about hierarchical power, the avoidance of a confrontation with Joe McCarthy was a virtual confirmation of his secret sympathies, especially since the elder Kennedy had a history of more than token congeniality with the demagogue from Wisconsin, and brother Bobby had worked for McCarthy's committee. John Kennedy had avoided all opportunities to vindicate himself by taking a forthright anti-McCarthy stand. Further, those with longer memories knew that Kennedy himself had once condemned the State Department for the "loss" of China, a charge that was one of the battle-cries of the fervent anti-communist crusaders. Therefore, it was not simply Kennedy's Catholicism that was viewed as a threat in many quarters but the association of his name with the reactionary stereotypes so frequently attributed to his co-religionists.

Others were put off by the currency of suspicions that Kennedy was not much better than Nixon, a man whose McCarthyite background and apparent lack of scruples had created resistance not only among liberals and moderates but even among many conservatives who were already turning to Senator Barry Goldwater of Arizona as a man with sincere convictions. Willis Robertson, who was again doubting the wisdom of openly defying his party's choices, viewed Nixon in terms that were strikingly akin to the way many liberals viewed Kennedy. Robertson wrote to a friend that Nixon was "both a shrewd and ambitious politician who is willing to go as far in behalf of civil rights legislation as political expediency dictates."[7] One who was even more skeptical about Nixon, journalist Murray Kempton, filed a dispatch from the Democratic convention in Los Angeles that asked: "Could you imagine anyone saying that Jack Kennedy, as he is now, makes you proud to be called a Democrat?"[8]

The emergence of Johnson as Kennedy's running-mate, however, was the greatest shock to the party's left-wing. The Michigan delegation, led by Governor Williams and heavily influenced by Walter Reuther, had greeted it with shouts of protest. Chairman Le Roy Collins' motion that the convention declare Johnson's nomination unanimous was carried despite the strong roar of "nays" that came from the floor of the Sports Arena.[9] Of all the possible candidates other than Kennedy and Stevenson, Johnson had been regarded as the most conservative, the man most potentially damaging to the liberal cause. In April, the ADA's national director had circulated a special memorandum detailing why, because of his record in such matters as civil rights, foreign policy, labor, and natural resources, Johnson would be the candidate least likely to "pursue new, vigorous domestic and international policies to pull us out of the stagnation of the last eight years."[10]

Still, when the convention had adjourned, there was a new spirit of confidence, helped in no small part by Kennedy's acceptance speech, the common determination to defeat Nixon, and the gradual realization that the choice of Johnson may have been the candidate's master stroke. Jim Warburg, revising his outlook, informed Galbraith that "we shall have a man of courage and decision in the White House and that, it seems to me, is the number one requirement." Later that fall, after Kennedy's narrow victory, Warburg admitted that he still did not know the senator's position on many major issues, but added that "we shall have a man in the White House who has intelligence, courage and energy, instead of a man who to my mind would have been little more than a weather vane."[11]

2

It was natural for men with ideals, men who believed that the principles of the Democratic Party afforded an adequate basis for renewing the vitality of liberalism, to convince themselves that in

John F. Kennedy they had a new brand of forward-looking man, who understood the ingredients of power and had the appetite and capability to assure its deployment—and who also shared their notions about lifting American society out of its dead-center Eisenhower-era rut.

One who was so convinced was James MacGregor Burns. A professor of political science at Williams College and noted biographer of Franklin D. Roosevelt, he had also contributed a precampaign book called *John Kennedy: A Political Profile.* Kennedy, Burns maintained, was not just another rich boy who was most comfortable impressing ladies at political teas. Despite that image, he was bright and serious. Most of all, he cared; he was willing to learn; he was far from the conventional playboy type; he preferred the solitude of his study and an evening with a good book to the company of politicians and was receptive to ideas that engaged an evident sense of humanity that had enabled him to mature well beyond the values of his powerful father. If he had failed to oppose Joe McCarthy, Burns insisted, it had not been through sympathy for the demagogue. Neither Kennedy nor Lodge had been sufficiently suicidal to take such risks during that 1952 senatorial campaign in a state that had a large core of McCarthyites. Besides, making open defiance of McCarthy during those days, *the* test of liberalism, would leave America with very few heroes. Kennedy's enlightened civil libertarian instincts had been exerted more quietly and effectively through his repeated Senate votes against *McCarthyism*, if not against McCarthy.[12] Kennedy was a man who should be appreciated and understood as a pragmatic liberal who, unlike the prophet the "egg-heads" had been courting during the 1950s, cared as much about how to make things work.

He was also, Arthur Schlesinger, Jr., had determined, not unlike Stevenson. An afternoon at the Kennedy compound at Hyannis Port on Cape Cod had emphasized the similarities. There, in August of 1960, the historian found much of "the same mood and tempo" and even the "same patrician ease of manners" as at Libertyville. Kennedy himself had used that afternoon to offer his own analysis of why he thought that Lyndon Johnson and Richard Nixon were very similar to each other while he was much more like Stevenson, a distinction between totally absorbed professional politicians and "those who took politics at a gentleman-intellectual's distance."[13] "The Democratic Party underwent a transformation in its years in the wilderness," Schlesinger explained that summer, and it was a transformation achieved almost singlehandedly by Stevenson. "More perhaps than either of them fully realizes, Kennedy today is the heir and executor of the Stevenson revolution."[14]

In 1959, Schlesinger, in a little pamphlet that was printed privately and circulated by Tom Finletter, had prognosticated about what lay at the end of the wilderness. Taking off from his father's essay that had presented a cyclic theory of American political behavior, Schlesinger speculated that there was "a spreading anxiety and frustration in our society; a confused, inchoate feeling that things aren't going right; a growing boredom with excessive self-congratulation and complacency" that was inevitably leading, if past rhythms offered any clue, to a new period. The new period would be more like the progressive era of the early twentieth century than the New Deal. "Instead of the quantitative liberalism of the thirties," he wrote, "we need now a *'qualitative liberalism'* dedicated to bettering the quality of people's lives and opportunities." The opportunity, then, was there. Leadership able to articulate a sense of public interest, as had Teddy Roosevelt, "will elicit a remarkable response." The challenge was to the party's resources of intelligence and creativity; and to meet it would require, "above all, *hospitality to ideas in the Democratic party, and the selection of Democratic candidates with the intelligence and imagination to anticipate the needs of the new period.*"[15] There were ideas, Schlesinger explained later, that "evidently corresponded to things which Kennedy had for some time felt himself."[16]

If that was Schlesinger's perception of Kennedy, it was still not shared by a wide segment of the public that considered the youthful politician a Democratic version of Nixon. "The 'managerial revolution' has come to politics," wrote Eric Sevareid, "and Nixon and Kennedy are its first completely packaged products. The Processed Politician has finally arrived."[17] Editor Peter Ritner of The Macmillan Company proposed to Schlesinger that he turn out a pamphlet explaining the differences between the Democratic nominee and the vice president. Schlesinger, burdened with other commitments, at first rejected the idea. Kennedy, however, read Sevareid's comments and persuaded him to change his mind, promising to provide his own analysis of the differences.[18] The resulting essay, which was published in a hardcover edition only a few weeks later, portrayed Nixon as the chameleon to whom issues were secondary to politics in contrast with Kennedy the man of conviction for whom politics was secondary to issues. Moreover, Kennedy was a liberal who had come to his faith by a path that was different from that taken by most liberals but one whose "conclusions are no less solidly grounded or less firmly held." Kennedy had the style and taste that raised him far above the level of his opponent, a man who could not be identified with any firm position. The Democrat was, simply, the one to help the nation "recover control over our national destiny and resume the movement to fulfill the real promise of American life, a promise defined not by the glitter of our wealth but by the splendor of our ideals."[19]

3

In trying to sell Kennedy as a more pragmatic and decisive Stevenson, the intellectuals were assuming a rational coexistence of both qualities. Whether applied to policymaking or strategy, however, the differences were much greater than the similarities. Kennedy was a virtual stereotype of the nonideological man who had come into vogue during the 1950s and stressed power and its implementation rather than ideas. To be effective one had first to win; without the necessary machinations and muscle-flexing, good intentions meant nothing. The existence of party diversity, with the multitudinous congressional and regional interests, required adroit quarterbacking and an efficient machine, not well-meaning platitudes. The country had had enough of that under Eisenhower. His presidency would offer leadership by executive action.

One of Kennedy's civil rights lawyers, Harris Wofford, has recalled that "he had a picture of a strong President who was giving leadership in all parts of our national life."[20] As much as he collected academicians, Kennedy was impatient with their tendency to theorize, to speculate in terms of philosophical or historical perspectives, to behave like "knee-jerk" liberals. In the Senate, he was much more compatible with a Paul Douglas, who could combine liberal domestic attitudes with an appreciation of the need for power against the international communist menace, than with such doctrinaire liberals as Joseph S. Clark, Jr., of Pennsylvania. Further, before the 1958–1960 period, it was hardly possible to regard Kennedy himself as a liberal.[21] Jim Loeb, Jr., analyzing the potential candidate in a letter to Chester Bowles nine months before the convention, wrote, "Jack Kennedy, as far as I could see, is playing both sides of the street. . . . He plays the North and the South, the liberals and the conservatives, the independents and the machine boys, the labor boys and the anti-labor farmers, etc."[22]

Bowles soon found himself able to confirm the accuracy of Loeb's perception. A letter from Kennedy in late January invited him to become the candidate's chief foreign policy adviser. Intrigued as he was with power, Kennedy could in no way have thought that he and Bowles shared a similar view of the world, but the invitation followed a decision that the candidate was suffering from a lack of names that could attract liberals and intellectuals; in other words, the sort of people who were devoted to Stevenson. At a Hyannis Port organizing session on October 28, 1959, the need to utilize Bowles "in some way in the campaign" was a command decision. Make him "some sort of advisor"; give him a title. Its exact wording was immaterial, but the function would not give him a direct connection with the campaign as a policymaker, only a prudent association.[23] It did not take long for Bowles to discover that some of Kennedy's "professional political campaign operators . . . were more interested in power than in ideas and . . . looked on the more liberal elements in the Democratic Party as competitors rather than working partners."[24]

Overcoming his reputation as a conservative would become, to Kennedy, as vital a part of campaign strategy as tactics designed to win any other sector of the electorate. The McCarthy matter always rankled, and would, unfairly, hound him until his death. Perhaps what kept it indelible was the tacit worry of many liberals that it merely confirmed their fear that Roman Catholics were inherently conservative, an awareness that Kennedy himself confirmed to associates when he observed that inclination in contrast to the liberal leanings of most Jews.[25] That fear was also implicit in a comment by Dr. Reinhold Niebuhr. The theologian, while explaining his preference for Humphrey over Kennedy, wrote, "I would like very much to vote for a liberal Catholic and destroy one of the Ghosts of American history."[26]

The circumstances of the 1956 convention had also furthered Kennedy's conservative reputation. Had Stevenson chosen him for the vice presidential slot, a substantial possibility at the time—one that had been developed through harmony between the Kennedy and Stevenson camps and by arguments that having a Catholic would be attractive to many Eisenhower Democrats—the senator's future as a national figure may have suffered. That had been the reason for Joseph P. Kennedy's farsighted attempts to discourage his son's candidacy. Dictating a letter after a visit with Clare Boothe Luce, the "founding father" advised the younger Kennedy that she also hoped he would not accept a vice presidential nomination. "She has many arguments," he reported, "not the least of which is that if you are chosen, it will be because you are a Catholic and not because you are big enough to do a good job. She feels that a defeat would be a devastating blow to your prestige, which at the moment is great, and non-partisan."[27] But the senator was encouraged by indications that he stood high on Stevenson's own list of possibilities.

Stevenson, however, was confronted with the conflicting ambitions of others. Since they included such figures as Humphrey, Kefauver, Symington, Albert Gore, and Mayor Robert Wagner of New York, he chose to resolve the dilemma by leaving the choice to the convention. While the move may be interpreted as yet another indication of his indecisiveness and was made over vehement opposition by Johnson and Rayburn, it nevertheless constituted a shrewd public relations demonstration of a departure from conventional political "bossism." It also provided an otherwise languid convention with its most memorable moments. Additionally, it gave Kennedy invaluable national exposure. At the same time, by pitting him through two ballots in what became a race against the progressive Kefauver that drew southern conservatives to his side in their desperate and ultimately successful move to stop the maverick Tennesseean, the convention provided additional fuel for liberal suspicions.

The civil rights battle of 1957 had also left scars. Southern demands that provisions for trial by jury in the case of those accused of interfering with voting rights were resisted by liberals fearful of having implementation of the law negated by segregationist juries. Kennedy had not shown any particular interest in racial matters, but he had stood with the liberals in supporting Title III of the original bill. That was designed to protect civil rights in areas other than education. Knocking that out, however, was one way of avoiding a filibuster, which still could not be broken very easily because of the two-thirds requirement for cloture contained in Rule XXII. Another part of the price, it became clear, was to go along with the jury-trial provision, a legal principle that many liberals found hard to oppose. Their dilemma was resolved, and misgivings satisfied, by the desire to remove all obstacles blocking the landmark legislation. Kennedy then voted for the compromise.

The Senate's original jury-trial amendment had been opposed by just nine Democrats and had been sponsored by Joseph O'Mahoney of Wyoming and co-sponsored by Kefauver and Frank Church of Idaho. Among the northern Democrats, only Wayne Morse voted no. Nevertheless, it was Kennedy, the Catholic with the reputation as a conservative and the stature of a potential presidential nominee, who found himself a target of civil rights forces. Among the more significant critics were NAACP leaders Clarence Mitchell and Roy Wilkins, who accused the senator of "rubbing elbows" with southern segregationists and deplored his vote, thereby minimizing his support for the more significant Title II powers of the original version. Indignant, Kennedy complained to Wilkins about having been "apparently singled out for attack by you and Mr. Mitchell from the nearly three dozen Senators from outside the South who voted for the jury trial amendment. This is particularly inexplicable to me in view of our correspondence which indicates that you have no basic objection to jury trial in cases of criminal contempt, which is what the bill finally provided."[28]

Kennedy soon found himself on the defensive against labor union criticism for his association with what became known as the Landrum-Griffin Labor Management and Disclosure Act of 1959. After his brother Bobby had been serving as a counsel to the McClellan Committee that had been investigating racketeering in unions, the senator accepted an invitation to join. Out of his participation, which involved much scrutiny of the legislative process and close examination of intricate labor law, came Kennedy-sponsored legislation aimed at corrupt practices. Finally, in 1959, the Kennedy-Ervin bill passed the Senate by a vote of 90 to 1. Becoming vulnerable to criticism from the labor leadership, particularly George Meany, Kennedy took the position that the much publicized corruption would inevitably help to create a much more extreme antilabor measure. Its subsequent legislative history, with a conservative, pro-business administration and a formidable southern Democratic-Republican congressional coalition all eager to exploit the popular hostility, justified that concern. Kennedy's version incorporated a series of measures designed to cleanse union activities while avoiding antilabor Taft-Hartley amendments, including provisions against secondary boycotts.[29]

Backed by the Eisenhower administration, however, after conditioning by the McClellan Committee's findings about union corruption, the legislation passed. Attacked for his own association with the measure, Kennedy could only explain that his efforts had been useful for preventing a far harsher version. He pointed to his success at eliminating fifteen restrictions on normal union activity. "But although the final version was on balance closer to the Senate bill," Ted Sorensen later wrote, Kennedy "thought it politic that it not bear his name." Sorensen, who had become the senator's chief speech writer and indispensable aide, was also candid about the Kennedy gain in the affair. In an era when conservative publicity had helped to further arouse the prejudices of a public already more suspicious of labor than of business, it would not hurt for the television public to become, as Sorensen put it, "increasingly familiar with the Kennedy brothers grilling dishonest union leaders or lecturing racketeers who had misused the funds of honest members."[30]

Even while conservative aspects of the Kennedy record were proving troublesome, he was not ready to permit rightists to regard him as a liberal. On the same day he wrote to Clarence Mitchell in defense of his civil rights position, he sent a letter to William Loeb, the reactionary president and publisher of the Manchester [New Hampshire] *Union Leader.* After thanking Loeb for editorials that agreed with his position on the federal budget and communist China, Kennedy took exception to the publisher's comparison of his liberalism with that of Senator Humphrey and the association of his voting record with the ADA. "I must say I was somewhat surprised myself to read that the A.D.A. rates me so highly as to approve 12 of my 14 votes on what they regard to be the key issues, particularly since many of their supporters have frequently accused me of being too moderate on liberal issues," Kennedy informed Loeb, adding that he could not interpret any of the votes as "in any way radical or inconsistent with the philosophical position I have always tried to occupy—that of a moderate Democrat who seeks on every issue to follow the national interest, as his conscience directs him to see it."[31]

In other ways, too, he had been cautious about keeping his standing with the party's center and right. He refused an early invitation to join the Democratic Advisory Council, explaining that he would have to stand for re-election in 1958 and that the interests of his state did not always coincide with national party views on some issues of most concern to the group.[32] He tried to maintain close ties with the South, which had enabled him to come so close to winning the vice presidency. Disturbed by complaints that he had not earned southern support because his attitude toward the region had been unfriendly, he privately assured Governor J. P. Coleman of Mississippi that that had not been the case, that despite having had to uphold different interests because of the flight of New England textile mills, he was "not opposed to industrialization of the South." Omitting any mention of civil rights, he added, "Let me assure you that I have never been 'anti-Southern' in any sense of the word."[33] An editorial in the Winchester *Evening Star*, which was run by Harry F. Byrd, Jr., prompted a letter of appreciation from Kennedy to the son of the Virginia political boss. The Byrd editorial had minimized Kennedy's unacceptability to the South by portraying him as merely a shade more liberal than Nixon, the difference between a moderate liberal with many conservative leanings and a moderate conservative with some liberal tendencies. Pushing the comparison between the two potential candidates, the Byrd paper had declared: "Neither is an extremist in any case."[34]

Before and after his nomination, Kennedy labored to demonstrate his ideological purity before southerners who, concerned about the force of the religious issue on the region's voting patterns, cared more deeply about the long-term significance of the senator's attitudes toward civil rights and labor. His vote for the jury trial amendment, of course, served him in good stead as he maintained close contacts with a wide array of leaders, most notably former governor John Battle of Virginia and his son William, as well as with several influential Georgians, including Senator Herman Talmadge and Atlanta attorney Robert Troutman. Bob Kennedy, keeping a close watch on the southern situation for his brother, at one point suggested that the attacks being made by Wayne Morse on Kennedy for being antilabor could be turned to good advantage by publicizing them in the South.[35] If further assurances were needed to placate southern conservatives about the party's liberal convention platform, the Kennedys were ready and willing. Two days before the convention opened, Willis Robertson, imploring John F. Kennedy to omit any civil rights plank stronger than that of 1956 to avoid embarrassing loyal Virginians, was told by the candidate, "I have got to carry Michigan." During a postconvention session with Byrd on August 19, he disavowed any responsibility for the party's labor plank that condemned "right-to-work" laws and offered assurances that he would never recommend legislation to overturn them.[36]

There should have been little surprise, then, at the contents of a confidential report to the Kennedys that was dated October 20, 1959, eight days before the organizational meeting at Bobby's Hyannis Port home. It advised, "There is a prevailing doubt in some circles that Kennedy is a bonafide liberal . . . he must identify as a 1960 liberal in clear and unmistakable terms."[37]

4

Once he had the party's nomination, Kennedy's pursuit of the liberals was relatively simple, aided to a large extent by the Republican selection of Richard Nixon. Only Joe McCarthy, who had died in 1957, was hated as much as was the vice president by the same groups that Kennedy now needed to win to his side. The candidate's appeal to the Democratic left finally represented a tying together of the main elements of the old coalition. Before the Los Angeles convention, however, it was not that certain.

Many still continued to have more confidence in Hubert Humphrey. Humphrey had appeared as a mainstay of party liberalism during the fifties, never quite shedding the reputation won for his civil rights efforts during the 1948 convention. Whatever reservations were expressed about his Communist Control Act of 1954 or his loyalty oath accommodation with John Battle prior to the 1956 convention were generally attributed to honest differences of opinion over the price that should be paid to blunt the old "softness toward communism" charges and to preserve party harmony during a period of great stress. The forces of liberalism, civil rights and labor had not been betrayed by the senator from Minnesota.

Before finally withdrawing from the campaign after his disastrous loss in West Virginia, where Kennedy won an astonishing 61 percent of the vote despite the state's overwhelming Protestant majority, Humphrey had also appealed as a sympathetic figure who was very much the underdog against the highly organized, well-financed, and well-staffed opposition. It was, in fact, a time of crisis for many liberals, who came close to intramural conflict as the two men faced each other in the important primaries. Watching the debates during those clashes, especially as they revolved around the sensitive religious issue—where its mere mention raised suspicions that it was being exploited by one side or the other—some worried about a schism that would leave the party in impossible shape for the fight against Nixon. Humphrey accepted the endorsement of West Virginia Senator Robert Byrd, who had been a Kleagle of the Ku Klux Klan and whose ties with that organization had been as recent as 1946.

Schlesinger, pointing out that Humphrey would have reacted with indignation had Kennedy accepted such support, lectured his ADA colleague about the need for the party's liberal leadership to resist behaving irresponsibly in even the most trying circumstances.[38]

But Kennedy, even before knocking Humphrey out of the race, disclaimed the Minnesota senator as a threat to his own candidacy. He felt that Humphrey was really serving the ends of Lyndon Johnson's efforts to stop the Kennedy machine. Although there were ample reasons for believing that Jim Rowe would have been legitimately happy to see Humphrey win the nomination, Rowe's closeness to Johnson nevertheless raised doubts about the sincerity of his involvement in the West Virginia campaign. There was also talk about Johnson money being used to help Humphrey's effort and sufficient bitterness resulting from the confrontation to prompt some of the Humphrey supporters to latch onto Stuart Symington as a way of stopping Kennedy.[39]

In contrast with the congressional record of the majority leader, who was silent about his own candidacy but nevertheless maintaining substantial support among the party's conservatives, especially in the South, Kennedy's West Virginia campaign aided the process of his acceptance as a sincere liberal. He employed the kind of rhetoric that was so effective in a state where photographs of Roosevelt were still common household objects. Constantly recalling the New Deal, specifically as well as by inference, he talked to crowds throughout the state about what Democrats had done for the unemployed in depressed areas, promising to make a strong effort in behalf of the Area Redevelopment Program that had been rejected twice by Eisenhower after passage by Democratic-controlled Congresses. At Mount Hope, speaking in his forceful, clipped manner, he declared, "So long as there is one hungry child—so long as there is one family without a decent diet—so long as any American is forced to get by on flour, rice and corn-meal—the Democrats care."[40] Although he had witnessed substantial poverty in his own state of Massachusetts, especially as a young congressional candidate going through the "triple-deckers" of Charlestown in 1946, his West Virginia experience encouraged the theme that he had had an initial and sobering encounter with what it was really like to exist in squalid circumstances.[41]

At the same time, the effort to get the blessing of Adlai Stevenson was viewed as a vital element in the wooing of the liberal community. Schlesinger, serving as one of Kennedy's liaison people to achieve that goal, informed the two-time candidate in mid-May that only some eighty to one hundred additional delegate votes were needed to secure the nomination. Considering the importance of creating the vital "atmosphere" for the urgent task of defeating Nixon in November, Kennedy was anxious to be put across at Los Angeles by the liberals rather than by the South, a source that he would otherwise have to tap. Since he regarded himself as the only liberal left in the competition, he felt that Stevenson was the key to being able to form a united front of the party's left, which would also make him indebted to that wing. All he wanted from the governor was to know whether he could count on his assistance at some definite point before the convention.[42] Stevenson, about to receive a visit from Kennedy at Libertyville, instead expressed concern for the possible effect of a recent statement by the Vatican newspaper, *L'Osservatore Romano*, which told Catholics that the Church "has the duty and the right" to tell them how to vote. Besides, Stevenson added, "The reaction to the liberal plea to support him lest the bosses, Southerners, et al. get control, is sometimes greeded [sic] by a cynical 'what a confession!' "[43]

Stevenson could not be moved, neither by those urging him to declare his own candidacy nor by overtures that he at least secure his position with a possible Kennedy administration. Instead, he seemed to resent the pressure from the senator's people, along with the insinuations that he was thwarting the Kennedy drive, that his very silence was aiding and abetting the stop-Kennedy movement. It was unfair, he complained, because he had done so much to help the man. He recalled that the "importance of retrieving the Catholic defectors" in 1956 had led him to desire the senator on his own ticket, an opportunity he had provided by throwing open the nomination and thereby helping to provide a source of exposure that had launched national interest in Kennedy. He had done so, he pointed out, while "thinking that Kennedy's chances would be at least as good" as Kefauver's. Now, by not announcing his own candidacy, and by not encouraging his friends to promote him for a third time (although several, especially Mike Monroney of Oklahoma and David Lawrence, were eager for a green light), he was making the Kennedy campaign possible. "With all this in mind," Stevenson wrote, "I have found the talk from his camp, albeit not from him, quite aggravating."[44] Arthur Schlesinger, Jr., after conferring with Kennedy about Stevenson's attitude, reported his response: "I think I understand for the first time that Adlai is helping me by doing nothing—that he could do me considerable harm by raising his finger."[45] Nothing that followed, however, seemed to confirm that he really believed that.

Stevenson's ambivalence was deeply perplexing, not only to Kennedy, but particularly to those liberals who, just as they would ultimately see Kennedy as the one man standing between themselves and Nixon in November, at that moment saw him as obviating their having to make a choice between Kennedy and Johnson. Few were as devoid of the influence of personality, or were as partisan, as Jim Rowe. Rowe informed Stevenson's law partner, Newton Minow, that "As long as the available mechanism is the Democratic Party, and the troops to command are Democrats, I do not think there would be much difference between the three men." Rowe added, "This is the reality and all the sound and fury of 'liberalism' and 'moderation' which all of your gentlemen indulge in are mere chimera."[46] Many liberals were clearly leaning toward Kennedy because, as California Governor Edmund Brown informed Agnes Meyer, "I don't want something else to happen," meaning a Johnson nomination.[47] Mrs. Roosevelt, meanwhile, continued to hold out hopes for the possibility of a Stevenson draft and found some encouragement from a telephone conversation in which Stevenson told her that he thought he had made amply clear in his public life that he would serve his party and country whenever called upon.[48] On June 15, Stevenson, reacting to Mrs. Roosevelt's public declaration that he really was a candidate, sent her a note that read:

> My dear Mrs. R-
> I surrender!!
> With love—
> Adlai

Enclosed was a New York *Times* column by Arthur Krock that explored the Latin origins of the word "candidate" and pointed out that to Webster a "candidate is one who offers himself, or is put forward by others," words which Stevenson had underlined with a red pencil.[49]

All that spring, and at the convention itself, Stevenson's behavior molded Kennedy's subsequent resentment and virtually killed any chance of his becoming secretary of state. Clearly, he would have been delighted to have been drafted again. He was thrilled by the eloquent nominating speech that was delivered by Senator Eugene McCarthy of Minnesota, an oratorical flourish that was easily the high point of the convention, even though its suspected real objective was as a last-minute attempt to coalesce the stop-Kennedy forces in behalf of Johnson. When McCarthy concluded by pleading, "Do not leave this prophet without honor in his own party. Do not reject this man," the Stevensonian-filled galleries roared and an enormous spontaneous demonstration rocked the sports arena in defiance of Chairman LeRoy Collins' attempts to restore order. A beautiful spectacle resulted when the hall was darkened to quiet the crowd and shafts of floodlight swept through the shadowy arena, providing an impressive scene for home TV viewers. The Stevensonians, who had been converging on Los Angeles all week, were finally having their moment, even though the last-ditch effort would obviously fail to upset the Kennedy bandwagon. "I think it is the most eloquent utterance I have ever heard," Stevenson later wrote to McCarthy in appreciation, "at least since Newton Baker's League of Nations speech back in 1924. Certainly it was for me my 'finest hour' and the pinnacle of a long and varied career."[50] For the Kennedy clan, however, what would linger would be the memory of how Stevenson had resisted efforts to entice him by virtually holding out the promise of a distinguished career in the new administration in exchange for his placing the senator's name in nomination; and how, instead, he had helped to spark the commotion by appearing on the floor of the sports arena and taking his seat as though he were just another delegate.[51]

That Stevenson was suffering from "inner turmoil," as Kenneth S. Davis has written, is undoubtedly correct, as it was also accurate to note that only a draft could have given him the nomination—although, of course, that was the last thing the powerful Kennedy forces would have permitted had their own man failed.[52] There is also considerable room for believing that Stevenson was torn between his own desires, however unrealistic they may have been at that late hour, and by assurances of neutrality he had given much earlier to other potential candidates.[53] As much as such close friends as Agnes Meyer and others tried to persuade him, he felt that he could not renege. As he reminded Mrs. Finletter on June 9, "to announce that I am a candidate is just what we agreed long ago at Chelsea I would not do, and I really can't do it now."[54]

Having extinguished the final Stevenson spark, Kennedy moved swiftly to win over those liberals who still hoped for the governor's selection as secretary of state. That strategy led him quite naturally to the reformers of the Lexington Club variety, who had since fallen behind Mrs. Roosevelt, Herbert Lehman, and Tom Finletter in the formation of the New York Committee for Democratic Voters. The committee, organized in early 1959 to blunt an incipient combination of dissident clubs that had been set up by Harriman-associate George Backer, was in the process of spearheading an all-out assault against the leadership of Carmine De Sapio and state chairman Michael Prendergast. While unable to unseat the Tammany regulars in 1959, they had made an impressive showing in the primaries. Of immediate concern to Kennedy, in addition to his desire to gain political mileage from proximity to personalities who were influential with liberal voters, was the fact that it had been the Lexington reformers who had controlled the Stevenson-for-president volunteers in 1956, a course that had resulted in a bitter schism with the regulars.

Considering, too, that New York State then had the largest number of electoral voters, forty-five, it was hardly wise to overlook the fact that its Democrats were divided; "not that this Liberal element will vote for Nixon," Robert Kennedy was advised, but leaving the leadership in the hands of the professionals could weaken the "spur necessary to get vigor and activity out of this Liberal element."[55] The younger Kennedy agreed and advised that the disparate groups should be dove-tailed at least for the duration of the campaign.[56]

In California, on the Friday after his nomination, presidential candidate John F. Kennedy, together with a large retinue of newspapermen and photographers, paid an early afternoon visit to Lehman's Beverly Wilshire Hotel suite. Asked about his support for the ticket, Lehman cited his expressed willingness to back any potential nominees. As yet unaware that Kennedy had met the day before with Mayor Robert Wagner, De Sapio, and Prendergast and had agreed not to sponsor or authorize the creation of an organization to run his campaign independent of the Democratic State Committee, Lehman stressed that the liberals and reformers would work only under an arrangement that would not make them subservient to the Tammany machine. When Kennedy suggested Wagner as a bridge between the reformers and the regulars, Lehman was pessimistic about the willingness of the independents to accept the mayor's leadership. Before the newsmen were called in to record the meeting between the candidate and the New Deal liberal, Kennedy indicated that he intended to create an independent committee to work with both groups.[57]

Later that month, in New York City, Robert Kennedy attended a series of meetings with reform leaders. At one of them, in Lehman's Park Avenue apartment, he told a group that included Mrs. Roosevelt, Lloyd K. Garrison, and Tom Finletter, "I don't give a damn for Carmine De Sapio and I don't give a damn about anyone in this room, either. All I want is to elect my brother president of the United States."[58] What finally emerged was an independent Kennedy-for-President committee, under the direction of Anthony Akers. Akers, a New York lawyer and twice-defeated congressional candidate, was not identified with the reformers but had close ties with their camp. The arrangement was accomplished with the acquiescence of both De Sapio and Prendergast, whose preconvention inclinations toward Johnson had left them in a weakened position for dealing with the new candidate.[59] The alliance, a tenuous one, just barely managed to survive through election day. But the Kennedy goal was achieved. He went on to win New York's forty-five electoral votes by a plurality of nearly 400,000.[60]

By August, however, Kennedy's standing with liberals was still precarious. At the start of the month, he received Stevenson at Hyannis Port and, without any discussion about a possible place for the governor in his administration, expressed concern about how to attract the liberal vote, especially that of the Jews and Negroes in New York and California, a process that Stevenson agreed to aid by undertaking a series of speeches in regions where his own prestige was particularly high.[61] In Washington for a special session of Congress that the Johnson-Rayburn leadership had planned before the convention, Kennedy's determination to secure that vote surpassed his familiarity with the issues. Driving his red convertible, with Harris Wofford in the passenger seat, and tapping his left hand on the door impatiently as he sped along, he said to Wofford, "Now, in five minutes, tick off the ten things that a President ought to do to clean up this goddamn civil rights mess." Kennedy seemed appalled at the intricacy of the issues and betrayed his ignorance of the subject.[62] Then, on the fourteenth of August, he visited Hyde Park for a meeting with Mrs. Roosevelt, who had complained that she had had to fight to see him alone, "as the Kennedy people are interested only in the publicity, photos, etc. they can get out of it."[63] With the former first lady, he put his best liberal sentiments forward. He revealed that he was beginning to understand what he was up against, especially after Florida's recently elected governor, C. Farris Bryant had told him, "I want you to know that I am a conservative, I am against integration, and I am for the Right-to-Work Law." Kennedy quoted

The new president, Harry S Truman, and Mrs. Eleanor Roosevelt at FDR's grave, Hyde Park, New York, April 15, 1945. *(U.S. Information Agency)*

LEFT TO RIGHT: James F. Byrnes, President Truman, and Henry A. Wallace at FDR's funeral. *(U.S. Office of War Information)*

The States' Rights Democratic presidential and vice-presidential candidates of 1948, J. Strom Thurmond (LEFT) and Fielding Wright. *(U.S. Information Agency)*

LEFT TO RIGHT: Vice President Alben Barkley, Speaker Sam Rayburn, House Majority Leader John McCormack, and Senate Majority Leader Scott Lucas looking at a copy of President Truman's Midyear Economic Report on July 11, 1949. *(U.S. Information Agency)*

Senator A. Willis Robertson of Virginia. *(Courtesy Earl Gregg Swem Library, College of William and Mary)*

Speaker Sam Rayburn. *(Courtesy Sam Rayburn Library)*

Chester Bowles as governor of Connecticut. *(U.S. Information Agency)*

Herbert H. Lehman with congratulatory telegrams after defeating Senator John Foster Dulles in 1949. *(U.S. Information Agency)*

President Truman was the surprise guest at a luncheon marking Speaker Rayburn's sixty-eighth birthday. *(U.S. Information Agency)*

Senate Majority Leader Scott Lucas meeting with colleagues Herbert Lehman (LEFT) and William Benton on January 5, 1950. *(U.S. Information Agency)*

Franklin D. Roosevelt, Jr., and former National Chairman Jim Farley meet at a Democratic victory dinner in New York City on January 29, 1950. *(U.S. Information Agency)*

Thomas K. Finletter being sworn in by Secretary of Defense Louis Johnson as secretary of the air force, April 24, 1950. LEFT TO RIGHT: Finletter; Stuart Symington, head of the National Security Resources Board; Secretary of State Dean Acheson; Mrs. Finletter; Secretary Johnson. *(U.S. Information Agency)*

New York's Mayor William O'Dwyer cutting the tape opening the Brooklyn-Battery Tunnel on May 25, 1950. Looking on (LEFT TO RIGHT) are Brooklyn Borough President John Cashmore, Francis Cardinal Spellman, Manhattan Borough President Robert Wagner, Jr., and Triborough Bridge and Tunnel Authority Chairman Robert Moses. *(U.S. Information Agency)*

Senator Estes Kefauver of Tennessee. *(U.S. Information Agency)*

Adlai Stevenson campaigning for the presidency at the Illinois State Fair in 1952. (*U.S. Information Agency*)

President Eisenhower received Democratic senators at the White House on March 4, 1953 in the midst of hurried conferences over the implications of the imminent death of Joseph Stalin. Assistant to the President, Sherman Adams, is at the far right in the rear row. *(National Park Service)*

Movie star Melvyn Douglas (LEFT) and labor leader George Meany in a scene from an AFL-CIO documentary film, *Land of Promise. (U.S. Information Agency)*

President Kennedy with two chairmen of the Democratic National Committee, John M. Bailey (LEFT) and Senator Henry Jackson, at the Mayflower Hotel, Washington, D.C., January 21, 1961. *(National Park Service)*

President Kennedy's first press conference, January 25, 1961. Press Secretary Pierre Salinger and his assistant, Andrew Hatcher, are seated at the right. *(National Park Service)*

The New Frontier's congressional leadership. SEATED: Sam Rayburn (LEFT) and Mike Mansfield; STANDING, LEFT TO RIGHT: John McCormack, Carl Albert, Hubert H. Humphrey. *(National Park Service)*

LEFT: President Kennedy with Ambassador Averell Harriman. *(National Park Service)* RIGHT: Attorney General Robert F. Kennedy and Vice President Johnson pose with civil rights leaders in June, 1963. Also in the front row (LEFT TO RIGHT): Benjamin Epstein of the Anti-Defamation League, Dr. Martin Luther King, Jr., of the Southern Christian Leadership Conference, and Roy Wilkins of the N.A.A.C.P. *(U.S. Information Agency)*

Harry Truman visits President Johnson in the White House. *(National Park Service)*

Senator Robert F. Kennedy at Greenwich, Connecticut, May 20, 1967. (*Herbert S. Parmet*)

Senator George McGovern campaigning on Long Island, September 23, 1972. *(Herbert S. Parmet)*

himself as having said to Bryant, "Why don't you join the Republicans?" He also told Mrs. Roosevelt that he had not realized just how seriously fragmented the party was and that he had learned that there was a complete absence of the unity that had existed in her husband's time. Mrs. Roosevelt, of course, suggested that Kennedy would be wise to appoint Stevenson as his secretary of state and received an inference that both he and Bowles would be offered places in the administration, but she did not press the matter beyond that. Most of all, she told him, he needed close identification with Stevenson.[64]

On the twenty-seventh, the ADA's national board met in Washington and endorsed the Kennedy-Johnson ticket. But it nevertheless offered little evidence that there was much enthusiasm in that liberal camp. Their attitude was expressed by a participant who said, "We don't trust Kennedy and we don't like Johnson; but Nixon is so terrible that we have to endorse the Democrats." Moreover, the endorsement was made only after the deletion of the following paragraph:

In the critical fields of human concern—foreign affairs, economic and social policy, civil rights—he has shown himself an aggressive champion of creative liberalism. He stands with deep conviction for national strength, for peace, for economic growth, for social welfare, for the guarantee to all our citizens of their constitutional rights. He has amply displayed the qualities of political skill and leadership essential in transforming platform pledges into national policy.[65]

In early September, Jack Kennedy telephoned Bobby and suggested, "We should plan at the appropriate time to have an ad run which would be of particular interest to the Jewish voters to be run in the *New York Times* and the *New York Post* signed by Herbert Lehman and Mrs. Roosevelt. We should also check a little into what radio programs the Italians and the Jewish voters listen to as well as what special newspapers they read."[66] But the Kennedy efforts were, at the same time, having unintended consequences. On August 25, Senator Richard Russell told Harry Byrd that the candidate intended to implement the liberal Democratic platform and, in the area of civil rights, even to go well beyond what the party had accepted at Los Angeles.[67]

5

Russell was regarded as one of the most perceptive among the southerners. His alarm was not baseless. His sensors had told him what was evidently true, that the region had little choice but to do what Paul Butler had outspokenly suggested not long before, either go along with the party's national position or find a new home. That, of course, meant either bolting once more or joining the Republicans.

The former had been unproductive in 1948; in fact, almost counterproductive, and the other was entirely unacceptable to Democrats convinced that they, and not the representatives of the urban coalition, were the upholders of the Jeffersonian faith. Further, not only had a Republican administration been charged with responsibility for the Brown decision, but a Republican president had outraged the South by implementing integration in Little Rock by using military force, and Republican congressional leadership had helped to write two civil rights acts within the past four years. Additionally, confirmed southerners still viewed Republicanism as hostile to their region's economic interests, as the exponents of the tariff protectionism that aimed to inhibit any chance to compete with northern industrialization. As Senator Robertson had written to a constituent, "If the Republicans of the North had had their way, everyone in the South would be raising cotton, tobacco and peanuts and buying all of their manufactured goods from the North and the Northwest."[68]

Conservatives who saw little difference between the two parties on the racial question nevertheless held to the advantages that had been accrued through seniority and Democratic congressional majorities. The Baltimore *Sun* put the matter very succinctly when it pointed out that "Among those who would certainly cheer a withdrawal of the Southerners from the national Democracy would be the labor extremists." Too many conservatives had become bound to the party's institutional advantages to begin any kind of mass desertion.

Nevertheless, after the 1956 elections there were persistent reports of contemplated third-party movements, usually associated with the potential leadership of such southern spokesmen as Russell, Byrd, Jimmy Byrnes, and Governor George Bell Timmerman, whose earlier efforts had failed to kindle a rebellion.[69] At Columbia, South Carolina, a conference of political leaders from nine southern states that had been heralded in some quarters as an incipient third-party movement promptly disavowed that goal and called, instead, for a concerted effort to defend themselves against Republican attempts to split the region.[70] Southerners were still more inclined to insist that they, and not the North and West, comprised the party's heartland. Mississippi's state chairman pointedly reminded Paul Butler that Stevenson had carried only 918 counties out of a national total of 3,068 and that only 155 were won outside thirteen southern and border states.[71] Finally, at the Los Angeles convention, there was amazingly little appetite for resistance to the adoption by the Platform Committee of an advanced civil rights plank.[72]

The more serious threat involved a different kind of tactic, one that utilized the mechanism that had been provided by the Founding Fathers to preserve the power of small states to influence the choice of presidents. By withholding enough votes, in a close election, the decision could be thrown into the House of Representatives, where each state would have an equal voice regardless of size. With precisely that in mind, Alabama's Democratic Executive Committee had voted on March 21, 1959, to free the state's electors from any obligation to support the party's nominees. The rules specifically stated that Democrats could become electors without any advance pledges to back the party's national ticket.[73] Backed by Gessner T. McCorvey, the architect of the 1948 bolt, six out of the state's eleven electors were chosen with the understanding that they would remain unpledged, a 1960 version of the Dixiecrat movement. And, as had been the case twelve years earlier, the opposition by senators Sparkman and Hill helped to prevent a clean sweep.[74] Mississippi followed with a slate of eight independent electors chosen to run as rivals to the eight loyalists. In urging all southern states to unify behind them, the speaker of the state's house of representatives suggested the nomination of a third candidate "in the event it should be determined that our best interests would be served by throwing the election into the House of Representatives."[75]

But none of the other states joined the scheme. Harry Byrd preferred to hold out for Johnson's nomination, even rationalizing the majority leader's support for the civil rights bills by crediting him with having helped to defeat the "most iniquitous parts," an argument reminiscent of the justification used by the liberals to explain Kennedy's relationship to the labor act of 1959.[76]

The clearest threat to Democratic unity in the South by 1960, then, was not the widespread defection of the party's leadership but the emergence of conservative forces that were beginning to resolve nearly a decade of wavering by veering more firmly toward the GOP. Eisenhower had not only helped to establish the respectability of breaking from traditional patterns and supporting what had been a loathesome association; he had enabled southerners to break through the psychological barrier against apostasy. Even more basic was the changing nature of the region itself. By 1960, the South had shifted from a predominantly rural economy to one that was increasingly urban and commercial. The rising power of industrial capitalism was converting the cities to northern patterns, with stronger middle classes and the influx of white-collar labor that, like the corporate managers, were more amenable to the conservative economic policies of Republicanism. Moreover, where capitalism was relatively new and the countervailing power of labor as yet was undeveloped, economic muscle was clearly with management, which had become the establishment within the large cities to a much greater extent than was usual in the North. Such major centers as Dallas, Houston, and Atlanta each had a well-established elite that controlled local government, newspapers, radio and television stations, and the calibre of public education. They were, moreover, dependent on attracting more capital and highly trained personnel, college-educated men and women who were reluctant to locate their families in regions of instability and provincialism. The emerging socioeconomic climate favored racial moderation rather than the methods of the KKK or even of the White Citizens Councils. Thus, in the border states, in particular—including Texas—integration was beginning to reach the take-off point; and even in Virginia, the administration of Governor Lindsay Almond, influenced by the more affluent elements in the counties adjacent to the District of Columbia and by the reality of an enlarged black electorate in the tidewater cities, suddenly defied Harry Byrd's resistance to racial progress and recognized the inevitability of change. In such a climate, the Republicans were no longer the villains of Reconstruction but appreciated as supporters of entrepreneurial growth. A *Wall Street Journal* correspondent was told by a Georgian, "Whatever the party in power when desegregation came, most of us knew it was coming, and the Democrats would have done the same thing."[77] Only an abrupt turnabout by the national Democracy, spurning the influence of the northern urban coalition, could have countered what could already be perceived as the inexorable southern advance toward a two-party system.

Such were the forces John F. Kennedy hoped to contain even as he worked to mobilize the elements that had been attracted to the party of Franklin D. Roosevelt. In early August, while his brother was organizing liberal support, Bobby Kennedy notified his brother-in-law, Sargent Shriver, "We are having a great deal of difficulty in the Southern states such as South Carolina, Mississippi, Texas, on the grounds that Jack's views are socialistic, and he wants the state to control both man and business," and suggested a concerted drive in Dixie by the candidate's Business Committee.[78]

Much of the credit for Kennedy's electoral vote success in the South ultimately went to Johnson. There was no question about the effectiveness of the majority leader, particularly his ability to deal with southern politicians and advise them in his not-so-subtle style about how much better off they would be with him as vice president than if he found himself still in the Senate because of them. Even that, however, had its limitations and its actual impact on the balloting is hard to assess. Further, his efforts were by no means universally appreciated, even in his own state, where conservative hostility jeopardized his ability to tread delicately between the political extremes. So heated was the opposition that a pre-election day appearance with Lady Bird Johnson at the Adolphus Hotel in Dallas provoked an ugly confrontation with a swearing, spitting, and placard-waving band of conservative protesters. The incident, which dramatized his lack of acceptance by the Texas rightists, was credited with having made it possible for the ticket to win the state's twenty-four electoral votes by a mere 46,000 vote plurality.[79]

Whether that really did make the difference in closely contested southern states is hard to prove, but whatever sentiments were drawn to the ticket by the Dallas incident were in addition to Johnson's ability to mobilize his own Mexican American constituents as well as by Kennedy's success in attracting the wavering black electorate back to the party.

In October had come the news that Martin Luther King had been arrested in Georgia on a technicality—driving beyond the maximum number of days permitted to a new resident who still held an out-of-state license. For that violation, he was sentenced to six months at hard labor and, despite the fact that his wife was in her fifth month of pregnancy, was sent to a remote state penitentiary. Subsequently, two personal telephone calls, one to the distressed Coretta Scott King by Senator Kennedy offering sympathy and any possible assistance she might request and the other to the judge by Robert Kennedy to secure the civil rights leader's release—a call that achieved its purpose—gained enormous attention. While the Republican presidential candidate was confined to silence as he attempted to woo the white South, accounts of what the Kennedys had done were offered from pulpits to black congregations throughout the country. In addition, there was the expeditious distribution of more than a million copies of a pamphlet called *The Case of "No Comment Nixon" Versus the Candidate with a Heart.*[80]

Before the incident, the black vote had been reportedly moving toward Kennedy largely because of his identification as a Democrat.[81] What had been a trend became a massive tide. In Texas, where it combined with a Mexican-American turnout of 91 percent, it went for Kennedy and Johnson by 84 percent. South Carolina, where 80 percent of the voting Negroes supported the Democrats, was won by a margin of less than ten thousand votes. Thus, the small majorities of those two states added up to thirty-two electoral votes, a number that became crucial when fourteen unpledged electors were chosen by Alabama and Mississippi. Had Texas and South Carolina gone for Nixon, the Democratic electoral lead would have been 271 to 261 and the required majority would have been in the hands of the fifteen men (including one from Oklahoma) who later cast their ballots for Harry F. Byrd.

While Byrd maintained his "golden silence," Virginia voted Republican again. At the same time, there were important leaders in his state, as elsewhere in the South, who did their best to see to it that the issue would not be decided in their region on religious grounds. Brooks Hays, whose moderation in the Little Rock integration affair was given exaggerated importance as an explanation for his inability to win another term in Congress, worked at trying to keep the Reverend Billy Graham from denouncing Kennedy's Catholicism.[82] In Virginia, Francis Pickens Miller managed to bring together a number of prominent leaders, including Governor Almond, Senator Robertson, and former governors Colgate Darden and John C. Battle for a joint statement upholding Jeffersonian principles of religious freedom for office-holders.

6

But, as many had feared, the religious issue was important. It was the consideration that threatened to overshadow substantive partisan matters. It was the issue that had, long before the Kennedy nomination, provoked endless speculation and re-examination of past experiences, including a memorandum drafted by Ted Sorensen and distributed by Connecticut Democratic leader John Bailey arguing that the concentration of Catholic votes in the more populous industrial states could give the candidate an advantage despite inevitable losses in Fundamentalist areas. It had also inspired a *Reporter* article by historian Richard Hofstadter demonstrating that Catholicism had not been responsible for Al Smith's defeat in 1928, that such factors as Prohibition and aversion to his Lower East Side dialect and mannerisms had also done much to alienate the solid South.[83] It was also the threat that had made such Catholics as Governor David Lawrence of Pennsylvania, himself a victim of bigotry while campaigning statewide, sufficiently dubious about gambling on a fellow Catholic to stick with Stevenson until the last minute. And it was the religious issue that had led Connecticut's Abraham Ribicoff, a Jew, to support Kennedy as early as 1956 with the hope that he could thereby help to open the presidency to other minority groups.[84]

From the preconvention primaries until election day itself, the issue refused to disappear. There had been hope that Kennedy's sensational victory in West Virginia would settle the matter; by going into that state, he had, after all, gambled. And he had won. But it refused to die. From all parts of the country, not only the widely advertised Bible Belt, countless publications warned of the imminence of papal power in America and about the inevitable subservience of a Catholic president to clerical dictation on such sensitive matters as church-state relations. They persisted even after Kennedy had made a bold midcampaign appearance before the Ministerial Association of Houston, a performance that was probably the most eloquent and effective one of his career, and stated forcefully that he intended to be a Catholic who was president rather than a Catholic president. Contrary to the fears that his candidacy was spearheading a Romanist plot to control the White House, such incidents as the Vatican newspaper's editorial asserting the Church's "duty" and "right" to tell Catholics how to vote (which made Kennedy remark that he could now understand why Henry VIII had established his own church), Cardinal Spellman's ostentatious support for Nixon, and a pre-election day order by the hierarchy of Puerto Rico directing all Catholics to vote against Governor Luis Muñoz Marín, raised serious questions about whether some of his coreligionists really thought their interests would be furthered by his presidency.[85] There was also little solid evidence that his bold confrontation with the issue, unlike Al Smith's comparative reticence, did much to allay the suspicions.

After it was all over, the University of Michigan's Research Center concluded that the religious issue had cost Kennedy a net loss of one and a half million votes. His victory, then, had been eked out with a narrow popular margin of 113,000, which was achieved despite his religion rather than because of it. In several areas, the influence of Kennedy's faith was obvious. Tennessee was a traditionally Democratic state that had had a brief flirtation with Eisenhower in 1952 before supporting Stevenson four years later, but Kennedy could not hold it against Nixon. The vice president also countered the national pro-Democratic trend by besting Ike's performance in Oklahoma and Georgia.[86]

Elsewhere, the importance of religion was less clear, so much so, in fact, that political scientist V. O. Key, Jr., cautioned against premature conclusions that "the election overruled once and for all the custom that excluded Catholics from eligibility to the Presidency."[87] Even among fellow Catholics, the effect was uneven and tended to correlate more with economic factors. Catholics were more loyal where unemployment was highest, especially in the industrial Northeast, and Irish Catholics gave him less support than did working-class Jews and other ethnic groups. Seven representative blue-collar districts in various parts of the country, each with a Polish American population of at least 75 percent, gave Kennedy an overall figure of nearly 87 percent.[88] Perhaps stronger than any single other factor was the uncertain state of the economy, with unemployment in some industrial centers exceeding 7 percent. That, rather than the size of the Catholic population, was a more reliable clue to the pattern of his vote. The coincidence of working-class areas with large numbers of Catholics helped to obscure the reasons for Kennedy's attraction, but an examination of counties with similar religious compositions elsewhere in the country fails to show correspondingly strong Democratic trends, except where the particular locality was also economically depressed.[89]

Explanations of the Kennedy appeal must emphasize less the religious considerations and more the attractions of a candidate who had managed to patch up the disparate components of the Democratic vote that had been falling apart since the 1930s. He represented a new generation of Democrats, untarred by McCarthyite charges and dissociated with the foreign policies that had placed his party on the defensive ever since World War II. To an America fearful of com-

munist aggression and deterioration of the "free world," and accepting of the virtual inevitability of a nuclear war, Kennedy offered a
1960 Democratic version of what Republicans had managed to sell at
the start of the decade, a pinpointing of responsibility for what most
voters believed was a continuing international threat. Americans
fearful of a Moscow-leaning Cuba and anxious about the collapse of
the incipient détente as a result of the U-2 spy plane incident heard
Kennedy stress strength and determination under vigorous new
leadership. His message was no more or less truculent than Nixon's,
but emphasizing the "loss" of American prestige, an alleged missile
gap, and the importance of firmness against military threats managed to relieve most doubts about Democratic determination. Even
his most unbelligerent foreign policy adviser, Chester Bowles, accepted the reality of the political climate by urging the candidate to
stick to the line that "regardless of how unhappy we are over ridicu-
lously exposed situation [sic] on Quemoy and Matsu we will not
retreat under fire," and labored to make the candidate immune from
the "softness on communism" issue.[90] Indeed, Kennedy's most
difficult moments had come earlier, before his nomination, when he
had responded to the news that Francis Gary Powers had been on a
spy mission by advising an expression of diplomatic regrets to the
Russians.

A subsequent decade of cold war, brought to a boil over the conflict in Southeast Asia, made it easy to forget that 1960 was a time
when few Americans, and no major politician, failed to share the
basic assumptions. Perhaps the most vigorous advocates of détente
were such businessmen as Inland Steel's Clarence Randall who
viewed East-West harmony as a spur for trade, but even they had to
mute such desires before the enormous consensus that remained
skeptical about alternatives to military strength. Kennedy's victory
had at least surmounted popular reluctance to return foreign policy
to Democratic hands. The narrowness of his election, sensitivity over
suspicions that he lacked the nerve to withstand cold-war challenges,
and his own acceptance of the basic assumptions behind American
foreign policy had made alternatives unlikely. Perceptions that he
lacked such qualities would have ensured his defeat.

Still, his inaugural address adroitly fused bellicose nationalism
with recognition of the existence of a compromise solution between
war and appeasement. The Democrats had at least partially reconsti-
tuted their majority, had emerged from the wilderness and re-entered
the White House, but only after the closest of elections. Moreover,

signs of any sort of mandate for the party were scarcer than usual, as they lost nineteen seats in the House and two in the Senate. The far right was already active, with the John Birch Society gaining new members daily and ultra-conservatives were looking beyond Richard Nixon and toward Barry Goldwater as their savior from communism and statism. If it was to be the start of a new era, Kennedy's New Frontier would have to contend with a foundation incomparably less secure than the one provided at the birth of the last Democratic reign.

PART THREE

★

The Politics of
Discontent

CHAPTER X

The New Frontier

1

Recalling the experience of the Republicans when control over the executive branch finally passed into their hands in 1953, the Democrats of the 1960s found their dilemma also vitiating the rewards of power. The "politics of expectation," as Henry Fairlie has sardonically described the Kennedy years, undoubtedly did much to minimize the hazards of responsibility and maximize the possibilities. Still, aside from the hopes that were manufactured by the incoming administration, there were circumstances that were mainly rooted in the inherent distinctions between the Democrats and the Republicans.

For one, there was the concept of the presidency itself. It had become an article of faith for liberal Democrats, in particular, to equate "strength" in the White House with success itself. The Democratic pantheon thus honored the activism of Wilson, Roosevelt, and Truman, upholding them as the chief surrogates of the "public interest" in opposition to the influences of private power and private greed. It was a tradition that had come to dominate the modern Democratic Party, and it looked to the presidency as a reformist institution. It was also a notion that was sufficiently well established, especially among the party's New Deal heirs, to become institutionalized regardless of what expectations may have been generated by the youthful and even romantic figure in 1600 Pennsylvania Avenue. A large corps of political scientists did their best to outline the innovative responsibilities of modern presidential leadership.

Quite apart from any Kennedy desires, however, as Arthur Schlesinger, Jr., had indicated in his 1959 pamphlet, substantial forces for change were already at work. The prominence of reform movements in various states, most notably New York, Michigan, Minnesota, Pennsylvania, and California, augured many "last hur-

193

rahs" for the old order. Michigan Democrats, under the leadership of Neil Staebler and Governor G. Mennen Williams, with essential support from Walter Reuther and his United Auto Workers, had already succeeded in rebuilding their moribund statewide party along liberal lines and, during the 1950s, in providing a contrast with the conservatism that prevailed in Washington. New York's reform challenge to the Carmine De Sapio-Mike Prendergast leadership, now further weakened by their preconvention resistance to Kennedy, was sufficiently serious for Mayor Robert F. Wagner, Jr., to heed the warning of the president of the Lexington Club that he must either become a leader of the reform movement or "fade out as a factor in New York City politics."[1] Taking that advice, the mayor won re-election the following year as an insurgent candidate in opposition to the "bossism" of De Sapio, his former supporter, while running in concert with the Roosevelt-Lehman-Finletter reformers. In Philadelphia, Richardson Dilworth was already installed as that city's second consecutive reform mayor, having succeeded Joseph S. Clark, Jr., an ADA liberal whose election in 1951 had followed extensive revelations about municipal corruption. Minnesota's Democratic-Farmer-Labor Party had become a bastion of upper midwestern liberalism, having elected such leaders as Governor Orville Freeman and both of the state's senators, Eugene McCarthy and Hubert Humphrey. California's reform impetus was already well under way, reaching a high point of success in 1958 with the victory of all but one of its statewide candidates who had run under the auspices of the California Democratic Council.[2] Similar stirrings elsewhere by new-breed reform Democrats, often from well-educated, upper-middle-class-establishment backgrounds, as were the Yankee liberals of Massachusetts in contrast with the South Boston working-class Catholics, provided further evidence that John Kennedy was not expected to be only an innovator but also the implementer of a departure from the Eisenhower consensus.

Such groups had, in effect, compiled a mandated legislative program, much of it emanating from Truman's Fair Deal proposals; and one, for national health care for the aged, was even traceable to Roosevelt's original efforts in behalf of social security. Having languished between Truman's 1948 victory and the outbreak of the Korean War, and having experienced the conservative dry spell of the Eisenhower years and the accompanying congressional leadership, much of the liberal program had at least managed to gain notice through the position papers of the Democratic Advisory

Council and, finally, as part of the party's national platform for 1960. Consequently, the virtues of economic growth had become as much of a sine qua non for liberals as balanced budgets continued to be for conservatives, with the methodology for stimulating productivity the most debatable point.

But the roster of desired legislation also included such specific items as expanded public housing and the Area Redevelopment Bill, both having already fallen before Eisenhower vetoes (the former to the embarrassment of Johnson and Rayburn, whose trimmings had supposedly made it palatable to the administration), as well as aid to all levels of education, public power development, extension of unemployment compensation, and the expansion of welfare services. Organized labor had virtually given up on even its rhetoric about repealing Taft-Hartley and was concentrating on trying to abolish the "right-to-work" laws. Currently on the books of seventeen states, their prohibition of union shops had made them the prime targets of the AFL-CIO (which had merged in 1955). Most of the same forces, representative of labor as well as intellectuals, were also emphasizing substantial civil rights measures to carry reform well beyond the two voting acts already passed, to provide for equality in employment, accommodations, and transportation. A series of student-led lunch-counter sit-in demonstrations, begun in North Carolina at the start of 1960, had spread rapidly throughout the South. Coming on top of efforts already associated with Dr. Martin Luther King, the protests and subsequent bitter resistance furthered liberal sentiment for getting something done. At several points during the campaign, Kennedy criticized Eisenhower for having failed to employ the "stroke of a pen" to end discrimination in public housing built with federal funds, a power within the purview of executive action.

Kennedy himself, in responding to such pressure, had begun significant preparatory moves well before his inauguration. During the campaign, he arranged for both Senator Joe Clark and Congressman Emanuel Celler of New York to draft legislative proposals for the civil rights program. He had also appointed a task force under Professor Paul Samuelson to make recommendations about the economy and had asked Paul Douglas to head a committee on area redevelopment.

Still, as Kennedy was to discover, intellectuals were not all that certain about what should be done. Intoxicated by the aura of affluence during the nineteen-fifties, they were also smitten with the notion that poverty had ceased as a national problem and that the ideological battles of the thirties belonged to the remote past. The concept gained credibility with Daniel Bell's *The End of Ideology*. Bell was preoccupied with the dynamics of a society in which the concerns with status and psychological adjustment had eradicated the relevance of traditional arguments. Subtitling his book *On the Exhaustion of Political Ideas in the Fifties*, Bell concluded:

In the West, among the intellectuals, the old passions are spent. The new generation . . . finds itself seeking new purposes within a framework of political society that has rejected, intellectually speaking, the old apocalyptic and chiliastic visions.[3]

Adlai Stevenson was impressed by the analysis offered by a political scientist and economist who had told him that the old liberal causes were obsolete, that "where we once had a problem of monopolies and trusts with identifiable fat boys, exploiters, we now have the politically more difficult problem of trade union power," and that where "we once had a familiar problem of poverty, we now raise questions about mental health."[4] In a post-Sputnik burst of national self-analysis, inspired more through fear of Soviet competition than perceptions of decay at home, two assemblages of experts produced papers devoted to the values implicit in American domestic and international policies. One group, chaired by Dr. Henry M. Wriston, was the President's Commission on National Goals; the other was sponsored by the Rockefeller Brothers Fund, Inc. Neither constituted a call for drastic action; neither urged basic reforms. Both, especially the Wriston Report, upheld the virtues of American morality and defended the wisdom of the federal structure and the system of private enterprise. "We have ever more closely approached a classless society," declared Wriston's presidential commission. Its section on racial equality, while noting the need for additional legislation at all governmental levels, emphasized the efficacy of the ballot box. One of the commissioners who felt its civil rights recommendations were too timid was George Meany. The labor leader added a dissent that complained that it had stopped "short of supporting the only realistic legislative step: an enforceable federal fair employment practices law, supplemented by similar state and federal laws."[5] The Rockefeller Report, at least, recognized the possible connection between FEPC legislation and the "stimulus to private reorientation of attitudes."[6] Such ambivalence even characterized the Samuelson recommendations to President-elect Kennedy. Issued two weeks before the inauguration, it fused "economic logic and po-

litical caution" by advocating economic stimulation while continuing to warn against "massive spending programs."[7]

If there was a popular consensus behind anything, it was not in
favor of a sweeping transformation of American life. Even in areas of
extraordinary deprivation, as Robert Kennedy noted rather wryly to
his staff during the primaries, "It is food, family and flag in southern West Virginia."[8] The American Institute of Public Opinion
polls of attitudes that were released during the month of the inauguration of the new president found support for anti-inflationary
policies and medical care for the aged coupled with a general desire
that the new president would follow a middle-of-the-road policy.
While there was great recognition that Ike had "kept the peace" as
his most outstanding accomplishment, the Gallup pollsters noted
that the public believed that Russia was winning the propaganda
war.[9] Meanwhile, the Lou Harris surveys had confirmed that voters
were mainly interested in the restoration of American prestige, a
theme that the winning candidate had pursued with considerable
enthusiasm. Concern about the need to stop the spread of communism, improving military defenses, and doing something about the
Castro regime in Cuba also dominated the responses.[10]

For the new president, the narrowness of the electoral victory and
the condition of public opinion ruled out any attempt to do much
beyond consolidating his own political support. Clearly, the strongest demands for reforms were sectarian calls from the Democratic
left. Hypersensitivity to advanced liberal positions would be contrary to his moderate, pragmatic instincts. With the state of the cold
war foremost in the minds of most Americans, the administration's
policies were, therefore, well prescribed even before the inauguration. It was an attitude that was telegraphed well in advance, on the
morning when his victory finally seemed secure. Speaking from Hyannis Port, Kennedy assured the public that he intended to keep
J. Edgar Hoover as director of the FBI and Allen Dulles at the head of
the CIA, a comforting consolidation to those who may have thought
a revolution had taken place at the polls.

Nor was it, in his eyes, the time to undertake the reversal of
essential cold-war policies; if anything, he would need to demonstrate his willingness and ability to react with determination. After
having spoken with Stevenson at Hyannis Port shortly after his
nomination about preparing foreign policy recommendations, Kennedy finally received one that called for a new emphasis on East-
West negotiations and disarmament, but the time was not ripe for

him to act on either approach and, later, Stevenson was shocked to hear the new president characterize attempts to mitigate the arms race as mere "propaganda."[11] Chester Bowles spoke for the incoming administration when he met with Soviet Ambassador Menshikov on November 30 and, citing the "massive administrative problems" about to be faced by Kennedy, made clear that they included severe domestic political problems. Bowles urged the Russian to get his government to relax tensions during the transition period instead of exerting further pressure in such sensitive spots as Berlin, Formosa, or Africa. Menshikov replied that, of course, the Russians also had to cope with internal pressures and hoped that the Americans would not try to exploit the transition by postponing at least preliminary discussions of some of the major questions of mutual interest.[12]

Such political circumstances undoubtedly influenced the eventual disposition of the appointment of a secretary of state, a matter that had remained one of considerable interest to Stevenson and his followers. Finally, the two-time candidate was offered merely the ambassadorship to the United Nations, an assignment that he informed Kennedy on December 8 was a disappointment. He had wanted the top spot in the State Department as his best way of performing valuable service to the administration and the country, he explained to Kennedy. Not until he telephoned the president-elect on December 10, nearly two weeks after the job had first been proposed, did he accept the offer—a delay that evoked considerable scorn from Kennedy. And, when he did, he attached a series of conditions: a voice in policymaking, cabinet-level rank, control over appointments to his staffs in Washington and New York, and concerted efforts to improve relations with third-world nations.[13]

With the possible exception of J. William Fulbright, who was temporarily the leading candidate to head the State Department, at least in Kennedy's mind (but was finally eliminated because of his identification as a segregationist and as a sympathizer with the Egyptian regime of Gamal Abdul Nasser), a Stevenson appointment would have offered the best chance to mitigate the hard-line cold-war policies that had been pursued since the Truman-Acheson era.[14] Subsequent explanations of his rejection have varied. Some depict the president-elect as bitter over Stevenson's conduct at the convention. There was also the likelihood that, having been elected by a tiny margin, Kennedy did not want to choose an established and potentially controversial political figure who, in addition, had his own constituency.[15] However, inconsistencies remain. His oft-stated preference for Fulbright was scotched by Bobby Kennedy's arguments that he would be unable to deal with the African states, which at least implied that the president-elect was willing to risk the certain criticism that would have come from Democrats who were primarily concerned about Israel, attacks that could have been particularly sharp since Stevenson also happened to be one of their favorites (although, privately, Agnes Meyer wrote to Herbert Lehman in 1961, "I think he [Stevenson] has a prejudice against Israel because that country made trouble for him in the 1956 election.").[16] More likely as an explanation is the awareness that there were significant temperamental and intellectual differences between the one who viewed international affairs in terms that emphasized morality and responsibility and one whose concept of *realpolitik* accepted what America had been preaching about the omnipotence of international communism and was certain that toughminded foreign policies were essential for political success at home. Having decided on his personal mission, and the need for presidential activism in foreign affairs, Kennedy chose a man remembered only vaguely as an assistant secretary of state under Truman and as president of the Rockefeller Foundation, as well as the recent contributor to *Foreign Affairs* of a hard-headed article on the presidency, Dean Rusk.

So the domestic and international political circumstances that launched the Kennedy-Johnson Democratic administration were in great contrast with that which had begun the last Democratic era. An uncertain political base and a mandate that offered only limited options were very different from a desperate nation eager to be shown the way up. The party's left would have to be patient.

2

Kennedy's inaugural address was largely a pointed repudiation of the leadership of the past eight years. The tone was one of a renaissance, of a rebirth of purpose, not merely, as he said, "a victory of party," but "a celebration of freedom—symbolizing an end as well as a beginning—signifying renewal as well as change." It was not just a new administration and he the thirty-fifth president, but the "torch has been passed to a new generation of Americans—born in this century, tempered by war, disciplined by a hard and bitter peace, proud of our ancient heritage. . . ." His leadership was of one of the few generations, he declared, that have been "granted the role of

defending freedom in its hour of maximum danger. I do not shrink
from this responsibility—I welcome it."

The applause was warm and sustained. Whatever the Eisenhower
years had signified, and whatever Kennedy meant by such phraseology as "Ask not what your country can do for you: Ask what you can
do for your country," it offered the possibility, at least, of being the
germ of what Stevenson had called the "New America"; only this
time it was under the newest Democratic appellation, to be called
the "New Frontier." Only a limited number of skeptical critics
wondered what the rhetorical flourishes implied, what he had really
said, if anything. Was it a conservative call for old-fashioned indi-
vidualism, a signal to abandon welfare economics for the virtues of
self-reliance; or was he suggesting the acceptance of responsibility for
all of society as the highest form of patriotism? Was the globe being
confronted with new opportunities for harmony or with new appe-
tites for aggression? "Let us never negotiate out of fear. But let us
never fear to negotiate."

The answer, of course, was that the address was perfectly suited for
the occasion, the end-product of a careful scrutiny of past inaugural
addresses, the successful achievement of the appropriate tone, and
fashioned by his chief speech-writer, Ted Sorensen. It had the sound
of dedication, the ring of patriotism, the sense of mission that whatever else it may have meant, it surely seemed to promise to fulfill his
campaign vow to "get America moving again." Shrewdly in contrast
with the style and image of the old general who was also the retiring
president, a man who carried with him his carefully preserved personal popularity, it marked a transition without disruption. If only a
delicate plurality had installed the new leadership, nothing heard
that day from the snowy capital would cause the nation to have any
regrets.

When, a little over a thousand days later, Kennedy was assas-
sinated in Dallas, the cynical critics still wondered how to evaluate
his brief reign. The promise had been so bright; but Tom Wicker
spoke for many when he wrote, "I believe he stood on the sidelines
. . . while the game was going on, measuring his performance, wryly
remarking upon it, not much impressed, not much deluded." Then
Wicker added: "Perhaps he knew all along that events could control,
action overwhelm, means fail to reach ends."[17]

The final irony, then, was that he had done only too well in his
efforts to arouse great expectations, an inspirational function inseparable from the process of educating the public. It was the kind of

rhetoric that was usually lamented by liberals for its absence; and when they complained about Eisenhower it was not only because he was too conservative, not only because he trusted businessmen, but that he had also failed to exert any presidential prerogatives, to place his popularity on the line when necessary, to buck the hopeless racists and reactionaries, to lead. From Kennedy, more was expected, and properly so. He had written about the virtues of political courage; he had expressed admiration for the integrity of a John Quincy Adams and an Edmund Ross that had moved them to resist pressures and follow their convictions. His inaugural address was designed to be inspirational; unlike the detailed legislative programs spelled out by States of the Union messages, that was its unique function, so it evoked inferences that tantalized the nation with a sense of dedication. It had succeeded in convincing such skeptics as Sam Rayburn that the young man deserved to be taken seriously.[18] Much was expected of the presidency, not only because much had been promised, but also because Democrats had promised to end the eight years of Republican drought.

Essentially, however, it was not the Democratic Party per se that had captured the White House: led by an attractive candidate who exuded change, it was under the sway of an efficient machine that had manipulated the controls and regulated the conduits through which had poured all the elements necessary for victory. Unlike European parliamentary systems, the president was not the legislative leader. Theoretically, at least, holding the White House was not dependent upon any such thing as party control of the House and the Senate. For Kennedy, it was quite clear at the outset that the first priority would have to be gaining the confidence of the nation, building popular support that might be able to negate the flimsiness of his victory. The nature of the presidency had made its power more personal than partisan, almost independent of the amorphous institution known as the Democratic Party. Therefore, it was essential that strategy be designed to first bolster his standing with the public and then aim toward a victory in 1964 that would eradicate all doubts about his authority.

On Kennedy's side, on Capitol Hill, Democrats enjoyed a smaller majority than during the Eighty-sixth Congress, one so precarious, in fact, that it was entirely vulnerable to the constant reforming of Republican-southern Democratic coalitions. It was the voting pattern in 1960, combined with the disproportionately heavy representation of rural areas, that had resulted in a situation in which most

members of Congress came from counties that had supported not
Kennedy but Nixon. So, as party leader, Kennedy had little choice
but to work with whatever forces promised loyalty, whether they
were reformers whose goals were compatible with the promises of
the New Frontier or whether their interests were more concerned
with maintaining local machines. The administration kept close ties
with Mayor Richard Daley of Chicago, especially since his ability to
deliver the disputed Illinois vote had been crucial in 1960 and might
be just as vital four years later. If New York could be kept together
more efficiently by the care and feeding of Peter Crotty and Charlie
Buckley, the Kennedy-assisted replacements for the fallen De Sapio-
Prendergast leadership, that would be better than tarrying with a
weak, narrow-based, and factious reform movement. Similarly, Kennedy gave the prestige of his attention to Congressman William J.
Green, the political boss of Philadelphia whose city machine had
supplied the Democratic majority that had easily overcome the deficit turned in by the rest of Pennsylvania. Pragmatically, too, Kennedy counted among his friends such conservative Democrats as
Florida Senator George Smathers, and his concern with keeping a
base in Texas led to peace-keeping efforts among the warring factions in the state that were led by John Connally and Ralph Yarborough. And, although he had won the admiration and loyal
support of "Mr. Sam," it was a temporary gain as Rayburn, stricken
with cancer, left Washington during the first of Kennedy's three
summers and died in Bonham that November.

The loss hurt. Rayburn's successor was Mike Mansfield, an Idaho
senator of impeccable integrity who had the respect of his colleagues; but, withal, inexperienced and not quite ready to handle
the administration's legislative desires with the fragile congressional
support. Eager to expedite matters, he misfired, especially when he
decided that Wilbur Mills fully intended to keep the Kennedy med-
icare program bottled up in the Ways and Means Committee.
Rather than follow the usual procedure, which would have meant
waiting for the Senate Finance Committee to first get from Mills the
bill to provide the financing of medical care through the Social Security system, Mansfield brought it to the floor via Clinton P.
Anderson. Anderson, in turn, introduced it as an amendment to the
Public Welfare amendments that had already been passed by the
House. But the power of the conservative coalition managed, just
barely, but dramatically, to defeat the maneuver by a four-vote margin. "The few defeats which were suffered in the Congress," Mansfield later explained, "were not the fault of the President but were

in some instances, as a matter of fact, my fault, because I tried to bypass committees on various proposals."[19]

But what Kennedy did have on his side to make his leadership credible was a bright and energetic White House staff of Ivy Leaguers and, in the House, such liberals as Richard Bolling and Frank Thompson, Jr. With Eugene McCarthy and Lee Metcalf, Thompson had already contributed the Democratic Study Group to the interests of forward-looking legislation. First set up at the end of the Eighty-fourth Congress, it was an informal group of congressional liberals, in a sense the Capitol Hill version of the progressive-reformist minority sentiment that was restless during the 1950s and had inspired both the "Finletter Group" and the Democratic Advisory Council. As Thompson later explained, "One purpose was really to educate our colleagues and ourselves on the issues."[20] Boosted by the simultaneous work of White House congressional liaison aide Larry O'Brien and Speaker Rayburn, their efforts helped Kennedy achieve his first and perhaps most dramatic legislative victory. That was the key fight, early in the new administration, to wrest control of the House Rules Committee, which had been the graveyard for countless pieces of liberal legislation. The maneuver was, in effect, also designed to overcome the dictatorial control of the committee's chairman, Howard W. Smith of Virginia.[21] Rayburn had been the one to point out that much of the obstruction could be circumvented by adding three members to the twelve-man committee, a scheme that would provide at least a precarious eight to seven pro-administration majority.

The subsequent battle split the party into fairly orderly liberal-conservative groups and made almost impossible the avoidance of what was, in effect, an ideological commitment. Even the president's father could not resist the fight. Ambassador Kennedy called Judge Smith and urged the chairman to oppose the administration's attempt to "stack" the committee.[22] Perhaps similar conflicts were in Kennedy's mind when he later faced the National Association of Manufacturers and, with considerable charm, observed that most industrialists had voted against him in 1960 except "for a very few who were under the impression that I was my father's son."[23] Most importantly, he had had his victory as the expansion of the Rules Committee carried by a five-vote margin. At the moment, it was a formidable boost to his popular standing.

The Rules Committee outcome was important. It seemed to confirm that the "new frontiersmen" were truly capable of extraordinary deeds; suddenly the hitherto invincible Judge Smith, friend and ally of Harry Byrd, upholder of the Southern Democracy, had been punctured. The triumphant outcome of what had also been a symbolic fight was a perfect contribution to Kennedy's early need to enhance his own stock. At the same time, the accomplishment would have its negative side. Once again, the expectation of future miracles had been created, an illusion that ignored the reality of what had been accomplished, that the great struggle had merely installed a tenuous pro-administration majority. It was neither sacrosanct nor guaranteed but dependent on the vagaries of individuals and shifting political requirements.

That was dramatized on the education aid bill. Of all presidents, Kennedy was least able to agree that there were merits to the arguments for helping parochial schools, even if that had been his private inclination. His advocacy of restricting assistance to public schools was much less provocative than the opposite position would have been, but he had aroused the ire of Catholics who were quickly realizing that there would have been fewer liabilities with a Protestant in the White House. The clamor became sufficiently intense for Cardinal Cushing of Boston, the president's friend, and the editors of *The Commonweal* to urge Catholics to recognize the political realities.[24] The divisions were sharpened when James Delaney, an Irish-Catholic member of the Rules Committee from New York City's Queens County, dissented from the administration's bill both for reasons of his personal conviction and the feelings of his constituents. Suddenly, the victory to enlarge the committee seemed futile.

There were similar frustrations in trying to put together committee majorities to save other measures that fared no better than if Judge Smith had never been defeated. Among them were a mass transportation bill, a measure to reduce the high rate of unemployment plaguing the nation's youth, and Kennedy's attempt to update the executive department by creating a Department of Urban Affairs. The last came amid the controversy created by Kennedy's announced intent to name Robert Weaver as the head of the new cabinet-level department. Weaver, whom the president had already installed as administrator of the Housing and Home Loan Agency, was also a black man. Suddenly, it seemed, a vote against urban affairs was synonymous with being anti-Negro. Republicans, caught between being accused of voting their racial prejudices or handing the administration a victory by default, risked the former and helped to defeat the move.

Still, on balance, considering the absence of a broad-based demand for reforms, the new administration did remarkably well with the Eighty-seventh Congress. In addition to the Area Redevelopment Bill, the minimum wage scale was raised to $1.25, and other hallmarks of a liberal administration were secured. Social security benefits were widened, the Peace Corps was established, localities were given support for their efforts to control water pollution, a vastly increased public works program was adopted, and Congress accepted a major manpower retraining program. Provisions were also made for an omnibus housing bill and, in 1962, Kennedy achieved the passage of the significant Trade Expansion Act—not bad, considering the size of his election victory.

Nevertheless, Kennedy left vital elements on the left discontented and disappointed, angry that the administration was compromising, especially by making concessions to the South. Undoubtedly already self-conscious about the region that had resisted him so strongly on religious grounds, he had omitted any mention of the need for civil rights legislation from proposals to be enacted by the Eighty-seventh Congress, despite the preliminary work that had been done at his request by Manny Celler and Joe Clark. If any push would be made in behalf of civil rights, it would come through actions of the Justice Department in enforcing voting regulations. Prudently, too, the effort to break the power of the filibuster by modifying Senate Rule XII found the administration on the sidelines. Other actions strengthened the impression that Kennedy, much as had Adlai Stevenson, was pursuing a southern strategy. Cotton price supports were raised, patronage flowed southward in abundance, and the first accomplishment under the Area Redevelopment Act was a grant for a water system in Arkansas.[25] The president also made a concerted effort to cultivate Harry Byrd, a bit of strategy that included making a dramatic descent by helicopter at the senator's birthday party celebration in Virginia. Further, although time was passing and reminders were becoming less restrained, the man who had criticized Eisenhower for failing to lift his pen to end discrimination in housing subsidized by federal funds also found political considerations conducive to his own procrastination. Not-so-subtle barbs from those who had not forgotten Kennedy's campaign statements came in the form of "pens for Jack" that began to arrive at the White House. When the executive order was finally signed, on November 20, 1962, existing housing was not included.

Nor were there bold departures on the diplomatic front. Instead, there was mounting evidence that the president's major fear was being considered inadequate in the face of challenges from the communist world. It was a conflict that tended to sacrifice his much-praised capacity for dispassionate and realistic judgments. Thus, instead of overruling the CIA's plot to overthrow Fidel Castro (which had been concocted during the Eisenhower administration), Kennedy assumed it would be politically far more prudent to avoid risking being blamed for having ordered the dismantlement of the invasion apparatus. He gave the operation the green light while attempting to conceal American participation by denying air cover to the operation, which provided a handy excuse for those who remained convinced that that had been a decisive factor. The resulting fiasco, the extraordinary naïveté in thinking that Cubans were awaiting the first opportunity to restore Batista, plus revelations of how anti-Castro refugees had been prevented by the CIA from having anything to do with the Bay of Pigs invasion, further damaged the administration's standing. Cold-war tensions were no less relieved later that spring when Kennedy returned from a meeting with Premier Khrushchev and stressed that their sessions in Vienna had revealed that the Russians were determined to press for a showdown over Berlin. The Soviets, it seemed, had every intention of turning over jurisdiction to East Germany. At a White House meeting with congressional leaders, right after the president's return from Europe, he appeared shaken because, as Mike Mansfield explained, "Khrushchev had looked upon him as a youngster who had a great deal to learn and not much to offer."[26]

The tensions were great that summer. Khrushchev was, in effect, daring the United States to start a nuclear war over maintaining access rights to West Berlin and Kennedy, as Ted Sorensen has put it, was determined to pursue the position that what was involved was not only the fate of that city "but a question of direct Soviet-American confrontation over a shift in the balance of power."[27] Nor was there any doubt that the sense of crisis was perfectly consistent with the popular mood, giving Kennedy the opportunity for the kind of leadership that satisfied American determination. A private report to the executive board of the National Committee for an Effective Congress provided ample confirmation of how the public was ready to respond. Findings from all over the country produced the startling conclusion that Americans were resigned to the inevitability and justification of a nuclear war to defend West Berlin. There was little agreement about what to do at home, but toward the Soviets there was little disagreement. The theme heard from all over was expressed by the words "stand firm"—"stand firm" even if it means war. The attitude was so intense, congressmen reported privately, that, as their fears were summarized, "it would be 'political suicide at home' to talk negotiation to resolve the Berlin crisis just as it would be physical suicide to engage in nuclear war." Intransigence and passionate domestic attitudes were, in short, threatening to drive the United States into a dangerous "chicken game." In the wake of the Bay of Pigs, Democrats were especially sensitive to the "appeasement" charges coming from the proliferating radical right.[28]

It was in the middle of that crisis, on July 25, that the president delivered a somber television address to the American people that reaffirmed the Western commitment to Berlin and accepted the need to risk war to defend the city. Fear that a nuclear clash was virtually imminent also intensified the national dilemma over air-raid fallout shelters, an interest Kennedy had inspired by his request for a new form of "survival insurance." By the end of the year, as Khrushchev hedged over his Berlin threats, a frightened public debated the practicable and ethical issues involved in trying to seal off themselves and their families from the coming incineration. Religious leaders and the press pontificated on the moral justification for the use of force in trying to keep desperate neighbors from sharing the means for survival. New York's Hammacher-Schlemmer store unfurled a deluxe family "shelter for living," which, for $14,000, provided a one-room unit, with a "wall covered in US Plywood's Charter Pecan Weldwood paneling," air conditioning, television, hi-fi unit, fold-away bed, a "discreetly, practically hidden" compact kitchen and bath, air filter, a four and a half pound tin of multipurpose food, and a portable plastic container with five gallons of water guaranteed to remain fresh for fifteen years.[29] Eleanor Roosevelt, somewhat less enthusiastic about psychological conditioning for the acceptance of war, was sent an assuring note by the president. "The prospect of a nuclear exchange is so terrible that I conceive that it would be preferable to be among the dead rather than among the living. The difficulty," he pointed out, "is that this has been the weapon on which we have relied for our security and without it as an ultimate action we are unprepared. We are going to attempt to improve this, however."[30]

Cuba and Berlin had clearly been the dominant areas of public concern, leaving most Americans almost oblivious to the remote conflicts in Southeast Asia. Still, the political and ideological questions involved in policymaking kept the administration committed to the full assumption of American responsibility for that corner of the world. The administration was in no mood for becoming the target of new "who lost China?" accusations. President Eisenhower, in his White House conference with Kennedy just before his retirement, outlined the problem his successor would face by summarizing the deteriorating situation in Laos. Fearful of a complete victory by the communist Pathet Lao, the new president gambled on conservative criticism at home and a crisis of confidence in Asia by accepting a coalition government under Prince Souvanna Phouma, a move made without any realistic confidence that its neutralist leadership would not soon capitulate to the Pathet Lao in any case. Coming as it did right after the Bay of Pigs episode and with the simultaneous need to demonstrate American determination in Berlin, there seemed to be no options available other than the renewal of emphatic commitments to the Diem government of South Vietnam, assurances that Vice President Johnson conveyed during his visit to Saigon that May.[31]

Despite the Bay of Pigs, Kennedy's cold-war leadership and domestic prudence had given him a strong centrist base. By year's end, the Gallup poll reported that his task of building personal popularity had succeeded. "No really great President gets 78 percent public support till he's dead," commented TRB in *The New Republic*. "We trust Kennedy's burning desire to be 'great' will take care of this."[32]

Almost inevitably, the dissent had begun to come from the political extremes. On the right, largely from Republican ranks but also appealing to a combination of Democrats that included northern Catholics, southern conservatives, and economically aggressive and newly wealthy professionals and businessmen, the John Birch Society was gaining enough strength to alarm moderates and liberals. Wyoming Senator Gale McGee was so upset by the success of their exploitation of the fear of communism, especially since it threatened to create Republican gains, that he urged Democratic National Chairman John Bailey to take immediate steps to produce propaganda to counter the effects of the widespread showing of the Birchite film, *Operation Abolition*.[33] In other parts of the country, vigilante-minded individuals called themselves "Minutemen" and began to train for the coming personal combat with the Red invaders.

At the same time, the fractures on the left were also undermining any possibility of a broad Kennedy consensus. Chester Bowles, in conflict with Secretary of State Rusk over the persistence of military solutions for the situation in Southeast Asia, was finally eased out of the State Department after more than a half year of bureaucratic tension. As Bowles later explained, "Having been charged with 'woolly-headedness,' 'softness on Communism' and similar crimes during the Republican Administration, they felt it necessary to demonstrate that they were, in fact, tough characters."[34] Bowles, of course, was a symbol of the party's most ardent liberals and, as Harris Wofford had warned Kennedy six months before Bowles' dismissal, "the firing of Bowles could be a signal to all his friends in the country—and to the supporters of Stevenson, Humphrey, Williams, and Reuther—that you are turning away from them and their views of the world."[35] Despondent over the failure of liberal voices, a group of liberals and left-wing intellectuals had already founded a Committee of Correspondence. Begun as a newsletter run off on a spirit duplicator in the Harvard University office of Professor David Riesman, the author of *The Lonely Crowd*, the responses to the Kennedy administration proved to be a boon to its circulation, warranting its evolution to a mimeographed and then a photostated publication. Under the editorship of Nathan Glazer, it offered dissenting views from such others as Lewis Mumford, Erich Fromm, Staughton Lynd, Robert Paul Wolff, and James P. Warburg. After less than five months of the new Democratic presidency, it asked editorially whether the New Frontier was a fraud and concluded, "The rhetoric of the inaugural address is now too deeply soiled to wash clean."[36]

3

If the Democratic left was but a fringe along the party's periphery, increasingly, especially in later years, it came to be regarded as their version of the GOP's radical right. Its ability to sway an administration devoted to gathering a middle-class centrist majority was nil. Apologists for the Kennedy reluctance to push ahead boldly, to press for even a semblance of the civil rights advances his campaign had suggested, asked for patient understanding. Faith in the administration's goodwill was, for many liberals, the only substantive argument for holding that their support was still deserved. And yet, two things were becoming clear: that the Democratic Party itself had little to do with policymaking; and, second, any gains that might be made would require extrapolitical methods.

Events, then, forced by the unleashing of pent-up frustrations and new expectations, striking outside impotent party structures, moved the cautious White House planners more rapidly than expediency had dictated. They pointed up that the lag had become inexcusable, that response to neglect simply could not await the creation of the comfortable consensus; if a national emergency and not a simple political victory was necessary to "get America moving again," one was already present; action was dependent not on an institution known as the Democratic Party but on Americans who were Democrats for want of a better partisan faith.

So the momentum was provided, during those first two Kennedy summers, by forces over which the administration had little control. The sit-ins of early 1960, desegregating a series of lunch-counters in a growing number of states, had matured to the level of more coordinated programs. Private resources, mainly backed by the Taconic and Field foundations and tacitly encouraged by the president, pressed a voter-registration campaign among southern blacks; faith in the power of the ballot box, backed by the Civil Rights Division of the Justice Department even without the active support of Attorney General Robert Kennedy, had become at least a temporary substitute for introducing new legislation.[37] Assistant Attorney General Burke Marshall and his deputy, John Doar, brought more than fifty suits to enforce voting-right provisions already on the books. James Farmer, the new national director of the Congress of Racial Equality, devised the idea of "freedom rides" to test discrimination in interstate transportation terminals. Buses went south, carrying biracial passengers, students, professors, and clergymen, along a carefully planned itinerary. Arrests and violence followed. The American Nazi Party countered with a "hate bus" dispatched from Washington. During the month of May, the demonstrations captured headlines nationally, so much so that on the twenty-fourth Attorney General Kennedy issued a plea for a "cooling-off" period, which Martin Luther King promptly rejected.[38] Rather than subsiding, the momentum increased, reaching a dramatic confrontation at the University of Mississippi in the fall of 1962 when two killings and rioting accompanied the struggle by James Meredith to become the first black man to enroll in Ole Miss. The civil rights movement was quickly becoming a revolution, a revolution for which neither political party had a program but merely the flexibility to respond to the obvious realities. In November, under such pressures, John Kennedy signed his housing order.

The question for Democrats was in the form of a choice between continuing to remain sensitive to its southern wing for more certain but limited legislative gains that could be placed before the voters in the midterm elections of 1962 and in 1964 or to respond to the obvious inequities by coming to the assistance of the minorities and acceding to the desires of the urban coalition. Both Kennedys had been attempting to live with the former, falling back on the promotion of voting rights as the most politic solution. But, as a confidential NAACP memorandum had urged in February 1961, "It is not necessary to choose as between executive and legislative actions. Neither alone is adequate to accomplish the goal; both are indispensable to it."[39]

But the silence from the White House was in tune with Eisenhower's years. It continued even while Senator Clark and Representative Celler introduced the civil rights measures that Kennedy had asked them to prepare.[40] "By going easy on civil rights legislation," James Reston explained, the president "has avoided an angry break with the Southerners in his own party."[41] And there was sufficient evidence in support of the administration's position, that the Eighty-seventh Congress had given Kennedy much of what he wanted only because enough southerners had voted to overcome Republican opposition. The minimum wage bill, a housing bill, the Area Redevelopment Bill, an emergency feed grains program, and measures involving travel taxes and stock dividend withholdings were all resolved in favor of the administration with the help of crucial southern votes.[42]

Still, before events had foreclosed options, there was much internal pressure for civil rights action. Assistant White House Counsel Lee White and Democratic National Committee Deputy Chairman Louis Martin called for presidential leadership, Martin reminding the administration that Negroes had come to expect better from northern Democrats. He pointed to the difficult elections ahead in the states of New Jersey and New York, hoped that that would strike a responsive chord, as warranting overtures to vital blocs of Negroes and minority groups.[43] In November, White sent the president a summary of thirteen possible legislative items.[44]

But Kennedy held back, trying to preserve his thin congressional margin, giving as little as possible beyond his housing order. To make no concessions, however, risked alienating the administration not only from the northern Democracy, which had become the basic fulcrum of the party's presidential wing, but also from newly franchised Negroes in Dixie. By February, Kennedy was ready to go before Congress with a voting bill prepared by the Justice Department. At its heart was authorization for the appointment of federal voting referees in communities where less than 15 percent of voting-age Negroes were actually enrolled, but with the requirement that assistance could be granted only where applicants had *first attempted* to register with state registrars. As the staff director of the Civil Rights Commission warned, "In the Mississippi counties which are of greatest concern to the Justice Department, the likelihood of violence and harassment will cut down the number of applicants for Federal registration." Moreover, there were dubious constitutional grounds, particularly those based on the argument that compelling district courts to appoint referees if less than 15 percent of the blacks in any particular county were registered would deprive the courts of their discretion. "The only effective answer to it is that you can't leave this matter to the discretion of the judges because the judges are no good," the commission pointed out, "But this is the one argument that cannot be publicly used." The crux of the memorandum that was sent to Lee White was summarized by the following dilemma:

This bill is needed for only one reason: There are Federal judges who have been appointed to the District courts who are so racially prejudiced that they will not obey their oaths of office and, therefore, some method is being in Congress sought to compel them to act. But this can not and will not be publicly stated.[45]

They also predicted that it would be impossible to pass a bill that nobody favored, that the only effective kind of legislation would be a bill drawing upon the authority to regulate federal elections by establishing a federal registration system completely independent of the courts. Their conclusion was that the "most pressing need is to deal with the 2,000 school districts which are still disobeying the Constitutional mandate to desegregate their schools. This is a problem which cannot be dealt with even indirectly, by voting legislation."[46]

One week after that critique, the president submitted the bill with a message to Congress, the first one devoted exclusively to civil rights. As expected, even the sympathetic were cool, dissatisfied with its prospects. While its legislative future remained clouded, attention was diverted by the outbreak of violence in different parts of the country, mainly in the South but also in some northern localities. In Alabama, there was trouble in both Selma and Birmingham, but the latter quickly became the sensation trouble-spot of all. Fought against the background of a disputed mayoral election between Albert Boutwell and Public Safety Commissioner Eugene "Bull" Connor, the spark was ignited by a Southern Christian Leadership Conference drive led by Martin Luther King to desegregate public facilities. Marching demonstrators, challenging the traditional Jim Crow patterns, became the targets of police dogs and high-power fire hoses. Connor obtained a sudden national reputation for his mob-control tactics; but the crowds were only more incited when bombs exploded at a motel being used as Dr. King's headquarters. Also in Alabama, a white civil rights worker was shot to death. Before a truce was finally declared in Birmingham, over two thousand persons had been arrested, and demonstrations that spring and summer in eleven southern states and about seventy-five cities resulted in 13,786 arrests, according to figures compiled by the Southern Regional Council. Meanwhile, the Justice Department counted 758 demonstrations throughout the country in the ten-week period after the restoration of temporary peace in Birmingham. In June, additional headlines were made by the murder of Mississippi NAACP Field Secretary Medgar Evers.

Exactly one week after the Evers murder, President Kennedy all but abandoned the temporizing quality of February's voting-rights request and urged Congress to pass a bill that not only attempted to uphold voting rights more effectively than was possible under the mild legislation that had been enacted in 1957 but also requested federal power to enforce school desegregation and the guarantee of equal access to public accommodations. Although he made no direct request for an FEPC, his message was accompanied by the endorsement of such provisions that were already pending on Capitol Hill. Further evidence that the president had joined the civil rights fight came in August when, after considerable White House disagreement over how he should respond, he welcomed the leadership of a massive March on Washington that brought over a quarter of a million people to the capital in support of the reforms.

The Kennedy identity had finally begun to crystallize; the Democratic president was finally moving to where his party's liberals had, from the start, thought he belonged. The new developments served to enhance the identity he had acquired from a number of other requests that were yet to be fulfilled by the Congress. His association with the efforts to obtain medical care through the social security system appealed to the majority of Americans whose approval of the plan was still being thwarted by the intense lobbying effort of the American Medical Association. At Yale University, he had delivered a commencement address that sought to enlighten the public about the pre-Keynesian myths regarding balanced budgets and the growth of big government. Accepting the concept of progress through economic growth, he had also called for reduced taxation as a stimulus; and, in recognition of the plight of America's cities, he also asked for the establishment of a cabinet-level Department of Urban Affairs.

Moreover, even Kennedy's cold-war diplomacy had undergone a shift. For his part, Khrushchev had permitted the Berlin scare to evaporate, contenting himself with the face-saving gesture of a rapidly constructed wall to reduce escapes to the city's western sector. Oddly helping to mitigate tensions, after creating what some feared was the imminence of nuclear disaster, was the Cuban missile crisis of October 1962. After weeks of rumors about Russian placement of missiles on the island, and challenges for a response by the administration delivered by several Republican leaders, most notably Senate Minority Leader Everett McKinley Dirksen and Senator Kenneth Keating of New York, confirmation that such weapons were being installed brought a dramatic American naval blockade of the island. Khrushchev's careful avoidance of a showdown and his subsequent removal of the missiles gave Kennedy a great victory that went far toward removing the onus of the Bay of Pigs. Instead of nuclear confrontation, the two leaders moved toward nuclear agreement, with Kennedy revealing his desires for a test-ban treaty during a major speech at American University on June 10, 1963, only a few weeks before the actual paper was signed. There was also some hope for an end to the difficulty in Southeast Asia, too. With some 16,000 American "advisers" already in South Vietnam, intensifying protests against the Diem regime, underlined by a series of self-immolations by Buddhists, prompted Kennedy toward a reappraisal of the American commitment. Facing CBS television cameras in September, the president told interviewer Walter Cronkite that "in the final analysis" the war belonged to the people of that country and that they would have to win it.[47]

4

"The domestic as well as the foreign behavior of the New Frontier seems to be motivated by masochism and national immolation," wrote a Virginia supporter to Harry Byrd.[48] Other southerners were telling the story about one Negro who said to another, "What is all this talk about electing a President next year? Ain't we got a President?" To which his friend replied: "Yes, but the white folks, they want a President."

The administration's standing in the South had slumped severely, precipitating a reaction that was perhaps predictable, one that had never been far beneath the surface. The period of tolerable relations with the Kennedy administration had never been more than a tenuous détente governed by the most blatant mutual self-interest. Now, however, the South was undergoing new burdens of political change. All the old walls were tumbling down, jarred further in 1962 by the Supreme Court's decision in the case of *Baker v. Carr* that ruled against the wildly disproportionate representation that weighed so heavily in favor of rural over urban areas. Georgia's Fulton County, containing Atlanta, had a 1960 population of 556,326 but, compounding the handicaps of the state's county unit system, had only the same number of state representatives as the 6,980 inhabitants of three rural counties.[49] Elsewhere in the South, where industrialization had created significant demographic changes, there were similar patterns, all of which had favored continued domination by rural politicians, a source of vital strength to Talmadge in Georgia. An anti-poll-tax amendment had also become an inevitability, having been passed by the Congress and sure to be ratified by the states before the 1964 elections. Already, the voter-registration campaigns that had been pushed by the Justice Department were achieving dramatic results in some localities. In Macon County, Alabama, the number of enrolled blacks had gone from a mere trickle to some 2,800. Duplicated elsewhere, it was a trend that could be checked only by continued defiance and intimidation and the counterforce of greater determination by whites to get out their own vote, a reaction that was already evident in some places. All such changes were traumatic to resentful southerners, especially the frightened, semiliterate poor whites. The most impoverished elements were the most susceptible to cries that the Kennedy administration's moves were part of the international communist conspiracy that they had heard so much about, and that Martin Luther King was a red devil in black skin.[50] On the defensive, vulnerable to the unsympathetic reportage by the northern press and national news media, they were especially swayed by appeals directed at resurrecting the "southern creed."

Moreover, it was easy to brand the Kennedys as the victims of change. Those northern Catholics who spoke with Harvard accents and came from a family of immense wealth were merely the latest oppressors. Joining Chief Justice Earl Warren and the Court on the hate list, they were victimizing the nation's poorest region, something that northern capitalists had done before. Hearing about administration plans to attempt a purge of thirteen obstructionist southern congressmen, who had joined ever more solidly with the conservative coalition to resist the administration's legislative program, the regional director of the Republican National Committee promised that "Southern voters will not tolerate the rich and mighty Kennedys dictating their nominees for any office."[51] Others regarded the brothers as akin to such wealthy civil rights supporters as Nelson Rockefeller, G. Mennen Willliams, Marshall Field, and Averell Harriman, who were simply revealing the self-conscious guilt common to men with giant unearned fortunes and encouraging them to pit "class against class and race against race." George Wallace, in winning Alabama's governorship in 1962, had combined Jim Folsom's old populist appeals to subsistence farmers and poor workers with vows to free the South from northern domination, even going so far as to promise in his inaugural address complete defiance of federal civil rights laws by declaring, "Segregation now! Segregation tomorrow! Segregation forever!" It was a position that left him with little choice but to be photographed as the symbol of resistance by standing in front of the doorway to the University of Alabama to thwart its integration.[52]

The signs that the South was on the verge of a full revolt that would facilitate a shift toward solid support for conservative Republican presidential candidates seemed to have been confirmed by the Alabama senatorial election of 1962. In what had been a one-party state, Lister Hill could manage no more than 50.9 percent of the vote against a conservative Republican. That was despite the fact that Hill had done best in those counties that had recently been forced to register large numbers of Negroes.[53] Still, Republican optimism was being tempered by the realization that prospects for success on the local level were still fairly bleak. Virginius Dabney pointed out that with Republicans committing themselves more

firmly to conservatism, Democrats on the right were starting to abandon their old party to the more liberal elements.[54] Whatever the prospects for converting the region into a two-party area, it had begun to
seem likely that considerable southern sentiment was moving behind
ultraconservative Republican Senator Barry Goldwater's presidential ambitions. The region was rapidly becoming the area of his
greatest strength.

Robertson was relieved that he would not be on the ticket in 1964
because the pro-Kennedy people and the proponents of "golden silence" would find themselves caught in a crossfire.[55] To an old
friend, the senator expressed alarm at the specter of Martin Luther
King bringing several hundred thousand Negroes to Washington
and having them swarm over the Capitol grounds and storming
congressional offices like a mob of barbarians, rather vivid hyperbole
for the old and dignified aristocrat.[56] Considerably less sober was
Frank Boykin. The Alabama businessman and land speculator, now
an ex-congressman, venting his anger at Attorney General Kennedy,
wrote that "this youngster has really gone wild, and we are in trouble." All through the South, he reported, from Baltimore to Mobile
Bay, he had never seen people so upset. He had also heard that the
Negroes planning that big protest march intended to tear up some of
the city's hotels, including the one built by his company and now
owned by his cousins, the Washington Hotel.[57] Dr. Edward Teller,
the nuclear physicist and strong opponent of the test-ban treaty, told
H. L. Hunt right after the president's American University speech
that there was no chance to get the Kennedys out unless they were
defeated in 1964. "The stake," explained Hunt to Harry Byrd, "is
the future of the nation." The Republicans must come to the rescue
by nominating Goldwater, if not somebody stronger. "I am writing
some other outstanding Democrats," advised the multimillionaire
Texan, "and would prefer that my name not be mentioned as you
discuss the best moves to save the nation with other prominent
Democrats of the South."[58] Chalmers Roberts reported in the
Washington *Post* that sources close to the president were admitting
that things had gone from bad to worse in the South. Further, there
was doubt about how much could be gained from the North, if
anything at all, to compensate for the expected loss.[59] At the same
time, there were indications that some southern Democrats were
starting to shift the way Dabney had noted, toward more liberal
positions by shaping alliances of white workers, poor farmers, intellectuals, and minority groups composed of Negroes and Mexican

Americans. "As conservatives move to the Republican Party and as Negroes vote in larger numbers, Southern Democracy inches leftward," Alan L. Otten observed in the *Wall Street Journal* on November 13, 1963.

Clear signs of such a development had already come from Texas. In Crystal City, where the population of 10,000 was comprised of 8,500 Mexican Americans, a ballot-box revolt in April had given an alliance known as PASO (the Political Association of Spanish-speaking Organizations, an offspring of the 1960 "viva Kennedy" movement) control of that community, thereby wresting local government from its traditional domination by the Anglo-Saxon minority. In June, that move was followed by the organization of the liberal Democratic Coalition, which was composed of liberals, organized labor, Negroes, and PASO. At the same time, the state's Republican Party was growing by absorbing conservative Democrats, who had formerly been able to overwhelm the liberals.[60] With a potentially solid base of voters in that state ready to support Kennedy in 1964 (and help him carry it as they had done before), and with the rest of the South becoming more uncertain daily, the importance of securing Vice President Johnson's home state's twenty-five electoral votes had magnified. But even that prospect was in jeopardy because of the continued squabbling among Texas Democrats. The contending leaders were John Connally who, after serving as Kennedy's secretary of the navy, had been elected as the state's governor in 1962, and liberal leader Senator Ralph Yarborough. For Kennedy, a trip to Texas to restore harmony before the 1964 campaign was of top-priority importance.

The president's trip to San Antonio, Houston, and, finally, Dallas was planned against a history of vehement right-wing opposition in the latter city. Lyndon Johnson had been their target at the Adolphus Hotel just before the 1960 election. Most recently, in October of 1963, Adlai Stevenson, in Dallas for a United Nations Day commemoration, was also the victim of a mob of hysterical anti-UN followers of General Edwin Walker. The American ambassador was spat upon and denounced with abusive language. "Actually," Stevenson wrote to Agnes Meyer a few days later, "I never had a warmer or more enthusiastic reception anywhere, and the idiot fringe was small if vocal and violent."[61] Stevenson then sent assurances for Kennedy that the president would have "an enthusiastic and sincere reception" in Dallas.[62]

On November 22, the day after his arrival in the state, the Detroit

News ran an editorial called "All Eyes on Texas" and, after explaining the efforts of the party to "cement an arrogant right and a liberal left wing to a common center," concluded with, "That's why the eyes of all the politicians are on Texas today."[63]

The next day, in Washington, White House Counsel Lee White prepared a two-page memorandum for Lyndon Johnson under the heading, "Items Requiring Decisions by the President."[64]

CHAPTER XI

The Ephemeral Consensus

1

Appropriately, Lee White's memorandum of November 23 devoted two of its eight items to what had clearly become the most pressing domestic need, civil rights. The violence in Dallas had followed by only two months the renewal of bloodshed in Birmingham, when a Sunday morning bombing of a black Baptist church killed four girls. Suddenly, political considerations seemed moot. The only question was how to proceed, as White pointed out by citing matters dealing with voter registration and the Kennedy civil rights bill. The sole doubt, at that moment—at least for those who knew little about the new president, pertained to his determination to complete what the administration had begun.

Chance had placed in the White House the man least acceptable to the proponents of civil rights. Lyndon Johnson's public record contained little room for encouragement. He had, of course, steered the 1957 and 1960 voting laws through the Senate, but both were weak, both were designed as compromises to pacify northern liberals while preserving southern patience. Both, further, were suspected of having been handy devices for Johnson's political ambitions, particularly the need to obscure his identification as a southerner. Although there was never the suggestion that he had ever been a rabid racist, the public record supplied enough evidence of support for segregationist traditions. As a member of the House, he had twice voted against federal lynching laws and had opposed attempts to do away with poll taxes not once, but on four different occasions. He had also joined with fellow southern Democrats in opposing attempts to remove the filibuster obstacle by modifying Rule XXII, the most recent instance occurring at the opening of the Eighty-eighth Congress. At that time, as vice president with the power to rule on whether the Senate was a continuing body or could adopt new procedures, he held that the matter was up to the Senate itself, a stance that provoked ADA attorney Joe Rauh to remark that Johnson had "demonstrated once again that his first loyalty is to the southern racists."[1]

Moreover, it seemed not only consistent with his own beliefs but also conveniently loyal. The administration was, after all, pursuing the strategy by doing what it could for civil rights without risk to its delicate congressional majority. And Vice President Johnson, suddenly quiescent, suddenly tamed, was behaving as a loyal member of the team and not betraying the difficulties of his new role and his personal strains with the president and the Kennedy staffers. To that end it was also easy to write off his public comments in behalf of racial justice, which began with the moment he delivered his vice presidential acceptance speech. On that occasion, he said he looked forward to a "new day of hope and harmony for all Americans regardless of religion, or race, or region," the last item being another attempt to equate his regional liabilities with other forms of discrimination. At Austin, too, in concluding his campaign, he had also visualized equal opportunities regardless of such inherent differences.[2] Since cynics automatically assumed that vice presidents merely mouthed their administrations' points of view, nothing Johnson said affected his reputation.

To those within the administration, and even to critics who got a more intimate view of him at work, there was another Johnson, the man whose own instincts for compassion and justice had long since won him the loyalty of Mexican Americans in Texas. As vice president, his actions were without publicity, removed from suspicions of political opportunism. Yet his interest was evident. First of all, there was his role as chairman of the President's Committee on Equal Employment Opportunity, a function that was generally minimized by civil rights activists who tended to ignore the significance of widening economic differences on frustration within black communities. In June of 1963, one week before preparing his major civil rights legislation, President Kennedy pointed out to Secretary of Labor Willard Wirtz and Anthony Celebrezze, who headed the Department of Health, Education and Welfare, that the vice president's experience as a member of that committee had convinced him "that the Federal Government should and could be doing much more to relieve Negro unemployment by additional and intensive job training programs for the unskilled, the illiterate and those on public welfare."[3] In preparing for a White House session with civil rights leaders concerned with the president's proposals, Johnson sent a confidential memorandum that, in addition to displaying his sensitivity to the extremist positions that were tending to widen racial conflicts, called for specific recommendations that would, in his words, "amount to a 'bill of rights' representing agreement between the President and the Negro community as to those things to which Negroes are legitimately entitled." His enumeration of areas of equality was precise: employment, education, housing, recreation, opportunity to move around the country freely, and protection under the law. But even such specifics were not enough, he warned. "The first step in solving any problem is always definition of the problem. This we do not now have."[4] At the subsequent meeting, held less than two weeks after that memorandum, it was Johnson and not the president who was most encouraging. Joe Rauh, after the specific FEPC endorsement that Kennedy had omitted from his recommendations of the eleventh, was both surprised and delighted to hear Johnson tell him to fight for it if he thought he could get the votes. As Leonard Baker has pointed out, "the civil rights people left the meeting believing they had received a more favorable response from Johnson than they would have received from John Kennedy."[5]

But President Kennedy's political fears were also being realized. Already at work was the building backlash to the administration's growing identification with civil rights. The southerners held the balance of power, of course, and they were determined to use their leverage to retaliate regardless of whether the specific measure had much to do with racial equality. It even hindered programs designed to relieve the poor of their own region, such as the 209 to 204 defeat given in the House to the administration's attempt to authorize additional funds for the Area Development Administration. The brief Kennedy-southern détente had ended. After having simmered since the 1930s and remained evident through the 1940s, the revolt of the Dixie Democrats against the urban coalition-dominated party was accelerating. Prospects of being able to vote for a conservative of the character of Barry Goldwater had become sufficiently attractive to diminish whatever resistance stood in the way of supporting a Republican for the presidency, especially if the Arizona senator seemed ready to turn the GOP into a white man's party.[6]

The political logjam was all-pervasive, let alone on civil rights legislation. All of Kennedy's requests were snarled; the more eager the administration the more stubborn the conservative bloc. In the face of the intraparty schism, the impasse began to raise new doubts about the government's ability to respond to the national crisis. Walter Lippmann wrote in October, "This is one of those moments when there is reason to wonder whether the Congressional system as it now operates is not a grave danger to the Republic."[7]

But even as the Lippmann column appeared, the blockade seemed to be lifting in response to administration pressure. On September 25, optimism was encouraged by the House's acceptance of the tax bill, which, along with civil rights, was Kennedy's top-priority item. After the liberals in Manny Celler's Judiciary Committee had added FEPC to the administration's original civil rights bill, despite White House pleas that a stronger version would guarantee its death, the president's personal intervention with Minority Leader Charlie Halleck succeeded in gathering enough Republican support to get it reported out by the end of October and delivered to the House on November 20. In the lower chamber, only the threat of a discharge petition induced Rules Committee Chairman Smith to promise action by January.[8] With the help of the liberals, it was considerably stronger than the administration had thought prudent. In addition to providing for equal employment opportunities, it gave the Justice Department broader powers to enforce desegregation. Once extricated from the Rules Committee and Judge Smith, its prospects seemed bright.

The issue with by far the leading emotional appeal, it was also the symbol of continuity. The new president, addressing a joint session of Congress on November 27, appealed for its passage along with the rest of the unfinished Kennedy program. "Today, in this moment of new resolve," he said in a brilliantly appropriate and emotional speech, "I would say to all my fellow Americans, let us continue." Determined to push civil rights, within the first two weeks of his presidency Johnson conferred with a succession of prominent black leaders. To Roy Wilkins of the NAACP, with whom he held his first such session, he "gave unmistakable notice that you had a friend and not an enemy in the White House for this legislation." Nor did he make any attempt to cool off the civil rights activists while the bill was pending.[9] Bull Connor's excesses in Birmingham, the Kennedy martyrdom, and Johnson's personal legislative skill and determination guided the bill through a congressional maze which was full of traps. On July 2, after the Senate for the first time defeated an anti-civil rights filibuster, the president signed the most significant guarantee of racial equality since Reconstruction. In what was to become characteristic of the Johnson presidency, the signing ceremony was performed as a "spectacular" for the benefit of national television cameras.

2

By any standard, the Johnson start was impressive. It heralded the return of strong presidential reform leadership by a Democratic administration. Also, the success with the Eighty-eighth Congress, still governed by the thin Kennedy majority, was particularly commendable; then, after the 1964 elections, the resolution of the legislative program was rated as an accomplishment on a par with Roosevelt's. Within just two years after Dallas, the Kennedy legislative program had been achieved. All that had been either stalled or about to be salvaged from the conservative bloc had been enacted into law. The list of additional credits contained, among others, tax reduction to stimulate the economy, a revised immigration law that finally discarded the quota system, a program of medical assistance for the elderly, federal aid to all levels of education, money for mass transportation, and, finally, the Voting Rights Act of 1965. The last item became closely identified as a Johnsonian reform, a process that was assisted by the president's vigorous identification with the cause of racial equality in a speech at Howard University.

Moreover, he was able to build upon the Kennedy beginnings in devising strategies to counter the persistent incidence of poverty. Much has been written about how Kennedy had been influenced by Michael Harrington's book, *The Other America*. But Johnson virtually remade the cause into a personal crusade and turned it into what he called a "war against poverty." With remarkable speed, after calling in Ann Arbor, Michigan, for help in "the battle to build the Great Society, to prove that our material progress is the only foundation on which we will build a richer life of mind and spirit," he obtained from Congress the Economic Opportunity Act. In his third State of the Union address, he rejected suggestions that the expanding Southeast Asian war would have to impair ambitious domestic programs and proposed additional reforms. That led Max Ascoli to editorialize in the *Reporter*: "This man is not a visionary or a radical: he is an exuberant middle-of-the-road extremist."[10]

The Ascoli description remained the most perceptive comment about Lyndon Johnson and his presidency. Its nuance differed only slightly from Hugh Sidey's observation that "Lyndon Johnson's Presidency is a very singular Presidency. . . . For Johnson it is singularly a one-man affair."[11] Both saw Johnson as the driving force, as the initiator, as the man who had salvaged the Kennedy impasse and, both conscious and resentful of the aura that surrounded the memory of his predecessor, had driven both himself and subordinates day and night to give the presidency his own peculiar style. His success in those first two years, especially after the thorough defeat of Barry Goldwater in 1964, was enough to give the appearance of a New Deal revival not only in the legislative sense but in reaffirming the Democratic Party as the great agency of reform. Suddenly, it seemed, only a few years after the wilderness period of the Eisenhower years, the resuscitation was so thorough that the most serious fear about the future of the two-party system related not to the viability of disparate, chaotic Democrats struggling to accommodate motley elements under the broad umbrella but to their opponents, the Republicans. Again, for awhile, it had begun to seem that the Democratic Party had become an invincible force, what Johnson liked to call "a party for all Americans," while the GOP was struggling to survive.

One month before the defeat of Goldwater, Senator Willis Robertson wrote ruefully that "the commentator who said that Franklin D. Roosevelt was Johnson's idol of a successful politician was right and that he also was right when he predicted that next year we will have a rebirth under different names of all the Roosevelt 'spend and spend—elect and elect' programs on a grandiose scale that will befit the Johnson 'Great Society' slogan."[12] Robertson had found the campaign painful, one that he had to suffer through quietly. To friends, he confided that not being up for re-election at least obviated having to make a public endorsement for Johnson, a move that would have been consistent with his concepts of loyalty but completely contrary to his convictions. Still, at the same time, as a Virginia conservative welcoming Barry Goldwater's messages, especially in behalf of states' rights and against "big government," Robertson was disturbed to find the Republican challenger campaigning in a manner inimicable to any pretense of making a genuine effort to win. He was distressed when Goldwater indicated his intention of placing former Vice President Nixon in his cabinet, a suggestion that he believed would hurt the ticket not only in Virginia but throughout the entire South. Robertson had heard from California Republican Senator Thomas H. Kuchel that Nixon was despised by the members of his own party in Sacramento; and associating him with Senate rulings to facilitate cloture against filibusters as well as with Eisenhower's use of federal troops and the administration's support of the civil rights acts of 1957 and 1960, he dismissed the vice president as a man who did not warrant confidence.[13]

Other developments contributed to the pessimism about electing Goldwater as the first presidential challenger since the New Deal to wage an out-and-out assault on its basic assumptions. Whatever loss Johnson may have suffered from the sudden but sensational arrest of one of his close aides on a morals charge was salvaged by the news from the Soviet Union about Nikita Khrushchev's fall from power. It was one of those events that provide pre-election assistance to an incumbent by assuming continuity in office as the best means to enter a period of uncertainty. But even more important was Goldwater's own contribution to the creation of an image that he could not be trusted with power, that he was even erratic. Waging the most truculent cold-war campaign of them all, Goldwater talked about carrying the Indo-China war north of the seventeenth-parallel dividing line by bombing North Vietnam and defoliating the jungles. Further, the racial voting balance had been altered by a constitutional amendment abolishing the Virginia poll tax, a development that Robertson speculated could bring as many as 100,000 new voters to the polls; half would be black, he guessed, a number large enough to offset the 46,000 majority that Nixon had received there in 1960.[14]

Robertson's immediate fears were justifiable. Goldwater could do no better than win six states, one of them his native Arizona, and all five others were in the Deep South. Further, the magnitude of the Democratic victory was enough to destroy the possibility of a conservative coalition being able to block the president's Great Society legislation. Not since the Seventy-fifth Congress would a liberal-dominated party have such power on Capitol Hill. Further, in Virginia the result was pretty much as Robertson had anticipated. Johnson carried the state with the help of an estimated 125,000 to 150,000 blacks, at least 95 percent giving him their support. That conclusion, however, tends to ignore the fact that many white Virginians were also swayed by considerations decisive for millions of other Americans, fear that Goldwater would sabotage the social security system and also reduce farm price supports; and, as elsewhere, voters in the Old Dominion perceived Johnson as the peace candidate and regarded Goldwater as potentially indiscriminate with the use of atomic bombs.[15] When the results were tabulated and showed that the president had been re-elected with over 60 percent of the national popular vote, Robertson suggested to Virginius Dabney that the name of the old nineteenth-century Whig Party ought to be revived as a home for conservative southern Democrats and conservative Republicans.[16]

For Johnson, the victory was a great triumph, an enormous source of personal satisfaction for a man still sensitive about many things— sensitive at being chided for having been chosen for the Senate back in 1948 by a niggardly eighty-seven-vote plurality over Coke Stevenson, sensitive about being regarded as a mere accidental caretaker fulfilling a predecessor's administration. So it must have been especially welcome for Lyndon Johnson to have his own new majority stand in such contrast to the Kennedy election. Now he was in full control, with a Congress apparently free to demonstrate Democratic responsiveness to social and economic needs long neglected under the burden of a Republican presidency and the conservative coalition. At last, legislative success was virtually guaranteed. Among the party's liberals, only extreme pessimists could suggest that a New Deal revival was not at hand, especially since the tide of popular sentiment seemed to be running strongly in behalf of equal rights and against the evident repression of racism. Polls confirmed consistent majorities in favor of the key elements of the New Frontier program, especially since Kennedy's martyrdom. All of these things had seemed obvious in 1964 as Barry Goldwater, adhering to his conservative convictions with a vengeance and cheered on by an increasingly vocal right-wing, stubbornly refused to make any of the concessions that were needed to strengthen his position with moderates and liberals.

And still, the thing that was hard to see at the moment, that would eventually become the most salient thing about the Democratic Party for at least another decade, was the shift already taking place toward ideological moderation rather than the formulation of radical or even of ultra-liberal responses to national needs. For all that would later be said about polarization and the absurdity of having prematurely proclaimed the end of ideology, the American majority had not changed that much from its moderate-conservative stance of the 1950s. After a brief fling with politics of compassion, post-New Deal normalcy was on the verge of returning. The elements that led the way were coexistent and defiant of neat enumeration within any particular sequence, but they were all there.

Part of the problem was Johnson's conception of the presidency. The national image of the big Texan as a man of intrigue, of wily political machinations all in behalf of intensely partisan goals was only partly accurate: the view of him as an intense partisan was fallacious. At the start of his administration, of course, such elements were visible. Having taken over suddenly, having vowed continuity, he worked to implement the efforts begun by Kennedy to achieve harmony within the party at all levels, even the wildly fragmented structure that marked such state organizations as in New York, Texas, Pennsylvania, and California. Attempting to patch up differences, whether reconciling reformers or recognizing the need for compromises elsewhere, he appealed with the request to "let us continue."[17] Generally overlooked, however, was that Johnson was not a partisan leader in the traditional sense.

More characteristic of his approach was the conception of Democrats as a "party of all Americans." He referred to the umbrella party as a "great tent" that could accommodate everybody. Having succeeded by his wits through the Byzantine factionalism of Texas—not really a one-party state but actually a jumble of personal organizations loyal to particular fiefdoms—he had not been schooled in the two-party politics that had been in the educational processes of most presidents. For Johnson, power was achieved by gathering crucial elements from each faction, satisfying their interests and catering to their influence, doing whatever was necessary to establish a broad coalition behind his personal leadership, a coalition that would emerge upon the national scene as a consensus. More effective in American politics than dogmatic ideology, it would offer each group what was necessary to win support, whether or not it obviated partisanship. Loyalists would find rather futile any protests that the administration was trucking too much with Republicans. If Johnson could pull under the same tent black and white southerners, businessmen and organized labor, intellectuals and traditionalists, offering to each some role in his conception of what America needed in the mid-sixties, that was the key to effective government. If he could enroll business interests to support the objectives that liberals had been fighting for, by offering them a "piece of the action" in the form of government contracts and other favors, both groups could be satisfied. Organized labor, which had grown increasingly conservative and indistinguishable from the establishment and becoming more distant from their social campaigns of the 1930s and 1940s, was similar to business in its parochial concerns with self-interest. Under

George Meany, there was chafing at the abandonment of efforts to repeal the right-to-work provision of the Taft-Hartley Act, but there was little true cause for discontent. Even the administration's response to the inflationary trend of the mid-sixties by imposing wage guidelines brought sniping but reluctance to bite the hand of the benefactors in Washington substantially. Under Johnson, labor could share with business the steady increase in the gross national product that had followed the slowdown at the start of the decade, and so there were few incentives for disloyalty. Both civil rights leaders and the white students from the North who were going South, particularly during that Freedom Summer of 1964, to register blacks and effectuate the final collapse of official Jim Crow restrictions could hardly find more satisfaction than they obtained from Johnson's administration.

All of this was entirely consistent with Johnson's own very personal conception of the presidency. Rather than the traditional argument about executive versus legislative powers, rather than any such academic constitutional considerations, it was really more of an extension of his own ego, undoubtedly derived in large part from his own considerable insecurities. That was the element that would render so intolerable for him recollections of the glories of Kennedy's thousand days, the portrayals of a Camelot, the sneers from eastern intellectuals at the contrast between the two presidents; they liked neither his accent, clothes, tastes, or style in any category. When he exposed his midriff to show news photographers the scar from a recent gall-bladder operation, he confirmed their suspicions that he was merely gauche, and they delighted at stories that he conferred with aides while seated on the toilet. They were of two different worlds. When he boasted that he had not bothered to read what they had written about him, he was letting them know what he thought of their power. He had used them to demonstrate continuity after Kennedy, had persuaded such luminaries of the intellectual establishment as Schlesinger to stay on for awhile with the new administration; but, in the end, he lost all except those who told him what he wanted to hear, including his fellow Texan, Bill Moyers, who has been described as one of the brightest of the lot. When he appointed Thomas Mann as assistant secretary of state for Latin American affairs, the elevation of an individual who was anathema to some New Frontier liberals was viewed as Johnson's declaration of his own "independence from the Kennedy foreign policy."[18] Later, contradicting his own campaign themes (which were intentionally deceptive) and moving toward Goldwater's prescription for "winning" the war in Vietnam, the strategy was a personal matter. He pored over the maps; he chose the bombing runs and the targets; he decided on the troop allocations as he slowly but steadily escalated the level of American participation in a war that, at the start of his administration, had not yet caught much popular interest. As the protests began to mount, and embarrassing questions were asked, he defied their opposition by suggesting that if a lack of patriotism was not their problem they were at least "nervous Nellies." Beginning with the suspect circumstance by which Congress had been persuaded to approve the Gulf of Tonkin resolution in August of 1964 ("I needed it," he later explained, "because once you send in our boys and there's shootin' and dyin', the support of Congress would close the door to the cowards who would start crying."[19]) and the start of American bombing just a few months after his election as the "peace" candidate, the war was his, just as thoroughly as both the presidency and his conception of the Democratic Party. He felt no need to make concessions to the fact that the most articulate dissent from the Senate was coming not from the opposing conservative Republicans but from the Fulbrights, Morses, Gruenings, and McGoverns within his own party; and, after all, only Democrats could conceivably block his nomination in 1968.

Consistent with his style of leadership, too, was the virtual dismantlement of the party's national committee. Kennedy had drawn complaints about such neglect; functions normally undertaken by the organization, however innocuous, were gradually delegated to the White House staff. The process was actually begun by Kennedy but was converted into policy by Johnson. Finally installed by the president was his chief lieutenant in charge of such decisions, a fellow Texan, Marvin Watson, Jr. Questions involving the allocation of funds for voter-registration programs, patronage, and other matters routinely handled through the machinery of the national committee in concert with the executive department were now entirely absorbed by the administration to serve its own and not partisan purposes. Even fund-raising was centralized under his aegis. Watson, accordingly, became the villain to those who complained that the oval office had been closed to them. At the same time, John Bailey, the national chairman of the party and a holdover from the Kennedy administration, rarely convened the committee despite regulations requiring at least two meetings a year. Actually, Bailey had wanted to resign right after the 1964 elections; but he suited Johnson's purposes, and the president convinced him to stay aboard. The Democratic leader from Connecticut not only represented continuity with the Kennedy era, but he had a more important asset: he was regarded as free from ties with ambitious personalities angling to succeed Johnson in 1972. As Meg Greenfield pointed out in a perceptive piece in the *Reporter*, the sudden multiplication of powerful Democrats in the nation—a direct result of the 1964 elections—had left two-thirds of the cities and thirty-three of the states in their hands; and that was an inflated roster of competitors for higher office.[20] Apprehensions that the party would be in poor shape for the midterm elections of 1966 as a consequence of his policies were shrugged off by the president. Despite the fact that it promised to be a difficult year in any event, particularly after the party's inflated gains two years earlier, Johnson remained confident that, somehow, his role as party leader would be confirmed at the polls. One month before the voting, Washington correspondent David Broder published an article in *The Atlantic* that offered the following explanation:

The decimation of the Democratic Party structure—the abolition of the centralized voter-registration effort that was the keystone of the Kennedy campaign, the 50 percent cutback in manpower at the Democratic National Committee, and the collapse of communications between Washington and state party chairmen—all these things have been described by critics as an expression of the antagonism to party organization that has been growing for eighteen years in Mr. Johnson, ever since he ended the first phase of his political career as a loyal Roosevelt agent within the Democratic Party.[21]

Shortly after the disastrous results of the election had been received, George Meany warned the president that field reports gathered by the AFL-CIO's Committee on Political Education (COPE) had provided evidence that the national committee was in chaotic shape. Success in 1968, he advised, depended on its rehabilitation.[22]

3

Had it been only that that weakened Johnson's position, however, he might have survived. For a time, his consensus was working very well, indeed, with just about the only grumbling coming from the far right and the last-ditch southern segregationists who still felt the obligation to make noises about the president's championing of civil rights legislation. But the forces were already endemic, even as he was basking in the satisfaction of his glorious victory; and they revealed more about the state of American society in the mid-1960s than about the Democratic Party per se. Johnson was not far off the mark, during those early days, when he considered the Democratic tent "a party for all Americans." And the "coming apart," as William O'Neill would characterize the decade, began to take place in the midst of both a rapidly expanding economy, which would feature a record period of continuous growth, and the most advanced legislation since the death of Roosevelt.

The first contradiction, and perhaps the touchstone for much of what followed, was the maturation of the civil rights movement into a full-fledged revolt. For white America, it was particularly shocking. Hadn't the government, albeit after an unconscionably long delay, finally responded to the most impassioned pleas of the established black leaders? Hadn't the bulk of the middle classes sympathized with the Freedom Riders of 1963 and the aspirations of those young people and clergymen who went south during that Freedom Summer of 1964? Further, there could hardly be much less than condemnation for the murderers of three young civil rights workers near Philadelphia, Mississippi. The following year, Dr. King's march to Selma, Alabama, a dramatic defiance of the vestiges of segregation, received additional sympathy thanks to the incredibly shortsighted intransigence of Sheriff Jim Clark, who, playing the role that Bull Connor had performed two years earlier, undoubtedly helped to condition both the Congress and the public to accept without much resistance the significant Voting Rights Act of 1965. Just as faith in the ability of a democratic society to respond to its obvious inequities seemed to be reaching its height, however, different sounds were coming from new black leadership, both North and South.

Suddenly, the momentum was beginning to pass out of the hands of established forces; a new consciousness, spurred perhaps by the optimism that time and power was on their side—or, simply, by the rising expectations—was bringing to the forefront charismatic young people such as Stokely Carmichael. Beginning with demonstrations in Mississippi, and threatening to wrest the reins from King's hands, was Carmichael's call for "black power." Few could define exactly what it meant; explanations were numerous, some meant to antagonize, or perhaps to goad, middle-class whites, some designed to reassure. But the slogan became the theme of the new consciousness.

More militant, more threatening to the white majority, was the black nationalist leader Malcolm X who, by the time of his assassination in 1965, had become the dominant figure among the younger generation of Negro activists. Most upsetting, perhaps, was the basic area of agreement between Carmichael and Malcolm X. Both rejected King's vision of turning the other cheek and working within the system as determined by white society. They, and such angry young men as John Lewis and Robert Moses of SNCC, seemed to be not only impatient at precisely the moment when most Americans considered progressive changes finally at hand, but were also contemptuous of the virtues of racial integration as their solution. Thus they began to assail the very aspiration that had been the fighting faith of liberals for the past two decades. No longer willing to accept progress on "Whitey's" terms, they provoked increasing complaints about "reverse racism." By 1967, a Richmond, Virginia, attorney and future associate justice of the United States Supreme Court, Lewis F. Powell, expressed a position that was consistent with the new national mood. Writing to the editor of the Richmond *Afro-American*, he warned, "If civil disobedience is pressed, the ultimate results will either be anarchy or a form of repressive reaction which may be totalitarian in its consequences. In either event, minority groups and races will be those who suffer the most."[23]

The so-called white backlash that Powell was suggesting had become a mature force on the American political scene, with enormous implications for the Democratic party. During the first part of the decade of the 1960s, especially until 1964, there was every indication that developments were bound to be favorable. In large areas of the South, before the Voting Rights Act of 1965, registration of blacks climbed sharply, zooming upward by some 500,000 during those four years alone, by far the greatest gain than at any time since the death of the white primary.[24] Not only in Virginia did the new vote make a difference for Johnson, but it appeared to have been a crucial factor in such other states as Florida, Tennessee, and Arkansas. Estimates of the percentage of eligible blacks registered to vote, according to figures supplied by the Southern Regional Council, went from 28 percent in 1960 to over 43 percent four years later.[25] The combined efforts of a sympathetic Justice Department, the Voter Education Project of the Southern Regional Council, the grass-roots efforts by local black activists aided by northern civil rights workers, and the Taconic Foundation, working with the legislation already enacted, succeeded in luring to the polls an electorate that was over-

whelmingly Democratic. Once aided by the 1965 law, the process
began to accelerate, so that by 1966 over half of all southern blacks
were eligible to vote. But the change itself contained ingredients
that brought frustration and reaction.

One state where progress had been retarded before 1964 was Mississippi. By 1972, however, some 270,000 were finally registered.
Even that improvement still represented just 59 percent of the black
population. But in the year of Johnson's victory, when the state went
for Goldwater, the total qualified Negro electorate stood at only
28,500.[26] Not surprisingly, it was there, too, where violence had
been commonplace, including against those attempting to exercise
simple rights of citizenship. In addition to occasional murders, such
as the deaths of Andrew Goodman, Michael Schwerner, and James
Chaney, numerous other accounts of brutality became known to the
public. Perhaps the most dramatic and moving was the testimony of
Fannie Lou Hamer of Ruleville. "They beat me and they beat me
with the long flat blackjack," she told the members of the Democratic Party's Credentials Committee before the opening of the 1964
nominating convention. "I screamed to God in pain. My dress
worked itself up. I tried to pull it down. They beat my arms until I
had no feeling in them. After a while the first man beating my arm
grew numb from tiredness. The other man, who was holding me, was
given the blackjack. Then he began beating me," she added, until
her sobs kept her from continuing.[27]

With only 7 percent of them eligible to vote, local blacks worked
with the active assistance of New York militant liberal Allard Lowenstein and organized a revolt that gave the White House an un-
expected dilemma. Thus was born the Mississippi Freedom
Democratic Party (MFDP), which suddenly came into national
prominence during the 1964 convention at Atlantic City. It conceived of itself as part moral crusade and part political force. Its basic
assumption was that the state's official Democratic Party was not a
loyal branch of the national organization; Mississippians who
wanted to support the kind of liberal programs that had been endorsed at the Los Angeles convention in 1960 and promulgated by
the Kennedy and Johnson administrations, whether they were black
or white, had no place to go. As they stated when applying for formal recognition as the official Democratic Party of Mississippi, "The
group which calls itself the Mississippi Democratic Party has for-
feited any claim it might make to such a position by its consistent
discrimination against Negro citizens and by its repeated and ex-

plicit disavowals of any connection with the National Democratic Party."[28] Not only had the official group refused to take the loyalty oaths promising to support the national candidates, but Mississippians were represented in the electoral college in 1960 by nothing better than an unpledged slate, a maneuver designed to defeat the party's presidential and vice presidential candidates. Nor, the MFDP charged, was there any indication for forthcoming support for the 1964 platform. More specifically, the resolution adopted by the regulars in Jackson on June 30, 1960, said not one word about loyalty to the national party and enumerated its continuing devotion to racial segregation of every aspect of society "and in all spheres of activity where experience has shown that it is for the best interest of both races that such separation be observed," a statement that, in effect, ignored the legality of the Supreme Court.[29] Further, if the state was a closed society, as Professor James Silver had charged in a book that was cited by the MFDP people, so was the local Democratic Party. In its challenge, the new group leveled the following accusation:

The Mississippi Democratic Party controls the legislative, executive and judicial branches of the government of the State. All 49 senators, and all but one of 122 representatives are Democrats. Repeatedly, the State legislature has passed laws and established regulations designed to discriminate against prospective Negro voters. The 1963 gubernatorial campaign was largely directed towards restricting the Negro vote. The state convention is being held in the Jackson Municipal Auditorium and the Heidelburg Hotel, both of which are segregated. In its devotion to racism and suppression and oppression of minority expression, the Mississippi Democratic Party prevents Negro Democrats and white persons who disagree with the party's racist stance from participating in party programs and decisions.[30]

The MFDP adopted a platform that was, additionally, a robust endorsement of racial equality as the first step "in solving the basic problems of poverty, disease and illiteracy confronting American society," and included an eleven-point resolution that constituted vigorous support of the domestic principles of the Kennedy and Johnson administrations. Further, they selected four candidates to oppose Senator John Stennis and Congressmen Jamie L. Whitten, William M. Colmer, and John Bell Williams. Thus, they prepared to wage a fight at Atlantic City by making their case, through a combination of moral and legal grounds, for the replacement of the party regulars by MFDP delegates.

Essentially, of course, the MFDP was idealistic, sectarian, reformist, and devoted to the singleminded purpose of forcing open the
state's closed political society to the previously disfranchised. Its
prime movers had those goals clearly in mind. Lowenstein, who was
only thirty-four in 1963, had already served on the staffs of Senator
Frank Graham of North Carolina and Hubert Humphrey. A lawyer
by profession, he also had that prime asset of reformers, independent
means, an advantage that he used energetically to promote liberal
causes. Intellectual, aggressive, and issue-oriented, and supporting
positions that sacrificed radical solutions for results, he was destined
to become one of those makers of history far better appreciated by
the historians than by the public. It was Lowenstein who went to
Mississippi in 1963 to assist with voter registration and who later
worked to organize the Freedom Summer. Working with members
of SNCC, he helped to originate a plan to educate potential blacks
in Mississippi as voters by staging a mock election in November of
1963 behind the "gubernatorial" candidacy of a Negro druggist, Dr.
Aaron Henry, a project that registered 83,000 blacks as an example
of the electorate that had been systematically excluded from the
state's political process. Another white attorney, Joe Rauh, Jr., better known for his service with the Americans for Democratic Action,
became the MFDP's lawyer. Rauh, an older liberal, was slightly to
Lowenstein's right but hardly less involved with the issues. The
heart of the new party, however, consisted of such people as Henry,
Fannie Lou Hamer, Edwin King, and Robert Moses, individuals
with bitter experiences with being black in Mississippi.

At a meeting in Jackson on April 26, 1964, the MFDP was formally established in the presence of about three hundred delegates,
and plans were made to undertake three major efforts: freedom registration, the promotion of Freedom candidates, and the challenge to
the regulars at Atlantic City. It promptly won endorsement from the
ADA, which called on the Democratic National Committee to seat
the "integrated Freedom Democratic Party delegation" and to
"refuse to seat the traditional segregated Democratic Party delegates from the state," as well as from Michigan's Democrats. Adding
to their prestige came support from Dr. King, who explained why
blacks should join the party. With the approach of the convention
scheduled for the last week of August, the MFDP seemed to be
enjoying considerable support. After all, the seating of rival Texas
delegates in 1944, splitting that state's vote, had provided an ample
precedent, and the New York *Times* ran an editorial on August 19

that suggested a similar solution to the new challenge.[31] As with all seating challenges, the issue was debated before the Credentials Committee before the convention met.

For the Johnson administration, it was a dilemma. Rauh appealed to the president to take a position of "benevolent neutrality," which, in effect, meant not supporting the Mississippi regulars; but the coming Goldwater campaign had already guaranteed that the administration would have its hands full trying to win the South as it was. Any thought that the matter could be ignored very easily was dispelled when millions of Americans saw and heard Mrs. Hamer's moving testimony. Her words eloquently drove home the reality of what life in America was actually like for some unfortunates. Hubert Humphrey, dispatched by the president to work out a satisfactory solution at Atlantic City, possibly to persuade the regulars to avoid a floor fight by taking a loyalty oath, came up with a three-point plan. It provided for seating the regulars upon signing such a pledge and for seating the MFDP without voting rights as "honored guests" of the convention. A further point was a promise that all future conventions would be open to blacks. Aaron Henry, however, called it a "back-of-the-bus compromise" and Martin Luther King said that Negroes would "go fishing election day" if the party were not seated.[32]

More congenial to the rebels was a plan advanced by a member of the committee, Congresswoman Edith Green, which called for both groups to take the loyalty oath and for the state's delegate vote to be divided proportionately. But the administration turned that down because it would give the MFDP the appearance of legal status. Then came a new plan from the White House, one containing five points: (1) the seating of any member of the regular delegation who took the loyalty oath; (2) the Freedom Party would be welcomed as honored guests of the convention; (3) Aaron Henry and Edwin King, chairman of the delegation and national committeeman of the Freedom Party, respectively, would be given delegate status in a special category of "delegates at large"; (4) the Democratic National Committee would obligate states by 1968 to select and certify delegates through a process without regard to race, creed, or color, or national origins; and (5) the chairman of the DNC would establish a special committee to aid the states in meeting standards set for the 1968 convention and a report would be made to the national committee for use by the next convention. Both the Credentials Committee and the full assemblage at Atlantic City then ratified the administration plan, thereby sparing Johnson the embarrassment of a floor fight.

Less easy to placate, however, were the determined protagonists. On the morning of August 25, the MFDP leaders gathered at the Union Baptist Temple Church to consider the compromise. The conflict was sharp. Established civil rights leaders such as Dr. King, attorney Rauh, Bayard Rustin, and James Farmer were treated with scorn for advocating its acceptance, almost as though, according to the most thorough student of the party, "they were arch-enemies of the Freedom Democrats." They were also prevented from addressing the grass-roots delegation before a decision could be made. Blocking them and holding out for total rejection were the militants led by Robert Moses, John Lewis, and James Forman, of SNCC and COFO (Council of Federated Organizations, an umbrella arm of civil rights groups in Mississippi), individuals who, as Leslie Burl McLemore has pointed out, "firmly believed that one should not compromise his principles. For them, it was a moral issue which took precedence over politics."[33] At the same time, the regulars were unwilling to surrender their own concepts of tradition, law, and morality. Upon hearing that the convention had adopted the five-point plan, most of them staged a new walkout, leaving only four members of the sixty-eight delegates and alternates left to take the loyalty oath and receive seating credentials. Finally, the Johnson administration concluded matters by selecting Aaron Henry and Edwin King as the two delegates at large, an appointment the two men accepted.

That seemed to close the affair, at least for the moment; but the MFDP had made a mark in several ways. Dramatizing their grievances, they had won recognition and acceptance of the need for reform in the selection of delegates for future Democratic conventions so that the party's selection process itself would be more consistent with the high principles professed by its most recent convention platforms. The subsequent appointment of a special commission under Governor Richard Hughes of New Jersey was designed to implement that goal by 1968. Also, by providing a base for black activism in Mississippi, they became the catalysts of that state's new born political competition. Thus, in Mississippi, it was after 1964 and not before, as elsewhere, that there was a real spurt of black voter participation. Registration rose sevenfold by 1967 to a new high of 190,000 and climbed another eighty thousand during the next five years.[34] It was also the MFDP that took the initiative, in early 1965, of challenging the seating of the five elected representatives from the state on the grounds that they had been chosen by voting carried out in defiance of the 1957 Civil Rights Act and of demanding that the seats be given, instead, to the winners of their own mock election held in November. Dropping that argument, however, in the face of Joe Rauh's advice that it was both of dubious legality and could lead to political chaos throughout the country if mock election groups were permitted to prevail, they pressed to have the results of the election vacated. But the House of Representatives, in a 276 to 148 test vote on January 4, 1965, turned back the second challenge, leaving behind, if not the highly publicized and televised drama of the Atlantic City confrontation, new proof that "Uncle Tom" was dead.

The case of the MFDP was, in the long run, important perhaps because it offered the most dramatic evidence of the emerging black spirit in the South, the very factor that set off a new chain of reactions, the inevitable response that, combined with other simultaneous events, soon sacrificed the politics of the 1960s and the fortunes of the national Democratic Party to the workings of the white backlash. There was the inevitable attempt to brand the new militants as communists. Thus, months after the congressional challenge had been resolved, Representative Colmer sent Speaker McCormack a "Fact Sheet on the Mississippi 'Contest' " that asserted, among other things, that the "revolutionary character of the Mississippi Freedom Democratic Party and many of its leaders has been pointed out by national columnists Evans and Novak, *Newsweek*, and others, and has not been denied. Some of its leaders quote Marx, some Mao, some Castro, some the late French Algerian author and intellectual Albert Camus, some author James Baldwin, whom *The Minority of One*—hardly a conservative or segregationist publication—called 'an unhappy Negro nancy.' Some by act, appearance and word show themselves to be simply anarchists."[35]

Further, it served to spur a force that was already becoming evident in the South. With its traditional lack of political competition, in addition to the legal obstacles for democratic participation by both races, the region's voter turnouts had, of course, been the lowest in the nation. Even before the dramatic assertions—and threats to the status quo—that were raised by the MFDP, there were signs of a countervailing force, one that was a reassertion of the response to the first challenge to political monopoly that had come in the 1940s. Senator Robertson advised Senator Spessard L. Holland of Florida in April of 1964 that his best strategy for running for re-election was to "forget about issues" but to "urge all of your leaders throughout the State to impress upon every White registered voter that next November is the time when every White voter in Florida should go to the polls and be counted."[36] With blacks threatening to partici-pate in the local Democratic Party structure, there were fears that its political machinery would slip out of the hands of the traditional leaders. An investment counsel of Charlottesville, Virginia, writing to Harry Byrd, expressed concern about the drift of the national Democratic Party which, he said, can now be called a Socialist-Labor Party and warned the senator that "conservative Democrats will not be able to retain control of the Party in Virginia when you, Senator Robertson, Judge Smith and a few others retire."[37]

On the defensive, then, before the new competition, it was white voting that began to rise. In Mississippi, where only 41 percent of whites had been registered in 1960, that figure jumped to 70 per-cent by 1970, an obvious response to the movement for black power. In Georgia, where Negro political expansion had been pronounced in the two years before the 1964 election, the greatest growth in white registration became a parallel force, and three times more whites than blacks were added to the rolls. A similar development in South Carolina provided further evidence of the effect of increased political competition.[38]

Increasingly, blacks, even the members of the MFDP angry at what they considered as intransigence on the part of those who had refused to compromise at Atlantic City and holding out little hope for success of an all-black MFDP versus on all-white regular state-wide organization, preferred to work within the official party to rebuild it along biracial lines. Joining with the prestigious Green-ville newspaperman, Hodding Carter II, and drawing other moder-ate support from organized labor and the NAACP, they formed, first, what they called the Mississippi Democratic Conference; when that ephemeral group failed to gain recognition from the national party, it was replaced by the Young Democratic Clubs of Missis-sippi, which operated under the same sponsorship and goals.[39] Tak-ing over the voter registration drive, and aiming toward participation in the 1968 convention, by the following year the integrated group had established itself as a substantial enough force to command re-spect, a direct consequence of their increased numbers. In March of 1966, Senator Robert Kennedy, encouraging the organization, criti-cized the state's traditional segregationist leadership in a speech at the University of Mississippi. Senator Walter Mondale of Minnesota, who had been chairman of the Credentials Committee in 1964 and had helped to write and win approval of the rule against segregated future conventions, addressed the Young Democrats at Biloxi and promised that there would be empty seats at the next convention if southern political leaders attempted to exclude Negroes.[40]

Whatever difficulties were experienced trying to achieve political integration in Mississippi and other states, and there were many, were counterbalanced by the increasing receptivity of old-line Democrats to the Republican Party. Thus, in 1964, the conservative Democratic Fourth District of Southside Virginia—the heart of the Old Dominion's former slave-holding region, where blacks had outnumbered whites—known as an area of tobacco farming and loyalty to the Democratic Party, succumbed to backlash politics and voted for the Republican presidential candidate.[41] While less dramatic elsewhere, it was nevertheless a pattern that held throughout the South, where all classes of the population drifted toward Goldwater, a candidate who seemed to embody the fighting values of old Dixie.[42] With voters in the Old Confederacy finding their way to the Republican column, it was also increasingly clear that the white majority, which had hitherto not exerted its full power at the polls but had plenty of numbers to spare, had more than enough strength to counter "black radicalism."

4

At precisely the same time, the black explosion spread to the North, not only in the form of school desegregation, which often involved de facto separatism through blatantly gerrymandered educational districts, but as outbursts of physical violence in the ghettos. An expression of economic and social frustration that came at the moment of fulfillment of liberal programs for advancement, they spilled over into arson and looting, destructive of their own blighted communities and frequently aimed at the local merchants and businesses regarded as exploitative. They erupted without any evidence of concerted planning, usually mushrooming out of seemingly innocuous incidents, and turned into veritable fire-storms, first beginning in Harlem during July of 1964 and spreading throughout the country. The greatest upheavals, the ones that provided home TV viewers with scenes of burning districts, heavily armed national guardsmen with military paraphernalia, occurred in the Watts section of Los Angeles, Chicago, and Detroit. But even such smaller communities as Plainfield, New Jersey, were not spared. Other urban centers were left with burnt-out districts, including Washington, D.C. The so-called "long hot summers" ran their course through 1967, when such other cities as Nashville, Toledo, Milwaukee, and Grand Rapids were also hit, and began to subside in 1968, becoming most evident that year after the murder of Martin Luther King in Memphis during early April.

The shock to white-middle-class America was difficult to measure with any kind of precision. It became abundantly clear that proximity to the danger zones had little relevance to the degree of fear and resentment, or simple hatred, that was unleashed. Old stereotypes were re-evoked. Politicians such as Governor George Wallace of Alabama were suddenly seen as having the appropriate solutions. Suddenly vindicated were those who believed all along that the Negroes were inherently incapable of conformity with middle-class standards, that they were hardly removed from the jungle. It was easier to counter with repression than to accept the arguments of those who held that the solution was to increase rather than reduce social programs.

Not surprisingly, then, the politics of the so-called white backlash began to enter the vocabulary, completely transcending partisan lines. President Johnson himself, after having commissioned a study of the conditions behind the urban upheavals, received the findings of the committee that had served under Governor Otto Kerner of Illinois in silence. The president even failed to take note of its conclusion that "Our nation is moving toward two societies, one black, one white—separate and unequal."

A specific victim of the backlash was the poverty program itself. Insufficiently funded at the outset, with the president having requested far less than its administrators had advised and with Congress granting even less, and with the Economic Opportunity Act having called for the "maximum feasible participation" of the poor —a phrase never clarified with much success—from the start it was more a demonstration of willingness to act than a realistic assault upon the problem. Local politicians, such as Mayor William F. Walsh of Syracuse, New York, profited from the backlash issue that was created by community-action programs on behalf of the poor. Other mayors complained that federal money was undermining their control, even as they worked to manipulate the program for their own political purposes, especially patronage, while shunting aside the intended beneficiaries of economic rehabilitation. The mayor of San Francisco complained that the Office of Economic Opportunity, which was directing the war on poverty, was "undermining the integrity of local government" by organizing the poor into militant groups and insisted that "elected city officials must retain control." Almost adopted by the Conference of Mayors in June 1965 was a resolution put forth by Mayor Sam Yorty of Los Angeles that charged Sargent Shriver, the program's director, with "fostering class struggle."[43] In early 1967, economist Robert Lekachman published an article that noted that "in an era of backlash, the War on Poverty looks suspiciously like a Negro-aid program, and is therefore ripe for destruction."[44] On Capitol Hill, too, the reaction had begun to set in, with some Republicans who had opposed the program from the outset, such as New York Congressman Charles Goodell, suddenly quick to exploit the obstacles that had been placed before it by urban politicians, who were mostly Democrats.[45] It was becoming clear, too, that congressional restrictions were in order, particularly as questionable handling of the Head Start Program, an experiment in early education for ghetto children, won wide publicity. The war on poverty, having been waged by enlisting business support, which included a 11.5-million-dollar contract with the Federal Electric Corporation to operate a job training center at Camp Kilmer, New Jersey, and a 13.4-million-dollar contract to Litton Industries, Inc., to operate a similar installation in California, was suddenly being devoured not only by local political reactions but by the growing problem of inflation and the racial backlash.[46]

President Johnson's attempt at personal government was beginning to fall apart. In the congressional elections of 1966, at least forty-five members of the House who had supported the poverty program lost their seats, an emphatic message to the survivors.[47] North as well as South, new political names, individuals less marked by partisanship than by the stridence of their responses to interracial conditions, began to enter the public consciousness: Lester Maddox, Rosemary Gunning, Louise Day Hicks, Ronald Reagan. Governor Nelson Rockefeller, running for a third term in New York, switched the tone of his campaign in its last three weeks to concentrate almost entirely on the issue of crime in the streets. In New York City, the concept of a civilian-controlled police review board, although endorsed by every single name politician from both major parties, went down to a disastrous two-to-one defeat. In Congress, after successful experiences for the major pieces of legislation designed to ameliorate the impact of racial discrimination, the Civil Rights Bill of 1966 was defeated without much difficulty. It had been designed for open housing and the protection of civil rights workers.

At the same time, contradicting his campaign pledges of 1964, Johnson was escalating the war in Southeast Asia. American bombing missions, moving north of the seventeenth parallel starting in early 1965, marked a new phase in the conflict, a commitment of national dedication rather than the more subtle, although pernicious, type of intervention that had existed during the Kennedy years. Despite the president's repeated insistence that the effort would not diminish the Great Society at home, that Americans could have both "butter and guns," the vast sums of money regarded as necessary to spare the administration from having to preside over still another communist gain in Asia, inevitably began to disrupt the domestic economy. Without the imposition of any kind of controls, even the mild regulations that the Truman administration had concocted during the Korean War, the inflationary trend became obvious. The coincidence of rising costs, disenchanting both business and labor, plus the white backlash all combined as a reaction against both the Great Society's assumptions and the president's leadership. Having, in effect, denied a role as a partisan political leader, he would soon find himself, additionally, coming under greater attack from Democrats than from Republicans.

Starting, most notably, with the "teach-in" at Ann Arbor, Michigan, in 1965, the energies of both students and academicians that had been exerted behind the civil rights movement were turned against the war and the president. With leadership provided on a growing number of campuses by the Students for a Democratic Society and with antiestablishment exposés gaining circulation through the pages of such new publications of the left as the New York *Review of Books* and *Ramparts*, there was a sharp reaction against both the Democratic Party and the assumptions of centrist liberalism. Less with regret than with satisfaction, two radical scholars subtitled their 1967 anthology of papers pertaining to the Great Society with the proclamation, "The Failure of American Liberalism."[48]

For Johnson, it was the broad consensus that was beginning to crumble while the core was still loyal but increasingly restless. Business, brought together by a Democratic administration more successfully than at any time since the New Deal, was becoming disturbed over both inflation and domestic spending. Labor was annoyed by the president's wage guidelines but, nevertheless, tended to vent its anger more at the new radicalism while workers, increasingly hostile to the black militancy and unable to afford the luxury of fleeing to the suburbs, understood what an ethnic politician in New York City meant when he castigated "limousine liberals." Jews, too, until then the white group most actively sympathetic with civil rights goals, became frightened by the anti-Semitic comments from some black extremists. With the moderately conservative middle classes becoming more impatient with reform, some saw a repetition of the reaction that had led to the end of the first Era of Reconstruction after the Civil War.[49]

The elections of November 1966 confirmed the pattern, not one of rightist reaction but of a return to centrist conservatism. With the decline of Johnson's popularity and the onset of inflation, losses in a midterm test were inevitable; two years after the abnormal gains that resulted from the Goldwater campaign, they were even more unavoidable. Accordingly, the GOP gained forty-seven seats in the House, three in the Senate, and picked up eight governorships, which dramatically shifted the balance in the state houses from a 33 to 17 Democratic majority to an even 25 to 25 division. Still, the Republican comeback was, for the most part, achieved while candidates rejected the more extreme Goldwater appeal of 1964 and competed for the allegiance of the moderate center. In California, former movie star Ronald Reagan felt the need to trim his strongly conservative image while winning election as California's chief executive by a plurality that approached one million votes. In Illinois, Paul Douglas, who had long been identified with the civil rights movement, was unseated in a senatorial campaign that, according to one careful observer, was "determined by a white rebellion against the drive for open occupancy in housing."[50] But he was defeated by a business executive who was immediately perceived as a moderately liberal Republican, Charles H. Percy. Southern voters, meanwhile, gave some shocks to the more liberal forces by selecting a primitive segregationist, Lester Maddox, as Georgia's governor over Ellis Arnell, while Alabamans ratified a caretaker administration for Lurleen Wallace since her husband was not permitted to succeed himself. In Florida, after Robert King High had won the Democratic gubernatorial primary with liberal support, he was defeated in November by a conservative Republican, Claude R. Kirk, Jr. Still, the southern pattern did not indicate a uniformly rightward shift.

The power of the black vote was clearly vital in preserving a considerable degree of moderation to the electoral changes, both as a result of the primary fights earlier in the year and in November. In the states of the Old Confederacy, it was a significant force in several contests; further, whereas only eleven Negroes had been seated in southern legislatures two years earlier, that figure rose to twenty. Even more symptomatic of change was the tone of campaigning as traditionally blatant racists responded to the prudent need to mute their comments about blacks.

In Virginia, as part of the heavily urbanized tidewater area around Norfolk and Newport News, Negroes contributed to the demise of the Byrd machine, the old symbol of resistance to liberal democracy. Harry Byrd himself had retired in 1965, whereupon outgoing Governor Albertis S. Harrison appointed Harry Byrd, Jr., as his successor. But the heir to the dynasty found himself having to battle for his own election as an outpouring of blacks, voting as a bloc, held his victory to a hair-line 50.9 to 49.1 percent margin. Byrd's challenger, Armistead L. Boothe, had long since been associated with the "Young Turk" challenge to the old order. The most emphatic change, however, occurred with the primary election defeats of both Howard Smith and Senator A. Willis Robertson, just about destroying what was left of the forces that had controlled Virginia for so many decades and altering the composition of the state's Democratic Party. They were defeated by the elements that had almost deprived the younger Byrd of his seat: a heavy concentration of black votes, some 90 percent going to Robertson's opponent; the turnout of a well-educated and increasingly numerous middle class that lived in the counties contiguous to the District of Columbia; and, most emphatically, the character of the new urban Democratic vote that had been growing in Virginia for two decades in the populous region that stretched from the Potomac to the tidewater cities. A further modification of the electorate was the movement of conservative white Democrats that November behind the candidacies of such Republicans as William L. Scott, who then managed to defeat the liberal who had unseated Smith.[51] Mills Godwin, who was elected as governor in 1966, would later regain his office as a Republican, and the younger Byrd would call himself an Independent.

The extremes on either end were clearly defecting from both Johnson and the Democrats. Harvard student Doris Kearns and Sanford Levinson contributed an article to *The New Republic* pointing out that the president could be removed by the formation of a third party that could displace the normal Democratic vote and effectuate the election of an "acceptable" Republican.[52] In the late summer of

1967, Joe Rauh circulated a memorandum among his ADA friends that insisted that "no responsible Democrat will associate himself with an effort to unseat the incumbent President." Less than three months later, Rauh nevertheless enlisted behind the insurgent candidacy of Eugene McCarthy.[53] Max Ascoli, loyally standing by Johnson's conduct of the war in Southeast Asia, even while his magazine was being submerged in the process, asked with bewilderment about the president, "What has he done to make himself the object of such revulsion?"[54]

CHAPTER XII

The "New Politics"

1

Rarely had a presidential speech taken the nation so much by surprise and, at the same time, come as such a fitting denouement. Indeed, it does not take much exaggeration to consider the night of March 31, 1968, as a landmark for the post-New Deal Democratic Party, as the moment when the old coalition finally yielded to the new fragmentation, when the old politics gave way to the new. For it was on that night that Lyndon Johnson, catching practically everyone in his national television audience unaware of what was coming, concluded his prepared speech with the following announcement: "Accordingly, I shall not seek and I will not accept the nomination of my party for another term as your President." Finally, after a quarter of a century, the Democratic Party was left to confront the reality that had been building ever since Roosevelt's death, the failure of the realignment to survive in any permanent, meaningful sense.

There is no reason to doubt the considerable evidence that Johnson had been contemplating retirement for a long time, that the building opposition had not been crucial to his decision. Still, with an individual as particularly volatile as the president, and one as fond of crossing up speculation, no move could possibly be regarded as sealed until actually made. His options were open until the end; and there were those who insisted that they were not actually foreclosed even on that night. Speculation about a last-minute change of mind continued until virtually the eve of the Humphrey nomination in Chicago that following August. Granting that the move had been contemplated for a long time, as Johnson himself insisted, it was a product of the national climate that March 1968.

A series of events that came to a head that month had apparently brought the inevitable result. General William C. Westmoreland's call for a major boost of the American military force in South Vietnam had run into firm opposition within the administration itself. Once lonely critics of military escalation who were close to Johnson had found themselves joined by a rapid succession of formidable figures, including Clark Clifford, Robert McNamara, McGeorge Bundy, and Johnson's long-time confidant and personal adviser, Jim Rowe. Dean Acheson and General Omar Bradley, also consulted, seconded the view, now that the course of the war was disastrous. So, through both memoranda and personal advisories, the mounting failure in Southeast Asia had been put to the president quite plainly: the bombing was futile, even counterproductive; to send in 206,000 additional Americans, as General Westmoreland had requested, was both politically and militarily inadvisable.

Further, the mounting cries for Johnson's head could hardly be dismissed as limited to the kooky, bearded, affluent students who delighted in playing poor and in staging rebellions in the streets and on the campuses. Sacrificing both hair and counterculture life-styles, they had poured into New Hampshire as part of the enormous "children's crusade" behind Senator Eugene McCarthy's maverick campaign for the presidency. Their mood was perhaps best illustrated by a note that David Halberstam found on a bulletin board in McCarthy headquarters that read: "Over 40 percent we go onto Wisconsin; 30 percent back to school; 20 percent we burn our draft cards; 10 percent we leave the country."[1]

While their candidate did not actually win, the results were interpreted as so triumphant for the poet-politician from Minnesota that perhaps few Americans realized that New Hampshire, hawkish, blue-collar, and Catholic—especially in the working-class districts of Manchester, where most of the state's Democrats were concentrated—had actually written in more votes for the president. Yet the fact remained that a relatively obscure senator, one whose most notable act had been his Stevenson nomination speech, had been able to draw 42.2 percent of the vote to the 49.4 percent for the man who was, after all, the president of the United States. In a way even more surprising, and revealing, were the additional 5,500 votes that McCarthy received that day in New Hampshire's *Republican* primary. As though that event were not sufficiently traumatic for the viability of the Democratic Party, it was followed almost immediately afterward by one of the most unfortunately ill-timed and clumsy moves in American political history, the announcement by Senator Robert F. Kennedy of New York that he, too, was entering the presidential

competition. Having determined well in advance of the New Hampshire voting that he would finally make the move, Bobby decided
that he could wait no longer, could not waste any more time than he
already had, and would simply endure the temporary criticism that
he was ruthlessly exploiting the McCarthy triumph.

The New Republic, more concerned with dumping Johnson than
with Kennedy's ethics, ran an editorial called "Welcome Aboard,
Bobby," and declared that "Many Democratic politicians who have
squirmed uncomfortably but kept silent, disliking Johnson and hat-
ing his policies in Vietnam but going along nevertheless, worried
lest a word against the President be used against them in their own
campaigns, may now speak their true thoughts. . . . Lyndon Johnson,
along with his miserable war in Asia, has nowhere to go but down."[2]
At about the same time, the Gallup organization was discovering
that popular approval of the White House leadership had dropped
to 36 percent, a figure veering uncomfortably close to the level of
another Democratic president sixteen years earlier. And, as with
Harry Truman, Lyndon Johnson had recognized the inevitable.
Both men would swear that their departures had been pre-planned.

2

The act effectively confirmed suspicions that there would hardly
be said to be such an organization as a national Democratic Party. Of
course, there was still a structure, a Democratic National Committee
composed of the men and women representing the partisan interest
in each of the states and territories. There were also the numerous
local leaders and officeholders, the state, county and city officials who
owed their jobs, affiliations, and influence to the national organization. Many of them, even if personally disaffected by the president's
military policy, would not for a moment consider rupturing their
quid pro quo relationships with the White House. That was a lesson
learned by Kennedy very early in his campaign. From California's
Central Valley, where he was traveling with the senator, journalist
Jimmy Breslin filed the following dialogue:

"What about Daley?" somebody said. Richard J. Daley, the mayor of Chicago and one of the few big city bosses left in the country. [sic]
   "He's been very nice to me personally," Kennedy said. "And he doesn't
like the war. You see, there are so many dead starting to come back, it
bothers him."

"Well then you should be all right with Daley," somebody said.

"It's very hard for him," Kennedy said. "He has been a politician for a long time. And party allegiances mean so much to him. It's a wrenching thing for him. We'll have to win primaries to show the pols."

"If you get Daley, where do you stand?" he was asked.

"Daley means the ball game," Kennedy said.[3]

And Kennedy may have been right. Daley was, after all, one of the most powerful Democrats in the country, perhaps the most significant holder of a bloc of delegates. In an era when national Democratic administrations had virtually permitted the party's organization to atrophy, the mayor ruled the country's most efficiently run political machine and had almost complete control over which Democrat would be supported by Illinois. In contemplating Daley's support, Kennedy undoubtedly also recalled how the strong man of Chicago had aided his brother. But the situation was different in 1968; the younger Kennedy, instead of trying to wrest the White House from a Republican, was going after an incumbent, a president with whom the mayor had established particularly close ties. Just how significantly Daley's private reservations about the war figured in comparison with the political requirements of the moment were revealed after the young senator telephoned him in an effort to get his support.

Daley's response was emphatic. In a press conference called soon afterward, he revealed Kennedy's overture and then added, "I said I would support the President of the United States if he is a candidate for re-election. I hope he is." While that was a full two weeks before Johnson's renunciation of another campaign, Daley nevertheless left no doubt that he was committed to the administration or its chosen heir. He masked his own feelings about the war and praised the president's efforts to find a "peaceable way to resolve the Vietnam situation." He also revealed that his requirement of each delegate to be chosen from Illinois included a pledge of support for the administration's Indo-China policy, a stipulation that prevented Illinois State Treasurer Adlai E. Stevenson III from joining Daley's slate.[4]

The schism also extended through the ranks of the nonprofessional supporters of the party, especially organized labor. David Dubinsky, then seventy-five years old and president emeritus of the International Ladies Garment Workers Union, was a member of the ADA's governing board. The liberal organization, then under the chairmanship of John Kenneth Galbraith, had recently voted by 65 to 47 to endorse McCarthy's candidacy, which prompted the withdrawal from the organization of such other prominent labor leaders as Dubinsky's ILGWU successor Louis Stulberg, I. W. Abel of the United Steelworkers, and Joseph A. Beirne of the Communications Workers of America. Dubinsky, responding to the rebellion, announced that his personal strategy involved remaining in the organization to fight for the president's renomination from the inside. At the same time, nine other unionists, including Walter Reuther, stood by the ADA's new anti-Johnson position.[5]

Such rebellions, however, were confined to a small minority of organized labor. Amid the splintering of the party, it was becoming clear that the major union leadership, overlooking differences over wage-price guidelines and the abandonment of efforts to repeal Section 14b protection for the right-to-work laws, had remained the most loyal supporters of the Democrats. The relatively higher paid workers of the skilled craft unions were, in fact, the hard-core loyalists, the least likely to defect. What perhaps was dawning very slowly among liberal intellectuals was the pronounced movement of the bulk of organized labor in America toward an establishment mentality, which not only supported the war but deeply resented, even hated, the privileged collegiate youth's criticism of American values. Thus there was the inevitable gap between the reality and the self-deception, the belief that big labor leadership lagged behind the more enlightened position of the rank-and-file. It was easy, when so deluded, to point to the most powerful unionist of them all, George Meany, as an aberration.

Meany, however, was more representative of his organization than his critics would acknowledge. First of all, as his biographer has made very clear, it was true not only that he was as bitter an anticommunist as any that the cold war had nurtured, but that he was also a superhawk, one on a par with Secretary of State Dean Rusk and Walt W. Rostow. Since 1965, he had devoted more public attention in numerous statements in support of the war than to any single issue, and the executive council of the AFL-CIO had issued nine statements consistent with that position. Moreover, the close rapport he had established with Johnson was a more intimate relationship than would normally be possible even with a Democratic president. During the unfortunate congressional election campaign of 1966, it had been the AFL-CIO's Committee on Political Education that had supplied the White House with the organizational muscle that might normally have been provided by the Democratic National Committee. There had never been much doubt about labor's stake in the Great Society, and there should have been even less about how it would react to the growing dissent that was coming from within the party. In 1967, right after McCarthy had announced his candidacy, an attempt by antiwar unionists to get the AFL-CIO to take a position on the war ended in disaster, as a peace proposal that was placed before a "National Labor Leadership Conference for Peace" by Charles Cogen of the American Federation of Teachers was overwhelmingly rejected in a standing vote. Of the two thousand delegates present, just six approved. Union members questioned by pollster John Kraft in January 1967, in a survey conducted for COPE, also responded emphatically behind the president's foreign policy, as did delegates who were polled at various state conventions later in the year. After the dramatic Tet offensive at the end of January 1968, during which the Vietcong confirmed their military capability despite all the American efforts, Meany convened a conference of labor officials in Washington and warned that anti-Johnson dissenters would only succeed in electing a Republican president. Moreover, he reminded them of the great success in winning social legislation from the administration since 1964.[6]

Meany's response to Johnson's withdrawal, then, was entirely consistent with both his personal course and that of the bulk of organized labor. Even before Hubert Humphrey's own official entry into the competition, and even without consulting his own executive committee, he issued a statement supporting the candidacy of labor's friend from Minnesota, the vice president. As Joseph Goulden has pointed out, Meany's early "prominence in the Humphrey coalition, and particularly his opposition to Bob Kennedy, excited the permanent enmity of the left wing of the Democratic party, the liberal intellectuals and doves who had wanted to purge the country of all vestiges of the Johnson Administration, and most certainly its Vice-President."[7]

That the Kennedy and McCarthy campaigns would confront enormous obstacles in combating the resistance from the machine leadership such as offered by the Mayor Daleys and the pro-administration loyalty of the Democratic center, which now included the hard core of organized labor, was very clear. Having formulated their positions around issues, they had attracted followers to whom ideas were more precious than party. Partisanship, to most of their youthful followers in particular, was an irrelevent vestige from the past, the prop of the fat boys with cigars in smoke-filled rooms who cared more about jobs, power, and accommodation in pursuit of their tactics. The time had come for purpose and morality to replace expediency, to substitute the "new politics" for the old, which had only served as a tool of the "establishment." From the South, at the same time, and spreading alarmingly throughout the Democratic strongholds elsewhere, the rebellion of George Wallace was threatening to split the party into a fourth part.

3

George Wallace, the "prime minister" of Alabama, the power behind Governor Lurleen Wallace, was beginning to impress the Gallup pollsters that spring. In May, they warned of the "strong possibility" that he could deprive either major candidate of a majority of the electoral votes. Quite simply, the entire election might be tossed into the House of Representatives, where mischief could be done through his ability to withhold the votes of crucial states. By July, the Wallace rating had risen to 16 percent and there were persistent reports of surprising strength in vital northern areas, communities where national Democrats traditionally received substantial majorities, all of which seemed to confirm the growing power of the earthy fighter from Alabama. That same month, no less an experienced observer of the American political scene than Gerald Ford, the Republican House minority leader, predicted that the election would indeed be settled by the House. An additional question was whether the Wallace candidacy would be more damaging to the Republicans or to the Democrats.[8]

Wallace had made his first serious impression as a national figure in 1964 by doing well in the primaries of three states outside the Deep South. In two northern states, Wisconsin and Indiana, he had drawn between 30 and 35 percent of the votes, and the border state of Maryland had given him about 45 percent. Suddenly, gone was the comfortable illusion that racial demagoguery could be dismissed as an aberration of Dixieland. The Wallace bravado, with such exhortations as, "Let 'em call me a racist. It don't make any difference. Whole heap of folks in this country feel the same way I do. Race is what's gonna win this thing for me."[9] Granting the assumptions that he was correct, that he spoke for a whole lot of people nationally as well as in the South, that regional differences were no longer significant, he could not be dismissed as just another southern racist. If there was any single development that kept Wallace, who was then

Alabama's governor, from attempting more conquests up North it was the presence of Barry Goldwater as the Republican hope. The Arizona conservative was attracting potential Wallace supporters and discouraging both the well heeled and the politically well situated from endorsing the maverick campaign. Since 1964, nothing had happened to dispel the view that he was already the most potent politico to come out of the South since the days of Huey Long.

His sensitive biographer, Marshall Frady, has called Wallace the "ultimate product of the democratic system."[10] Frady could have taken that one step further by adding that he was the ultimate product of an American egalitarian democracy that, with a party system poorly organized along ideological lines expressive of particular interests, was peculiarly vulnerable to fluid realignments. As his career moved through the 1950s and the 1960s, Wallace was far less representative as a product of the party system than of the stresses that tore at domestic life. As increased numbers of Americans dissociated themselves with either major party, it was Wallace who best voiced their sense of futility and cynicism as well as, paradoxically enough, their native optimism about the efficacy of the popular will. The crowds understood him perfectly when he said, "You get a bayonet in yo back with the national Democrats, and yo get a bayonet in yo back with the national Republicans."[11]

George Corley Wallace's first prerequisite was something he already had in abundance, ambition. If there was a central theme in his career, it was his recognition of what was necessary to expedite personal success and a willingness to seize the opportunities. There was the story of how he did not even wait for his army discharge before flooding future constituents in Barbour County with Christmas cards, thus establishing a base for a presence he later exploited when running for the state legislature. At the 1948 Democratic national convention, not only was Wallace seated as a delegate who was also a member of the state's legislature, but he was also there as a close associate of Governor Jim Folsom, an identification that had been furthered by his sponsorship of a progressive vocational program. When Handy Ellis led the famous walkout, Wallace remained with the loyalists and helped to reorganize the delegation, ultimately casting his presidential nomination ballot for the regional favorite, Richard Russell. Through the subsequent Alabama administration of Gordon Persons, Wallace retained his reputation as a liberal, even as a racial moderate. Folsom himself later recalled: "George wasn't no race bigot either back yonder. Me 'n' George were always close.

My uncle and his granddaddy were Populists together. George ain't nothing but an old Populist himself."[12] When Folsom permitted liquor to destroy what should have been a brilliant career, Wallace broke with his former hero. Running for the governorship in 1958, he found himself competing against a man who, four years after the Brown decision, had made the cool calculation that appeals to bigotry were the surest means to the voters' hearts. John Patterson, Wallace's opponent, accepted Ku Klux Klan support and ran a race that helped to raise the state's massive resistance decibels. Wallace, meanwhile, issued a careful repudiation of KKK support that shrewdly included the disclaimer that not *all* Klansmen were bad and won the endorsement of both the NAACP and the state's Jewish minority.[13] But Patterson's pitch was the more successful, leaving the young legislator with the belief that he had been, as he put it, "out-niggered," something he vowed would never happen again.

His new formula was to become his stock in trade. It worked beautifully when he ran again in 1962. That winning campaign was blatantly segregationist, villifying the federal government and with promises to "stand in the schoolhouse door" to prevent integration. His inaugural address was a throwback to the darkest days of a Theodore Bilbo. The strident appeal warned against Americans becoming "a mongrel unit of one under a single all-powerful government," and, he declared, "In the name of the greatest people that have ever trod this earth, I draw the line in the dust and toss the gauntlet before the feet of tyranny." Then, in a battle-cry that could never be forgotten: "And I say, Segregation now! Segregation tomorrow! Segregation forever!"[14] During a tape-recorded confrontation with Attorney General Robert Kennedy in his Montgomery office, Wallace labored to provoke a threat that federal troops would be employed if necessary to integrate the University of Alabama. When the attempted entry of black students took place, he did make the dramatic gesture of "standing in the schoolhouse door," complete with a lectern from which to issue his prepared statement of defiance. But of little surprise to him or to anyone else was his inability to thwart the collapse of segregation in the state's system of higher education, a development that followed his well-publicized gesture by just four hours. Just as futile, but of equal political value, was his use of state troops to delay the desegregation of Alabama's public schools.

His administration succeeded in strengthening its hold on both the special interests and the voters. Wallace initiated an extensive public works construction program, especially in the area of education. Further, he began the practice of supplying Alabama's schoolchildren with free textbooks. Thus, his appeal to the plain people of the state was substantial and led Jim Folsom to recall the administration as the realization of "the fondest dreams of every liberal in the state. He did what all the Populists have always dreamed of doing."[15] At the same time, of course, his building program also provided a bonanza for his cadre that was necessary to cement his political structure. After the legislature thought the appropriation was for the creation of five junior colleges and five trade schools, the state ultimately wound up with fourteen junior colleges and fifteen trade schools, and for a price that was more than double the initial allocation.[16] Meanwhile, Wallace was isolating the Alabama party from the national Democratic organization and creating a personal powerhouse, one that did not hesitate to use brazen, extravagant measures against the few open opponents. During the Wallace years, Alabama had become the most tyrannical state in America.

One of Wallace's great problems was the local constitutional prohibition against governors succeeding themselves for a second term. In 1964, there were rumors that he had been on the verge of becoming a Republican when Senator J. Strom Thurmond of South Carolina suddenly switched and beat him to the move. For Wallace, apparently, it was to be nothing less than the South's number one Republican. The House Republican *Congressional Newsletter* reported that he put out feelers in 1965 about switching parties so he could run for Senator John Sparkman's seat.[17] Still left with the problem of his own succession, he tried to force the legislature to amend the Alabama constitution for his convenience and came close to success. Then, as a final solution for the dilemma, he hit upon the idea of having his wife Lurleen run as his stand-in; not that Mrs. Wallace was in the least qualified, not that they even had a particularly close recent relationship, but that she could, nevertheless, serve as a surrogate for his power. He had, by then, become sufficiently heroic before his fellow Alabamans for even that gothic ploy to succeed without much trouble. It may also be added that Lurleen Wallace's final months of life, before she died of cancer in 1968, constituted one of the more melancholy examples of how a woman permitted her own personal degradation in the interest of her husband's goals.

By 1968, the time had long since passed when there could be much doubt that George Wallace was the shining hope of the South.

More than any single individual, even more than Orval Faubus of Arkansas, he had become the spokesman for defiance against a dominant and domineering North. While his very extremism incidentally gave northern liberals the ammunition for passing much of the civil rights legislation of the 1960s, it voiced the frustrations of ordinary southerners, especially poor whites who could neither understand nor accept the elements of social and economic change. It gave them the means of flailing out against the national Democrats without having to turn to the Republican Party. George Wallace was telling the people that he was for them and for their way of life, that they need not surrender themselves to either Washington or Wall Street. The mixture of race and economic displacement was again producing a vigorous spokesman, one who could make the business elites in Birmingham wince with trepidation about their state's future and who could, at the same time, offer enough to keep them in line while also satisfying the masses. The big question in early 1968, then, was not whether Wallace had strength, but whether it would damage the national Democrats or the Republicans. Giving him the electorate that had gone to Goldwater four years earlier would surely undermine the GOP, but so, too, could Democrats be hurt if he could duplicate his appeal elsewhere as he had begun to demonstrate might be possible.

4

It has been suggested that George Wallace became a presidential candidate in 1968 largely as a warm-up for 1972.[18] Along with most others, he had harbored the natural expectation that Lyndon Johnson would attempt another term. Any kind of projection beyond that point must have made it appear logical to Wallace that the left-wing of the Democratic Party would triumph by 1972 and that its natural nominee would be Bobby Kennedy. That would provide an ideal confrontation between what Wallace saw as the two basic forces in American life, the "pointy-headed intellectual morons" who, along with communists and other assorted radicals, were engineering a federal take-over of what had been local prerogatives, and, on the other hand, the vast majority of Americans who were paying the price for their architecture.

Whether Wallace would seek to have his name advanced by a so-called third party or would actually fight it out at the convention was, of course, a source of early speculation—and significance. A traditional fight waged at Chicago by the rules of the game would, in ordinary circumstances, bring either victory or defeat; or the possibility of neither, which could be in the form of his designation by the winner as the vice presidential candidate, a not farfetched assignment for a leading southerner. Or it could, in the tradition of 1948, lead to an abandonment of the party by the rebellious. Almost overlooked was the fact that such considerations would be of small consequence in the real world, that is, the future allegiance of voters who had customarily thought of themselves as Democrats. The fact is that, with party loyalties weaker than ever, the familiar emblems alongside the voting-machine levers mattered less than the individual candidates. In the case of George Wallace, it seemed clear that his followers, regardless of where on the ballot they would ultimately have to opt for him, included enormous numbers of Democrats. Almost without exception, they, as Wallace himself, had inherited their political consciousness from the era of the New Deal. There was, in short, little less awe of FDR among Democratic Wallaceites than in the governor's own political disposition.

To a remarkable degree, they tended to be among the more poorly educated, the less affluent, those who had partaken of the postwar abundance only enough to get a taste of comfort without the luxury of security. In the South, they were traditional Democrats upset by the racial changes of the past two decades and susceptible to populistic appeals directed at the urban coalition establishment; but in the North they tended to concentrate along the zones of conflict caused by social change. Wallace sympathizers were, to be sure, plentiful in some of the conservative Republican suburbs, such as Garden City on Long Island; but large numbers of his supporters also came from among those whites who could not afford to escape from the expanding areas of changing neighborhoods and schools by fleeing to grass-surrounded little bastions in more responsive tax districts. So, in the North, Wallace had a message that reached close to much of the white working-class. Both his appeals to visceral anti-communism, which was practicularly attractive to traditional concepts of patriotism, and his carefully coded rhetoric that meant the preservation of schools, homes, and ancient values had inevitable attractions. He worked hard, and with considerable success, to present himself as the only national politician who truly understood the "little guy." Thus, not only in such blue-collar enclaves as the Chicago suburb of Cicero and South Boston would there be many who

could find much to like about Wallace, but also among other workers, largely Democrats and often of Irish, Slavic, and Italian descent,
who had to cope with the frustrations of a changing society over
which they felt they had pitifully little control: crime, busing to
promote integration, and increasing welfare rolls (which they readily attributed to indolence) while their incomes were being taxed
disproportionately and they were receiving few social services. Already, Mrs. Louise Day Hicks had come close to defeating Kevin
White for the mayoralty of Boston. In New York City, Negro and
labor animosities had been exacerbated by a school strike against a
black local board of education's actions.

If conditions were strikingly favorable for Wallace in 1964, they
were that much better by 1968, when local "law and order" candidates had already begun to proliferate. Even New York City, the
home of liberal Democrats, would witness a primary election victory
for Comptroller Mario Proccacino as an opponent for Republican-
Liberal Mayor John V. Lindsay. Proccacino would gain fame for
using the phrase "limousine liberals," as well as for the not-so-
fortunate remark to a Harlem audience that "my heart is as black as
yours." After all, it was a period that had followed three "long hot
summers." The civil rights movement had long since flared into
open rebellion. If Martin Luther King was too radical for the appetite of much of the working class, there had nevertheless been a
strong sense of justice that right was right, that if blacks were still
not welcomed as neighbors every American still deserved basic constitutional rights. But all that, flimsy as it was, had begun to erode.
Both the rising vitriol of the black leadership and the perceptions of
spreading lawlessness, whether due to an expanding teenage population or to ghetto culture, were tailor-made for Wallace's appeal. To
one newspaper correspondent, he said, "They're all concerned about
crime and property rights. You take a working man, if he lives in a
section where law and order break down, he can't just up and move
like rich folks can."[19]

The campus rebellions also played into his hands. Student unrest,
spreading from the "free-speech" movement in Berkeley and lashing
out against both institutions and the war in Vietnam, offended those
who, like Wallace, were angered by their hostility toward authority.
Perhaps envious of their opportunities as students, of the privileges
that had resulted from the middle- and upper-middle-class birth, it
was easy for workers to feel deep revulsion against their disdain for
the institutions where they were supposed to be engaged in serious

study and against their sometimes violent, and often irrational, anti-Americanism. Such behavior provoked a typical Wallace response, the sort of comment he would repeat endlessly: "I would have the Justice Department grab them by the long hair—these intellectual morons, these professors, these students tearing up their draft cards, raising money and blood for the Viet Cong—and have them charged with treason, have them tried and put away. . . . We're at war. It doesn't matter whether Johnson had the legal right to send the troops over there."[20]

The Johnson renunciation of March 31 somewhat confused the Wallace timetable, as it did in the case of the other hopefuls. But it was a most temporary period of reassessment. For one, the antiwar activism only accelerated after that point rather than desisted, seeking thereafter to control the party itself as their principal instrument for ending the war.[21] And, as though to further spark the Wallace drive, the assassination of Dr. Martin Luther King in a Memphis motel on April 4 was followed by a renewed outbreak of burning and looting, creating more fertile ground for the governor's campaign. From that point until the early fall, his popularity ratings showed a steady rise, moving to just over 20 percent.

Wallace finally became the candidate of the American Independence Party. In some states, because of the intricacies of local laws and splinter parties, he was forced to appear under different labels. It was, however, all incidental to the fact that, whatever his insignia, the candidate had become a serious threat to the Democrats in the North as well as to Republican hopes for repeating Goldwater's southern electoral success. That spring and summer, the Wallace forces pushed hard. With a core of workers from Alabama fanning out throughout the country, and with considerable support from dissident right-wing elements—the Ku Klux Klan, the John Birch Society, the White Citizens Council, and anti-Semitic fringe zealots such as Gerald L. K. Smith—none of which he renounced, the push was organized and money was raised. Temporarily slowed down by the terminal illness of his wife Lurleen, and brought to a momentary halt by her death on May 7, Wallace nevertheless was able to maintain his momentum. For awhile, it was as though Huey Long (only one who made a far more racist appeal) was waging a national battle. Both before and after the Democratic convention in late August, persistent reports, supported by public opinion polls, had the governor making remarkable inroads into the party's normal blue-collar backing in northern industrial areas. However exaggerated some of the accounts turned out to be, organized labor could no longer be complacent.

American workers had to be educated about George Wallace's real colors, about his masquerading as a populist friend of the working man. Consequently, with COPE and Walter Reuther's United Auto Workers (UAW) leading the way, a vigorous educational campaign was launched. Workers were informed about the hostile climate toward organized labor under the Wallace regime in Alabama, a state with right-to-work legislation. They were reminded that, for all his common-man pitch, the state had a pathetic ranking among the others in the nation, near or at the bottom in such public service categories as education, per capita income, and literacy.[22] The burden of the labor offensive was to dissuade workers from forgetting the pocketbook issue while falling victim to their social anxieties. But, contradicting the simple conclusion that white northern unionists could be seduced by racism alone, the auto workers—many of whom came from the South—were also reminded that Wallace was trying to exploit racial fears. According to the Harris poll, the Alabaman's appeal never exceeded 16 percent among union members outside the South.[23]

By early October, when labor was on the counteroffensive and with Humphrey and Nixon already established as the candidates of the two major parties, the Wallace surge was a clear threat to the electoral college majority for either camp. If Wallace was a parochial candidate, capitalizing on the internal agitation of the era, he was nevertheless the one man whose position was clear-cut. About the only compromise he made was avoidance of blatant racial appeals by the substitution of euphemisms that conveyed his meaning to audiences with sufficient clarity. His strength seemed capable of permanently retaining the disaffected of either party, the elements who felt that Democratic and Republican compromises sacrificed their interests. As election day approached, however, Wallace began to decline, a process that may be traced to two factors.

The first was the usual hazard that befalls minor-party candidates who attract a segment of the majority electorate. While Wallace's ideological position was firm, it was one that had no realistic chance of victory; yet, at the same time, it offered an outlet for the views that were not accommodated by the establishment parties. Had he been designated as the candidate of either the Democrats or the Republicans, his appeal would have been given a much better test. As it was, however, the final days of the campaign saw Americans turning more to the traditional concern with supporting one of the more credible candidates, meaning, of course, one who had a realistic chance of actually winning. Wallace, then, as had been the case with other third-party figures, declined rapidly by the second Tuesday in November.

Perhaps as fatal in Wallace's case was that the American people, however much frustrated by the situation in Vietnam, and however angry at the antiwar protests that had been growing for the past two years, were still not ready to risk a nuclear war. That did not mean that the public was dovish. Quite the contrary. Polls continued to show only small majorities favoring withdrawal from Vietnam; considerable support remained for the president's position, with more actually favoring a vigorous offensive rather than de-escalation. That, they believed, was the real way, the only effective and honorable way, to end the war. A study conducted by the University of Michigan's Survey Research Center showed that, in New Hampshire, 60 percent of the supporters of Eugene McCarthy believed that Johnson was wrong on Vietnam, not because of the bombing raids and the steady build-up of ground forces, but because he was not hawkish enough.[24] Still, withal, there was tacit acceptance of a limitation for military action. While the public was for a quick military solution, it balked at the prospect of nuclear war. That was a principal reason for Goldwater's disaster in 1964, as the Democrats were certainly aware of when they circulated TV commercials showing a little girl picking flowers and having that bucolic scene dissolve against the horrors of an atomic mushroom cloud. They chose Johnson because he was the peace candidate; he was the man who could be trusted with ending the conflict as soon as possible, responsibly, if not by withdrawal then at least by a controlled military victory that would not involve a third world war.

Wallace's reputation as an extremist made him especially vulnerable, then, for what followed after he made the disastrous choice of an air force general, Curtis Le May, as his running mate. Introduced to the press on October 3 as the vice presidential candidate, the general virtually gave Wallace apoplexy by insisting on discussing the feasibility of using nuclear weapons in Vietnam. "I don't believe the world would end if we exploded a nuclear weapon," said the general, while Wallace stewed at his side. In rhapsodic terms, he pointed out that, after all, atomic bombs had not been so destructive to the Bikini atoll. "The fish are all back in the lagoons; the coconut trees are growing coconuts; the guava bushes have fruit on them; the birds are back. As a matter of fact, everything is about the same except the land crabs."[25]

So much for the Wallace campaign and for serious speculation about the election having to be decided by the House of Representatives.

5

While the Wallace boom continued to mount that spring, the McCarthy-Kennedy competition constituted an assault not only upon the president but against the relevance of the Democratic Party, as though, suddenly, the party of change, the party that had just authored the economic and social legislation of the Johnson years, had become evil and obsolete. Somewhere, between 1965 and 1968, a great transformation had occurred. What had been a civil rights revolt had, seemingly, become dissipated in the flames of burning ghettos, and the youthful brigades enlisted in the fight for equality had suddenly become an inchoate force, disinterested in the old cause and turning to a new target to vent moral indignation, while the politicians had begun to modify the rhetoric of liberal reforms and had begun to adopt the coded language of the backlash. The clearing of the smoke from the nation's Detroits and Newarks revealed that they had been abandoned to themselves, deserted for a new target, the waging by Americans of a war in Southeast Asia. It was a cause that brought together the "new politics" and the New Left, the idealists for whom a better world could be salvaged through "the system" and the romanticism of Marxism and Maoism that enticed the radicals of the new generation.

The new politics seemed to represent the coming of age of the reform movements that had been simmering in the Democratic Party's "silk-stocking" districts since the late 1940s. The New York reformers, the California reformers, the Pennsylvania reformers, etc., each rising and falling with the vagaries of leadership and issues, each bucking the power of machine regulars and the obstacles of diffused loyalties, had been replenished by the Stevenson "enthusiasts." More recently, they had been inspired by the promise of the New Frontier and the expectations offered by the Great Society. Of more importance, however, was their greater affluence, giving them independence from traditional bread-and-butter worries. For them, issues and ideas were what patronage and favors had been to the professionals. Intellectuals, for the most part, and often connected with the academic community, they were as likely to find themselves at home within Democratic ranks as business executives were among Republicans. The Democratic Party, then, which had provided the leadership for both civil rights and the commitment of troops to Vietnam in the early 1960s, was finding itself, as in the case of George Wallace, providing resistance against the first and, in the campaigns of McCarthy and Robert Kennedy, posing new alternatives for the latter.

Unlike what later happened in the case of Richard Nixon and the Watergate scandals, the undercutting of Lyndon Johnson came in the form of a rebellion from within his own party. Here and there were some Republicans who had begun to question the wisdom of the State Department and the military establishment, but the strongest dissent on Capitol Hill was coming from the Democrats. The heart of the attack was centered in the Senate Foreign Relations Committee. Under the chairmanship of J. William Fulbright, who had already bristled over the president's intervention in the Dominican Republic in 1965, the Democratic majority had begun to ask embarrassing questions. In addition to Fulbright, who had already established himself as the administration's gadfly, other committee members who had questioned either the bombing or the military calculations were such Democrats as Frank Church, Eugene McCarthy, Wayne Morse, Joseph Clark, Albert Gore, and Claiborne Pell. On January 27, 1966, McCarthy had joined with fourteen other Democratic senators in signing a public letter to the president urging him not to resume the bombing. Making his first formal statement on the war in the Senate that same day, he suggested that the debate over the war was a "proper point for the beginning of a much deeper and much more extensive discussion not only of Vietnam but also of the whole role of America in this second half of the twentieth century."[26]

Vehement opposition was not consistent with McCarthy's style. The senator was widely regarded as a moderate liberal at best, one who commanded considerable respect from his southern colleagues. His voting record was hardly calculated to please the devotees of the "new politics." He had been forthright in support of defense appropriations, even oppressing George McGovern's 1966 effort to slash military aid funds by $250 million. He voted against reducing the tax depletion allowance for the oil companies, against reducing the subsidy to the National Rifle Association for rifle-practice, against reducing appropriations for the House Un-American Activities Committee, against abolishing the Subversive Activities Control Board, and against the Senate's inquiry into the questionable financial dealings of Thomas Dodd of Connecticut.[27] Nevertheless, he had been a prime mover in getting the liberal House Democratic Study Group organized in the 1950s. His colleagues considered him a highly intelligent and well-informed legislator who, for all his independence, was regarded as a liberal spirit. Yet he could never quite escape the suggestion that his moves contained ulterior motives. For instance, his Stevenson nominating speech was widely regarded as an effort to block John F. Kennedy in order to help Lyndon Johnson. After he had announced his own presidential candidacy on November 30, 1967, there would be gossip that it had been motivated by pique at having been passed over for the vice presidency in 1964. Eugene McCarthy was not a conventional politician and there was nothing conventional about his decision to challenge an incumbent president.

McCarthy's decision to run was, in a way, another project of Allard Lowenstein's. The New Yorker, already a veteran of the Mississippi Freedom Democratic Party and the Freedom Summer, had decided in the spring of 1967 to forward his plans to get rid of Johnson and, in effect, to almost singlehandedly engineer the remaking of the Democratic Party. Laying out his own money and enlisting in his cause such other dissenters as Gerald N. Hill, the president of the California Democratic Council, Curtis Gans of the ADA, and Harold Ickes, the son of FDR's secretary of the interior, Lowenstein moved to weld together the "dump Johnson" sentiment. In August, with Hill, he formed the Conference of Concerned Democrats. The only political figure of any significance he could get to announce openly as actively involved in an anti-Johnson movement was the state chairman in Michigan, Zoltan Ferency, an antiorganization, "new politics" type. Lowenstein's most significant search was for a candidate around whom the movement could coalesce, a candidate willing to become a credible contender for the presidency against Johnson. Several individuals were approached, including George McGovern and Robert Kennedy. Finally, since there were no other takers, McCarthy accepted and made his announcement.

McCarthy would retain the faithful because he was first. Whatever reservations his followers had, that fact could not be denied. It would enhance his mystique and ensure their devotion, preventing the massive defections from his cause that had seemed inevitable when Kennedy declared his own candidacy. Above all, and what few observers were perceptive enough to detect at the outset, Eugene McCarthy made an appeal that was surprisingly effective with a considerable segment of the electorate. It stood up in his initial surprise showing in New Hampshire on March 12, and, just two days after Johnson's withdrawal, again in Wisconsin. Once confronting the other antiwar candidate, Kennedy, who was far better known, more glamorous, and endowed with what had clearly become a valued political pedigree, he suffered from his handicaps, winning only in Oregon and losing primary battles in Indiana, Nebraska and, finally, in early June, the dramatic clash in California.

After the assassination of Robert Kennedy in Los Angeles the night the returns were coming in, McCarthy's challenge was the major obstacle to Humphrey. By mid-July, a Harris poll showed that he had become the candidate most capable of defeating either likely Republican opponent, Richard Nixon or Nelson Rockefeller, running well ahead of Humphrey in separate match-ups against both men.[28] Once Nixon had been nominated, with the consequent post-convention boost to his popularity, a Gallup poll on the eve of the Democratic gathering at Chicago indicated that McCarthy had fallen five percentage points behind the former vice president. Humphrey, however, was trailing by sixteen points.[29]

When such polls were confined to Democrats, the story was different. McCarthy could never be shown as their favorite. As late as August 7, the Gallup organization reported that those identifying themselves with the party that McCarthy hoped to take over were behind Humphrey by a substantial 53 to 39 margin.[30] There would thus be substantial room for the belief that, for all the complaints of the new-politics people about how the traditionalists had controlled the Chicago convention, they did select the candidate most representative of the rank-and-file. Others would also be able to maintain, with equal justification, that McCarthy would have had a better chance of defeating Nixon had he been given the opportunity to compete in the general election.

McCarthy evidently came across with far more nonpartisan appeal than as a Democrat. Thus he polled a substantial GOP write-in vote in New Hampshire, was suspected of having obtained a generous crossover endorsement in Wisconsin, and was clearly acceptable to many Republicans. Recalling that Robert Kennedy was able to get almost the solid vote of the minorities, he added, "They showed

again that I could get votes for the Democratic party in 1968 that
other candidates could not get."[31] His bid was to none of the Democratic power centers, neither to the Jewish, black, Catholic, or
unionist components of the urban coalition; nor, for that matter, to
the rural poor and the numerically small but strongly Democratic
Mexican Americans. To southerners, he was not as repugnant as
memories of civil rights fights still rendered Humphrey in certain
quarters, and neither did he carry his colleague's stigma for having
been out in front in the fight for organized labor and social reforms;
but his demeanor and intellectuality and frequent use of poetry (he
often traveled with Robert Lowell as a campaign companion), combined with a contention that the war was wrong because it was
immoral and indefensible, was not what that region was yet ready to
accept. Among Democrats, McCarthy's support was centered with
the antiwar youth and new-politics intellectuals. A Roman Catholic,
and somewhat of a theological scholar, he nevertheless appeared as
an aristocratic WASP. Richard Goodwin has observed that "Anybody looking at McCarthy on television, whether he talked about
fiscal policy or the gold standard, could look at that man and know
he wasn't a communist, and was probably a conservative."[32]

Additionally, his attempt to take over the party must be seen as a
curious kind of quixotic battle. If that was his real purpose, he
nevertheless ran as a virtually nonpartisan Democrat, a peculiar way
of winning over the organization. More conventional strategy would
have dictated a blatant partisan appeal before the convention and a
shift toward independents and Republicans during the fall campaign. Had that been his disposition, however, it undoubtedly
would have undermined much of his stature among the new-politics
admirers. Accordingly, pursuing a position that issues were more
important than partisanship, he subordinated such connections. Facing the Conference of Concerned Democrats on the night of December 2, 1967, in his first major address as a candidate for the
nomination, he mentioned the party just once, at the outset and
then only to link it with Adlai Stevenson, and made not a single
reference to it thereafter. Such mentions were indeed rare. Even
when speaking before a large audience at Boston University, in the
heart of a traditionally Democratic stronghold, he went on to identify himself with the civil rights, health, and educational programs of
the past decade without once using the word Democrat. The closest
he usually came toward establishing his political identity was
through reciting the names of the party's past heroes. When appear-

ing before delegates from the various states at Chicago, as McCarthy himself has revealed, he refused to say he would support whatever choice they might ultimately make simply because of the demands of party loyalty.[33]

His personality and style also appealed to reformers because it recalled someone who had brought many of them into politics in the first place, Adlai Stevenson. By the summer of 1968, the party's former titular leader had been dead for three years, having collapsed on a London street. But there was Eugene McCarthy, witty, unashamed of being bright, unorthodox, reluctant to cater to crass ethnic or group interests, and liberal without being strident. The man who had become the darling of the Stevensonians for his oratory at the 1960 convention had also become the natural successor, an identification McCarthy himself invoked at that Chicago appearance on December 2 by devoting a long introductory section of the speech to Stevenson's memory. The association was also of sufficient attraction to draw back into politics, as his finance chairman and one of his key campaign strategists, the old Stevenson associate and Democratic national chairman, Steve Mitchell.[34] It was also purely Stevensonian of McCarthy to chafe at the strident oratory used by Allard Lowenstein, who preceded him as a speaker before the National Conference of Concerned Democrats. Remembering his annoyance at the time, he later recalled that it was an "overstatement of the case against Lyndon Johnson and which was not in the spirit of the campaign which I intend to wage." Then he added: "It was not a time for storming the walls, but for beginning a long march."[35] Fearful of escalating the rhetoric and increasing the chances of serious violence, he also demanded that Lowenstein call off a massive demonstration in Chicago involving thousands of citizens in an effort to inundate the delegates with evidence of popular demand for McCarthy.[36] Coolly, while the challenges to the regulars were being fought at the convention itself, McCarthy preferred to remain in his Conrad Hilton suite with his brother Austin, a surgeon, playing mock baseball. Repeatedly, on August 28, just as Stevenson before him had been urged to seize the opportunities, Mitchell implored McCarthy to go to the convention floor to do battle for his cause, at that moment the contest over acceptance of the "peace" plank that had been advanced by the McCarthy-George McGovern-Ted Kennedy forces. While Mitchell was hopeful that it would not only advance their position on the war for acceptance by the party but might also create a sudden rush of enthusiasm toward the candidate, the senator feared that the already heated-up convention would boil over still more.[37]

In contrast with McCarthy, Robert Kennedy was the candidate of passion, the one who could more readily evoke the emotional responses of the mass of Americans. Also unlike McCarthy, his appeal was essentially partisan: he could be as easily hated as loved. The man who had left the Johnson administration after tense months following his brother's death and had been elected as a senator from New York by defeating Republican incumbent Kenneth Keating also offered the hope that he was the one individual who might command the support of the new-politics people while also drawing from the traditional bedrock sources of New Deal Democratic strength. Whereas McCarthy could never hope to compete with Wallace on the same ground, Kennedy might offer serious competition for the loyalty of blue-collar workers and, at the same time, render Humphrey's attraction to minorities as passé. His youth, close association with a martyred brother, record as attorney general, and developing sensitivity to the social issues that were bothering so many Americans were perceived as substantial assets. He might fill the need for a Democrat who could represent both the mood of reaction against the excesses of the cold war and the kind of liberalism that had not made much headway since the Roosevelt era. Only in their common identification with the new politics and opposition to the war did he resemble McCarthy.

There was little doubt about Kennedy's confidence that, ultimately, he would become president. Kennedys simply did not lose, as his brother Ted had also demonstrated by defeating John McCormack's nephew to represent Massachusetts in the Senate. As had John Kennedy before him, he, too, could count on the advantages of a well-endowed and loyal family, together with countless young people to whom there was still more magic in the Kennedy aura than in any single source, including the Democratic Party. After all, his brother had somehow inspired the masses, had finally evoked their humane instincts. And the belief was that Bobby was well in advance of Jack's social commitments, that the younger man was less inclined to surround himself with such traditional pragmatists as Ted Sorensen, whose 1950s concern with the mechanism of political success was making him hopelessly conservative in the eyes of the new-generation intellectuals. To those hopeful that the new politics could find its most eloquent voice in Bobby Kennedy, it was heartening that his surroundings were more likely to be populated by such issue-oriented types as Adam Walinsky, Richard Goodwin, Al Lowenstein, Peter Edelman, Frank Mankiewicz, Jack Newfield, and even SDS founder Tom Hayden, an association that the senator kept discreet. A new Kennedy take-over of the Democratic Party could, in that case, finally give the poor, the blacks, the workers, the city people, the kind of America that had been compromised away so often. It was not surprising, then, that *Fortune* magazine appeared that March with the statement that businessmen considered him the least popular presidential politician since Roosevelt.

The idea of running had been pressed on him for a long time. When Lowenstein approached him in 1967, he replied, "I would have a problem if I ran first against Johnson. People would say that I was splitting the party out of ambition and envy. No one would believe that I was doing it because of how I felt about Vietnam and poor people. I think Al is doing the right thing, but I think that someone else will have to be the first one to run."[38] Although such veterans as Sorensen and John Bailey saw matters the traditional way and advised that a campaign not be undertaken without the explicit support of the party professionals, such as Mayor Daley, the new-politics advisers were urging him to test his popularity in the primaries. Success there, they reasoned, might induce Johnson to step aside. Opposition to the war was gaining sufficient strength, especially when Selective Service dispensed with college deferments and the draft began to hit the middle classes, for articulate and charismatic leadership to mobilize such opinion into a political force. The senator, for awhile, reasoned that the president was so contrary that he might prolong the war because of his opposition.[39] There were those around Kennedy with the impression that this had actually become the most persuasive reason for his not running. Not too significant was the opposition from his brother Ted, which led Bob to say to an aide, "I don't have anybody to do for me what I did for my brother."

As to the possibility of McCarthy doing the job, that filled Kennedy with little confidence. For one thing, there was the lingering resentment over the role the Minnesotan had played at the 1960 convention; loyalty would always be a prime virtue among the Kennedys. Additionally, he considered McCarthy to be unreliable. In Kennedy's view, he was a lazy senator, one who could never be counted on to deliver the vote when most needed. Further, McCarthy's role on the Senate Finance Committee had left Kennedy with the impression that he had certainly gone out of his way to represent the special interests, which accounted in good part for the well-financed campaigns of a man who had no personal wealth. So Kennedy finally appraised McCarthy as a poor senator who was willing to compromise himself to make sure he was at least adequately financed.[40]

There is substantial evidence that Kennedy finally decided to enter the presidential competition at least one week before McCarthy's New Hampshire triumph. At a dinner gathering of regional Democrats that was held in Des Moines, Kennedy found himself surrounded by some forty politicians. No journalists were present. Safe and off-the-record, and led by governors Harold Hughes of Iowa, Warren E. Hearnes of Missouri, William L. Guy of North Dakota, and Robert Docking of Kansas, as well as Congressman John Culver and others from the surrounding area, they expressed uninhibited feelings about Johnson. Without actually saying that Kennedy should be the one to take on the job, they were emphatic that the president had to go. Some recounted their inability to get any kind of cooperation from the White House, while others made the point that the war was dividing their constituents. The situation, they feared, was getting so desperate that it had become questionable that any of them could get re-elected. Finding that opposition to both the president and the war coming from a conservative part of the country convinced Kennedy that the time had come. En route to California, where he was to meet with César Chavez on March 10 to induce the United Farm Workers Union leader to abandon what was already a long fast, he mentioned his decision to aides. His wife, Ethel, then telephoned both Arthur Schlesinger, Jr., and Ken Galbraith with the information.[41]

On March 13, the day after the New Hampshire primary, Kennedy informed a group of reporters outside a Senate hearing room that he was reassessing his position about whether to run against Johnson, adding, "I think that the election in New Hampshire has indicated a good deal of concern in the Democratic party about the direction our country is going."[42] That was on Wednesday. On Thursday, Kennedy went to see McCarthy but returned angry because, as he related it, McCarthy had said to him, "Well, Bob, if you step aside for me this year, I'll step aside for you in seventy-two." It was, Kennedy thought, the height of chutzpah.[43]

That Saturday, Robert Kennedy told a press conference that he was a candidate for the nomination and would be entering a number of primaries. As his aides had feared, the move looked like such a blatant exploitation of New Hampshire's primary results that it brought indignant protests ranging from cries of "foul" to agreement that his much publicized "ruthlessness" had been confirmed. Steve Mitchell, then not yet with the McCarthy campaign, sent the Minnesotan a one-hundred-dollar contribution and a note expressing his disgust with Kennedy. "If he were half the man he claims to be," he wrote, "he would be supporting you without reserve instead of opposing you and placing such heavy burdens upon your struggle."[44] Some did defect from McCarthy. Dick Goodwin, who had been writing speeches for the senator, switched to the Kennedy camp. One prominent Connecticut Democrat informed Mitchell that he still preferred Kennedy because, as he wrote, "RFK reminds me very much of TR, and also of J. Q. Adams—thorny, intense, dedicated and gutsy. I like that. This is a time for seeing and saying things as they really are. To me, RFK sees and says more sense than either Gene McCarthy or Happy Hubert Humphrey."[45]

Mainly, the two men appealed to two different kinds of Democrats, each, in effect, leading a party of his own. Whereas McCarthy appeared as the nonpartisan, WASP-ish-looking intellectual, expressing in moderation the moral revulsion of respectability against the war, Kennedy was the tough Irish kid with flair and heart, the one whose social commitments seemed capable of mobilizing Americans more along class rather than racial lines. During the Indiana primary, while winning 86 percent of the state's black voters, his victory was made possible by a sweep of the seven largest counties that had gone to George Wallace in 1964 and the urban centers of Gary, East Chicago, South Bend, and Hammond, where the white backlash was strongest.[46] In California, a confidential survey made for Kennedy early in the campaign by the Pacific poll showed that his greatest weakness was among the white voters, while the black and Chicano districts were overwhelmingly on his side. A representative sampling of largely Negro neighborhoods, ranging from Los Angeles to the San Francisco-Oakland area, showed Kennedy favored by anywhere from 88 to 75 percent of the population, while two Mexican-American neighborhoods preferred him by 64 and 69 percent. An analysis of the Caucasian sentiment according to religious differences also showed how the two men stood. In mid-April, with the vote divided three ways because of the presence of delegates pledged to Attorney General Tom Lynch, which was a stand-in slate for Hymphrey, and with the further complication of a large undecided group, McCarthy was running strongest among the Protestants, with 34 percent, fol-

lowed closely by the Jews, with 33 percent, while his own co-religionists were giving him 29 percent. Kennedy, meanwhile, was first
among the Catholics, with 33 percent, followed by 21 percent of the
Jewish vote, and just 18 percent among the Protestants.[47] With
close to one-third of all white voters still undecided, the mission of
both candidates was self-evident.

Their effort to cater to the preferences of Orange County, just
south of Los Angeles and one of the most conservative in the state,
illustrated how, in a pinch, the new politics succumbed to the old
expediency. Appearing together on June 2 during a televised debate,
McCarthy explained that it was unrealistic to rejuvenate the ghettos
simply by constructing better housing. "What we have got to do is to
try to break that up," he explained. "Otherwise, we are adopting a
kind of apartheid in this country, a practical apartheid. . . . Some of
the housing has got to go out of the ghetto so there is a distribution
of races throughout the whole structure of our cities and on into our
rural areas." Kennedy responded as though on cue. "You say you are
going to take 10,000 black people and move them into Orange
County," he answered, although McCarthy never said quite that,
and proceeded to argue that "if you are talking about hitting this
problem in a major way, to take those people out, put them in the
suburbs where they can't afford the housing, where their children
can't keep up with the schools, and where they don't have the skills
for the jobs, it is just going to be catastrophic." McCarthy then
accused Kennedy of injecting "scare tactics" into the campaign.[48]
The bitterness between the Kennedy and McCarthy camps was then
exacerbated by subsequent accusations of how each side had rushed
to exploit racial sensitivities. McCarthy, charged Kennedy's people,
had circulated in the black Watts section the recorded voice of
Martin Luther King speaking approvingly of the senator from Minnesota, thus giving the impression that the civil rights martyr had
granted his endorsement. At the same time, Kennedy campaigners
were accused of using sound trucks in Orange County to play back
the tape of the so-called "Orange County Remarks."[49]

On the night of June 5, Robert Kennedy never was able to learn
the final results of the California primary, but when he addressed his
followers in the Hotel Ambassador, he knew he had won. Some
people, including Kennedy press secretary Frank Mankiewicz,
turned to George McGovern; others had notions of drafting Ted;
but, on the road to Chicago, the only serious challenger to Hubert
Humphrey was Eugene McCarthy.

6

For Steve Mitchell, the political amateur who became a veteran by heading the Democratic Party until Paul Butler took over, the Mc-Carthy campaign was an entirely different sort of affair. This time his efforts were in opposition to the political establishment, a power still very much dominated by President Johnson. Even if the new-politics candidates had really forced his retirement, there was little doubt that LBJ could still dominate the convention. The very choice of a site, Chicago, was made at the president's insistence, with more than just a passing notion of consideration for the loyalty of Mayor Daley. Further, despite the difficult primary battles between McCarthy and Kennedy that lasted until the tragedy in Los Angeles, the man who still controlled the Democratic machinery helped to guarantee that, in state after state, quietly and without the publicity given to the maverick candidates, the vice president would get the bulk of the delegates. Even while he was being repudiated by a sizable force within his own party, his efforts were directed toward securing both his man and the vindication of his policies, namely, the conduct of the war.

Through all this, Mitchell, who joined the McCarthy campaign in May, had to maneuver a most unorthodox campaign. First of all, nobody was better aware than Gene McCarthy of the virtual impos-sibility of victory; unlike the old politics, however, the new talked in terms of principles and issues as paramount considerations, prefer-ring to contemplate long-range reforms rather than expedient com-promises for immediate victory. Therefore, to the senator, the nomination was bound to end in a triumph for Hubert Humphrey who was, after all, the vice president. Not only was Johnson behind him, but so were the elements through which the president worked: organized labor, the big city bosses, the loyal state machines. More-ever, the McCarthy campaign organization itself was inexperienced and often chaotic. Mitchell, thinking of himself as a comparative professional, privately referred to the bands of his youthful volun-teers as "McCarthy's Coxey's Army." To one correspondent, he wrote, "The McCarthy campaign has all of the organizational head-aches that go with amateur efforts."[50]

The funding, too, was largely dependent upon sources that repre-sented elements that were never highly partisan, that were not given with the expectation of making an investment for future special considerations. One of Jim Warburg's sisters, for example, gave five thousand dollars to help Ken Galbraith defray the expenses involved in his labors for the senator, largely organizational and educational efforts, including the production of a pamphlet on the Vietnamese war.[51] Extensive use was made of mailing lists that were obtained from a variety of anti-administration sources. By the middle of June, $652,456.17 had been received from such individuals, who included the subscribers to radical publications like the New York *Review of Books* ($3,446.50) and *Ramparts* ($58,968.22), Businessmen vs. Vietnam ($3,595.00), the Student Non-Violent Coordinating Committee ($4,799.00), Lawyers for McCarthy ($4,527.00), Faculty for McCarthy ($51,262.83), and Republicans for McCarthy ($2,320.00). An ad in the New York *Times* had brought 795 respondents who were good for $15,053.15.[52]

Not only did Mitchell have to deal with a grass-roots type of mobilization, but where other experienced individuals were involved, there was always the danger that the ephemeral nature of the drive would make them cautious about staking very much on McCarthy's success. Thus Mitchell was depressed about his relationship with Tom Finney. Finney was also a Stevenson veteran, his association having come during the 1960 last-minute drive at Los Angeles. An Oklahoman who had worked for the Central Intelligence Agency, he had also been a law partner of Clark Clifford, until the latter became Johnson's secretary of defense. Finney, whose expertise as a political strategist was well established, advocated making the challenge at Chicago by liquidating the reliance on McCarthy's "Coxey's Army" and working to merge their forces with the regulars, a blending, in other words, of the new politics with the old. Mitchell, however, for all his reservations about McCarthy's legions, preferred to continue with the preconvention organization, arguing that there was little point in trying to compete with Humphrey for control of the regulars.[53] There was undoubted frustration and jealousy among the two men. Mitchell began to suspect that Finney was at heart a "Washington lawyer-lobbyist who realizes and figures that he will be on hand to whoever wins the nomination and the election and he will have to deal with life as he finds it then." Moreover, Mitchell wrote in a private memorandum, "I have also come to suspect that Finney's ties and sympathies with Johnson and with Humphrey and with the Oklahoma leaders and other political people on the Hill and Congress are too strong to permit him to run any risk even if he [sic] his loyalties to Gene might make him wish to do so." He even suspected that Finney was "an operative in the McCarthy camp for the President and Humphrey."[54] Such were the realities of the distribution of power.

To Mitchell, it was clear that the only hope to accomplish any of the objectives of the movement lay in a direct challenge at Chicago to the party's apparatus, an operation that could be done by attacking both the establishment's domination of the convention machinery and the commitment to ideological principles. An additional bonus, the possible result of a crusade that could rally the most liberal forces, might even be a last-minute rush toward McCarthy. His first tactic involved the unit rule, a device that was used to bring certain state delegations under the total voting domination of a segment that might be able normally to muster only a slender majority, an efficacious means of keeping control in the hands of certain powerful state leaders.

Actually, only nine delegations were bound by the rule, while its use was optional among nine others. Numerically, there was little reason to suspect that even getting rid of it could do much to change the outcome of the convention. But Mitchell, leading the strategy, had other things in mind. On June 2, meeting with McCarthy in San Francisco's Fremont Hotel, he presented his proposal to the senator. "He grasped it and all of its implications immediately," Mitchell noted a few days later, "in fact he said I will go further and release all of my delegates and we might even have a pro-forma first ballot." McCarthy was so enthusiastic that he wanted to announce the plan in a speech, but Mitchell wanted the greatest dramatic impact and publicity and urged that it be saved for Chicago.[55]

Mitchell's plan was basically aimed at the huge 104-vote Texas delegation, a body that was under the firm control of Governor John Connally. Far greater stakes than the mere handful of votes that might be rescued from Texas, however, were in Mitchell's mind. First of all, there was the three-way relationship that involved Connally with his long-time political ally in the Lone Star State's power struggles, Lyndon Johnson, who, in turn, was important for helping to keep power out of the hands of Connally's chief rival, Senator Ralph Yarborough. Second, an assault on the unit rule would present a dilemma to Hubert Humphrey. Already on the defensive for his loyal support of the administration's war policies and thoroughly suspected by northerners on the party's left of adhering to an outmoded liberalism that belonged to the old politics, the vice president would, by opposing the reform, merely confirm his conservative course and further alienate his opposition. The McCarthy campaign could then argue, with some additional persuasion, that he was not in touch with the new mood and that he was, indeed, the creature of the political bosses. If, however, the vice president endorsed the change, he risked offending not only the southern delegations where the device was used most widely but the single individual most essential to his ability to capture control of the party, President Johnson. In Mitchell's mind, there was also the possibility that an assault on the unit rule could make Connally amenable to a bargain for at least a portion of the delegation, and possibly to a move that would exploit McCarthy's good standing with relatively conservative and middle-class voters, having the Texan join the ticket as its vice-presidential candidate. In short, Mitchell had devised a strategy that was an old-politics ploy to achieve new-politics results.

On the eighth of July, the Texas leader of the state's McCarthy-for-president organization notified him of plans to send at least two hundred McCarthy supporters to Chicago as a rump delegation, largely to dramatize the fact that, as he argued, fewer than 5 percent of Texans controlled the selection of the Connally delegation. Mitchell himself, having won McCarthy's approval for the strategy, informed a Fort Worth supporter that he hoped also to spend some time in Texas and "on the possibilities there may be a deal with the Connally delegation in Chicago for the benefit of Senator McCarthy." Then he added, "perhaps we can make a virtue and an advantage out of the Johnson-Connally boss control which they have achieved at the expense of individual rights and with the help of the unit rule. One of our major efforts will be a proposal to abolish the Unit Rule." McCarthy himself later wrote that the Mitchell strategy was the heart of the basic attack to be used at the convention.[56]

Predictably, Humphrey came under the pressure of northern liberals to support its abolition. The vice president, who had already promised Connally he would uphold it, was caught in the crossfire, just as Mitchell had hoped. Nevertheless, Humphrey then changed his mind and word went out that he favored the reform. That led to a near revolt by southern delegates, with the explicit threat that they might yet turn to President Johnson as their own candidate.[57] Meanwhile, the convention's Rules Committee heard arguments on both sides, with Mitchell presenting the case against the unit rule and calling it "infamous" and Connally defending it as the "essence of pure democracy."[58] On the Saturday night before the convention opened, Dick Goodwin went to Connally. The governor, who was by

then piqued by Humphrey's reversal, was asked about joining forces
with McCarthy. While the Texan made no decision during the two-
hour conversation, Goodwin came away feeling that he would be
agreeable. McCarthy was then asked if he wanted the presidency
badly enough to take John Connally as a running mate and
promptly replied, "The answer is no."[59]

Opposing both Johnson and Connally on the unit rule had threatened Humphrey with a last-minute loss of what had seemed so secure. Even as George S. McGovern of South Dakota made a serious
effort to enter the competition as a more liberal alternative to Mc-
Carthy, and talk about renominating the president mounted, others
began to search for additional possibilities. Jesse Unruh, the powerful leader of the big California delegation, had been in McCarthy's
corner since the death of Bobby Kennedy; but now, getting together
with Mayor Daley, who was decidedly cool toward Humphrey at that
point, he found that he and the Illinois Democratic boss could agree
on just one man. That was the third Kennedy brother, Edward
Moore (Ted) Kennedy. But on Tuesday, a statement came from
Steve Smith, Kennedy's brother-in-law, that the young senator, who
was still at his Hyannis Port home, would have his name withdrawn
if actually placed in nomination.[60] Also on that day, McGovern
appeared in a joint debate with Humphrey and McCarthy before
the California delegation and emerged as the clear winner for his
vigorous attacks upon the administration's war and the attendant
sacrifice of domestic programs. "It is to correct that situation, to end
the war in Vietnam and to be about the business of reconstructing
our own country that I seek the nomination at this convention," he
told them at the conclusion of arguments that won several standing
ovations. Humphrey's reception was the coolest.[61]

With the threats to his nomination suddenly becoming so real,
Humphrey moved to reassert his strength. He notified the Texas
delegation of another switch on the unit-rule debate, that he now
favored instituting changes for future conventions rather than in
1968. He also felt he could not afford even a compromise position on
another challenge made by the McCarthy-McGovern-Kennedy forces,
a platform plank offering an alternative to the administration's
conduct of the war. The recent invasion of Czechoslovakia by Soviet
troops had further compounded the difficulty of taking a dovish
position. The antiwar proposal, with its call for a negotiated withdrawal of all American and National Liberation Front (NFL) troops
from the south, an unconditional end to the bombing of North

Vietnam, the encouragement of negotiations between the government in Saigon with the NFL toward the establishment of a coalition
regime, and the early withdrawal of a significant number of American troops by a reduction of military offensives in the Vietnamese
countryside was clearly intolerable to Johnson. Again using his influence, the president dispatched Charlie Murphy to the scene. With
Murphy's guidance, the draft that both Humphrey and the convention then accepted called, instead, for the United States to "stop all
bombing of North Vietnam when this action would not endanger
the lives of our troops in the field; this action should take into
account the response from Hanoi."[62] Its passage, by a vote of 1,567 to
1,041, was a crucial test, if any were needed, of the convention's inclination. Humphrey then went on to an easy first-ballot nomination,
defeating McCarthy by 1,760¼ to 601, while McGovern received
146½, and a scattering of votes went to six other names. Promptly,
the vice president's choice of Senator Edmund Muskie of Maine was
endorsed as his running-mate.

Still, in spite of the control of the convention and its apparatus by
the regulars, the 1968 session made some significant breakthroughs.
In the one big surprise at Chicago, the delegates voted by 1,350 to
1,206 to uphold the position of the minority on the Rules Committee that rejected the unit rule as binding on the delegates for the
1968 convention. For 1972, it would no longer be valid at the pre-
cinct levels, either. Then, too, although the reformers were badly
outnumbered on the Credentials Committee as well and could
hardly have expected overwhelming success, additional points were
scored. Supported mainly by the McCarthyites, attempts were made
to implement the guidelines that had been established in 1964,
when, as part of the compromise that had ultimately permitted the
seating of two delegates from the Mississippi Freedom Democratic
Party, states had been placed on notice that future delegates would
have to be chosen without regard to race, creed, color, or national
origins. As early as 1967, Governor Richard Hughes of New Jersey,
placed at the head of a subcommittee to implement the commitment
to equal opportunity, had reminded state party chairmen about the
requirement. But noncompliance was still common. Outnumbered,
the McCarthy people were nevertheless able to get enough northern
pro-Humphrey liberal supporters to override the segregationist Mississippi delegation led by Governor John Bell Williams and installed
the biracial challengers. They also secured the sharing of the Georgia vote by rival groups led by black Atlanta state Representative

Julian Bond and the segregationist forces of Governor Lester G. Maddox, although most of the latter group then spurned the settlement and walked out. While defeated on other challenges, most notably to the Texas delegation, where a Yarborough group competed with the Connally forces, they nevertheless had forced wide open the entire issue of party representation as well as voting. As David Broder observed, they may have thereby set "the important precedents for an interracial or even Negro-led Democratic party in the South."[63] At least as important for subsequent years were decisions to establish two commissions, one to deal with party structure and delegate selection and the other to take up convention rules.

Unfortunately, the week's most memorable developments occurred not within the amphitheater but on the streets of Chicago. From all over the country, Mayor Daley's huge lakefront city was flooded by some ten thousand antiwar militants, a number that would undoubtedly have been higher had McCarthy not countered Lowenstein's more ambitious plans. They were an assortment of protesting youth; many were in the category of the so-called crazies, the irrational, revolutionary and anarchistic, members of such extreme groups as the Yippies; others were affiliated with more conventional New Left movements, present to vent their anger at the war-supporting vice president, the Democratic Party, and the war machine developed by the United States; some were hippies with unconventional life-styles, while still others flaunted the mores of the society and, more immediately, of the Chicago police by carrying obscene signs and shouting profanities; policemen found themselves the targets of urine and feces-filled bags, and of young girls who goaded them while lifting their dresses provocatively; and there was also love-making in the open and the carrying of the red-and-black flags of the Viet Cong. And yet, as the Walker Commission subsequently concluded, most of the demonstrators had been merely intent "on expressing by peaceful means their dissent either from society generally or from the administration's policies in Vietnam."[64] The mayor had refused to give them permits either to march or to camp overnight in the city's parks.

The simultaneous violent confrontation that then took place, beginning at the start of the week and becoming most vicious on the night of Wednesday, August 28, consisted of a series of battles between the young people and Daley's law-enforcers, clashes that the Walker Commission later termed a "police riot." Millions of Americans looked on horrified before television sets while they watched club-swinging charges by policemen, some of whom had become insanely unrestrained, frequently smashing the heads and cameras of newsmen as indiscriminately as the skulls of young men and women. The scenes rendered nihilistic manifestations of the bitterness that was taking place inside the amphitheater, of the intensity that was dividing Americans and threatening to rip apart the Democratic Party.

For Humphrey, the subsequent campaign was an uphill battle. The events in Chicago, especially what had happened on the streets, had left McCarthy incensed. His own youthful workers had been abused by a police raid in their Conrad Hilton Hotel suite, and he felt that he could not support the vice president without betraying his "children's crusade." Meanwhile, George Wallace appeared to be making sharp inroads into the blue-collar vote, a following that, in normal circumstances, Humphrey could have taken for granted. With the polls showing Nixon the front-runner by a comfortable margin and Wallace chillingly near Humphrey, and with both opponents exploiting the recent turbulence by placing themselves at the forefront of the "law-and-order" issue, the healing of Democratic Party wounds was particularly vital.

Steve Mitchell, with a statement that "After a period, the wounds will be less painful and the wounds will be dry," had already announced his support of the vice president.[65] To George McGovern, Mitchell wrote in mid-September, "I only hope that Hubert will find a basis for a credible accommodation to the minority position on Vietnam that Gene and you and Ted Kennedy . . . have espoused."[66] The Reverend Channing Phillips of Washington, a black man who had drawn 67½ votes for the presidency at Chicago, argued, "We have to reform the Democratic Party, but we have no right to endanger the lives of black people."[67] Such views were, of course, prompted by fear of Wallace being able to send the choice to the House of Representatives, or, in the event of a Nixon victory, the likelihood of a conservative administration being able to appoint as many as four new justices to the Supreme Court.

But Humphrey's dilemma was similar to the tightrope he had been forced to walk during the convention, where he had attempted to compromise on both the unit rule as well as the peace plank. Suddenly abandoning his support of the war would further vitiate his links with President Johnson, which had already become severely strained. Such a change of position could, additionally, expose his earlier views as insincere and make him vulnerable to charges of opportunism. Moreover, they would also offend the backing coming from organized labor as well as the powers in such important states as Texas. And yet he needed to reconcile the differences.

Finally, at the end of September, the vice president spoke in Salt Lake City and, still trying to maintain the balance between the new-politics antiwar crowd and the sensitivities of the president and his followers, he offered a revised view. If elected, he promised, he would stop the bombing, but only *after* being assured of communist willingness to restore the demilitarized zone. He would also reserve the right to resume bombing if he deemed that necessary.

For those looking for a rationale to support Humphrey, an opening had been created. Four days after his speech, the ADA, which had backed McCarthy early in the preconvention campaign, joined the discernible shift to the vice president. Humphrey himself began to battle with renewed confidence, almost as though he had been liberated from his fetters. A massive infusion of AFL-CIO money and personnel helped to offset the inadequate performance of the party machinery which, weakened during the past several years, was still largely ineffectual.[68] Further, the combination of General Le May's nuclear contemplations and the efforts being made by organized labor was beginning to frighten northern workers away from Wallace. Of great assistance to the Humphrey campaign was the performance of Senator Edmund Muskie, especially in comparison with Nixon's unfortunate and inept running-mate, Spiro T. Agnew.

On October 29, while peace talks between the Americans and the North Vietnamese seemed to be making progress in Paris, Senator McCarthy announced his support for Humphrey. Two days later, the president revealed that he had ordered the cessation of bombing of enemy territory as of November 1, four days before the election, thus accepting a key part of the defeated minority plank. Last-minute voter surveys showed Humphrey making rapid gains, with the Harris poll actually placing him ahead of Nixon. At just that point, however, the outcome was further confused by the news from Saigon that the government there had condemned Johnson for the "betrayal of an ally" and would not participate in the peace talks. There was immediate speculation about the connection between the role played in that affair by Mrs. Anna Chennault and the Nixon campaign. Mrs. Chennault was the co-chairwoman of the Women for Nixon-Agnew Committee and, as the China-born widow of General Claire Chennault of World War II fame, retained close ties with Asian diplomats. It became known that she had intervened in encouraging the South Vietnamese to reject the steps toward peace. Johnson quickly moved to satisfy himself that Nixon had had nothing to do with her actions and Humphrey, convinced that his rival would not stoop to such chicanery, made no use of it in his campaign. Had he done so, the difference may well have been decisive.[69]

As it turned out, he drew a lot closer than most people had anticipated. His popular vote deficit was a slender half million, although the electoral college was, as usual, much more decisive. With the exceptions of Hawaii, Minnesota, Texas, and Washington, Nixon enjoyed a commanding sweep west of the Mississippi. Helped by an additional seven states from the South, the winner emerged with 302 electoral votes. That left Humphrey with 191, the bulk coming from Michigan and the Northeast. While the Wallace third-party effort cut into both Democratic and Republican votes, the greatest damage was clearly done to Nixon because the governor took forty-five votes from the Deep South (plus a solitary Republican elector from North Carolina). Still, Wallace did far less well than had been feared, winding up with 13.5 percent of the popular vote.

More ominous for the Democratic Party was the fact that nearly 57 percent of the American people had chosen either Nixon or Wallace. While it was true that the Republicans, despite gains in both houses of Congress, had still failed to gain control over the legislature, the outlook for the Democratic Party could not, at that point, have been described as bright. Of the once solid South, the national ticket had carried only Texas as the others split among Nixon and Wallace. Elsewhere, the strong conservative trend among white middle-class voters raised doubts about the electorate that had emerged from families that had voted Democratic strongly in the 1930s. Further, while Humphrey did less well among blacks than had Johnson in 1964, he was still their overwhelming favorite but received only some 38 percent of the white vote.[70] The experience of 1968 left much room to accommodate the thesis being formulated by Kevin Phillips that "an emerging Republican majority" was in the making. What the tattered Democratic umbrella would look like in the future was less clear.

★

CHAPTER XIII

Repairing the Umbrella

1

At no time since the New Deal had the condition of the party come under closer scrutiny. There were the inevitable questions about the future of parties themselves as meaningful political institutions, as more Americans had become reluctant to express firm partisan commitments. Indeed, while Democrats remained the leading choice, no longer was it with majority support, and the "independent" category had edged ahead of those identifying with the GOP. Moreover, Hubert Humphrey's defeat, unlike the setbacks of 1946 and 1952, had raised new questions about coalitions rather than majorities. Both the presidential tabulations and the performance of candidates in statewide and local races had provided enough evidence to demonstrate that, in sheer numbers, Democrats could still get out the vote. There even might have been a Humphrey victory had the campaign lasted only a few more days. So, in spite of the impressive-looking "conservative mandate" apparently implicit in the combined Nixon-Wallace vote, the Republican triumph was surprisingly fragile. And that was despite the turmoil at Chicago.

The conventional view of what had happened was that Nixon had harnessed the rebellious middle class. They had lashed out not against the party's principles but, rather, its associates, not for a return to pre-New Deal conservatism but against the years of violence and street crime as well as the antipatriotic war protesters and the eccentricities of the counterculture. They were, in other words, moved by what was identified as the "social issue." Having accommodated himself to the views of Strom Thurmond, Nixon had moved to restore his standing in the South by implying that he was the more credible man to do the job that George Wallace was talking about. Without making the crude suggestion of a Wallace that he would drive his car right over anyone who would try to block his way, his message was clear. And the South listened. Virginius Dabney and Willis Robertson, both of whom had done their best to support the party's loyalists in 1948, overcame their fidelity and their aversion to Nixon and the Republicans by hoping that Wallace would not keep him from winning.[1] Running strongly in the South and the more affluent suburbs, Nixon was clearly the candidate of the status quo.

The Humphrey loss had been in confirmation of the view that the Democratic Party was plagued by the "crazies" on the left just as the Republicans were hindered by the "kooks" of the right. Without having to accept any responsibility for either the war or the domestic condition, Nixon had managed to dominate the center, a particularly attractive sector amid such turbulence. That advantage made the Republican candidate especially eager to adopt as his own slogan the message he had seen on a homemade campaign sign in Ohio: "Bring Us Together Again." Recalling the circumstances that had surrounded the 1968 campaign, George McGovern concluded that the Democrats had not, for once, been bothered by a cantankerous southern minority but by "something like half the delegates who were profoundly disaffected."[2]

Additionally, the party's structure was abysmally weak, possibly enough to have made the difference between winning and losing for Humphrey. Gone were most of the strong political machines of the past. The power of a Mayor Daley was an exception rather than the norm. Many species of reformers, North and South, large numbers of them adherents of the new politics, had challenged and frequently defeated boss control. At the national convention itself, the issues that had first been raised by the Mississippi Freedom Democrats in 1964 were broadened at Chicago, resulting in upsets to "regular" delegations from both Georgia and Mississippi, and the unit rule had been defeated by what amounted to a coalition of liberal supporters of all three candidates. Proposals to reform the entire delegate selection process, the inequities of which were documented by Governor Harold Hughes' compilation of practices within all the states, promised to further undermine the old sources of power.

Kevin P. Phillips, a conservative Republican analyst who had been close to Nixon campaign manager John Mitchell, read the returns as projecting an "emerging Republican majority," or as critics were quick to point out, at least an "emerging Nixonian majority." In Phillips' view, the 57 percent Nixon-Wallace vote was the seed of future conservatism. He saw the Wallaceites as strays who were merely in motion "between a Democratic past and a Republican future." Reduced to its core "liberal establishment," Democrats would be too innovative to win presidential elections but would become "a vital and creative force in national politics . . . inserting a needed leavening of humanism into the middle-class *realpolitik* of the new Republican coalition."[3] For Nixon to win again in 1972, and to win comfortably, would mean pursuing southern votes even more vigorously than he had in 1968. Wooing the Wallaceites meant exploiting the issues of crime and racial integration, especially school busing, that were also agitating northerners.

Joining the new debate were elections experts Richard M. Scammon and Ben J. Wattenberg, the latter an aide to Senator Henry Jackson. The Scammon-Wattenberg thesis, which projected the importance of the "social issue," was argued with some passion and clarity. To them, Democratic presidential candidates were having trouble putting together national majorities, despite the party's numerical advantages, because they were losing sight of the average voter, who was, as they put it, "unyoung, unpoor, and unblack." More people were like their hypothetical machinist's wife. Living in the outskirts of a mid-American city—for example, Dayton, Ohio— she was forty-seven years old and had a "somewhat different view of life and politics from that of a twenty-four-year-old instructor of political science at Yale," who cannot know much about politics unless he understands her problems and her circumstances. Had she and other white northerners gone to the polls in the same numbers as they had in 1964, they wrote, underscoring their words, *"Hubert Humphrey would have received a greater popular vote than Nixon."*[4]

Many of the essentials of the Scammon-Wattenberg thesis were borne out during Samuel Lubell's continuous monitoring of popular trends. There seemed little doubt that orthodox consensus ideology—if it could be said to be an ideology—was the most certain to bring victory in national elections. Yet, as Lubell pointed out, applying it was quite another matter, for the very combinations of blocs giving the party their strongest bases of support contained the powerful centers of interest that constantly threatened to exert themselves individually. Enough of them falling out simultaneously would threaten the life of the coalition.[5] And, while the Republicans had their fractures, the Democrats were ahead in sheer diversity.

One who had been close to both John and Robert Kennedy, Fred Dutton, approached the matter from a new-politics point of view by analyzing what he called the "sources of power" likely to be exerted during the 1970s. Emphasizing the importance of the new youth vote, particularly since eighteen-year-olds would be eligible to participate at the polls in 1972, Dutton saw that electorate as a spin-off from the middle class. He concluded that there was no such thing as a stable centrist position that could be held intact. "The principal tensions wracking the country," he wrote, "are still coming to bear most directly among key groups recently in the loose Democratic coalition."[6] The middle classes were spawning conservatism, all right, but also radicalism, especially since the younger generation was seeking new directions that were most decidedly headed in a forward path. Indeed, the center could hardly be static with the widening inroads of collegiate education becoming the chief vanguard for change. Therefore, far from an electorate split along conservative-liberal lines by economic divisions, the "key political struggle of the decade could well turn out to be as much over the nature of our culture as the politics of the 1930s were over the nature of the economy."[7] The principal opponents of the momentum for change, Dutton agreed, were the low-income blue- and white-collar whites, a contradiction of left-wing faith in the working classes as the promoters of social progress.[8]

Collectively, they were saying that the Democratic Party had a choice. It could seek to unify around a centrist coalition that would hold out the bait of national success every four years or it could sacrifice components of the coalition for ideological purity. The first might well be impossible, as both Lubell and Dutton suggested. To placate the machinist's wife would not only be negative but could also offend important other segments of the coalition. Conciliation of all divergent views, even if possible, would bring only a dubious prospect of party victory; but for what purpose? To gain offices and all the advantages of access to power. But, given the profile of the Democratic umbrella, it would only result in further decimation of the coalition without promising positive progress. Even the evidence of the most recent convention had shown that the party had no real choice. For all the support that clinched Humphrey's nomination, there were enough votes from the vice president's own delegates joined with the McCarthy-Kennedy-McGovern crowd to carry the day for the major reforms that came out of the convention. With southern conservatism much less of a factor than before, and the party in that region becoming an organization of blacks and liberals, the national party was finding itself released from inhibiting compromises. Let the Republican inheritors of the Dixie conservatives permit themselves to move ever onward toward the right while Democrats become a Kennedy-McGovern-centered party.

So began the post-1968 version of the new politics, an effort to improve matters not according to some New Left prescriptions, not by destroying the system or even by starting a new party, but by reshaping the Democrats, inheriting it from the bosses and ward-healers who cared little about either war and peace or bread and butter and making it responsive to the needs of modern American society. Enough Democrats had been for McCarthy, Kennedy and, in the last days at Chicago, for George McGovern to form the nucleus of a new liberal force. Further, there were countless progressives who had gone along with Hubert Humphrey after the convention largely to solidify the effort to defeat Nixon. Having been forced to compromise their principles, they would welcome liberation. While 1968 had been a disaster, there was the hopeful reality that 1972 was but four years away.

The movement began long before the appearance of Dutton's book; in fact, the tumult at Chicago was still taking place when the idea of uniting the dissident forces began to germinate. Right after the convention, Percy Sutton, the black borough president of Manhattan, publicly announced that he and other leaders were planning to form a "new coalition" to restructure the party in New York State. Operating entirely outside the Humphrey campaign, he said it would strive to make the party an outstanding example of "participatory democracy." Sutton emphatically denied that it would merely attempt to resurrect New York's reform movement.[9]

Their eagerness to shed the "good-government" reform image nevertheless made them distinctive from the "old" reformers of New York's Lexington Club and the Lehman-Finletter-Eleanor Roosevelt brand, as well as from such movements as the California Democratic Council. They were younger and were also more likely to have non-white representation, although the latter were still a distinct minority among the predominantly college-educated white middle-class membership. In fact, at the first big conference to organize themselves as a national body, the paucity of "third-world" representation was noted as a matter for future correction.

That meeting was held a full month before the Nixon-Humphrey election, as though the outcome was either a far-gone conclusion, or, to a large portion of those assembled, a Humphrey victory would not alter the prescriptions of what the Democratic Party needed. It was a two-day affair, convened at the Dyckman Hotel in Minneapolis in early October. The central component consisted of the veterans of the McCarthy campaign: Allard Lowenstein, Dartmouth Professor David Hoeh who had managed the senator's New Hampshire primary, and Gerald N. Hill of the California Democratic Council. Unlike the usual composition of elite reform groups of the past, there was a smattering of representation from peace, labor, and minority groups, including such new leaders as Julian Bond and Herman Badillo, the Puerto Rican-born Bronx borough president. Others were veterans of the Robert Kennedy campaign and were still bitter about Eugene McCarthy. But, said Professor Hoeh, McCarthy nevertheless was the "spiritual leader" of the coalition. The senator was not present.[10]

Their basic support came from the local dissident organizations that had been established as part of the antiwar movement's attempt to dump Johnson. Most recently, they had been active in opposition to Humphrey's nomination. Hopefully, the tactics that had been used in McCarthy's campaign could be mobilized for the purpose of taking the party's machinery out of the hands of the old leadership. Calling themselves the New Democratic Coalition (NDC), the 225 delegates who had come from forty states promptly declined to endorse Humphrey's election. Their emphasis was not so much on defeating Nixon in November as on reforming the Democratic Party to make it more responsive to the "will of the voters" on the issues, especially the war and the domestic needs that could be attacked once the fighting had finally ended.[11]

While there could be no complete agreement about every detail of what New Coalition Democrats assumed or hoped to achieve, certain aspects may be deduced as central to the cause. They agreed that politics "belonged to the people." A restructuring of the party, "participatory democracy," would make that a reality. Underlying this faith was a conviction of many, albeit one that cannot be demonstrated as true, that both the Humphrey and Nixon nominations were denials of the men preferred by most Democrats and Republicans. Such injustices could be corrected, within their own party, by replacing the "old coalition" of city bosses, conservative southerners, and entrenched labor. The authors of a New Democratic Coalition discussion draft, for example, made a charge that was becoming current among new-politics people: now that the labor movement has basically achieved its end—a good economic standard of living for its members—it has become conservative; the movement shares little with the social revolution of rising expectations among the impoverished of the nation. Declaring that the "present liberalism of the Democratic party is stale and irrelevant," the purpose of the NDC should be to transform the party from "a machine to get people elected to an instrument of public service." Since parties were becoming obsolete because most of their traditional functions were being carried out by either the government or by the candidates and their personal supporters, they should become more responsive to the needs of the people by functioning as "an instrument of public service." The paper suggested the establishment of local "Social Action Committees." All could be undertaken by welding together the new generation of dissident Democrats, peace and civil rights groups, "enlightened" labor and business and such leaders of the "New South" as Bond, Charles Evers, and John Cashin, the chairman of a group that had been formed in early 1968 to challenge the Wallace Democrats of Alabama and had been legally chartered as the National Democratic Party of Alabama.[12] The new movement prompted a comment from Dick Goodwin, the former Kennedy and McCarthy speech-writer, who said, "I've always felt that things like the New Democratic Coalition were a great mistake because they were an effort simply to say, 'Look, we're better guys than those guys.' I don't think you can start a political movement in this country from that basis."[13]

By the end of 1968, local NDC clubs had been started in some twenty states. One year later, with chapters in more than half of the states, the national organization was nevertheless fragmented and disorganized. Its national office had closed down in early 1970, leaving behind more than $20,000 in unpaid bills. Blair Clark, Gene McCarthy's campaign manager in 1968, had resigned as its treasurer with the comment that anticipated contributors had seen no real need for a national organization. When some three hundred NDC members met in Chicago in mid-February 1970, McCarthy refused an invitation to attend, explaining that the Democratic Party was "beginning to look pretty good, beginning to look like the party I was describing back in 1968."[14] While local chapters remained strong in certain states, and would continue to spur new-politics activities in such places as New York City, Wisconsin, and California, McCarthy did have a point: the Democrats were starting to make structural reforms of a magnitude that the NDC people would have been proud to have accomplished.

2

Even while the NDC was groping its way toward significance, the reform decisions that had been made in Chicago were bringing a sharp departure from the way business had always been conducted. The national party was moving toward similar changes with the assumption that running the Democrats should not be the exclusive preserve of elite power brokers, whether politicos or spokesmen for special interest groups, but that the response must be that the "best cure for democracy is more democracy." Therefore, nothing was more essential than modernizing both the selection of delegates and the rules governing the national conventions. The institutionalization of such changes, despite the interests of established centers of power, illustrated both the weakness of the old order and the reformist zeal of the new breed of Democrats.

The consequences of the MFDP seating battle turned out to have far more implications than merely the question of justice for that particular state's delegation. It opened an examination of the methods used to select representatives of Democrats for national conventions in every single state. At the request of the Credentials Committee, Governor Harold Hughes of Iowa, well known for his interest in reform, organized a commission that prepared elaborate documentation of the procedures then in use. Never before had there been such a thorough study of how individuals came to be seated. The Hughes Commission thereby both provided evidence of what was wrong and forwarded recommendations for change, all of which served, in turn, as the basis for the subsequent work of the Commission on Party Structure and Delegate Selection. Both the later group and a Commission on Rules were then approved by the delegates, constituting at least a partial response to the conflicts within the convention hall and on the streets of Chicago. The membership of the commissions was left to the party's national chairman.

Initially, their composition became temporarily bogged down in the politics of the moment. The chairman, Larry O'Brien, showed little haste about making the choices. In the midst of the election campaign, O'Brien was disinclined to offend the national committee. At the same time, and precisely because the campaign for the presidency was taking place, Humphrey was eager to demonstrate his support for reform by being able to bless their formation. Therefore, the senator and his friends pressed O'Brien for early compliance with the convention's directive. They felt that having the organization would be of great attraction to those still reluctant to support the candidate. As Steve Mitchell put it, it would help to harmonize matters by getting their minds off the "stop the bombing" issue and move closer to Humphrey.[15] But O'Brien could not be moved during those crucial weeks. Finally, in early 1969, his successor, Senator Fred Harris of Oklahoma, staffed the two bodies. Representative James O'Hara, a liberal from Michigan, became the chairman of the Rules Commission; and the Commission on Party Structure and Delegate Selection, which became the more controversial of the two, was placed under the chairmanship of Senator George McGovern. Looking back upon his successor's choices, O'Brien noted that both were "clearly weighed toward the liberal wing of the party, rather than being representative of the party as a whole."[16]

During the spring and summer of 1969, the McGovern Commission held a series of open hearings in seventeen cities and took testimony from over five hundred witnesses. Not surprisingly, many suggested the outright abolition of the convention system. They pointed out that most of the selections had been predetermined so that the quadrennial gatherings were nothing more than expensive charades that posed the additional mischief of creating more divisions than harmony. One possible alternative that found support was a system of national nominating primaries for each party. Reluctance to do anything that drastic, however, and the persisting conviction that the conventions did provide much-needed opportunities for scrutinizing both ideas and candidates, led to the inevitable conclusion that the conventions themselves were not to blame. The problem was with the methods used to choose the delegates.

In its subsequent report to the national committee, published under the title of *Mandate for Reform*, a long list of deficiencies was enumerated.[17] They included the following conditions:

1) At least ten states had no written party rules and others were so vague about the delegate selection process that important decisions were in the hands of a few elected or appointed officials.

2) Proxy voting, largely unregulated, "was a source of much real and felt grievance in 1968." One Missouri party official cast 492 unwritten proxies in a township caucus.

3) Delegate selection frequently took place without any notification to the voters that such a process was being held.

4) Slate-making was an abuse by an official decision-making

body that had the virtually unchecked power to ratify a complete list from among one or more slates of prospective delegates.

5) There was a pattern of discrimination against blacks, women, the young, and the poor. In 1964, although 94 percent of all blacks voted Democratic and Negroes constituted over 11 percent of the population, they comprised only 2 percent of the delegates. In 1968, when 85 percent of black voters supported the Humphrey-Muskie ticket, their percentage at the convention was 5.5. More than a dozen states and territories had no black delegates whatsoever. In every state, women were seriously under-represented and they comprised just 13 percent of the voting delegates at Chicago. Only one woman, Representative Edith Green, chaired a delegation. Sixteen delegates had no voting members younger than thirty and eight had an average age of over fifty. Widespread imposition of assessments helped to eliminate those who were not wealthy. In Indiana and Iowa, each delegate was assessed $250 by the state party, and the former added another $250 to defray the cost of the state party's hospitality suite. The $500 still did not take care of the personal expenses involved in attending the convention.

6) Party committees were used in about one-fifth of the states to select some or all of the delegates. In every case, the voters played absolutely no role in their choice.

7) California's "winner-take-all" primary afforded absolutely no place to the loser's delegates even though the 1968 vote was split between Kennedy and McCarthy by 46 to 42 percent while an additional 12 percent was cast for the Lynch slate.

8) In at least twenty states, half or even 100 percent of the delegates were chosen before the calendar year in which the convention occurred. As the report stated, "This means that the day Eugene McCarthy announced his candidacy nearly one-third of the delegates had in effect already been selected."

By September 1969, the McGovern Commission (later chaired by Representative Donald Fraser after the senator stepped down a few days before declaring his candidacy for the presidency) adopted a set of guidelines. Besides reaffirming what the 1968 convention had already decided about eliminating the unit rule at all levels, most items were remedies that were too self-evident to stir much controversy. One major change, however, was the requirement that all delegates be chosen by some kind of an election and that none obtain a seat by virtue of holding public or party offices.

But the most sensitive areas were in sections A-1 and A-2. This first directed state parties to "overcome the effects of past discrimination by affirmative steps to encourage minority group participation, including representation of minority groups on the national convention delegation in reasonable relationship to the group's presence in the population of the State." Section A-2 required overcoming "the effects of past discrimination by affirmative steps to encourage representation on the national convention delegation of young people . . . and women in reasonable relationship to their presence in the population of the State."

The catch-words were "reasonable" and "affirmative steps." Carefully placed footnotes explained that it was the "understanding of the Commission that this is not to be accomplished by the mandatory imposition of quotas." But nobody could explain how a "reasonable relationship" could be achieved without the application of a formula containing quotas or how the "effects of past discrimination" could be rectified without basing delegations on formulas that consciously gave a disproportionate amount of weight to the formerly deprived elements. Further, if such traditionalists as O'Brien thought the commission was stacked in the first place, they felt even more aggrieved that guidelines A-1 and A-2 had been adopted by a mere 10 to 9 vote of the twenty-eight-member commission. The representative of organized labor, I. W. Abel, president of the United Steelworkers of America, had boycotted the session in protest and the moderates had contributed only sporadically, leaving the field open to the new-politics sympathizers.[18]

On February 19, 1971, the national committee adopted the guidelines and included them as part of the Preliminary Call for the 1972 convention. The O'Hara Commission Report on Rules, adopted later, contained a series of provisions to streamline the conventions. They also included a directive that committee members chosen by the states had to be in balance among the sexes and with "due regard to the race and age of the men and women elected."

It was obvious that the party had made the most significant changes since the elimination of the two-thirds rule in 1936. But, aside from the question of "reasonable" measures and "affirmative steps," two serious problems remained. Special-interest groups, particularly organized labor, could no longer be assured of a dominant role, especially since states that had convention systems were required to select at least 75 percent of their delegates at congressional-district or small-unit levels. Also created was the probability that old and established, and often respected, leaders within their states would suddenly find themselves challenged for the right to be seated as delegates. For some veterans, stepping aside would be easier than contending with what they would consider the humiliating spectacle of being challenged by youthful newcomers. As far-reaching as many of the New Democratic Coalition ideals, the reforms thus led the party toward another presidential election with a set of regulations that were not always understood or accepted. If the changes had been designed to counter the new-politics criticism of the party's structure that had grown out of the last two conventions, it soon became evident that an entirely new element of dissenters had been created. On June 28, 1972, only days before the opening of the national convention at Miami Beach, House Democrats held a closed caucus and approved by 105 to 50 a resolution offered by Frank Annunzio of Illinois that denounced the reforms as "not in the best interests of the Democratic party," and called for "further investigation and study." One member, Wayne Hays of Ohio, declared that "the Democratic party is in shambles, and this isn't going to make it a better shambles." But, for others, it was easy to dismiss the resolution, especially since Annunzio was a loyal Daley man. It merely proved that Congress was out of step with the times.[19]

3

The McGovern nomination triumph of 1972 was essentially the new-politics revenge for 1968, the culmination of reformist, new-breed activism that represented the mobilization of the antiwar movement as one final, desperate attempt to win the presidency. Their failure to compete credibly against Nixon in the fall campaign was far less astonishing than the process by which the nomination itself had been won. Turned back at the polls, left with victories in only Massachusetts and the District of Columbia, the antiwar activism, the youth crusade, the counterculture suddenly folded up and evaporated. Less certain was the failure of the new politics. Two years after the McGovern disaster, Lanny J. Davis, who had served with Senator Edmund Muskie as National Youth Coordinator in 1972, remained optimistic about an alternative to the prescriptions of Kevin Phillips and the Scammon-Wattenberg new conservatism. Wrote Davis: "There is, I suggest, a third alternative to the Democratic Party: the building of a new . . . majority coalition, a new center, uniting the forces of the New Politics, with its new areas of political support in formerly Republican and independent voter constituencies, with the traditional Democratic base of working-class and middle-class-income people, of all races and in all regions of the country."[20] Once more there was the formulation of a new winning coalition, presumably one that would form behind another new messiah. Once again, there was reluctance to be discouraged by the conventional assumptions of the American party system.

George McGovern, too, had his ideals. From a conservative state, South Dakota, he nevertheless had compiled a voting record that was comparable with that of any liberal in the country. As a congressman during the 1950s, he had been instrumental in helping to create a party in a state dominated by conservative Republicans and represented in the Senate by Karl Mundt and Francis Case. Leaving the House to challenge Mundt in 1960, he lost but made a credible showing against the entrenched incumbent. President Kennedy then named McGovern as the director of the Food for Peace Program. In 1962, with a plurality of just 597 votes, he won election to the Senate. Never a flamboyant liberal and certainly not a radical, he had succeeded in part by his ability to convince even his conservative constituents that he was sincere and cool-headed, the very absence of the kind of charisma that was thought to handicap his ability to make a national race.

Yet, when he declared himself for the presidency on January 18, 1971, it was as a "peace" candidate and with the pledge that he would effectuate the early withdrawal of American troops from Vietnam. "The people are not centrist or liberal or conservative," he declared in a televised address. "Rather, they seek a way out of the wilderness."[21] An opponent of the war as immoral, his critique dated as far back as 1963 when he took the Senate floor to warn that Vietnam was a trap that "will haunt us in every corner of the revolutionary world." Still, he went along with the Johnson administration, not joining Wayne Morse and Ernest Gruening in opposition to the Gulf of Tonkin Resolution and even opposing the subsequent attempt to get it repealed. Thus, he kept a discreet balance between his views toward the fighting and the requirements of his constituency. His colleagues in the Senate, however, regarded him as a dove. After the assassination of Robert Kennedy, he decided to go for the presidency.

At Chicago, McGovern won the support of the anti-McCarthy Kennedy people. In his debate with Humphrey and Eugene McCarthy before the California delegation, he emerged the clear winner. At a meeting with his close advisers who gathered at his farm on Maryland's Eastern Shore during the summer of 1970, the decision to go for the 1972 nomination was sealed. By January, one week after resigning his chairmanship of the McGovern Commission, he solicited support by sending a letter to the thousands of names that had been assiduously accumulated. It declared, in part, "I believe that my nomination as our party's presidential candidate offers the best chance of heading off a fourth-party movement by Democrats still fuming with impatience over the mistakes of past leadership. . . . I intend to be as completely forthright as a presidential candidate as I have been as a Senator."[22]

To make possible a candidacy that few could take seriously, some basic assumptions had to be accepted. Ted Kennedy, undoubtedly the most popular Democrat, had been taken out of competition by the Chappaquiddick tragedy of 1969 that had cost the life of Mary Jo Kopechne and had yet to be explained to the full satisfaction of the public. Hubert Humphrey was a spent politician, a symbol of outmoded liberalism, who simply could not reunite the party. Yet he could not be ignored, especially with a Gallup Poll in late 1971 showing that, with Kennedy out of the race, the former vice president was the first choice among all Democratic possibilities.[23] If he could not resist the temptation to enter the race, however, he would perform the service of checking the man widely recognized as the front-runner, Senator Edmund Muskie of Maine, a role that Humphrey did eventually play.

That same Gallup poll showed Muskie right behind Humphrey; in fact, they ran 34 and 31 percent with the drop-off then going all the way down to 8 percent for both McGovern and that recent convert to the Democratic Party, Mayor John V. Lindsay of New York. As Humphrey's running-mate in 1968, Muskie had in many ways emerged as the most impressive candidate on either ticket, and he was immediately regarded as a strong contender for 1972. Just before the midterm elections of 1970, he boosted his stock further by delivering a Lincolnesque talk filled with appeals to reason and good sense that was in sharp contrast to the strident law-and-order campaign speech by the president. Muskie, having the good fortune to be shown on television screens speaking right after Mr. Nixon's law-and-order speech, spoke calmly and deliberately from a home in Maine. Adding additional luster to Muskie's performance, as well as hope for the Democrats, was the lack of evidence that the voters had gone to the polls with any firm intent to confirm a sharp right-wing trend that had been feared. While not a clearcut Democratic triumph, especially for the party out of power, the most significant gains came in winning control over the statehouses as eleven governorships were picked up. With the reapportionment of congressional seats due as a result of the 1970 census, the party would have the advantage of being able to supervise most of the new mapping of district lines that would go into effect before the 1972 elections. All in all, by the end of 1970, Democratic hopes were high. So were Muskie's—so much so, in fact, that frightened occupants of the White House formed a Committee to Re-Elect the President to prepare for the coming defense of the incumbency. But, for the moment, Muskie was the target of McGovern and those Democrats who hoped that the senator from South Dakota might at least perform the function of helping to check the front-runner.[24]

Eugene McCarthy was also expected to run, but his followers had become considerably disenchanted since 1968. Seemingly unwilling to maintain his leadership, he had resigned from the Foreign Relations Committee and had voted against Ted Kennedy as the Senate whip. Then he voluntarily retired from elective office, his seat consequently won by Humphrey in 1970. Others still resented his belated endorsement of Humphrey during the 1968 campaign. So no longer did he appear as a serious contender.

Instead, the maverick with the large following was George Wallace. His strength was clearly not confined to the South, but also in those northern areas of great fear and hostility toward busing to remedy the effects of racial imbalances. Entering the Democratic primaries instead of running as an independent, Wallace commanded both votes and attention all spring. In Florida, he opposed such rivals as Muskie, Senator Henry Jackson, Lindsay, and McGovern, and, despite the heavy field, finished far out in front with 42 percent of the total vote. Early in May, he won the North Carolina primary by defeating that state's liberal ex-governor, Terry Sanford; one week later, he swept to victory in Maryland. But on that same day, May 15, he also won his first big northern victory, a massive sweep of Michigan, overwhelming both McGovern and Humphrey. Aided by heavy support from Republicans and independents in a state without party registration, he triumphed as the champion of the working classes and suburban middle-class whites who were resisting school busing.[25]

Also on that same day, in a shopping center in Laurel, Maryland, another assassin, this time one who fell just short of his goal, influenced the course of recent American politics. Arthur Bremer, a twenty-one-year-old Milwaukee man, fired several shots into the governor at close range, paralyzing him from below the waist and effectively removing him as a serious contender, at least for 1972. The steady stream of prominent politicians who subsequently rushed to be photographed at his bedside provided evidence that, if anything, the shooting had helped to enhance his respectability. One of the visitors was President Nixon, who would obviously be the big gainer.

Meanwhile, McGovern continued to forge ahead as a candidate with only minority support by appealing to the majority among the new wave, the youth and antiwar blocs. A fresh anti-establishment figure, he capitalized on emphasizing his frequent denunciations of the Vietnamese war. He talked positively of granting amnesty for war-resisters. He appeared on as many college campuses as possible to convey to the new generation, the first eighteen-year-old voters, that he understood their feelings on issues appalling to the very people Nixon had termed the "silent majority," such issues as abortion and marijuana, without saying that he favored the complete legalization of either. Taking a lesson from the McCarthy campaign, he knew that the young people were the best workers he could get. Intelligent, dedicated, their strength was disproportionately great. Moreover, the man who had headed the McGovern Commission certainly understood that the delegation selection would have to conform to the new guidelines. And that had inherent advantages for a leader who could command the former McCarthy-Kennedy following, the young, the women, the minorities, all of whom would, at Miami Beach, be more prominent than ever before at a national nominating convention.

Gathering his following, raising large sums from small contributors, McGovern entered the primaries. As the Watergate testimony later confirmed, in such places as New England and Georgia, in particular, he had covert assistance from the president's men, who employed their "dirty tricks" squad to weaken his rivals in the belief that McGovern would be the easiest man to defeat in November. Most damaging was a spurious letter used to condemn Muskie in the pages of William Loeb's Manchester *Union Leader*, which led the senator to an emotional defense of his wife's supposed pejorative reference to the local French-Canadian population. Reports that he had cried while speaking in the falling snow outside the newspaper's office helped to compound the perception that had been growing for months that Muskie was too weak to act forthrightly. His position on the issues seemed to lack a sense of firm commitment. As McGovern's pollster later revealed, the change in public attitudes about Muskie had begun to occur many months earlier, and that many "who had perceived him after the '70 speech as being a very decisive individual, a person who had some substance, began to get the feeling that there wasn't much there—that he was not taking stands and was all over the place. Our feeling by late December was that he was in very serious trouble."[26] New Hampshire turned in a disappointing first-place vote for him, while McGovern finished with surprising strength in second place.

But even while the primaries drew the headlines, in state after state McGovernites used the new guidelines to the hilt while Muskie continued to rely on the professionals for his support. Consequently, McGovern began quietly to accumulate large numbers of delegates. Finally taken seriously, outpolling all his rivals, his rank-and-file standing rose. A late-June Gallup poll, just before the convention opened, showed him with a 30 to 27 to 25 percent lead over chief rivals Humphrey and Wallace.[27]

McGovern waged his new-politics campaign with a combination of the new egalitarianism and continued recognition of the utility of the old tactics. Thus, in New York, with the assistance of writer Jimmy Breslin, he sought and won important organizational endorsement from an unlikely source. Matthew Troy, a city councilman and leader of the populous Queens County Democrats, announced for McGovern as early as the summer of 1971. Of all New York City politicians, Troy was one of the least likely to identify himself with McGovern. A conservative Democrat and critic of the antiwar movement, he had indulged in such gestures as climbing out to the flagpole atop City Hall to restore the stars and stripes after Mayor Lindsay had ordered it to be lowered in cooperation with protests against military policies in Asia. Yet, for Matty Troy, McGovern was handy. The New York City Democratic Coalition was overwhelmingly for the senator. Coming out for him was a way of bridging, Troy hoped, the gulf between himself and the new-politics people, a useful preparation for a possible citywide race in the future.[28] The McGovern camp, in turn, made no attempt to minimize their delight over the Troy support. Frank Mankiewicz, the campaign director, complained to the New York *Times* that the importance of the news had not been given proper appreciation in its pages.[29] Late in the primary campaign, Mankiewicz received an urgent call that McGovern was the only candidate in New York's delegate-selection contest whose slate was not in compliance with the McGovern Commission guidelines.[30]

But the outstanding discrepancy between conventional practical politics and the ideals of the "new" involved the situation in California. The McGovern Commission had seen fit to denounce that state's "winner-take-all" primary as an example of the denial of fair representation for a minority point of view. Still, when the Humphrey people fought to permit the seating of 151 Californians who had not been actually won by McGovern but had claims by virtue of that state's unit rule, they encountered the major contest of the convention. After an adverse ruling by the Credentials Committee, one that would have given Humphrey 106 seats with the other forty-five split among minor candidates, the McGovern forces regained their point on the floor of the convention. In an interesting reversal of roles, the anti-McGovern lawyers argued that the California law violated the "spirit of reform," while the senator's people fought for the "sanctity" of the state's law.[31]

The California case helped the South Dakotan over the top but the process, in competition with Humphrey, actually began his downfall. In a state heavily dependent upon the defense industry, Humphrey denounced criticism of the high military budget. That became the single most damaging point he was able to make.[32] He also weakened McGovern in attempts to get a clear explanation of the South Dakotan's plan to give a $1,000 income maintenance allowance to every needy American. What had been projected as a 20 percent McGovern advantage at the start of the California campaign finally ended in a victory by a narrow 5 percent margin. So even before Miami Beach and the unorthodox convention, McGovern's credibility had begun to decline. The convention itself, which was abhorrent to many conservative viewers, included three times as many women and blacks as in 1968 and had a fivefold greater participation by young people.

Further, having won the nomination, McGovern then had to seek an election victory over Nixon by adhering to the old rules. When confronted by the embarrassment of the revelation that his running-mate, Senator Thomas Eagleton of Missouri, had had a history of nervous breakdowns requiring shock treatments, he initially said he stood by the vice presidential candidate "one thousand percent" and then, instead of meeting the issue by appealing to the enlightened understanding of what was involved in such medical histories, surreptitiously began to prepare the way for his removal from the ticket.

That Eagleton was forced off is clear. As he explained in an interview only a few months later, "Some of the telephone calls I gather Senator McGovern was receiving, not only from key fund raisers, and key financial distributors, but from his advisory command as well, was that Eagleton ought to go off the ticket, that he would be a drag on the ticket." He added, "I would have been more of an asset on the ticket than a liability. I went on the ticket as a rather national unknown quantity, but the publicity that had been generated made me more of a national figure, which would have enhanced the ticket rather than detract from it."[33] After several embarrassing attempts to replace him with a prominent Democrat, which resulted in rejections from such people as Ted Kennedy, Muskie, and Abe Ribicoff, McGovern settled for Sargent Shriver.

Then McGovern tried to patch up matters with the traditional sources of power whom the new-politics people had offended. Mayor Daley and his slate had been successfully challenged at Miami Beach and dramatically denied seats because of nonadherence with the guidelines. Still, the candidate then sought his support, getting at least some perfunctory recognition acknowledging the mayor's awareness that the senator was alive. He also visited the LBJ Ranch, where he received a tepid endorsement from the former president. In a major address on Wall Street, he announced a major modification of his $1,000 income maintenance plan, which had caused his prolonged embarrassment. But his attempt to broaden his base had its distinct limitation as George Meany resorted to his own "golden silence" while cracking down on unions that dared to endorse McGovern. All over the country, millions of Democratic voters prepared to cast ballots, however reluctantly, for Richard Nixon.

The McGovern failure was readily predictable. He never had a chance. Even the news that there were White House ties with the burglars who were caught red-handed in a midnight break-in at Democratic headquarters at the Watergate complex in Washington— which McGovern tried to present as a major issue—influenced hardly any voters. Nixon had gone to both China and Russia; the old cold warrior, who had been so instrumental in having exacerbated the domestic hysteria over communism, was getting credit for creating a new détente. At the same time, he had mined the waters outside North Vietnam's major port and bombed the outskirts of Hanoi without drawing retaliation from either the Chinese or the Russians. To most Americans, having promised "peace with honor," he was the peace candidate. Also, having pursued a "southern strategy" through various means since assuming office, he was obviously locking up the vote in that region, especially with Wallace now out of the way. He had also made a blatant play for the Catholic vote, which included expressions of support for federal aid to parochial schools and a tactical letter to Terence Cardinal Cooke of New York that stated his opposition to that state's advanced abortion law.[34] Just as ardent was his play for the Jewish vote. He emphasized that his administration was more firmly committed to Israel's survival than McGovern would be, and America's ally in the Middle East cooperatively let it be known that they, too, believed Nixon was best for their interests.

McGovern had tried to have it both ways. He had employed the new-politics momentum to win the nomination. Having succeeded so remarkably, he tried to pull together the conventional forces to win an election that, basically, still had to be played according to the traditional rules. It could not be done, especially against the enormously well-financed and adroit tactics of a shrewd incumbent. The ability to brand McGovern as hypocritical as well as a "radical," and the threat to conventional cultural values implicit in the life-styles of much of the senator's following compounded the disaster. Postelection analyses showed that Nixon had cut heavily into the old Democratic coalition, not only in the South, but had taken 57 percent of the blue-collar vote and 52 percent of Catholics. Over a third of the Jewish vote, an exceptionally high figure, went for him. Even households with labor-union members supported him by 54 percent.[35] Winning 61.8 percent of the two-party vote, Nixon left McGovern with just seventeen electors.

4

"Win, lose or draw, the Democratic party can be counted on to tear itself apart, in internal wrangling whenever there is no election to concentrate on—and even an election rarely stills the bickering," began a postelection lead editorial in the New York *Times*. A Stewart Alsop column was entitled "The Nekkid Democrats."[36]

Torn by acrimony, largely inspired by bitterness at the McGovernites for having led toward destruction, and with the parallel resentment from the left that the center and right-wing of the party had followed much of organized labor into the Nixon camp, the Democratic Party found itself with the materialization of all its nightmares. Despite their numerical survival as the dominant force on Capitol Hill for the organization of the Ninety-third Congress, having resisted the Nixon sweep at least on that level, they were leaderless. McGovern himself hardly qualified for recognition as a titular leader. Suddenly, the man who had led the insurgency that had brought off an astonishing political coup in July was the target of recriminations within his own party. And the scapegoats were hit almost immediately.

Within a month after the election, Democrats rushed to purge themselves of the McGovernite leadership of the national committee. The committee itself had been reformed and greatly expanded during the previous summer, a reshaping that had added substantial McGovern influence to its ranks in key states. Nevertheless, Chairwoman Jean Westwood of Utah, a McGovern appointee, came under severe pressure that soon forced her to resign to give the party "a new sense of direction." At a meeting of the national committee on December 9, she was replaced by a fifty-four-year-old Texas lawyer and businessman, Robert Strauss. Strauss had served as the party's treasurer and was a good friend of John Connally, who had spent the campaign leading Democrats for Nixon. On the day of his election, Strauss said to the committee, "I am a centrist, a worker, a doer, a putter-together, and those talents belong to you."[37] A pragmatist rather than an ideologue, his new mission was to put the party together again by creating a more hospitable atmosphere for the Daleys, Meanys, and even, in one last effort, for John Connally, who later declared himself a Republican.

Inevitably, there were other ideas about the future shape of the party. In the wake of McGovern's defeat, a group composed principally of the supporters of Humphrey and Henry Jackson, who had campaigned during the primaries with a newfound conservative image, organized themselves as the Coalition for a Democratic Majority. With close ties to the AFL-CIO's Alexander Barkan and his Committee on Political Education, they constituted a centrist force, an attempt to recapture the party from the new politics. Penn Kemble, the coalition's executive director and Meany's executive assistant, explained, "It's been demonstrated in this campaign that they want to take over the Democratic Party, even if it means throwing out the labor movement," a statement that ignored the considerable number of less well-heeled unionists who had voted for McGovern.[38] To the left of the coalition, rose another group, this one led by Michael Harrington, who had come to prominence as the author of

The Other America. Harrington had resigned as national co-chairman of the Socialist Party during the campaign because their endorsement of McGovern had been given in a manner that, as Harrington complained, was "reluctant and backhanded."[39] On one of the coldest nights of the winter, some two hundred sympathizers met with Harrington in an auditorium on the campus of New York University and held what was billed as a National Conference of the Democratic Left. "We have ideas that can speak to the needs of the vast majority of the American people, if only we will speak to one another and work them out," he told them. The group became the nucleus of the Democratic Socialist Organizing Committee, which was devoted to exerting a left-wing influence within the Democratic Party to achieve progressive majorities in 1974 and 1976.

On Capitol Hill that January, as the Ninety-third Congress met to organize itself, elected Democratic legislatures were far less certain that there could be a central purpose to the party. Herman Badillo was one of the charter members of the New Democratic Coalition and now a congressman from New York City with a large black and Puerto Rican constituency. Highly intense, with an intellect that betrayed an impatience with frivolities verging on arrogance, his mood was one of despair over the complete hopelessness of ever getting the federal government to assist with the rehabilitation of his blighted South Bronx district. There was, he argued, nothing to counter the Republican administration's indifference to the cities. As to the opposition, "There really is no Democratic Party," he explained. In the House, he had found little real resistance to Nixon even from the Democratic side. "Albert," said the congressman, referring to the Democratic Speaker, "is a consistent supporter of Nixon. Most of the committee chairmen, all of the southern congressmen, almost invariably with very few exceptions support the president now even more strongly than they did last year." Rarely looking up from his desk, bitter and angry, he added: "Now Nixon carried the southern states, so that you put together the southern congressmen, the Republican congressmen from the Midwest, and you have a majority of the Congress. Therefore, I don't see any likelihood that there will be any attempt to have a Democratic Party in Congress that will seek to provide an alternative to the Republican Party in domestic and foreign policy." The Nixon victory and the Democratic congressional success, he explained, had resulted from "a split, an ideological split, because most of the Democrats and Nixon are really on the same side."[40]

One of Badillo's opposites within the party was equally disenchanted. Louisiana's John Rarick, who had been stripped of his seniority for having endorsed George Wallace in 1968 and was considered by some as the most reactionary member of the entire Congress, was among those particularly incensed about efforts to reshape the party. Sitting in an office decorated with right-wing bumper stickers (SUPPORT YOUR LOCO PROFESSORS), he deplored any effort of the party to "become a closed society" by trying to force agreement. "Then they overlook the fact that there is no such thing as a political party," he said. "Political parties are people. The party doesn't make the people do things; and when any political party comes under such regimented control that it feels that it can boss the people around, the people are going to punish it."[41]

Congressman Richard Bolling, one of the members of the new Coalition of Concerned Democrats and a former ADA field director, explained that American parties are "umbrella parties because the United States is a very complicated, difficult country. The people of the United States are more different from each other, from region to region, then, let's say, the Germans are from the French." The democratic process itself, he added, is much more complex and difficult than any theory of democracy; but he did agree that Democrats had splintered themselves by their failure to move swiftly enough on the issues.[42]

There was little doubt that the upholders of the umbrella were in the majority. Such people as congresswomen Edith Green and Martha Griffiths both stressed the need for Democrats to attend to the needs of middle-class voters, holding that that was the real political battleground and that any move to drive the party toward a rigid doctrinaire position would be suicidal. Said Ms. Green, in her final term as congresswoman from Oregon, "I think the Democratic Party has to make it abundantly clear that we represent the working guy as well as the guy on welfare, or the person that obviously needs help." Griffiths of Michigan, one of the prime movers of the Equal Rights Amendment and also completing her career, saw herself as representing "a middle-income level who is really paying for everybody else, and they would like to see some corrections made." Rather than what should be the heart of the Democratic constituency, she complained, "you apparently have people who have been running the party, who ran the convention, who ran the campaign, who had the ridiculous idea that you could put the very poor, the very deprived, make the sole appeal to these people. Well, you can't. I mean, they don't comprise that much of the population." A southern veteran, Senator John Sparkman, also agreed. "I'll predict we're going to consolidate the Democratic Party," he said. "That doesn't mean it's going to be a party of left-wingers or right-wingers, but it'll be a party that can appeal to the different groups that we represent in this country. There's one thing you've got to remember that has characterized the Democratic Party through the years, and that is that it is a nationwide party." And Thomas Eagleton welcomed Robert Strauss' recent overture to John Connally to return to the fold by saying that the "penitent sinners" should be received with open arms, but "I would not reward them by giving them a role in the party."[43]

But what that party could, should, or was willing to do remained a mystery. Without leadership from the White House, without a single spokesman, with both ex-presidents dead, with neither Majority Leader Mike Mansfield nor House Speaker Carl Albert temperamentally inclined toward forceful pace-setting—and neither very attractive to the party's urban liberal heartland in the North—there were plenty of followers without a messiah. Most liberals seemed as vague as the conservatives. Repeatedly, they talked about the Democratic traditions, the Democratic—or New Deal Democratic—traditions of "helping the poor." Hardly anything, however, remotely resembled a program, or the restructuring of both the party and the political system to expedite fulfillment of their expressed ideals. Such matters seemed to have been given little thought. With the outstanding exceptions of Badillo and Congressman Michael J. Harrington of Massachusetts, who worried about the nation's international assumptions, clichés were dominant. Democrats were still described as the "party of Roosevelt" that enabled them to glory in the "accomplishments of the New Deal." Lacking anything more substantial to say, a Democrat could usually get away with such banalities as, "we care about people while the Republicans care about money and property," all too reminiscent of Eisenhower's hope that the GOP would be constructive about money but liberal toward people. Their commitment to the concept of a party seemed tepid at best, most of them acknowledging its greatest importance was in organizing the new session of Congress. Even the majority leader, in a debate with his Republican counterpart over implications of the presidential pardon granted to Richard Nixon by Gerald Ford in September of 1974, declared: "I am sure that the Senator knows that I am just about as close to becoming nonpolitical or a apolitical Senator as I can, and I would not wish the implication to go to the country that this is a matter of politics."[44]

Thanks to the astonishing Watergate revelations and the economic debilities of an inflation later combined with a severe recession and mounting unemployment but not to any leadership taken by the Democrats as a party, an upturn in elective fortunes soon followed. In early 1974, a series of special elections signaled trouble for the Republicans. On August 8, Richard Nixon resigned from the presidency and was succeeded by Vice President Gerald Ford, who had earlier replaced the discredited Spiro Agnew. One month later, the new president, after having gone far toward consolidating his support during the transition period, suddenly stirred outraged reactions by announcing that he had pardoned Nixon without even awaiting a trial. With a national feeling of revulsion toward what had seemed a capricious act of injustice, and with the persistence of high prices and high unemployment, the Democrats commanded a favorable position during the midterm elections of 1974.

Suddenly, then, from all over the country, from New England to California, the totals seemed to indicate that the coalition had resurfaced. Workers, blacks, Chicanos, women, Catholics, farmers, small businessmen, had all voted Democratic. From Michael Dukakis, Hugh Carey, Ella Grasso, and Richard Stone in the East and South to Jerry Apodaca, Gary Hart, and Jerry Brown in the West, Democratic candidates had won offices on the remnants of old New Deal power. Recovering from the Nixon-McGovern disaster, the party had returned to a commanding majority. They would control two-thirds of the House, three-fifths of the Senate, and three-fourths of the governorships. The launching position for a sweep that could take them right through the presidency seemed secure. *Time* magazine, commenting on the returns from New York State, declared that "a Democratic candidate was finally putting back together the old Roosevelt coalition of labor, liberals and minorities." Theodore H. White, the journalist and chronicler of presidential campaigns, projected the results nationally and agreed that the party may finally have "resumed its movement."[45]

The figures did justify the optimism. Sixty percent of the voters had chosen Democratic congressional candidates. Furthermore, of the seventy conservatives on the House Republican Steering Committee, only thirty survived the rebellion while the moderates and liberals who belonged to the ad hoc Wednesday Group lost just one of their thirty members. Often, long-term Republicans fell to

younger, more liberal challengers. The pro-Nixon members of the
House Judiciary Committee, the only body that had been compelled
to vote on the question of presidential impeachment, were particularly hard hit. Four were defeated, one by the wife of a former
governor of New Jersey. Other women, without prior family connections in politics, made significant gains, rendering them very much a
part of all the other formerly disfranchised Americans now helping
to comprise the "emerging Democratic majority."

Democrats seemed to be coming out of the wilderness. Speaker
Albert could hardly be blamed for saying that it was not "just a
victory," it was "a mandate."[46] But the consensus that followed the
voting seemed to disagree; it sounded almost as though the Democrats had lost while winning. *The Christian Science Monitor* ran a
page-one banner headline that read: DEMOCRATS RULE—BUT WILL
THEY UNITE? Carl Albert also betrayed anxiety about the future.
"Now we're in the saddle," he said, "and also have the responsibility." Other comments, by both the press and individuals, constituted
an ominous chorus: "Democrats beware! Now you have to deliver"
(Hubert H. Humphrey). "The heat's on us now" (Walter Mondale). "I see nothing more than disillusionment, frustration and
near-chaos by the middle of next year" (Congressman Michael J.
Harrington). "The vote was less an act of faith than a rite of exor-
cism" (*Newsweek*). "Most Democrats recognized that they had received no mandate from the American electorate" (*Time*). "I don't
believe in this mandate stuff. A guy runs for office and gets elected.
All of a sudden he's got a mandate. Two votes less and he's nothing"
(George Meany).[47] Before the election itself, a warning had come
from Democratic pollster Peter Hart. Hart held that the size of the
victory would be meaningless. It would simply certify the protest
against Watergate and current economic conditions rather than a
renewal of faith in the party's wisdom and leadership.[48]

Virtually everybody agreed: That was the only consensus. Of
course, the old Roosevelt coalition had regrouped; but for what?
Neither they nor anyone else had much confidence that the problems plaguing the nation were within the competence of any single
party or individual. So they must have voted not to rekindle the
New Deal or for social democracy but to punish the Republicans.
And, even more precisely, they wanted to penalize those most obviously pro-Nixon and poisoned by Watergate and its sordid ramifications. If the president had chosen to pardon the principal defendant
on his own, the public would at least have *its* say. So it was probably

correct to say, as some did, that it was really Nixon's last election. With the voting out of the way, Democrats convened in early December in Kansas City to hold the sort of midterm conference that Paul Butler had urged twenty years earlier. Decided upon over the serious reservations of Chairman Strauss, it posed a challenge to the ability of the party to heal the wounds that had been caused by the resentment over the new delegate-selection guidelines and the leadership of McGovern and his followers.

5

On June 1, 1974, the incongruous Tenth Congressional District of Massachusetts held its Democratic caucus. Originally carved out to preserve a sanctuary for Joe Martin, the powerful Republican minority leader and speaker, the district was a microcosm of coalition headaches. At the northern end, along busy Route 128, were the affluent Boston suburbs, highlighted by Wellesley, the land of WASPs and elegance. Far to the south, stretching to the Atlantic Ocean and the Rhode Island border, it included the industrial cities of Taunton and Fall River. Their working-class populations were mostly of French Canadian, Portuguese, Italian, and Irish extraction. In an area devastated by the southward flight of textile mills, most were underemployed, undereducated, underpaid, and overtaxed.

In the spacious and modern auditorium of the Joseph Martin Middle School in Taunton, Francis J. Gillan addressed 161 other delegates. Gillan, who had been city chairman of Attleboro for the past six years, was trying to win a seat as one of the Tenth Congressional District's three delegates to the party's forthcoming midterm conference at Kansas City. Calling himself a "Truman Democrat," he stressed traditional values. Listening to his talk, it seemed as though nothing much had changed since the 1940s. Indeed, he reminisced back to 1928 when, as a child, he had hitched a ride on Al Smith's runningboard. His other unforgettable memory consisted of having talked to Bobby Kennedy fifteen minutes before Sirhan Sirhan pulled the trigger.

Gillan continued. "Politics is my vocation and avocation," he told them. "My dedication is to the people, the little people. I'm not impressed with the few intellectuals, the ultra-liberals. I like John Q. Public. I like the guy that needs help, the guy in the street, and that's the guy I'm looking to represent." After four ballots finally produced enough majority votes to complete the district's quota, Frank Gillan won the right to pay his own way to Kansas City.

Thus the district's Democrats were completing a ritual that was being repeated in almost half the states during the first part of 1974. When the Taunton session had ended, there was much self-congratulating, satisfaction that all had gone smoothly, that the three delegates were truly representative of the voters and, above all, that Democrats had shown their eagerness to shed the divisiveness of the past few years. Those chosen to be Gillan's Kansas City colleagues, Joan Menard of Somerest and Bertram Yaffe of Fall River, were two of the people at the caucus who had been more friendly to the McGovern campaign. Yet, neither could be described as members of the Citizens for Participation in Political Action (CPPAX), the state's new-politics committee. Yaffe, in fact, went out of his way to laud the virtues of slate-making and called for tickets that can balance ideologies along with geography, age, race, and sex. Ms. Menard asked for a new spirit of compromise and a willingness to negotiate and warned that Democrats must complete their work at Kansas City without abandoning the party's basic principles. She then challenged her fellow delegates, all of whom had been chosen for the session by election in their precincts, to prove that "if a woman is dedicated and willing to work for the Democratic Party, she can be elected to represent you at the national midterm convention. Prove that to me today," she concluded. On the second ballot, she led the field. Already eliminated from the original eleven nominees were the very young and inexperienced, an oldtime party worker, and a middle-aged contender whose brief speech was straight out of an American Legion hall circa 1948. As in Ms. Menard's talk, what was most obvious and voiced by virtually every formal and informal comment in the auditorium, was the need to avoid the extremes of the past and to forge a party capable of winning in 1976 without, at the same time, sacrificing basic objectives. Meanwhile, parked outside on the school lot was a Fiat with Massachusetts license plates that read "T E D—76."[49]

Such desires for compromise were, of course, the greatest wish of Robert Strauss as he approached the Kansas City conference with trepidation. The sessions, officially devoted to the adoption of a permanent charter for the party, were widely anticipated to become another example of Democratic disarray. Already dissension had taken place. The final meeting of the new Democratic Charter Commission, led by Terry Sanford, had broken up in mid-August with the walkout of the black and reform members. They had used parliamentary tactics to resist efforts supported by Strauss and the national committee, with the vigorous endorsement of the Coalition for a Democratic Majority, to roll back key advances of the Mc-Govern-Fraser guidelines. Defeated were attempts to restore the unit rule and "winner-take-all" primaries, an effort to rescind the requirement for the election of national convention delegates within the same calendar year as the convention itself, as well as other revisions.[50] Moving toward placating the critics, however, the Sanford Commission had already replaced the stipulation that delegates be chosen according to "reasonable representation" of the population and specifically forbade the use of "mandatory quotas." Participation of the traditionally underrepresented was to be encouraged through "affirmative action." State committees were given the right to elect up to 25 percent of their delegations, but the members of such committees themselves had to be chosen through open elections. With organized labor, particularly the George Meany-Alexander Barkan AFL-CIO faction, at loggerheads with the new-politics people, Strauss labored behind the scenes to prevent the predicted blow-up at Kansas City. The clash that existed between those who stressed representative democracy and those who insisted on participatory democracy was a basic schism that seemed insoluble.

Yet, by the December 6 opening of the three-day convention at Kansas City's Municipal Auditorium, as two thousand delegates arrived in the city, Robert Strauss' pragmatism had found the way. There was ample assistance from the delegates, who seemed to share the conciliatory spirit of the Taunton people. Richard Daley was greeted with warm applause, and so was George McGovern whose speech was the high point of the oratory, even though it was called "There Can Be No Compromise." George Wallace, confined to a wheelchair, entertained visitors in his suite and received a civil reception. What finally emerged was amazingly placid, another "Missouri Compromise," achieved in an atmosphere of staged conviviality. Even Mayor Daley went along with much of what he disliked. "I recognize when power moves," he reportedly told the Illinois caucus. "I recommend the compromise."[51] With the "reasonable representation" clause out once and for all, and with quotas banned in the text rather than in just a footnote, many of the new-politics people were unhappy; but so were the conservatives at their failure to win any substantial dilutions of the guidelines. The very least they now wanted was to eliminate any selection process that, whatever the actual wording might be, could open the way to the use of quotas. But, to head off a walkout of blacks and reformers, which would have been the kind of embarrassment to the Democratic conference that its critics were hoping for, Strauss reversed an earlier understanding with the laborites and agreed to remove a clause that would have placed the burden of proof on those challenging state parties for failure to take "affirmative action."

Still, not only could the phrase be used for a variety of interpretations, the provision would not go into effect until the 1980 convention and could be amended at any time by a two-thirds vote of the national committee.[52]

And yet, wrote Curt Gans a few days later, "Nothing happened in Kansas City to alter or to bridge the fundamental divide."[53] Barkan had stalked out, angry. Labor had, in effect, been told that it had no choice but to go along, that the party was now composed of a wide variety of groups that insisted on participatory democracy. Having lost his series of battles to repeal the reforms, less than a week later George Meany was reportedly contemplating an open break.[54] The next spring, after several hopefuls had already declared their candidacies for the 1976 nomination—including Henry Jackson, who had been labor's top choice—Meany was asked by a group of businessmen whom he would like to see elected president and replied, "Harry Truman."[55]

Moreover, the essentials of coping with the issues had been submerged for the sake of superficial harmony. The fundamental differences over foreign policy, which had plagued the party for the past three decades, were not permitted to receive public airing, and no clearcut position was taken as Averell Harriman deftly handled the panel discussion dealing with that sensitive issue.[56] Nor was there an attempt to come up with a firm party policy to cope with such other basic problems as inequitable taxation and, as Gans pointed out, the "mechanisms for social and economic planning that would place the long-term public interests above that of the short-term self-interest of various large and organized segments of the society.... But they did not try, and while they put issues of process behind them, the Democrats emerged from Kansas City without leadership, without program and without unity, and still deeply in jeopardy of losing their third successive Presidential election."[57] While delegate-selection and convention-rules reforms had their significance, they did not confront the essential problems of the Democratic Party.

6

Much had changed since 1945. But nothing was so significant as the fact that Democrats and Republicans had grown more dissimilar. Whereas the solid South had served to leaven the more liberal northern interests, that had been transferred to the Republicans. The GOP's former restraint upon its ultra-conservative pressures had been in its eastern establishment, most notably centered in New York. That had now become subordinated to the new southern constituency. Since the Goldwater take-over of the party in 1964, the great conservatism of the Republicans, along with constantly increasing success in the South, had become very apparent. Democrats were, at the same time, left with a black and white liberal core in Dixie. Elsewhere, they were dependent upon a coalition of liberal labor unions, upper- and middle-class reformers, minorities, academicians, and most workers engaged in public-service activities. Gone, then, was the greatest countervailing force against progressivism. Not surprisingly, the last years of the era saw a considerable number of prominent politicos changing party affiliations.

The Democratic umbrella was thus becoming redefined and being given a new focus. Its ideological options would inevitably become narrower, its ability and even its willingness to accommodate a wide range of diversity considerably reduced. Still, there would remain the temptations to try to put it "all together again" for the purpose of winning national elections, to accommodate the subscribers of the Scammon-Wattenberg centrist thesis. Yet, it would seem unlikely that such an effort, however great the enticements, would be productive of credibility and party success in the long run. Changed conditions, the new rate of progress in an altered world, would be bound to vitiate gains made through compromise of principle, as they had over and over again in the past. The risks of third or even fourth or fifth parties would have to be taken. The Democrats were showing every indication of maturing from the pragmatic progressivism of the New Deal that had inspired their modern foundations and were becoming, instead, intellectually devoted to giving substance to the rhetoric that Democrats are the party that "care about people." Instead of debilitating programs designed for the sake of keeping everybody within the "big tent," they would have to substitute demonstrated leadership capable of coping with the domestic and international conditions in a manner consistent with the best interests of their constituents. The formulation of such policies would have to become a prime party responsibility. No other agency could be expected to do the job for the nation.

7

It is no accident that the party's main luminaries, from FDR on down, were those who appeared most responsive to the needs of ordinary people. Harry Truman did not become a hero until he took on the "good-for-nothing Eightieth Congress" and espoused his Fair Deal program. Adlai Stevenson won a devoted following because he at least indicated a desire to appeal to intelligence, decency, and candor at home and abroad; and only when his ideals were at their highest were his worshipers most devoted. John Kennedy, had he been cut down one year earlier, before his efforts to mitigate a cold war he had embraced all too enthusiastically and before joining the movement for equal rights, would hardly have been remembered with such devotion in America and overseas. And his brother Bobby did not become legendary until he had shed his McCarthy Committee background and authoritarian mentality and become a sensitive respondent to the needs of human welfare. Only then did he rise to a position where it could even have been speculated that, if he had lived, he might have given common leadership to the forces that were otherwise divided by the so-called social issue. Lyndon Johnson, as he well understood and preferred to remember, had also reached his finest moments when he helped to achieve the realization of much of the outstanding post-New Deal legislation; he descended to a pitiful figure when the stubborn pursuit of a bankrupt war decimated his social programs. George McGovern, too, appeared to be nearing that height, but his chief difficulty lay less in the vulnerability of his programs than in his attempt to achieve new-politics goals by old-politics means in an old-politics world.

And so the leadership that is central to winning national elections must be in the hands of those who are aware that there is a real Democratic constituency and are willing to find and use it. As the 1976 election year neared, a large crop of names inevitably appeared willing to challenge either President Ford or whatever choice the Republicans might present. With the North, South, and West furnishing an abundance of possibilities to complement such old hands as Humphrey, Muskie, McGovern, and Jackson, the party will, nevertheless, have to select a candidate more in tune with the Democracy emerging after three decades of wandering. Once again, the desire to appeal across the spectrum, to open the umbrella until the seams strain, will be great; but, once again, it will become vulnerable to the common tactic of Republicans, unable to compete on the basis of domestic economic and social welfare issues, to move to siphon off Democratic strength by appealing to the jingoistic instincts of supernationalism and the internal fears of the insecure. Democrats cannot afford to depend upon Republican blunders. They did that in 1974 and profited from Watergate and the mishandled economy. But building a party in a far more sophisticated era implies a willingness to take stands for progress and to be prepared to pay the price.

Notes

PROLOGUE

1. New York *Times*, January 24, 1973.
2. *Ibid.*, October 18, 1974.
3. Washington *Post*, January 24, 1973.
4. Lyndon B. Johnson, Interview, June 30, 1970.
5. Robert Sherrill, *The Accidental President* (New York: Pyramid Books, 1968), p. 140.
6. Robert Weaver, Interview, November 4, 1973.
7. *Newsletter of the Democratic Left*, March 1973, p. 5.

CHAPTER I

1. Harold L. Ickes, *The Secret Diary of Harold L. Ickes* (3 vols.; New York: Simon and Schuster, 1954), vol. 2, p. 288.
2. Herbert S. Parmet and Marie B. Hecht, *Never Again: A President Runs for a Third Term* (New York: Macmillan, 1968), p. 279.
3. Warren Moscow, *Politics in the Empire State* (New York: Alfred A. Knopf, 1948), p. 40.
4. *The Catholic World*, December 1944, pp. 193–194.
5. Frank Freidel, *FDR and the South* (Baton Rouge: Louisiana State University Press, 1965), pp. 47–48.
6. Ellis Arnall, *The Shore Dimly Seen* (Philadelphia: J. B. Lippincott Co., 1946), p. 151.
7. Robert A. Garson, *The Democratic Party and the Politics of Sectionalism, 1941–1948* (Baton Rouge: Louisiana State University Press, 1974), p. 52.
8. Roland Young, *Congressional Politics in the Second World War* (New York: Columbia University Press, 1956), pp. 9, 13.
9. Proceedings of the Democratic National Committee, July 22, 1944, pp. 9–10, Democratic National Committee Papers, John F. Kennedy Library, Waltham, Massachusetts.
10. Chester Bowles to Henry A. Wallace, September 16, 1943, Wallace Papers, Franklin D. Roosevelt Library, Hyde Park, New York.
11. New York *Times*, March 2, 1945.
12. Stella C. and Byron H. Hornbeck to Roosevelt, January 17, 1945, Wallace Papers, University of Iowa.

13. New York *Times*, March 2, 1945.
14. *The Tablet*, January 13, 1945.
15. Alben Barkley to Franklin D. Roosevelt, January [?] 1945, Barkley Papers, University of Kentucky, Lexington, Kentucky.
16. W. K. Kittell to Remmie L. Arnold, January 24, 1945, Harry F. Byrd Papers, University of Virginia.
17. New York *Times*, March 2, 1945.
18. *The Tablet*, January 27, 1945.
19. *New Republic*, February 5, 1945, p. 167.
20. Grace G. Hudson to Franklin D. Roosevelt, January 16, 1945, Wallace Papers, University of Iowa.
21. Martin S. Anderson to Wallace, April 11, 1945, Wallace Papers, University of Iowa.
22. John Nance Garner to Sam Rayburn, April 18, 1945, Sam Rayburn Library, Bonham, Texas.

CHAPTER II

1. William S. Battle, Jr., to Harry Byrd, May 9, 1945, Byrd Papers, University of Virginia.
2. A. Willis Robertson to Harry B. Dyche, Sr., Robertson Papers, Swem Library, College of William and Mary.
3. George H. Gallup, *The Gallup Poll* (4 vols.; New York: Random House, 1972), vol. 1, pp. 397–398.
4. Garson, *Democratic Party*, p. 52.
5. Richard M. Dalfiume, "The 'Forgotten Years' of the Negro Revolution," *Journal of American History* (June 1968), p. 106.
6. Virginius Dabney to Mrs. Jessie Daniels Ames, July 12, 1945, Dabney Papers, University of Virginia.
7. Virginius Dabney to George Watts Hill, May 3, 1945, Dabney Papers, University of Virginia.
8. Dalfiume, "Forgotten Years," p. 101.
9. Dabney to Hill, May 3, 1945, Dabney Papers, University of Virginia.
10. Guy B. Johnson to Virginius Dabney, January 4, 1945, Dabney Papers, University of Virginia.
11. Virginius Dabney to Dr. J. Skelton Horsley, February 22, 1945, Dabney Papers, University of Virginia.
12. Mrs. Ames to Dabney, July 10, 1945, Dabney Papers, University of Virginia.
13. Dabney to K. M. Newton, August 2, 1945, Dabney Papers, University of Virginia.
14. P. B. Young to Dabney, June 18, 1945, Dabney Papers, University of Virginia.
15. Gary Clifford Ness, "The States' Rights Democratic Movement of 1948," unpublished Ph.D. dissertation, Duke University, 1972, pp. 14–19.
16. Joe Ervin to Sam Rayburn, July 31, 1945, Rayburn Papers, Sam Rayburn Library.
17. Joe Ervin to Fred Vinson, August 6, 1945, Vinson Papers, University of Kentucky.

18. Robert L. Pritchard, "Southern Politics and the Truman Administration: Georgia as a Test Case," unpublished Ph.D. dissertation, University of California in Los Angeles, 1970, p. 91.
19. Billington, "Truman and the South," p. 128.
20. Francis Pickens Miller, *Man from the Valley* (Chapel Hill: University of North Carolina Press, 1971), p. 168.
21. *Ibid.*, p. 169.
22. J. Harvie Wilkinson III, *Harry F. Byrd and the Changing Face of Virginia Politics, 1945–1966* (Charlottesville: University Press of Virginia, 1968), p. 28.
23. Abram P. Staples to A. Willis Robertson, January 24, 1945, Robertson Papers, Swem Library, College of William and Mary.
24. A. Willis Robertson to Howard Smith, February 3, 1945, Swem Library, College of William and Mary.
25. Cf. William D. Barnard, *Dixiecrats and Democrats: Alabama Politics, 1942–1950* (University, Ala.: University of Alabama Press, 1974), *passim.*
26. *Ibid.*, p. 41.
27. *Ibid.*, p. 69.
28. Pritchard, "Georgia," p. 174.
29. Byrd to Porter Graves, March 27, 1946, Byrd Papers, University of Virginia.
30. Byrd to Watkins Abbitt, March 27, 1946, Byrd Papers, University of Virginia.
31. Edward L. Breeden, Jr., to Harry Byrd, October 11, 1946, Robertson Papers, Swem Library, College of William and Mary.
32. James R. Boylan, "Reconversion in Politics: The New Deal Coalition and the Election of the Eightieth Congress," unpublished Ph.D. dissertation, Columbia University, 1971, p. 225.
33. E. R. Combs to Harry Byrd, November 6, 1946, Byrd Papers, University of Virginia.
34. Combs to Byrd, September 17, 1946, Byrd Papers, University of Virginia.
35. Roy G. Allman to Mr. and Mrs. Duvall Martin, October 30, 1946, Robertson Papers, Swem Library, College of William and Mary.
36. Boylan, "Reconversion," pp. 83–84.
37. James R. Sweeney, "Byrd and Anti-Byrd: The Struggle for Political Supremacy in Virginia, 1945–1954," unpublished Ph.D. dissertation, University of Notre Dame, 1973, p. 50.
38. Virginius Dabney to Alvin E. White, June 10, 1946, Dabney Papers, University of Virginia.
39. Numan V. Bartley, *From Thurmond to Wallace, Political Tendencies in Georgia, 1948–1968* (Baltimore: Johns Hopkins Press, 1970), p. 25; Pritchard, "Georgia," p. 10.
40. Arkansas *Democrat*, June 28, 1946.
41. Theodore Bilbo to Harry Byrd, August 20, 1946, Byrd Papers, University of Virginia; Boylan, "Reconversion," p. 222.
42. V. O. Key, Jr., *Southern Politics* (New York: Alfred A. Knopf, 1950), p. 74.
43. Transcript of Debate with Tom Sweeney, Kilgore Papers, Franklin D. Roosevelt Library.
44. Pritchard, "Georgia," p. 73.
45. Remmie L. Arnold to Harry S Truman, January 23, 1946, Byrd Papers, University of Virginia.

46. Remmie L. Arnold to Harry Byrd, February 11, 1946, Byrd Papers, University of Virginia.

47. Southern States Industrial Council, "A Statement to the Businessmen and Industrialists of the South," March 12, 1946, Byrd Papers, University of Virginia.

48. Tyre Taylor to Officers and Directors of the SSIC, November 12, 1945, Byrd Papers, University of Virginia.

49. William Harold Sadler to Brooks Hays, June 18, 1946, Hays Papers, John F. Kennedy Library.

50. *The Nation*, April 13, 1946, p. 417.

51. Charles E. Marsh to Henry Wallace, August 13, 1946, Wallace Papers, University of Iowa; John Gunther, *Inside USA* (New York: Harper & Row, 1947), pp. 841, 856–858; David M. Chalmers, *Hooded Americanism* (Garden City, N.Y.: Doubleday, 1965), p. 325; Pritchard, "Georgia," p. 42.

52. W. B. Twitty to Eleanor Roosevelt, August 4, 1946, Eleanor Roosevelt Papers, Franklin D. Roosevelt Library.

53. Wilkinson, *Byrd*, p. 53.

54. Wright Patman to Sam Rayburn, November 7, 1946, Rayburn Papers, Sam Rayburn Library.

55. F. Edward Hébert to Rayburn, November 22, 1946, Rayburn Papers, Sam Rayburn Library.

56. Carter Manasco to Sam Rayburn, November 27, 1946, Sam Rayburn Papers, Rayburn Library.

CHAPTER III

1. Agnes Meyer to Adlai Stevenson, October 8, 1955, Stevenson Papers, Princeton University.

2. *The Nation*, October 26, 1974, p. 390.

3. Michael Novak, *Choosing Our King* (New York: Macmillan, 1974), p. 89.

4. Andrew Greeley, *Building Coalitions: American Politics in the 1970s* (New York: New Viewpoints, 1974), p. 196.

5. Currin Shields, *Democracy and Catholicism in America* (New York: McGraw-Hill, 1958), p. 4.

6. Matthew and Hannah Josephson, *Al Smith: Hero of the Cities* (Boston: Houghton Mifflin, 1969), p. 459.

7. Kevin P. Phillips, *The Emerging Republican Majority* (New Rochelle, N.Y.: Arlington House, 1969), p. 153.

8. *America*, November 4, 1944, pp. 90–91.

9. Samuel Lubell, *The Future of American Politics* (3rd ed.; New York: Harper Colophon Books, 1965), p. 213.

10. Letters to Wendell Willkie dated August 28 and September 4, 1940. Willkie Papers, privately held; Charles J. Tull, *Father Coughlin and the New Deal* (Syracuse, N.Y.: Syracuse University Press, 1965), p. 191; Sheldon Marcus, *Father Coughlin: The Tumultuous Life of the Priest of the Little Flower* (Boston: Little, Brown, 1973), p. 229.

11. James A. Farley, Interview, January 19, 1973, and Columbia University Oral History Interview.

12. Francis L. Broderick, *Right Reverend New Dealer: John A. Ryan* (New York: Macmillan, 1963), p. 261.

13. Samuel Lubell, *Revolt of the Moderates* (New York: Harper & Row, 1956), pp. 71–72.

14. Peter H. Irons, " 'The Test is Poland': Polish-Americans and the Origins of the Cold War," *Polish American Studies*, 30 (Autumn 1973), p. 9; Arthur H. Vandenberg, Jr., *The Papers of Senator Vandenberg* (Boston: Houghton Mifflin, 1952), p. 148.

15. John Lewis Gaddis, *The United States and the Origins of the Cold War* (New York: Columbia University Press, 1972), p. 143; John Morton Blum (ed), *The Price of Vision: The Diary of Henry A. Wallace, 1942–1946* (Boston: Houghton Mifflin, 1973), p. 388.

16. *The Tablet*, October 21, 1944.

17. *America*, October 28, 1944, p. 70.

18. *The Catholic World*, August, 1944, p. 5.

19. Vandenberg, *Papers*, p. 124.

20. H. Bradford Westerfield, *Foreign Policy and Party Politics* (New Haven, Conn.: Yale University Press, 1955), pp. 189–90.

21. Gaddis, *Cold War*, pp. 61, 149.

22. *America*, November 4, 1944, p. 83.

23. *The Tablet*, February 3, 1945.

24. Ed Flynn, *You're the Boss* (New York: Viking Press, 1947), p. 185.

25. George N. Shuster, Interview, July 3, 1974.

26. Vandenberg, *Papers*, p. 150.

27. *America*, February 24, 1945, p. 411.

28. Donald F. Crosby, "The Angry Catholics: American Catholics and Senator Joseph R. McCarthy, 1950–1957," unpublished Ph.D. dissertation, Brandeis University, 1973.

29. *The Tablet*, May 26, 1945.

30. Irons, "Poland," p. 54.

31. *Ibid.*, p. 49.

32. Robert C. Hartnett, "Dumbarton Oaks and Catholics," *America*, November 25, 1944, pp. 144–45.

33. *The Tablet*, December 16, 1944.

34. *America*, April 28, 1945, p. 67.

35. *The Commonweal*, November 29, 1946, p. 156.

36. Mortimer Hays to James Loeb, Jr., July 16, 1945, ADA Papers, Historical Society of Wisconsin.

37. Hays to Edward R. Stettinius, February 28, 1945, ADA Papers, Historical Society of Wisconsin.

38. Blum, *Wallace*, p. 535.

39. Athan Theoharis, *The Yalta Myths* (Columbia: University of Missouri Press, 1970), p. 40.

40. John J. Kane, *Catholic-Protestant Conflicts in America* (Chicago: Regnery, 1955), p. 7.

41. *Ibid.*

42. George P. West, "The Catholic Issue," *The New Republic* (March 1, 1943), pp. 278–80.

43. *The New Republic*, June 7, 1943, p. 751.

44. Harold E. Fey, "Can Catholicism Win America?" *The Christian Century* (November 29, 1944 to January 17, 1945), *passim*.

45. *The Tablet*, January 6, 1945.

46. Walter Goodman, *The Committee* (New York: Farrar, Straus and Giroux, 1968), pp. 167–70.

47. *The Tablet*, June 9, 1945.

48. *America*, October 6, 1945, p. 14.

49. *The Tablet*, July 7, 1945; *America*, July 20, 1946, p. 360.

50. Robert I. Gannon, *The Cardinal Spellman Story* (Garden City, N.Y.: Doubleday, 1962), p. 336.

51. *America*, August 3, 1946, p. 415.

52. Vandenberg, *Papers*, p. 314.

53. Allan D. Harper, *The Politics of Loyalty* (Westport, Conn.: Greenwood, 1969), pp. 22–25.

54. Carl D. Smith and Stephen B. Sarasohn, "Hate Propaganda in Detroit," *Public Opinion Quarterly* (Spring 1946), pp. 45–48.

55. Sam Rayburn to John McCormack, September 25, 1946, Rayburn Library.

56. Kenneth Wilson Underwood, *Protestant and Catholic* (Boston: Beacon Press, 1957), p. 295.

57. Milwaukee *Journal*, October 2, 1946.

58. Rayburn to McCormack, September 25, 1946, Rayburn Library.

59. Warren Moscow, Interview, August 3, 1974.

60. Lubell, *American Politics*, p. 200.

CHAPTER IV

1. New York *Times*, November 7, 1946.

2. Wallace to Sid Blatt, November 14, 1946, Wallace Papers, University of Iowa.

3. Boylan, "Reconversion," p. 331.

4. Earl Mazo, *Richard Nixon: A Political and Personal Portrait* (New York: Harper & Row, 1959), pp. 46–47.

5. New York *Times*, November 6 and 7, 1946.

6. Boylan, "Reconversion," pp. 392–94; Berman, *Civil Rights*, p. 54.

7. Lubell, *Moderates*, p. 68; Boylan, "Reconversion," pp. 388, 390, 394.

8. Oscar Chapman to Herbert Lehman, November 7, 1946, Lehman Papers, Columbia University.

9. Lehman to Chapman, November 9, 1946, Lehman Papers, Columbia University.

10. Wallace to Sid Blatt, November 14, 1946, Wallace Papers, University of Iowa.

11. *America*, September 21, 1946, p. 601.

12. Hamby, *Truman*, pp. 16, 34–35.

13. James G. Patton and James Loeb, Jr., "The Challenge to Progressives," *The New Republic*, February 5, 1945, p. 204; *The Nation*, August 5, 1944.

14. Blum, *Wallace*, p. 374.

15. Wallace to Frances Perkins, July 30, 1945, and Perkins to Wallace, August 27, 1945, Wallace Papers, University of Iowa.

16. Patton and Loeb, "Challenge to Progressives," p. 202.

17. George Horsely Smith and Richard P. Davis, "Do the Voters Want the Parties Changed?" *Public Opinion Quarterly* (Summer 1947), p. 238.

18. Joseph P. Lash, *Eleanor: The Years Alone* (New York: Norton, 1972), p. 141.

19. Wallace to David Schneck, August 22, 1946, Wallace Papers, University of Iowa.

20. Curtis D. MacDougal, *Gideon's Army* (3 vols.; New York: Marzani & Munsell, 1965), vol. 1, p. 117.

21. *Harland Allen Economic Letter*, February 1, 1946, Brooks Hays Papers, John F. Kennedy Library.

22. A. N. Spanel to Wallace, July 23, 1945, Wallace Papers, University of Iowa.

23. Blum, *Wallace*, p. 601.

24. Cf. *ibid.*, pp. 612–628, 661–669; James F. Byrnes, *All in One Lifetime* (Harper & Row, 1958), pp. 371–372; Harry S Truman, *Year of Decisions* (Garden City, N.Y.: Doubleday, 1955), pp. 557–560; Norman D. Markowitz, *The Rise and Fall of the People's Century: Henry Wallace and American Liberalism, 1941–1948* (New York: The Free Press, 1973), pp. 181–184.

25. Blum, *Wallace*, p. 669n.

26. Markowitz, *Wallace*, p. 184; Ronald Radosh and Leonard P. Liggio, "Henry A. Wallace and the Open Door," in Thomas G. Paterson (ed.), *Cold War Critics* (Chicago: Quadrangle Books, 1971), pp. 76–107, provides a more sophisticated analysis.

27. Blum, *Wallace*, p. 618.

28. *The Commonweal*, September 27, 1946, p. 563.

29. Boylan, "Reconversion," p. 282.

30. William C. Ethridge to Wallace, September 26, 1946, Wallace Papers, University of Iowa.

31. *Ibid.*, p. 286.

32. John McCormack to Sam Rayburn, September 29, 1946, Rayburn Library.

33. Reinhold Niebuhr to Herbert Lehman, November 19, 1946, Lehman Papers, Columbia.

CHAPTER V

1. Transcript, UDA Conference, Washington, D.C., January 4, 1947, ADA Papers, Historical Society of Wisconsin.

2. Gael Sullivan to Paul Porter, January 27, 1948, McGrath Papers, Truman Library; Clifton Brock, *Americans for Democratic Action* (Washington, D.C.: Public Affairs Press, 1962), p. 24.

3. Richard Bolling to James Loeb, Jr., May 15, 1947, ADA Papers, Historical Society of Wisconsin.

4. G. Theodore Mitau, "The Democratic-Farmer-Labor Party Schism of 1948," *Minnesota History* (Spring 1955), pp. 192–194; Allan H. Ryskind, *Hubert: An Unauthorized Biography of the Vice President* (New Rochelle, N.Y.: Arlington House, 1968), p. 117.

5. William Carrol Bumpers to Brooks Hays, March 13, 1948, Hays Papers, John F. Kennedy Library.

6. Arthur M. Schlesinger, Jr., Open Letter, July 1, 1948, ADA Papers, Historical Society of Wisconsin.

7. William Batt, Jr., to Clark Clifford, April 15, 1948, Clifford Papers, Truman Library.

8. Herbert S. Parmet, *Eisenhower and the American Crusades* (New York: Macmillan, 1972), p. 17.

9. ADA Research Memorandum, undated, ADA Papers, Historical Society of Wisconsin.

10. Chester Bowles, *Promises to Keep* (New York: Harper & Row, 1971), p. 173.

11. David Lloyd to Adlai Stevenson, March 23, 1952, Stevenson Papers, Princeton.

12. William Graf, *Platforms of the Two Great Political Parties, 1932–1948* (Washington: U.S. Government Printing Office, 1950), p. 436.

13. *Ibid.*

14. Chester Bowles to Leon Henderson, July 22, 1948, ADA Papers, Historical Society of Wisconsin.

15. William Batt, Jr., to Gael Sullivan, April 20, 1948, Clifford Papers, Truman Library.

16. Brock, *ADA*, p. 102.

17. Allan J. Matusow, *Farm Policies and Politics in the Truman Years* (Cambridge, Mass.: Harvard University Press, 1967), pp. 178–185.

18. Ness, "States' Rights," pp. 100–102.

19. Transcript of the Proceedings of the Democratic National Convention, Sixth Session, July 14, 1948, Democratic National Committee Files, John F. Kennedy Library.

20. Arkansas *Democrat*, July 20, 1948.

21. Robertson to G. Fred Switzer, March 18, 1948, Robertson Papers, William and Mary.

22. Jack Redding, *Inside the Democratic Party* (Indianapolis and New York: Bobbs-Merrill, 1958), pp. 139–140.

23. New York *Times*, September 8, 11, 1948.

24. Key, *Southern Politics*, p. 336.

25. Robertson to Douglas S. Freeman, March 16, 1948, Robertson Papers, William and Mary.

26. Robertson to General E. Walton Opie, April 24, 1951, Robertson Papers, William and Mary.

27. T. Coleman Andrews to Harry Byrd, July 8, 1948, Byrd Papers, University of Virginia.

28. Pritchard, "Georgia," pp. 157–159; Ness, "States' Rights," pp. 200–202.

29. Frank Watts Ashley, "Selected Southern Liberal Editors and the States' Rights Movement of 1948," unpublished Ph.D. dissertation, University of South Carolina, 1959, *passim.*

30. Ness, "States' Rights," p. 170.

31. Lubell, *American Politics*, p. 201.

32. Rose A. Moran to Eleanor Roosevelt, January 19, 1948, Eleanor Roosevelt Papers, Franklin D. Roosevelt Library.

33. Irwin Ross, *The Loneliest Campaign: The Truman Victory of 1948* (New York: New American Library, 1968), p. 66.

34. Richard S. Kirkendall, "Election of 1948," Arthur M. Schlesinger, Jr., and Fred Israel (eds.), *History of American Presidential Elections, 1789–1968* (4 vols.; New York: Chelsea House, 1971), vol. 4, p. 3122.

35. Robert A. Divine, *Foreign Policy and U.S. Presidential Elections* (2 vols.; New York: New Viewpoints, 1974), vol. 1, pp. 181, 259.

36. Ellen E. Brennen, "Last-Minute Swing in New York City Presidential Vote," *Public Opinion Quarterly* (Summer 1949), p. 296.

37. Redding, *Democratc Party*, pp. 143–44.

38. Joseph R. Starobin, *American Communism in Crisis, 1943–1957* (Cambridge, Mass.: Harvard University Press, 1972), pp. 171, 173.

39. New York *Times*, July 17, 1948.

40. Brennen, "New York City Presidential Vote," p. 287n.

41. MacDougall, *Gideon's Army*, p. 426.

42. Wallace to Dr. John G. Rideout, July 12, 1948, Wallace Papers, University of Iowa.

43. Brock, *ADA*, p. 79.

44. Cf. Allen Yarnell, *Democrats and Progressives* (Berkeley and Los Angeles: University of California Press, 1974), *passim*.

45. Robert A. Divine, "The Cold War and the Election of 1948," *Journal of American History* (June 1972), p. 109.

46. Paul T. David, *Party Strength in the United States, 1872–1970* (Charlottesville: University Press of Virginia, 1972), pp. 288, 290, 294.

47. Lubell, *American Politics*, pp. 201–203.

48. Philleo Nash to Truman, November 6, 1948, Clifford Papers, Truman Library.

49. Robert Kerr to Robertson, March 21, 1951, and Robertson to Kerr, March 22, 1951, Robertson Papers, William and Mary.

50. Robertson to Arthur D. Davidson, April 23, 1951, Robertson Papers, William and Mary.

51. Robertson to James Duff, January 8, 1952, Robertson Papers, William and Mary.

52. *The Commonweal*, vol. 54 (1951), p. 542.

53. Parmet, *Eisenhower*, p. 50.

CHAPTER VI

1. Cf. Barton J. Bernstein, "Election of 1952," in Schlesinger, Arthur M., Jr., and Fred L. Israel, *History of American Presidential Elections, 1789–1968* (4 vols.; New York: Chelsea House, 1971), vol. 4, pp. 3236–3239; Kenneth S. Davis, *The Politics of Honor* (New York: G. P. Putnam, 1967), pp. 253–274; Walter Johnson, *How We Drafted Adlai Stevenson* (New York: Knopf, 1955), *passim*.

2. Stevenson to Rexford G. Tugwell, February 29, 1952, Stevenson Papers, Princeton; Stevenson to James P. Warburg, April 25, 1952 and May 30, 1952, Warburg Papers, John F. Kennedy Library.

3. Stevenson to Dean Acheson, July 31, 1952, Stevenson Papers, Princeton.

4. Phillips, *Republican Majority*, p. 163.

5. Louis L. Gerson, *The Hyphenate in Recent Politics and Diplomacy* (Law-

rence: University of Kansas Press, 1964), p. 214; Walter Johnson and Carol Evans, *The Papers of Adlai Stevenson* (4 vols.; Boston: Little, Brown, 1972–1974), vol. 4, p. 231.

6. Harvey Wheeler, "The End of an Era," *Reporter*, February 3, 1953, p. 31.

7. Stevenson to Sam Rayburn, August 11, 1952, Sam Rayburn Library.

8. Neil Staebler to Stevenson, November 17, 1952, Staebler Papers, Bentley Library, University of Michigan.

9. Stuart Gerry Brown to Stevenson, November 17, 1952, Stevenson Papers, Princeton.

10. Adolph Berle, Jr., to Stevenson, November 7, 1952, Stevenson Papers, Princeton.

11. Stevenson to Herbert Lehman, November 26, 1952, Lehman Papers, Columbia University, and Stevenson to Frank Altschul, December 29, 1952, Stevenson Papers, Princeton.

12. Chester Bowles to Stevenson, June 5, 1953, Stevenson Papers, Princeton.

13. Herbert Lehman to Lyndon Johnson, January 13, 1955, and Johnson to Lehman, January 17, 1955, Lehman Papers, Columbia University.

14. Paul H. Douglas, *In the Fullness of Time* (New York: Harcourt Brace Jovanovich, 1971), p. 307.

15. Douglas Scrapbooks, Douglas Papers, Historical Society of Chicago.

16. Marvin Rosenberg to Hubert Humphrey, August 23, 1954, ADA Papers, Historical Society of Wisconsin.

17. Eleanor Roosevelt to James Doyle, September 2, 1954, ADA Papers, Historical Society of Wisconsin.

18. Douglas, *Fullness of Time*, p. 231.

19. New York *Times*, March 7, 1954.

20. *Ibid.*

21. Johnson and Evans, *Stevenson Papers*, vol. 4, p. 346.

22. Stephen A. Mitchell to Harry Barnard, March 23, 1955, Mitchell Papers, Truman Library.

23. L. M. C. Smith to Stephen A. Mitchell, December 18, 1953, ADA Papers, Historical Society of Wisconsin.

24. New York *Post*, December 29, 1953.

25. Violet Gunther to Walter Reuther, January 7, 1954, ADA Papers, Historical Society of Wisconsin.

26. Arthur M. Schlesinger, Jr., to Stevenson, January 4, 1954, Stevenson Papers, Princeton.

27. Susanna H. Davis to Ed Lahey, November 5, 1954, ADA Papers, Historical Society of Wisconsin.

28. Violet Gunther to Harlan Noel, December 10, 1954, ADA Papers, Historical Society of Wisconsin.

29. Joseph Rauh, Jr., to Averell Harriman, January 6, 1955, Stevenson Papers, Princeton; Washington *Post*, November 1, 1955.

30. Eleanor Roosevelt to Stephen A. Mitchell, January 6, 1954, Mitchell Papers, Truman Library.

31. James Rowe, Jr., to Carl McGowan, January 27, 1954, Stevenson Papers, Princeton.

32. Allan Shivers, Johnson Library Oral History Interview.

33. "Report from Texas," August 15, 1955, ADA Papers, Historical Society of Wisconsin.

34. Violet Gunther to Arthur M. Schlesinger, Jr., June 16, 1955, Stevenson Papers, Princeton; "Reports from Texas" by George Lambert, August 1955, ADA Papers, Historical Society of Wisconsin.

35. "Notes from George Lambert," July 8, 1953, and "Confidential Memo on Texas Political Scene," January 1954, ADA Papers, Wisconsin.

36. Douglas Cater, "The Trouble in Lyndon Johnson's Back Yard," *Reporter*, December 1, 1955, p. 34.

37. *Ibid.*, p. 32.

38. New York *Times*, November 23, 1955.

39. Joseph Rauh, Jr. to Michael Straight, June 24, 1955, ADA Papers, Historical Society of Wisconsin.

40. Hale Boggs, Johnson Library Oral History Interview; Allan Shivers, Interview, January 10, 1975.

41. Johnson and Evans, *Stevenson Papers*, vol. 4, p. 445.

42. Adlai E. Stevenson, *Major Campaign Speeches* (New York: Random House, 1953), p. 293.

43. Johnson and Evans, *Stevenson Papers*, vol. 4, p. 581.

44. Arthur M. Schlesinger, Jr., to Stevenson, February 15, 1955, Stevenson Papers, Princeton.

45. Stephen A. Mitchell, Private Memorandum, November 11, 1958, Mitchell Papers, Truman Library.

46. Stephen A. Mitchell to Hyman Raskin, August 26, 1955, Stevenson Papers, Princeton.

47. "Report from Texas," November 1955, Stevenson Papers, Princeton.

48. Alfred Steinberg, *Sam Johnson's Boy* (New York: Macmillan, 1968), p. 422.

49. Stevenson to Rayburn, September 30, 1955, Sam Rayburn Library.

50. New York *Times*, October 17, 1955.

51. *Ibid.*, October 18, 1955.

52. Mitchell to Stevenson, October 19, 1955, Mitchell Papers, Truman Library.

53. Edward Hollander to Mrs. Eleanor Roosevelt, October 10, 1955, ADA Papers, Historical Society of Wisconsin.

54. Mitchell to Stevenson, October 24 and 28, 1955, and Mitchell to James Finnegan and Hyman Raskin, October 24, 1955, Stevenson Papers, Princeton.

55. Lyndon Johnson to A. Willis Robertson, October 25, 1955, Robertson Papers, Swem Library, College of William and Mary.

56. Johnson to Stevenson, November 9, 1955, Stevenson Papers, Princeton.

57. "Report from Texas," November 1955, Stevenson Papers, Princeton.

58. James Rowe, Jr., unsigned and undated memorandum, Box 500, Stevenson Papers, Princeton.

CHAPTER VII

1. A. Willis Robertson to Colgate Darden, Jr., June 5, 1956, Robertson Papers, Swem Library, College of William and Mary.

2. Gallup poll release, May 5, 1954.

3. Chester Bowles to Thomas Finletter, January 18, 1956, Bowles Papers, Yale University.

4. John Brademas to Arthur M. Schlesinger, Jr., September 16, 1955, Stevenson Papers, Princeton.

5. Gallup poll releases, June 16, 1954, and January 21, 1955.

6. Edward Hollander to Arthur M. Schlesinger, Jr., October 2, 1956, ADA Papers, Wisconsin.

7. Chester Bowles to Hubert Humphrey, August 16, 1955, Bowles Papers, Yale University.

8. Chester Bowles, "The Foreign Policy Issue and the Democratic Party," mimeographed memorandum, December 1, 1955, Bowles Papers, Yale.

9. Hubert Humphrey to William McCormick Blair, Jr., November 11, 1955, Stevenson Papers, Princeton.

10. Paul M. Butler, "A Democratic National Convention in 1954?" Mimeographed statement presented at Chicago, March 31, April 1, 1953, Stevenson Papers, Princeton.

11. Arthur M. Schlesinger, Jr., to Adlai Stevenson, November [?] 1953, Stevenson Papers, Princeton; New York *Times*, April 29, 1953.

12. Edward Hollander to James E. Doyle and Arthur Schlesinger, Jr., August 12, 1953, ADA Papers, Historical Society of Wisconsin.

13. Johnson and Evans, *Stevenson Papers*, vol. 4, p. 439.

14. Stevenson to Agnes Meyer, July 10, 1955, Stevenson Papers, Princeton.

15. *Reporter*, December 29, 1955, p. 7.

16. Stevenson to Hubert H. Humphrey, December 16, 1955, Stevenson Papers, Princeton.

17. Arthur M. Schlesinger, Jr., to Archibald Alexander, December 30, 1955, Stevenson Papers, Princeton.

18. Sweeney, "Byrd and Anti-Byrd," pp. 206–207.

19. Stevenson to Arthur Schlesinger, Jr., November 11, 1954, Stevenson Papers, Princeton.

20. Stevenson to Hubert H. Humphrey, July 8, 1955, Stevenson Papers, Princeton.

21. Stevenson to Agnes Meyer, February 8, 1956, Stevenson Papers, Princeton.

22. Herbert Lehman to Stevenson, February 11, 1956, Lehman Papers, Columbia University.

23. Stevenson to Eugene Meyer, February 20, 1956, Stevenson Papers, Princeton.

24. Chester Bowles to Stevenson, February 29, 1956, Bowles Papers, Yale.

25. Harry S. Ashmore to Stevenson, March 30, 1956, Stevenson Papers, Princeton.

26. Charles S. Murphy to Stevenson, September 22, 1953, and J. K. Galbraith to Stevenson, September 23, 1953, Stevenson Papers, Princeton.

27. Thomas K. Finletter to Chester Bowles, October 9, 1953, Bowles Papers, Yale.

28. Chester Bowles to Stevenson, November 25, 1953, Bowles Papers, Yale; Averell Harriman to Stevenson, February 1, 1954, John Sharon to Stevenson, November 24, 1953, and John Sharon to Wilson Wyatt, September 28, 1953, Stevenson Papers, Princeton.

29. Schlesinger to Stevenson, December 7, 1953, Stevenson Papers, Princeton.

30. Agnes Meyer to Stevenson, December 19, 1955, Stevenson Papers, Princeton.

31. Agnes Meyer to Stevenson, November 12, 1955, Stevenson Papers, Princeton.

32. Arthur M. Schlesinger, Jr., Interview, January 16, 1975.

33. Stevenson to John F. Kennedy, October 29, 1955, Stevenson Papers, Princeton.
34. Allan Shivers, Interview, January 10, 1975; "Texas Reports," March 18 and March 26, 1956, ADA Papers, Historical Society of Wisconsin.
35. Telegram, Sam Rayburn to Lyndon Johnson, March 7, 1955, Sam Rayburn Library.
36. Lyndon Johnson to Stevenson, September 6, 1956, Stevenson Papers, Princeton.
37. Allan Shivers, Interview, January 10, 1975.
38. Stevenson to Agnes Meyer, October 14, 1955, Stevenson Papers, Princeton.
39. Sally Oleon, "David L. Lawrence, Mayor of Pittsburgh: Development of a Political Leader," unpublished Ph.D. dissertation, University of Pittsburgh, 1958.
40. New York *Times*, July 13, 1956.
41. Chester Bowles to Stevenson, June 21, 1956, Bowles Papers, Yale.
42. St. Louis *Post-Dispatch*, March 1, 1953; Louisville *Courier-Journal*, March 13, 1953.
43. James Rowe, Jr. to Carl McGowan, January 29, 1953, Stevenson Papers, Princeton.
44. Johnson and Evans, *Stevenson Papers*, vol. 4, pp. 290–291.
45. *Ibid.*, p. 590.
46. Stevenson to R. Keith Lane, November 16, 1955, and F. P. Miller to Stevenson, March 13, 1956, Stevenson Papers, Princeton; Howard W. Smith to William Colmer, November 18, 1955, Sam Rayburn Library.
47. Stephen A. Mitchell to Stevenson, May 28, 1953, and Francis Pickens Miller to Stevenson, July 23, 1953, Mitchell Papers, Truman Library; Atlanta *Constitution*, November 7, 1954.
48. Independent Editorial Services, Ltd., *News Letter*, November 9, 1954.
49. New York *Times*, September 22, 1953; Atlanta *Constitution*, September 22, 1953.
50. C. A. H. Thomson and F. M. Shattuck, *The 1956 Presidential Campaign* (Washington, D.C.: The Brookings Institution, 1960), pp. 118–119.
51. Helen Berthelot to Margaret Price, March 1, 1959, Price Papers, Bentley Library, University of Michigan.
52. A. Willis Robertson to G. Fred Switzer, December 8, 1954, Switzer Papers, University of Virginia.
53. Joseph L. Rauh, Jr., to Arthur M. Schlesinger, Jr., September 22, 1953, ADA Papers, Historical Society of Wisconsin.
54. Arthur M. Schlesinger, Jr., Memorandum, September 6, 1955, Stevenson Papers, Princeton.
55. Stevenson to Agnes Meyer, November 23, 1955, Stevenson Papers, Princeton.
56. "The White Citizens Councils vs. Southern Trade Unions," Confidential Memorandum, March 12, 1956, Sleeping Car Porters Papers, Library of Congress.
57. Unsigned memorandum, July 24, 1956, Johnson Papers, Johnson Library.
58. James Loeb, Jr., to Joseph Rauh, Jr., Robert Nathan, *et al.*, n.d., ADA Papers, Historical Society of Wisconsin.
59. Chester Bowles to Stevenson, March 29, 1956, Bowles Papers, Yale.

60. Chester Bowles, Interview, January 23, 1975.

61. Alfred H. Corbett to Mrs. Edison Dick, March 14, 1956, Stevenson Papers, Princeton.

62. A. Willis Robertson to Virginius Dabney, July 15, 1963, Dabney Papers, University of Virginia.

63. Robertson to Lyndon Johnson, August 8, 1956, Robertson Papers, Swem Library, College of William and Mary.

64. "Resolution of the Platform and Resolutions Committee of the South Carolina Democratic Convention," March 21, 1956.

65. Washington *Star*, July 15, 1956.

66. New York *Times*, August 2, 1956.

67. Harry Ashmore to Stevenson, August 2, 1956, Stevenson Papers, Princeton.

68. Thomson and Shattuck, *1956 Presidential Campaign*, p. 39; Harry Ashmore to Adlai Stevenson, April 18, 1956, Stevenson Papers, Princeton.

69. Thomson and Shattuck, *1956 Presidential Campaign*, p. 55.

70. Stevenson to Eleanor Roosevelt, June 15, 1956, Eleanor Roosevelt Papers, Roosevelt Library.

71. Joseph Rauh, Jr., to Eleanor Roosevelt, July 24, 1956, ADA Papers, Historical Society of Wisconsin.

72. Rauh to Mrs. Roosevelt, August 2, 1956, ADA Papers, Historical Society of Wisconsin.

73. New York *Times*, August 8, 1956.

74. Stephen A. Mitchell, Memorandum, August 9, 1956, Mitchell Papers, Truman Library.

75. Agnes Meyer to Stevenson, April 15, 1958, Stevenson Papers, Princeton.

76. Arthur M. Schlesinger, Jr. to Stevenson, October 10, 1955, Stevenson Papers, Princeton.

77. Merle Miller, *Plain Speaking* (New York: G. P. Putnam, 1974), pp. 115 and 117.

78. New York *Times*, August 15, 1956; Thomson and Shattuck, *1956 Presidential Campaign*, p. 135.

79. *Ibid.*, p. 148.

80. *Ibid.*; *Reporter*, September 6, 1956, p. 12.

81. Willis Robertson to Sam Ervin, Jr., August 10, 1956, Robertson Papers, Swem Library, College of William and Mary.

CHAPTER VIII

1. John Stennis to Lyndon B. Johnson, August 27, 1956, Johnson Papers, Johnson Library; Stevenson to Johnson, September 1, 1956, Stevenson Papers, Princeton; A. Willis Robertson to W. Pat Jennings, September 10, 1956, and Robertson to George Smathers, September 25, 1956, Robertson Papers, Swem Library, College of William and Mary; Washington *Post*, October 10, 1956.

2. Parmet, *Eisenhower*, p. 492; Moses Rischin, *"Our Own Kind": Voting by Race, Creed, or National Origin* (Santa Barbara, Calif.: Center for the Study of Democratic Institutions, 1960), pp. 33–34.

3. Rischin, *"Our Own Kind,"* pp. 23, 27, 32; Heinz Eulau, *Class and Party in the Eisenhower Years* (New York: The Free Press, 1962), p. 2.

4. Adlai E. Stevenson, *The New America* (New York: Harper & Row, 1957), p. 11.

5. *Ibid.*, p. 189.

6. *Ibid.*, p. 262.

7. Eleanor Roosevelt, *On My Own* (New York: Harper & Row, 1968), p. 173.

8. Dean Acheson to Adlai Stevenson, October 9, 1956, Stevenson Papers, Princeton.

9. Willis Robertson to J. William Fulbright, October 29, 1956, Swem Library, College of William and Mary.

10. James S. Ottenberg, *The Lexington Democratic Club Story* (New York: Lexington Democratic Club, 1959), p. 7.

11. Lloyd K. Garrison, Interview, June 19, 1974.

12. George E. Hopkins, "The Airpower Lobby and the Cold War, 1945–54," paper delivered before the Organization of American Historians, Boston, Massachusetts, April 19, 1975.

13. Arthur M. Schlesinger, Jr. to William McCormick Blair, Jr., August 16, 1954, Stevenson Papers, Princeton.

14. Oleon, "David L. Lawrence," p. 102.

15. Stevenson to Arthur M. Schlesinger, Jr., August 16, 1954, Stevenson Papers, Princeton.

16. New York *Times*, December 5, 1954.

17. *Time*, December 20, 1954, p. 13.

18. *Ibid.*, August 27, 1956, p. 19.

19. Hale Boggs, Oral History Interview, Johnson Library; Sidney Hyman, "The Collective Leadership of Paul M. Butler," *Reporter*, December 24, 1959, p. 10.

20. *America*, December 20–27, 1958, p. 362; New York *Times*, April 17, 1959.

21. Truman to Rayburn, July 8, 1959, Sam Rayburn Library.

22. Fitzhugh Lee Ford to Harry Byrd, September 10, 1959, Byrd Papers, University of Virginia.

23. New York *Times*, September 17, 1959.

24. *Ibid.*, December 8, 1959.

25. Charles Tyroler II, Interview, May 30, 1973.

26. Humphrey to Margaret Price, November 16, 1956, Price Papers, Bentley Historical Library, University of Michigan.

27. Democratic National Committee Resolution on Advisory Council, February 15, 1957, Charles S. Murphy Papers, Truman Library.

28. Charles Tyroler II, Interview, May 30, 1973.

29. Lyndon Johnson to Rayburn, December 3, 1956, Sam Rayburn Library.

30. Overton Brooks to Paul Butler, December 11, 1956, Butler Papers, University of Notre Dame, South Bend, Indiana.

31. Paul Butler to Turner Catledge, December 20, 1956, Butler Papers, University of Notre Dame.

32. Charles Tyroler II to Stevenson, July 2, 1957, and Finletter to Stevenson, August 21, 1957, Stevenson Papers, Princeton.

33. Charles Tyroler II, Interview, May 30, 1973.

34. *Ibid.*

35. New York *Herald Tribune*, May 22, 1960.
36. Democratic Advisory Council, "Statement on the Little Rock Controversy," September 15, 1957.
37. Democratic Advisory Council, " 'Right-to-Work' Statement," May 5, 1957.
38. Cornelius P. Cotter and Bernard C. Hennessy, *Politics without Power* (New York: Atherton Press, 1964), p. 221.
39. Rayburn to Paul Butler, December 2, 1958, Butler Papers, University of Notre Dame.
40. Julius C. C. Edelstein to Herbert Lehman, July 25, 1959, Lehman Papers, Columbia University.
41. Helen Berthelot to Margaret Price, March 1, 1960, Price Papers, Bentley Historical Library, University of Michigan.
42. Charles S. Murphy to Author, February 19, 1975, and Leon H. Keyserling to Author, February 26, 1975, and March 24, 1975.
43. Charles Tyroler II, Interview, May 30, 1973; Chester Bowles, Interview, January 23, 1975.
44. Dean Acheson to Chester Bowles, August 22, 1957, Bowles Papers, Yale.
45. Dean Acheson and Paul Nitze, draft statement on "The Democratic Approach to National Defense," September 18, 1957, Staebler Papers, Bentley Historical Library, University of Michigan.
46. Democratic Advisory Council, "The Democratic Approach to Foreign Policy and the United States Defense," October 19, 1957.
47. "Notes on Comments Made by Members of the Advisory Committee on Foreign Policy of the Democratic Advisory Council at their Meeting in Washington on Saturday, September 28, 1957, under the Chairmanship of Mr. Dean Acheson," Butler Papers, University of Notre Dame.
48. James P. Warburg to Sidney H. Scheuer, March 10, 1958, Warburg Papers, John F. Kennedy Library.
49. Charles Tyroler II, Interview, May 30, 1973.
50. J. Kenneth Galbraith, "Next Steps in Public Welfare (The Next New Deal)," October 15, 1957, Stevenson Papers, Princeton.
51. *Consumption—Key to Full Prosperity* (Washington, D.C.: Conference on Economic Progress, 1957), p. 36.
52. Leon H. Keyserling to Author, February 26, 1975.
53. Sidney Hyman, "Can a Democrat Win in '60?" *Reporter*, March 5, 1959, p. 14.
54. Confidential sources.
55. Charles Tyroler II, Interview, May 30, 1973.
56. George Reedy to Lyndon Johnson, July 12, 1957, Civil Rights Papers, Johnson Library.
57. Rowland Evans and Robert Novak, *Lyndon B. Johnson: The Exercise of Power* (New York: New American Library, 1966), pp. 139–140.
58. Johnson to Jack W. Ferrill, September 5, 1957, Civil Rights Papers, Johnson Library, and Dean Acheson to Johnson, February 2, 1959, Civil Rights Papers, Johnson Library.

CHAPTER IX

1. James P. Warburg to Stevenson, April 11, 1960, and Warburg to Daniel Nugent, June 2, 1960, Warburg Papers, John F. Kennedy Library.
2. "An Important Message of Interest to All Liberals," June 17, 1960, Stevenson Papers, Princeton.
3. Stevenson to Mrs. Thomas Finletter, June 9, 1960, Stevenson Papers, Princeton.
4. New York *Post*, June 11, 1960.
5. Agnes Meyer to Stevenson, June 21, 1960, Stevenson Papers, Princeton.
6. Truman to Rayburn, June 30, 1960, Sam Rayburn Library.
7. Robertson to Dabney, January 9, 1960, Dabney Papers, University of Virginia.
8. Murray Kempton, *America Comes of Middle Age* (Boston: Little, Brown, 1963), p. 274.
9. Arthur M. Schlesinger, Jr., *A Thousand Days* (Boston: Houghton Mifflin, 1965).
10. Violet Gunther to All Chapters and Board Members, April 6, 1960, Lehman Papers, Columbia University.
11. Warburg to J. K. Galbraith, July 18, 1960, and Warburg to Matthew Robinson, November 11, 1960, Warburg Papers, John F. Kennedy Library.
12. James MacGregor Burns, *John Kennedy: A Political Profile* (New York: Avon Books, 1960), p. 140.
13. Schlesinger, *Thousand Days*, p. 23.
14. Arthur M. Schlesinger, Jr., *Kennedy or Nixon: Does It Make Any Difference?* (New York: Macmillan, 1960), pp. 33–34.
15. Arthur M. Schlesinger, Jr., *The Shape of National Politics to Come* (printed and circulated privately, 1959), pp. 6–7, 10, 17, 23.
16. Schlesinger, *Thousand Days*, p. 18.
17. Schlesinger, *Kennedy or Nixon*, p. 1.
18. Schlesinger to Archibald Cox, August 8, 1960, Democratic National Committee Papers, John F. Kennedy Library.
19. Schlesinger, *Kennedy or Nixon*, pp. 19, 26, 51.
20. Harris Wofford, Oral History, John F. Kennedy Library.
21. Meyer Feldman, Oral History, John F. Kennedy Library.
22. James Loeb, Jr., to Bowles, November 8, 1959, Bowles Papers, Yale.
23. Minutes of Meeting, Hyannis Port, Massachusetts, October 28, 1959, Robert F. Kennedy Papers, John F. Kennedy Library.
24. Bowles, *Promises to Keep*, p, 293.
25. Meyer Feldman, Oral History, John F. Kennedy Library.
26. Reinhold Niebuhr, "Humphrey for President?" *The New Leader*, December 29, 1958, p. 5.
27. Joseph P. Kennedy to John F. Kennedy, May 25, 1956, Sorensen Papers, John F. Kennedy Library.
28. John F. Kennedy to Roy Wilkins, July 18, 1958, Sorensen Papers, John F. Kennedy Library.
29. Kennedy to George Meany, May 28, 1959, Sorensen Papers, John F. Kennedy Library.

30. Theodore C. Sorensen, *Kennedy* (New York: Harper & Row, 1965), p. 54.
31. Kennedy to Loeb, July 10, 1957, Sorensen Papers, John F. Kennedy Library.
32. Kennedy to Paul Butler, February 7, 1957, Sorensen Papers, John F. Kennedy Library.
33. Kennedy to J. P. Coleman, November 1, 1956, Sorensen Papers, John F. Kennedy Library.
34. Winchester (Virginia) *Evening Star*, February 15, 1957.
35. Robert F. Kennedy, Private Memorandum, November 16, 1959, Robert F. Kennedy Papers, John F. Kennedy Library.
36. Robertson to Harry C. Stuart, November 3, 1960, and to James J. Kilpatrick, August 20, 1960, Robertson Papers, Swem Library, College of William and Mary.
37. Report by J. Miller, "Some Modest Realignments in the Kennedy Image," October 20, 1959, Robert F. Kennedy Papers, John F. Kennedy Library.
38. Schlesinger to Humphrey, May 2, 1960, Sorensen Papers, John F. Kennedy Library.
39. Schlesinger, *Thousand Days*, p. 26; Arthur M. Schlesinger, Jr., Interview, January 16, 1975; Lawrence F. O'Brien, *No Final Victories* (Garden City, N.Y.: Doubleday, 1974), p. 70.
40. Transcripts of Speeches at Charleston, Huntington, and Mount Hope, W.Va., April 20, 1960, Kennedy Pre-Presidential Papers, John F. Kennedy Library.
41. Dave Powers, Interview, April 18, 1973.
42. Schlesinger to Stevenson, May 16, 1960, Stevenson Papers, Princeton.
43. Stevenson to Schlesinger, May 20, 1960, Stevenson Papers, Princeton.
44. Stevenson to Arthur and Marian Schlesinger, June 7, 1960, Stevenson Papers, Princeton.
45. Schlesinger to Stevenson, June 8, 1960, Stevenson Papers, Princeton.
46. Rowe to Newton Minow, June 7, 1960, Stevenson Papers, Princeton.
47. Edmund Brown to Agnes Meyer, June 13, 1960, Stevenson Papers, Princeton.
48. Eleanor Roosevelt, Private Memorandum, June 13, 1960, Eleanor Roosevelt Papers, Roosevelt Library.
49. Stevenson to Mrs. Roosevelt, June 15, 1960, Eleanor Roosevelt Papers, Roosevelt Library.
50. Stevenson to Eugene McCarthy, August 10, 1960, Stevenson Papers, Princeton.
51. Sidney Hyman, *The Lives of William Benton* (Chicago: University of Chicago Press, 1969), pp. 530–531.
52. Davis, *Politics of Honor*, p. 427.
53. Hyman, *Benton*, pp. 530–531.
54. Stevenson to Mrs. Thomas Finletter, June 9, 1960, Stevenson Papers, Princeton.
55. James M. Landis to Robert F. Kennedy [?], Robert F. Kennedy Papers, John F. Kennedy Library.
56. Robert F. Kennedy to Landis, June 27, 1960, Robert Kennedy Papers, John F. Kennedy Library.
57. Herbert Lehman, Private Memorandum, July 15, 1960, Lehman Papers, Columbia University; New York *Times*, July 15, 1960.
58. Lloyd K. Garrison, Interview, June 19, 1974.
59. Schlesinger, *Thousand Days*, p. 16; New York *Times*, August 2, 1960.

60. Warren Moscow, *The Last of the Big-Time Bosses* (New York: Stein and Day, 1971), p. 168.
61. Stevenson to Mrs. Roosevelt, August 7, 1960, Eleanor Roosevelt Papers, Roosevelt Library.
62. Harris Wofford, Oral History Interview, John F. Kennedy Library.
63. Agnes Meyer to Adlai Stevenson, August 11, 1960, Stevenson Papers, Princeton.
64. Mrs. Roosevelt's Report of Talk with Jack Kennedy to Ruth Field, August 1960, Stevenson Papers, Princeton.
65. Arthur M. Schlesinger, Jr., to Kennedy, August 30, 1960, Stevenson Papers, Princeton.
66. John F. Kennedy, dictated by telephone to Robert F. Kennedy, September 3, 1960, Robert Kennedy Papers, John F. Kennedy Library.
67. Harry Byrd to Jimmy Byrnes, August 25, 1960, Byrd Papers, University of Virginia.
68. Robertson to John L. Whitehead, October 18, 1956, Robertson Papers, Swem Library, College of William and Mary.
69. *U.S. News and World Report*, October 11, 1957; Frank McCulloch to Rev. Charles G. Hamilton, October 11, 1957, Paul Douglas Papers, Historical Society of Chicago.
70. Charlotte (North Carolina) *Observer*, August 6, 1958; Jackson (Mississippi) *Daily News*, August 11, 1958.
71. Bidwell Adams to Paul Butler, February 27, 1957, Butler Papers, Notre Dame.
72. Paul T. David (ed.), *The Presidential Election and Transition, 1960–1961* (Washington, D.C., The Brookings Institution, 1961), p. 33.
73. Birmingham *News*, March 22, 1959.
74. Gessner T. McCorvey to Harry Byrd, June 9, 1960, Byrd Papers, University of Virginia.
75. Walter Sillers to Byrd, June 1, 1960, Byrd Papers, University of Virginia.
76. Byrd to Sillers, May 26, 1960, Byrd Papers, University of Virginia.
77. *Wall Street Journal*, July 17, 1959; Pat Watters, *The South and the Nation* (New York: Pantheon, 1970), pp. 71–134; William C. Havard (ed.), *The Changing Politics of the South* (Baton Rouge: Louisiana State University Press, 1972), pp. 53–54; Dewey W. Grantham, Jr., "The South and the Reconstruction of American Politics," *Journal of American History* (September 1966), pp. 233, 239; Avery Leiserson (ed.), *The American South in the 1960s* (New York: Praeger, 1964), pp. 25, 27.
78. Robert F. Kennedy to Sargent Shriver, August 4, 1960, Robert Kennedy Papers, John F. Kennedy Library.
79. Evans and Novak, *Johnson*, pp. 302–303.
80. Coretta Scott King, *My Life with Martin Luther King, Jr.* (New York: Holt, Rinehart and Winston, 1969), pp. 193–197; Harris Wofford, Oral History Interview, John F. Kennedy Library.
81. Jesse M. Unruh to Robert F. Kennedy, October 6, 1960, Robert F. Kennedy Papers, John F. Kennedy Library.
82. Brooks Hays, Oral History Interview, John F. Kennedy Library.
83. Richard Hofstadter, "Could a Protestant Have Beaten Hoover in 1928?" *Reporter*, March 17, 1960, pp. 31–33.

84. Abraham Ribicoff, Interview, February 5, 1973.
85. Sorensen, *Kennedy*, p. 209.
86. David, *Presidential Election*, p. 156.
87. *Ibid.*, p. 175.
88. John T. R. Godlewski, Report on Polish-American Voting, n.d., Robert Kennedy Papers, John F. Kennedy Library.
89. David, *President Election*, pp. 159, 166.
90. Bowles to John F. Kennedy, October 15, 1960, and October 17, 1960, Democratic National Committee Papers, John F. Kennedy Library.

CHAPTER X

1. George R. Donahue to Robert Wagner, Jr., September 29, 1960, Robert Kennedy Papers, John F. Kennedy Library.
2. Neal R. Pierce, *The Megastates of America* (New York: Norton, 1972), p. 585.
3. Daniel Bell, *The End of Ideology* (rev. ed.; New York: The Free Press, 1962), p. 404.
4. Stevenson to Herbert Lehman, June 15, 1959, Lehman Papers, Columbia University.
5. The American Assembly, *Goals for Americans* (Englewood Cliffs, N.J.: Prentice-Hall, Inc., 1960), pp. 4, 29.
6. The Rockefeller Panel Reports, *Prospect for America* (Garden City, N.Y.: Doubleday, 1961), p. 381.
7. James L. Sundquist, *Politics and Policy: The Eisenhower, Kennedy, and Johnson Years* (Washington, D.C.: The Brookings Institution, 1968), pp. 35–36.
8. Report of Meeting, April 8, 1960, Robert Kennedy Papers, John F. Kennedy Library.
9. Gallup poll releases, January 8, 11, 13, 29, 1961.
10. Harris Survey Reports, Boxes 12–13, Robert Kennedy Papers, John F. Kennedy Library.
11. Schlesinger, *Thousand Days*, p. 479; Stevenson to Kennedy, November 11, 1960, Stevenson Papers, Princeton.
12. Bowles to Kennedy, November 30, 1960, Bowles Papers, Yale.
13. Stevenson, Private Memoranda, December 8 and 10, 1960, Stevenson Papers, Princeton.
14. Haynes Johnson and Bernard M. Gwertzman, *Fulbright: The Dissenter* (Garden City, N.Y.: Doubleday, 1968), pp. 170–171.
15. Arthur M. Schlesinger, Jr., Interview, January 16, 1975.
16. Agnes Meyer to Lehman, January 24, 1961, Lehman Papers, Columbia University.
17. Tom Wicker, *Kennedy without Tears* (New York: Morrow, 1964), p. 60.
18. Richard Bolling, *Power in the House* (New York: E. P. Dutton, 1968), p. 211.
19. Mike Mansfield, Oral History Interview, John F. Kennedy Library.
20. Frank Thompson, Jr., Interview, January 24, 1973.
21. Bolling, *Power in the House*, p. 208.
22. Frank Boykin to Harry Byrd, *et al.*, January 20, 1962, and June 25, 1963, Byrd Papers, University of Virginia.

23. *The New Republic*, January 1, 1962, p. 2.
24. Sorensen, *Kennedy*, p. 363.
25. Sundquist, *Politics and Policy*, p. 85.
26. Mike Mansfield, Oral History Interview, John F. Kennedy Library.
27. Sorensen, *Kennedy*, p. 585.
28. Maurice Rosenblatt to the Executive Board of the National Committee for an Effective Congress, August 1, 1961, Warburg Papers, John F. Kennedy Library.
29. New York *Times*, November 12, 1961.
30. Kennedy to Mrs. Roosevelt, July 28, 1961, Eleanor Roosevelt Papers, Roosevelt Library.
31. Senator Gravel edition, *The Pentagon Papers* (5 vols.; Boston: Beacon Press, 1971), vol. 2, pp. 3–4.
32. *The New Republic*, January 8, 1962, p. 2.
33. Gale McGee to John Bailey, August 24, 1961, Sorensen Papers, John F. Kennedy Library.
34. Bowles, *Promises to Keep*, p. 344.
35. Harris Wofford to John F. Kennedy, July 17, 1961, Sorensen Papers, John F. Kennedy Library.
36. *Newsletter*, Committee of Correspondence, May 12, 1961 and David Riesman to Warburg, February 6, 1961, Warburg Papers, John F. Kennedy Library.
37. Victor S. Navasky, *Kennedy Justice* (New York: Atheneum, 1971), pp. 96–97.
38. Cf., Louis Lomax, *The Negro Revolt* (New York: Signet Books, 1963), pp. 144–159.
39. Arnold Aronson and Roy Wilkins, "Priorities in an Effective Federal Rights Program," February 6, 1961, Sorensen Papers, John F. Kennedy Library.
40. Louis Martin to Ted Sorensen, May 10, 1961, Sorensen Papers, John F. Kennedy Library.
41. New York *Times*, May 17, 1961.
42. Atlanta *Constitution*, May 5, 1963.
43. Louis Martin to Sorensen, May 10, 1961, Sorensen Papers, John F. Kennedy Library.
44. Lee White to the president, November 13, 1961, Sorensen Papers, John F. Kennedy Library.
45. Berl I. Bernhard and William L. Taylor to Lee C. White, February 21, 1963, Sorensen Papers, John F. Kennedy Library.
46. *Ibid.*
47. Robert Divine, "John F. Kennedy," in Frank J. Merli and Theodore A. Wilson (eds.), *Makers of American Diplomacy* (New York: Scribner's, 1974, p. 342.
48. Harry Vranian to Byrd, October 16, 1963, Byrd Papers, University of Virginia.
49. Bartley, *From Thurmond to Wallace*, p. 15.
50. *Ibid.*, p. 43.
51. New York *Times*, April 14, 1963.
52. Robert Sherrill, *Gothic Politics in the Deep South* (New York: Grossman, 1968), p. 277; Marshall Frady, *Wallace* (New York: World Publishing Company, 1968), p. 142.
53. Alexander M. Bickel, *Politics and the Warren Court* (New York: Harper & Row, 1965), p. 59.

54. Atlanta *Constitution*, May 4, 1963.
55. Robertson to Thomas B. Stanley, July 11, 1963, Robertson Papers, Swem Library, College of William and Mary.
56. Robertson to Virginius Dabney, July 1, 1963, Robertson Papers, Swem Library, College of William and Mary.
57. Frank Boykin to Harry Byrd, Howard Smith, *et al.*, June 25, 1963, Byrd Papers, University of Virginia.
58. H. L. Hunt to Byrd, July 11, 1963, Byrd Papers, University of Virginia.
59. Washington *Post*, July 21, 1963; *The Christian Science Monitor*, August 14, 1963.
60. New York *Times*, September 18, 1963; *Wall Street Journal*, September 18, 1963.
61. Stevenson to Agnes Meyer, November 1, 1963, Stevenson Papers, Princeton.
62. Stevenson to Kenneth O'Donnell, November 4, 1963, Stevenson Papers, Princeton.
63. Detroit *News*, November 22, 1963.
64. Lee C. White, Memorandum, November 23, 1963, Sorensen Papers, John F. Kennedy Library.

CHAPTER XI

1. Leonard Baker, *The Johnson Eclipse* (New York: Macmillan, 1966), p. 225.
2. *Ibid.*, p. 12.
3. John F. Kennedy to Willard Wirtz and Antony J. Celebrezze, June 4, 1963, Sorensen Papers, John F. Kennedy Library.
4. Johnson to Sorensen, June 10, 1963, Sorensen Papers, John F. Kennedy Library.
5. Baker, *Johnson*, p. 228; Evans and Novak, *Johnson*, p. 377.
6. A. Willis Robertson to William W. Wharton, July 8, 1963, Robertson Papers, Swem Library, College of William and Mary.
7. Lyndon B. Johnson, *The Vantage Point* (New York: Holt, Rinehart and Winston, 1971), p. 34.
8. O'Brien, *No Final Victories*, pp. 144–146; Schlesinger, *Thousand Days*, p. 973.
9. Roy Wilkins, John F. Kennedy Library Oral History Interview.
10. *Reporter*, January 27, 1966, p. 22.
11. Hugh Sidey, *A Very Personal Presidency* (New York: Atheneum, 1968), p. 245.
12. A. Willis Robertson to Virginius Dabney, October 7, 1964, Dabney Papers, University of Virginia.
13. Robertson to Walter H. Carter, October 2, 1964, Robertson Papers, Swem Library, College of William and Mary.
14. Robertson to Mike Mansfield, October 16, 1964, Robertson Papers, Swem Library, College of William and Mary.
15. Wilkinson, *Byrd*, pp. 258, 260–261.
16. Robertson to Virginius Dabney, November 12, 1964, Robertson Papers, Swem Library, College of William and Mary.
17. *The New Republic*, December 28, 1963, pp. 7–8.
18. Evans and Novak, *Johnson*, p. 397.

19. Lyndon B. Johnson, Interview, June 30, 1970.

20. New York *Herald Tribune*, March 14, 1965; Meg Greenfield, "LBJ and the Democrats," *Reporter*, June 2, 1966, p. 9.

21. David Broder, "Consensus Politics: End of an Experiment," *The Atlantic*, October 1966, p. 63.

22. Joseph C. Goulden, *Meany* (New York: Atheneum, 1972), p. 366.

23. Lewis F. Powell to Preston M. Yancy, November 9, 1967, Virginius Dabney Papers, University of Virginia.

24. Donald R. Matthews and James W. Protho, *Negroes and the New Southern Politics* (New York: Harcourt, Brace & World, 1966), p. 18.

25. *Ibid.*, p. 17; Reese Cleghorn and Pat Watters, "The Impact of Negro Voting on Southern Politics," *Reporter*, January 26, 1967, p. 25.

26. Neal R. Peirce, *The Deep South States of America* (New York: Norton, 1974), p. 187.

27. Len Holt, *The Summer That Didn't End* (New York: Morrow, 1965), pp. 168–169.

28. Mrs. Annie Devine and Edwin King to Heber Ladner, July 20, 1964, Sleeping Car Porters Papers, Library of Congress.

29. Platform and Principles of the Mississippi State Democratic Party, Adopted in Convention in the City of Jackson, June 30, 1960, Sleeping Car Porters Papers, Library of Congress.

30. Challenge of the Mississippi Freedom Democratic Party, n.d., Sleeping Car Porters Papers, Library of Congress.

31. Leslie Burl McLemore, "The Mississippi Freedom Democratic Party: A Case Study of Grass-Roots Politics," unpublished Ph.D. dissertation, University of Massachusetts, 1971.

32. *Ibid.*, p. 147.

33. *Ibid.*, p. 149.

34. Peirce, *Deep South States*, p. 187.

35. William Colmer to John McCormack, June 18, 1965, McCormack Papers, Boston University.

36. Robertson to Spessard L. Holland, April 7, 1964, Robertson Papers, Swem Library, College of William and Mary.

37. Derwood S. Chase, Jr. to Harry Byrd, June 24, 1964, Byrd Papers, University of Virginia.

38. Peirce, *Deep South States*, pp. 187, 317; Bartley, *Thurmond to Wallace*, pp. 9, 11; Chester W. Bain, "South Carolina: Partisan Prelude," in Harvard, *Politics of the South*, p. 604.

39. Charles N. Fortenberry and F. Glenn Abney, "Mississippi: Unreconstructed and Unredeemed," in Harvard, *Politics of the South*, p. 494; New York *Times*, August 10, 1965.

40. Washington *Post*, July 7, 1966, and August 27, 1966.

41. Wilkinson, *Byrd*, p. 261.

42. George Brown Tindall, *The Disruption of the Solid South* (Athens: University of Georgia Press, 1972), p. 64.

43. Barbara Carter, "Sargent Shriver and the Role of the Poor," *Reporter*, May 5, 1966, pp. 18–19.

44. Robert Lekachman, "Death of a Slogan," *Commentary*, January 1967, p. 60.

45. Barbara Carter, "Sargent Shriver," p. 20.
46. Jerald terHorst and Wayne Welch, "The Business Role in the Great Society," *Reporter*, October 21, 1965, pp. 26–32.
47. John C. Donovan, *The Politics of Poverty* (New York: Pegasus, 1967), p. 89.
48. Marvin E. Gettleman and David Mermelstein, *The Great Society Reader: The Failure of American Liberalism* (New York: Vintage Books, 1967), *passim.*
49. Daniel Patrick Moynihan, "The President and the Negro," *Commentary*, February 1967, p. 31.
50. Richard C. Wade, "Blacklash in the Percy Campaign," *Reporter*, January 12, 1967, p. 37.
51. Wilkinson, *Byrd*, pp. 333, 336; Harvard, *Politics of the South*, pp. 67–71.
52. Doris Kearns and Sanford Levinson, "How to Remove LBJ in 1968," *The New Republic*, May 13, 1967, p. 13.
53. *The Commonweal*, December 22, 1967, p. 375.
54. *Reporter*, November 2, 1967, p. 12.

CHAPTER XII

1. David Halberstam, *The Unfinished Odyssey of Robert Kennedy* (New York: Random House, 1969), p. 59.
2. *The New Republic*, March 23, 1968, p. 8.
3. Chicago *Sun-Times*, March 26, 1968.
4. *Ibid.*, March 15, 1968.
5. New York *Post*, February 13, 1968.
6. Goulden, *Meany*, pp. 337–338, 352–353, 356–357, 359–360.
7. *Ibid.*, p. 364.
8. Lewis Chester, Godfrey Hodgson, and Bruce Page, *An American Melodrama: The Presidential Campaign of 1968* (New York: Viking Press, 1969), pp. 293, 654; Richard M. Scammon and Ben J. Wattenberg, *The Real Majority* (New York: Coward-McCann, 1970), p. 191.
9. Frady, *Wallace*, p. 7.
10. *Ibid.*, p. 14.
11. *Ibid.*, p. 26.
12. *Ibid.*, p. 116.
13. *Ibid.*, p. 126.
14. *Ibid.*, p. 142.
15. *Ibid.*, p. 137.
16. Robert Sherrill, *Gothic Politics in the Deep South* (New York: Grossman Publishers, 1968), p. 291.
17. *Ibid.*, p. 293; Chester, Hodgson, and Page, *American Melodrama*, p. 657.
18. Chester, Hodgson, and Page, *American Melodrama*, p. 657.
19. Tom Wicker, "George Wallace: A Gross and Simple Heart," *Harpers*, April 1967, p. 46.
20. Sherrill, *Gothic Politics*, p. 270.
21. John G. Stewart, *One Last Chance* (New York: Praeger, 1974), p. 43.
22. New York *Times*, May 5, 1975; *Wall Street Journal*, April 28, 1975.

23. Chester, Hodgson, and Page, *American Melodrama*, pp. 707, 709.
24. Scammon and Wattenberg, *Real Majority*, pp. 90–91.
25. Chester, Hodgson, and Page, *American Melodrama*, p. 699.
26. Eugene McCarthy, *The Year of the People* (Garden City, N.Y.: Doubleday, 1969), p. 22.
27. Jeremy Larner, *Nobody Knows* (New York: Macmillan, 1970), pp. 73–75.
28. *Ibid.*, p. 155.
29. Gallup, *Polls*, vol. 3, pp. 3155–3156.
30. *Ibid.*, p. 2152.
31. McCarthy, *Year of the People*, p. 173.
32. David Gelman and Beverly Kempton, "New Issues for New Politics: An Interview with Richard N. Goodwin," *The Washington Monthly*, August 1969, p. 28.
33. McCarthy, *Year of the People*, p. 208.
34. Stephen A. Mitchell, Personal Memorandum, April 22, 1968, Mitchell Papers, Truman Library.
35. McCarthy, *Year of the People*, pp. 58–59.
36. Arthur Herzog, *McCarthy for President* (New York: Viking Press, 1969), p. 256.
37. *Ibid.*, p. 274.
38. Jack Newfield, *Robert Kennedy: A Memoir* (New York: E. P. Dutton, 1969), p. 186.
39. Peter B. Edelman, John F. Kennedy Library Oral History Interview.
40. Confidential Source.
41. Halberstam, *Kennedy*, p. 65.
42. McCarthy, *Year of the People*, p. 89.
43. Confidential Source.
44. Stephen A. Mitchell to Eugene McCarthy, March 29, 1968, Mitchell Papers, Truman Library.
45. Ten Eyck Lansing to Mitchell, May 20, 1968, Mitchell Papers, Truman Library.
46. Newfield, *Kennedy*, p. 81.
47. The Pacific Poll, April 13, 16, 1968, Robert Kennedy Papers, John F. Kennedy Library.
48. Scammon and Wattenberg, *Real Majority*, pp. 138–139.
49. *Ibid.*, p. 140.
50. Stephen A. Mitchell, Private Memorandum, July 9, 1968, and Mitchell to Mrs. Gertrude Van Tijn, July 1, 1968, Mitchell Papers, Truman Library.
51. J. Kenneth Galbraith to James P. Warburg, July 9, 1968, Warburg Papers, John F. Kennedy Library.
52. June Oppen Degnan to Eugene McCarthy, June 17, 1968, Mitchell Papers, Truman Library.
53. Larner, *Nobody Knows*, p. 142.
54. Stephen A. Mitchell, Private Memorandum, July 9, 1968, Mitchell Papers, Truman Library.
55. Mitchell, Private Memorandum, June 18, 1968, Mitchell Papers, Truman Library.
56. Don W. Allford to Mitchell, July 8, 1968, and Mitchell to Mrs. Jack Carter,

July 6, 1968, Mitchell Papers, Truman Library; McCarthy, *Year of the People*, p. 193.

57. Theodore H. White, *The Making of the President 1968* (New York: Atheneum, 1969), pp. 278–279.

58. Herzog, *McCarthy*, p. 250.

59. *Ibid.*, p. 259; Albert Eisele, *Almost to the Presidency: A Biography of Two American Politicians* (Blue Earth, Minn.: The Piper Company, 1972), p. 349.

60. New York *Times*, August 28, 1968.

61. *Ibid.*

62. *Ibid.*

63. David Broder, "The Election of 1968," in Schlesinger and Israel (eds.), *Presidential Elections*, vol. 3, p. 3734.

64. National Commission on the Causes and Prevention of Violence, *Rights in Conflict* (New York: Bantam Books, 1968), p. 4.

65. New York *Times*, September 4, 1968.

66. Stephen A. Mitchell to George McGovern, September 10, 1968, Mitchell Papers, Truman Library.

67. *The Nation*, November 4, 1968, p. 462.

68. Stephen A. Mitchell to [?], October 14, 1968, Mitchell Papers, Truman Library.

69. Broder, "Election of 1968," p. 3750.

70. *Ibid.*, p. 3751.

CHAPTER XIII

1. Virginius Dabney to A. Willis Robertson, September 12, 1968, Dabney Papers, University of Virginia.

2. George McGovern, "The Lessons of 1968," *Harper's,* January 1970, p. 43.

3. Phillips, *Republican Majority*, pp. 463, 472.

4. Scammon and Wattenberg, *Real Majority*, pp. 36, 70–71.

5. Samuel Lubell, *The Hidden Crisis in American Politics* (New York: Norton, 1970), p. 278.

6. Frederick G. Dutton, *Changing Sources of Power* (New York: McGraw-Hill, 1971), p. 239.

7. *Ibid.*, p. 225.

8. *Ibid.*, p. 222.

9. New York *Times*, September 2, 1968.

10. *Ibid.*, October 8, 1968.

11. *Ibid.*

12. Steve Denlinger and Jim Durham, "The New Democratic Coalition and the Revitalization of the Democratic Party," included with William W. McKinstry to Stephen A. Mitchell, November 14, 1968, Mitchell Papers, Truman Library; Washington *Post*, January 28, 1968.

13. Gelman and Kempton, "Interview with Richard N. Goodwin," p. 19.

14. New York *Times*, February 15, 1970.

15. Mitchell to Wayne Whalen, October 11, 1968, and Mitchell to Eugene McCarthy, October 21, 1968, Mitchell Papers, Truman Library.

16. O'Brien, *No Final Victories*, p. 289.

17. All references to *Mandate for Reform* were taken from the reprint edition of its insertion in the *Congressional Record* of September 22, 1971, made available through the Democratic National Committee.

18. Stewart, *One Last Chance*, p. 51.

19. New York *Times*, June 29, 1972.

20. Lanny J. Davis, *The Emerging Democratic Majority* (New York: Stein & Day, 1974), p. 207.

21. New York *Times*, January 19, 1971.

22. McGovern letter to Constituents, January 15, 1971, in author's possession.

23. New York *Times*, December 26, 1971.

24. Frank Mankiewicz to Staff, July 23, 1971, Mankiewicz Papers, John F. Kennedy Library.

25. New York *Times*, May 17, 1972.

26. Ernest R. May and Janet Fraser, *Campaign '72* (Cambridge, Mass.: Harvard University Press, 1973), p. 47.

27. New York *Times*, July 10, 1972.

28. Mankiewicz to Gary Hart and George McGovern, June 14, 1971, Mankiewicz Papers, John F. Kennedy Library.

29. Mankiewicz to A. M. Rosenthal, August 27, 1971, and September 2, 1971, Mankiewicz Papers, John F. Kennedy Library.

30. William Haddad to Mankiewicz, June 6, 1972, Mankiewicz Papers, John F. Kennedy Library.

31. New York *Times*, June 30, 1972 and July 10, 1972.

32. *Ibid.*, June 8, 1972.

33. Thomas Eagleton, Interview, January 11, 1973.

34. Theodore H. White, *The Making of the President 1972* (New York: Atheneum, 1973), pp. 229–230.

35. Stewart, *One Last Chance*, p. 16.

36. *Newsweek*, February 5, 1973, p. 92.

37. New York *Times*, December 10, 1972.

38. *Wall Street Journal*, December 8, 1972.

39. New York *Times*, October 23, 1972.

40. Herman Badillo, Interview, January 11, 1973.

41. John R. Rarick, Interview, January 8, 1973.

42. Richard Bolling, Interview, January 24, 1973.

43. Interviews: Edith Green, January 18, 1973; Martha Griffiths, January 17, 1973; John Sparkman, January 23, 1973; Thomas Eagleton, January 11, 1973.

44. *Congressional Record*, 93rd Congress, 2nd Session, September 9, 1974, p. S-16088.

45. *Times*, November 18, 1974, p. 8.

46. *Wall Street Journal*, November 7, 1974.

47. *The Christian Science Monitor*, November 7, 1974; New York *Times*, November 10, 1974; *Wall Street Journal*, November 7, 1974; *Newsweek*, November 18, 1974, p. 25; *Time*, November 18, 1974, p. 8; New York *Times*, November 8, 1974.

48. *Wall Street Journal*, October 31, 1974.

49. Author's personal observation, Taunton, Mass., June 1, 1974.

50. New York *Times*, August 19, 1974.

51. *Ibid.*, December 9, 1974.

52. *Ibid.*, December 10, 1974; R. M. Koster, "Surprise Party," *Harper's* (March 1975), p. 30.

53. New York *Times*, December 14, 1974.

54. *Ibid.*, December 13, 1974.

55. *Wall Street Journal*, May 23, 1975.

56. *Ibid.*, January 28, 1975.

57. *New York Times*, December 14, 1974.

Bibliography

INTERVIEWS

Herman Badillo, January 11, 1973
Lloyd Bensten, Jr., January 23, 1973
Mario Biaggi, January 17, 1973
Jonathan Bingham, February 10, 1973
Richard Bolling, January 24, 1973
Chester Bowles, January 23, 1975
Emanuel Celler, March 21, 1973
William Dunfey, August 7, 1973
Thomas Eagleton, January 11, 1973
James A. Farley, February 19, 1973
Charles Ferris, January 19, 1973
Lloyd K. Garrison, June 19, 1974
Edith Green, January 18, 1973
Martha Griffiths, January 17, 1973
Michael J. Harrington, January 23, 1973
Henry Helstoski, January 11, 1973
Lyndon B. Johnson, June 30, 1970
Phil Landrum, January 16, 1973
Allard Lowenstein, June 16, 1975
Warren Moscow, August 3, 1974

Frank Moss, January 24, 1973
Claude Pepper, January 23, 1973
Dave Powers, April 18, 1973
John Rarick, January 8, 1973
Ogden Reid, January 18, 1973
Abraham Ribicoff, February 5, 1973
Benjamin Rosenthal, January 9, 1973
Arthur Schlesinger, Jr., January 16, 1975
Allan Shivers, January 10, 1975
George N. Shuster, July 3, 1974
John Sparkman, January 23, 1973
Neil Staebler, June 28, 1974
Samuel Stratton, January 23, 1973
Herman Talmadge, January 18, 1973
Frank Thompson, Jr., January 24, 1973
Charles Tyroler II, May 30, 1973
Sidney Woolner, January 18, 1973
Sidney Yates, January 16, 1973

ORAL HISTORY INTERVIEWS

Boston University:
  John McCormack

Columbia University:
  Paul H. Douglas
  Julius Edelstein
  James A. Farley

  W. Averell Harriman
  Hubert H. Humphrey
  Estes Kefauver

Columbia University *(cont'd):*
  Herbert H. Lehman
  Wayne Morse
  New York Elections of 1949
  Charles Poletti

  Eleanor Roosevelt
  Anna Rosenberg
  Sam Rosenman
  Roy Wilkins

Harry S. Truman Library:
  Samuel Brightman
  Oscar Ewing
  Joseph G. Feeney
  Donald Hansen

  Charles S. Murphy
  Sam Rosenman
  Roger Tubby

John F. Kennedy Library:
  Richard Bolling
  Paul H. Douglas
  Ralph Dungan
  Peter Edelman
  Meyer Feldman

  Albert Gore
  George Meany
  Maurine Neuberger
  Herman Talmadge
  Harris Wofford

Lyndon B. Johnson Library:
  J. Lindsay Almond
  Hale Boggs
  Charles Diggs
  Allen J. Ellender
  Francis Keppel

  Clarence Mitchell
  Allan Shivers
  John Sparkman
  Roy Wilkins

MANUSCRIPTS

Boston University,
  Boston, Massachusetts:
  John McCormack Papers

Chicago Historical Society,
  Chicago, Illinois:
  Paul H. Douglas Papers

College of William and Mary,
  Williamsburg, Virginia:
  A. Willis Robertson Papers

Columbia University,
  New York, New York:
  Herbert H. Lehman Papers

Franklin D. Roosevelt Library,
  Hyde Park, New York:

Democratic National Committee
  Papers
  Harley M. Kilgore Papers
  Eleanor Roosevelt Papers
  Henry A. Wallace Papers
  Aubrey Williams Papers

Harry S. Truman Library,
  Independence, Missouri:
  Alben Barkley Papers
  William Boyle, Jr., Papers
  Clark M. Clifford Papers
  Kenneth Hachler Papers
  William D. Hassett Papers
  Charles Jackson Papers
  David Lloyd Papers

Harry S. Truman Library *(cont'd):*
J. Howard McGrath Papers
Stephen A. Mitchell Papers
Charles S. Murphy Papers
Philleo Nash Papers
Harry S. Truman Papers

Historical Society of Wisconsin,
    Madison, Wisconsin:
Americans for Democratic Action
    Papers

John F. Kennedy Library,
    Waltham, Massachusetts:
Democratic National Committee
    Papers
Brooks Hays Papers
John F. Kennedy Pre-Presidential
    Papers
Robert F. Kennedy Papers
Frank Mankiewicz Papers
Theodore Sorensen Papers
Drexel Sprecher Papers
James P. Warburg Papers

Library of Congress,
    Washington, D.C.:
Brotherhood of Sleeping Car
    Porters Papers
Emanuel Celler Papers
Tom Connally Papers
Donald R. Richberg Papers

Lyndon B. Johnson Library,
    Austin, Texas:
Senate Congressional File, U.S.
    Senate, and Civil Rights Pa-
pers of Lyndon B. Johnson

Princeton University,
    Princeton, New Jersey:
John Foster Dulles Papers
Adlai E. Stevenson Papers

Sam Rayburn Library,
    Bonham, Texas:
Rayburn Papers

University of Iowa,
    Iowa City, Iowa:
Henry A. Wallace Papers

University of Kentucky,
    Lexington, Kentucky:
Alben Barkley Papers
Fred Vinson Papers

University of Michigan,
    Bentley Historical Library,
    Ann Arbor, Michigan:
Margaret Price Papers
Neil Staebler Papers
G. Mennen Williams Papers

University of Notre Dame,
    South Bend, Indiana:
Paul Butler Papers

University of Virginia,
    Charlottesville, Virginia:
Harry Byrd Papers
Virginius Dabney Papers
G. Fred Switzer Papers

Yale University,
    New Haven, Connecticut:
Chester Bowles Papers

UNPUBLISHED DISSERTATIONS

Ashley, Frank Watts, "Selected Southern Liberal Editors and the States'
    Rights Movement of 1948," Ph.D., University of South Carolina, 1959.
Boylan, James Richard, "Reconversion in Politics: The New Deal Coali-
    tion and the Election of the Eightieth Congress," Ph.D., Columbia
    University, 1971.

Crosby, Donald F., "The Angry Catholics: American Catholics and Senator Joseph R. McCarthy, 1950–1957," Ph.D., Brandeis University, 1973.

Dunfey, William L., "A Short History of the Democratic Party in New Hampshire," M.A., University of New Hampshire, 1954.

Haney, Richard Carlton, "A History of the Democratic Party of Wisconsin Since World War Two," Ph.D., University of Wisconsin, 1970.

Hargrove, Kenneth Dewey, "Sam Rayburn: Congressional Leader, 1940–1952," Ph.D., Texas Technical University, 1974.

Little, Dwayne Lee, "The Political Leadership of Speaker Sam Rayburn, 1940–1961," Ph.D., University of Cincinnati, 1970.

McLaurin, Ann Mathison, "The Role of the Dixiecrats in the 1948 Election," Ph.D., University of Oklahoma, 1972.

McLemore, Leslie Burl, "The Mississippi Freedom Democratic Party: A Case Study of Grass-Roots Politics," Ph.D., University of Massachusetts, 1971.

McMillan, Edward Lee, "Texas and the Eisenhower Campaigns," Ph.D., Texas Technical University, 1960.

Ness, Gary Clifford, "The States' Rights Democratic Movement of 1948," Ph.D., Duke University, 1972.

Oleon, Sally, "David L. Lawrence, Mayor of Pittsburgh: Development of a Political Leader," Ph.D., University of Pittsburgh, 1958.

Pritchard, Robert L., "Southern Politics and the Truman Administration: Georgia as a Test Case," Ph.D., University of California at Los Angeles, 1970.

Sweeney, James R., "Byrd and Anti-Byrd: The Struggle for Political Supremacy in Virginia, 1945–1954," Ph.D., University of Norte Dame, 1973.

ARTICLES

Ader, Emile, "Why Dixiecrats Failed," *Journal of Politics* (August 1953), pp. 356–369.

Baggaley, Andrew R., "Religious Influence on Wisconsin Voting, 1928–1960," *American Political Science Review* (March 1962), pp. 66–70.

Belknap, George and Angus Campbell, "Political Party Identification and Attitudes toward Foreign Policy," *Public Opinion Quarterly* (Summer 1951), pp. 601–623.

Bendiner, Robert, "The Compromise on Civil Rights—I," *Reporter* (September 6, 1956), pp. 11–12.

Billington, Monroe, "Civil Rights, President Truman and the South," *Journal of Negro History* (April 1973), pp. 127–139.

Boskin, Joseph, "The Revolt of the Urban Ghettos, 1964–1967," *The Annals* (March 1969), pp. 1–14.

Broder, David S., "Consensus Politics: End of an Experiment," *The Atlantic* (October 1966), pp. 60–65.

———, "The Democrats' Dilemma," *The Atlantic* (March 1974), pp. 31–40.

———, "The Fallacy of LBJ's Consensus," *Washington Monthly* (December 1971), pp. 6–13.

Carter, Barbara, "Sargent Shriver and the Role of the Poor," *Reporter* (May 5, 1966), pp. 17–20.

Cater, Douglas, "Estes Kefauver, Most Willing of the Willing," *Reporter* (November 3, 1955), pp. 14–18.

———, "What's Happening to the Democratic Party?" *Reporter* (May 10, 1962), pp. 23–26.

———, "Who Will Speak for the Democrats?" *Reporter* (November 29, 1956), pp. 22–23.

Center, Judith A., "1972 Democratic Convention Reforms and the Party Policy," *Political Science Quarterly* (June 1974), pp. 325–350.

Cleghorn, Reese and Pat Watters, "The Impact of Negro Votes on Southern Politics," *Reporter* (January 26, 1967), pp. 24–32.

Converse, Philip E., Angus Campbell, *et al.*, "Stability and Change in 1960: A Reinstating Election," *American Political Science Review* (June 1961), pp. 269–280.

Cort, John C., "Catholics and Liberals," *The Commonweal* (June 16, 1950), pp. 242–244.

Cosman, Bernard, "Republicanism in the South: Goldwater's Impact upon Voting Alignments in Congressional, Gubernatorial, and Senatorial Races," *Southwestern Social Science Quarterly* (June 1967), pp. 13–23.

Dalfiume, Richard M., "The 'Forgotten Years' of the Negro Revolution," *Journal of American History* (June 1968), pp. 90–106.

Divine, Robert A., "The Cold War and the Election of 1948," *Journal of American History* (June 1972), pp. 90–110.

Fey, Harold E., "Can Catholicism Win America?" *The Christian Century* (eight-part series, November 29, 1944–January 17, 1945).

Gelman, David and Beverly Kempton, "New Issues for the New Politics: An Interview with Richard N. Goodwin," *Washington Monthly* (August 1969), pp. 18–29.

Grantham, Dewey W., Jr., "The South and the Reconstruction of American Politics," *Journal of American History* (September 1966), pp. 227–246.

Greenfield, Meg, "LBJ and the Democrats," *Reporter* (June 2, 1966), pp. 8–13.

———, "The War in Washington: The Temper of the Capital," *Reporter* (March 10, 1966), pp. 29–33.

Halberstam, David, "The Man Who Ran Against Lyndon Johnson," *Harper's* (December 1968), pp. 47–66.

Havard, William C., "Protest, Defection, and Realignment in Contemporary Southern Politics," *The Virginia Quarterly Review* (Spring 1972), pp. 161–184.

Hofstadter, Richard, "The Pseudo-Conservative Revolt," *The American Scholar* (Winter 1954–1955), pp. 9–27.

Hyman, Sidney, "Can a Democrat Win in '60?" *Reporter* (March 5, 1959), pp. 11–15.

———, "The Collective Leadership of Paul M. Butler," *Reporter* (December 24, 1959), pp. 8–12.

Irons, Peter H., " 'The Test is Poland': Polish-Americans and the Origins of the Cold War," *Polish American Studies* (Autumn 1973), pp. 5–63.

Kemble, Penn and Josh Muravchik, "The New Politics and the Democrats," *Commentary* (December 1972), pp. 78–84.

Keyserling, Leon, "Eggheads and Politics," *The New Republic* (October 27, 1958), pp. 13–17.

Koster, R. M., "Surprise Party," *Harper's* (March 1975), pp. 18–31.

Lekachman, Robert, "Death of a Slogan—The Great Society 1967," *Commentary* (January 1967), pp. 56–61.

Lipset, Seymour Martin and Earl Raab, "The Election and the National Mood," *Commentary* (January 1973), pp. 43–50.

Lowry, W. McNeil, "Douglas of Illinois, Liberal with a Difference," *Reporter* (April 17, 1951), pp. 6–10.

McGovern, George, "The Lessons of 1968," *Harper's* (January 1970), pp. 43–47.

Mitau, G. Theodore, "The Democratic-Farmer-Labor Party Schism of 1948," *Minnesota History* (Spring 1955), pp. 187–194.

Moore, John, "The Conservative Coalition in the United States Senate, 1942–1945," *Journal of Southern History* (August 1967), pp. 368–376.

Moynihan, Daniel P., "Bosses and Reformers: Profile of the New York Democrats," *Commentary* (June 1961), pp. 461–470.

———, "The President & the Negro: The Moment Lost," *Commentary* (February 1967), pp. 31–45.

Obenshain, Richard D., "Virginia Election: Direction for the South?" *National Review* (November 9, 1973), p. 1230.

Patterson, James T., "The Failure of Party Realignment in the South, 1937–1939," *Journal of Politics* (August 1965), pp. 602–617.

Patton, James G. and James Loeb, Jr., "Parties: Obstacles to the Formation of a National Third Party," *The New Republic* (February 5, 1945), pp. 202–205.

Raskin, A. H., "Labor's Political Frustrations," *Reporter* (April 7, 1966), pp. 26–33.

Reeves, Richard, "Campaign '72 Windup: A Grass-Roots Report from Queens," *New York* (November 6, 1972), pp. 42–47.

Reichley, A. James, "The Time Bomb Inside the Democratic Party," *Fortune* (February 1972), pp. 126–131.

Royster, Vermont, "American Politics: 1932–1972," *The American Scholar* (Spring 1973), pp. 205–214.

Salmond, John A., "Postscript to the New Deal: The Defeat of the Nomination of Aubrey W. Williams as Rural Electrification Administrator in 1945," *Journal of American History* (September 1974), pp. 417–436.

Sanford, Fillmore H., "Public Orientation to Roosevelt," *Public Opinion Quarterly* (Summer 1951), pp. 189–216.

Schlesinger, Arthur M., Jr., "Which Road for the Democrats?" *Reporter* (January 20, 1953), pp. 31–34.

Sitkoff, Harvard, "Harry Truman and the Election of 1948: The Coming of Age of Civil Rights in American Politics," *Journal of Southern History* (November 1971), pp. 597–616.

Smith, Carl D., and Stephen B. Sarasohn, "Hate Propaganda in Detroit," *Public Opinion Quarterly* (Spring 1946), pp. 45–48.

Smith, George Horsley and Richard P. Davis, "Do the Voters Want the Parties Changed?" *Public Opinion Quarterly* (Summer 1947), pp. 236–243.

Strong, Donald S., "Presidential Election in the South, 1952," *Journal of Politics* (August 1955), pp. 343–389.

terHorst, Jerald, "The Business Role in the Great Society," *Reporter* (October 21, 1965), pp. 26–30.

Walsh, Warren B., "What the American People Think of Russia," *Public Opinion Quarterly* (Winter 1944–1945), pp. 513–522.

West, George P., "The Catholic Issue," *The New Republic* (March 1, 1943), pp. 278–280.

Wheeler, Harvey, "The End of an Era," *Reporter* (February 3, 1953), pp. 31–36.

Wicker, Tom, "George Wallace: A Gross and Simple Heart," *Harper's* (April 1967), pp. 41–49.

Williams, T. Harry, "Huey, Lyndon, and Southern Radicalism," *Journal of American History* (September 1973), pp. 267–293.

Wills, Gary, "What Happened to the Democratic Coalition?" *National Review* (April 8, 1969), pp. 325–327.

Wolfinger, Raymond, "The Development and Persistence of Ethnic Voting," *American Political Science Review* (December 1965), pp. 896–908.

BOOKS

Anson, Robert Sam, *McGovern: A Biography.* New York: Holt, Rinehart and Winston, 1972.

Arnall, Ellis G., *The Shore Dimly Seen.* Philadelphia: J. B. Lippincott, 1946.

Bailey, Stephen, *Congress Makes a Law: The Story Behind the Employment Act of 1946.* New York: Columbia University Press, 1950.

Baker, Leonard, *The Johnson Eclipse.* New York: Macmillan, 1966.

Barnard, William D., *Dixiecrats and Democrats: Alabama Politics, 1942–1950.* University, Ala.: University of Alabama Press, 1974.

Bartley, Numan V., *From Thurmond to Wallace: Political Tendencies in Georgia, 1948–1968.* Baltimore: Johns Hopkins Press, 1970.

———, *The Rise of Massive Resistance: Race and Politics in the South During the 1950's.* Baton Rouge: Louisiana State University Press, 1969.

Berman, William C., *The Politics of Civil Rights in the Truman Administration.* Columbus: Ohio State University Press, 1970.

Bernstein, Barton (ed.), *Politics and Policies of the Truman Administration.* Chicago: Quadrangle Books, 1970.

Bickel, Alexander M., *Politics and the Warren Court.* New York: Harper & Row, 1965.

Binkley, Wilfred E., *American Political Parties, Their Natural History.* 2nd ed.; New York: Knopf, 1951.

Blum, John Morton (ed)., *The Price of Vision: The Diary of Henry A. Wallace, 1942–1946.* Boston: Houghton Mifflin, 1973.

Bolling, Richard, *House Out of Order.* New York: E. P. Dutton, 1965.

———, *Power in the House.* New York: E. P. Dutton, 1968.

Bowles, Chester, *Promises to Keep: My Years in Public Life, 1941–1969.* New York: Harper & Row, 1971.

Brock, Clifton, *Americans for Democratic Action.* Washington, D.C.: Public Affairs Press, 1962.

Broderick, Francis L., *Right Reverend New Dealer: John A. Ryan.* New York: Macmillan, 1963.

Burner, David, *The Politics of Provincialism: The Democratic Party in Transition, 1918–1932.* New York: Knopf, 1968.

Burns, James MacGregor, *The Deadlock of Democracy.* Englewood Cliffs, N.J.: Prentice-Hall, 1963.

———, *John Kennedy: A Political Profile.* New York: Avon Books, 1960.

———, *Roosevelt: The Soldier of Freedom, 1940–1945.* New York: Harcourt Brace Jovanovich, Inc., 1970.

Byrnes, James F., *All in One Lifetime.* New York: Harper & Row, 1958.

Campbell, Angus, Philip E. Converse, *et al., The American Voter.* New York: John Wiley & Sons, 1960.

———, *Group Differences in Attitudes and Votes.* Ann Arbor, Mich.: Survey Research Center, University of Michigan, 1956.

Campbell, Angus, Gerald Gurin, and Warren E. Miller, *The Voter Decides.* White Plains, N.Y.: Row, Peterson and Company, 1954.

Carmichael, Stokely and C. V. Hamilton, *Black Power.* New York: Random House, 1967.

Chalmers, David M., *Hooded Americanism*. Garden City, N.Y.: Doubleday, 1965.

Chambers, William N. and Walter Dean Burnham, *The American Party
Systems: Stages of Political Development*. New York: Oxford University Press, 1967.

Chester, Lewis, Godfrey Hodgson, and Bruce Page, *An American Melodrama: The Presidential Campaign of 1968*. New York: Viking Press,
1969.

Clark, Thomas D., *The Emerging South*. New York: Oxford University
Press, 1961.

Cochran, Bert, *Harry Truman and the Crisis Presidency*. New York: Funk
& Wagnalls, 1973.

Cosman, Bernard, *Five States for Goldwater: Continuity and Change in
Southern Voting Patterns*. University, Ala.: University of Alabama
Press, 1966.

Cotter, Cornelius P., and Bernard C. Hennessy, *Politics Without Power*.
New York: Atherton Press, 1964.

Dalfiume, Richard M. (ed.), *American Politics since 1945*. Chicago: Quadrangle Books, 1969.

———, *Desegregation of the U.S. Armed Forces*. Columbia: University of
Missouri Press, 1969.

David, Paul T., *Party Strength in the United States, 1872–1970*. Charlottesville: University Press of Virginia, 1972.

——— (ed.), *The Presidential Election and Transition, 1960–1961*. Washington, D.C.: The Brookings Institution, 1961.

——— (ed.), *Presidential Nominating Politics in 1952*. 5 vols.; Baltimore:
Johns Hopkins Press, 1954.

Davidson, Chandler, *Biracial Politics: Conflict and Coalition in the
Metropolitan South*. Baton Rouge: Louisiana State University Press,
1972.

Davis, Kenneth S., *The Politics of Honor*. New York: G. P. Putnam, 1967.

Davis, Lanny J., *The Emerging Democratic Majority*. New York: Stein
and Day, 1974.

Divine, Robert A., *Foreign Policy and U.S. Presidential Elections*. 2 vols.;
New York: New Viewpoints, 1974.

Donald, Aida DiPace, *John F. Kennedy and the New Frontier*. New York:
Hill & Wang, 1966.

Donovan, John C., *The Politics of Poverty*. New York: Pegasus, 1967.

Dorough, C. Dwight, *Mr. Sam*. New York: Random House, 1962.

Douglas, Paul H., *In the Fullness of Time*. New York: Harcourt Brace
Jovanovich, 1971.

Dutton, Frederick G., *Changing Sources of Power*. New York: McGraw-
Hill, 1971.

Eisele, Albert, *Almost to the Presidency: A Biography of Two American Politicians*. Blue Earth, Minn.: The Piper Company, 1972.

Eulau, Heinz, *Class and Party in the Eisenhower Years*. New York: Free Press of Glencoe, 1962.

Evans, Rowland and Robert Novak, *Lyndon B. Johnson: The Exercise of Power*. New York: New American Library, 1966.

————, *Nixon in the White House: The Frustration of Power*. New York: Random House, 1971.

Fairlie, Henry, *The Kennedy Promise: The Politics of Expectation*. Garden City, N.Y.: Doubleday, 1973.

Farley, James A., *Jim Farley's Story: The Roosevelt Years*. New York: McGraw-Hill, 1948.

Fenton, John H., *Midwest Politics*. New York: Holt, Rinehart and Winston, 1966.

————, *Politics in the Border States*. New Orleans: Hauser Press, 1957.

Flynn, Ed, *You're the Boss*. New York: Viking Press, 1947.

Frady, Marshall, *Wallace*. New York: World Publishing Company, 1968.

Freidel, Frank, *FDR and the South*. Baton Rouge: Louisiana University Press, 1965.

Fuchs, Lawrence H., *John F. Kennedy and American Catholicism*. New York: Meredith Press, 1967.

————, *The Political Behavior of American Jews*. Glencoe, Illinois: The Free Press, 1956.

Gaddis, John Lewis, *The United States and the Origins of the Cold War*. New York: Columbia University Press, 1972.

Gallup, George H. (ed.), *The Gallup Poll: Public Opinion, 1935–1971*. 4 vols.; New York: Random House, 1972.

Gannon, Robert I., *The Cardinal Spellman Story*. Garden City, N.Y.: Doubleday, 1962.

Garson, Robert A., *The Democratic Party and the Politics of Sectionalism, 1941–1948*. Baton Rouge: Louisiana State University Press, 1974.

Gaston, Paul M., *The New South Creed: A Study in Southern Mythmaking*. New York: Knopf, 1970.

Gerson, Louis L., *The Hyphenate in Recent American Politics and Diplomacy*. Lawrence: University of Kansas Press, 1964.

Gettleman, Marvin E. and David Mermelstein (eds.), *The Great Society Reader*. New York: Vintage Books, 1967.

Geyelin, Philip, *Lyndon B. Johnson and the World*. New York: Praeger, 1966.

Glazer, Nathan and Daniel P. Moynihan, *Beyond the Melting Pot*. Cambridge, Mass.: M.I.T. Press, 1963.

Goodman, Walter, *The Committee*. New York: Farrar, Straus and Giroux, 1968.

Gore, Albert, *Let the Glory Out: My South and its Politics*. New York: Viking Press, 1972.

Gorman, Joseph Bruce, *Kefauver: A Political Biography*. New York: Oxford University Press, 1971.

Gosnell, Harold F., *Grass Roots Politics: National Voting Behavior of Typical States*. New York: Russell & Russell, 1970.

Goulden, Joseph C., *Meany*. New York: Atheneum, 1972.

Grantham, Dewey W., *The Democratic South*. Athens: University of Georgia Press, 1963.

Greeley, Andrew, *Building Coalitions: American Politics in the 1970s*. New York: New Viewpoints, 1974.

Griffith, Winthrop, *Humphrey: A Candid Biography*. New York: Morrow, 1965.

Gunther, John, *Inside USA*. New York: Harper & Row, 1947.

Halberstam, David, *The Best and the Brightest*. New York: Random House, 1972.

———, *The Unfinished Odyssey of Robert Kennedy*. New York: Random House, 1969.

Hamby, Alonzo L., *Beyond the New Deal: Harry S Truman and American Liberalism*. New York: Columbia University Press, 1973.

Harper, Allan D., *The Politics of Loyalty*. Westport, Conn.: Greenwood, 1969.

Hart, Gary Warren, *Right from the Start*. Chicago: Quadrangle, 1973.

Havard, William C. (ed.), *The Changing Politics of the South*. Baton Rouge: Louisiana State University Press, 1972.

Hays, Brooks, *A Moderate Speaks*. Chapel Hill: University of North Carolina Press, 1952.

Heard, Alexander, *A Two-Party South?* Chapel Hill: University of North Carolina Press, 1952.

Herzog, Arthur, *McCarthy for President*. New York: Viking Press, 1969.

Hilsman, Roger, *To Move a Nation*. Garden City, N.Y.: Doubleday, 1967.

Hofstadter, Richard, *The Paranoid Style in American Politics and Other Essays*. New York: Knopf, 1965.

Holt, Len, *The Summer That Didn't End*. New York: William Morrow, 1965.

Hyman, Sidney, *The Lives of William Benton*. Chicago: University of Chicago Press, 1969.

Johnson, Haynes, and Bernard M. Gwertzman, *Fulbright: The Dissenter*. Garden City, N.Y.: Doubleday, 1968.

Johnson, Lyndon B., *The Vantage Point*. New York: Holt, Rinehart and Winston, 1971.

Johnson, Walter, *How We Drafted Adlai Stevenson*. New York: Knopf, 1955

Johnson, Walter and Carol Evans (eds.), *The Papers of Adlai Stevenson*. 4 vols.; Boston: Little, Brown, 1972–1974.

Josephson, Matthew, and Hannah Josephson, *Al Smith: Hero of the Cities*. Boston: Houghton Mifflin, 1969.

Kane, John J., *Catholic-Protestant Conflicts in America*. Chicago: Regnery, 1955.

Kempton, Murray, *America Comes of Middle Age*. Boston: Little, Brown, 1963.

Key, V. O., Jr., *Southern Politics*. New York: Knopf, 1950.

Larner, Jermey, *Nobody Knows*. New York: Macmillan, 1970.

Lash, Joseph P., *Eleanor: The Years Alone*. New York: Norton, 1972.

Latham, Earl, *The Communist Controversy in Washington*. Cambridge, Mass.: Harvard University Press, 1966.

Lee, R. Alton, *Truman and Taft-Hartley: A Question of Mandate*. Lexington: University of Kentucky Press, 1966.

Leiserson, Avery (ed.), *The American South in the 1960's*. New York: Praeger, 1964.

Levy, Mark R., and Michael S. Kramer, *The Ethnic Factor: How America's Minorities Decide Elections*. New York: Simon & Schuster, 1972.

Lomax, Louis E., *The Negro Revolt*. New York: Signet Books, 1962.

Lubell, Samuel, *The Future of American Politics*. 3rd ed.; New York: Harper Colophon Books, 1965.

————, *The Hidden Crisis in American Politics*. New York: Norton, 1970.

————, *Revolt of the Moderates*. New York: Harper & Row, 1956.

MacDougal, Curtis D., *Gideon's Army*. 3 vols.; New York: Marzani & Munsell, 1965.

McCarthy, Eugene, *Year of the People*. Garden City, N.Y.: Doubleday, 1969.

McCoy, Donald R., and Richard T. Ruetten, *Quest and Response: Minority Rights and the Truman Administration*. Lawrence: University of Kansas Press, 1973.

McKinney, John C., and Edgar T. Thomspon (ed.), *The South in Continuity and Change*. Durham, N.C.: Duke University Press, 1965.

McPherson, Harry, *A Political Education*. Boston: Little, Brown, 1972.

Mailer, Norman, *Miami and the Siege of Chicago*. New York: World Publishing Company, 1968.

Marcus, Sheldon, *Father Coughlin: The Tumultuous Life of the Priest of the Little Flower*. Boston: Little, Brown, 1973.

Markowitz, Norman D., *The Rise and Fall of the People's Century: Henry Wallace and American Liberalism, 1941–1948*. New York: The Free Press, 1973.

Matthews, Donald R., *U.S. Senators and Their World*. Chapel Hill: University of North Carolina Press, 1960.

Matthews, Donald R. and James W. Protho, *Negroes and the New Southern Politics*. New York: Harcourt, Brace & World, 1966.

Matusow, Allen J., *Farm Policies and Politics in the Truman Years*. Cambridge, Mass.: Harvard University Press, 1967.

May, Ernest R. and Janet Fraser (eds.), *Campaign '72: The Managers Speak*. Cambridge, Mass.: Harvard University Press, 1973.

Mayer, George H., *The Republican Party, 1854–1966*. 2nd ed.; New York: Oxford University Press, 1966.

Mayhew, David R., *Party Loyalty among Congressmen*. Cambridge, Mass.: Harvard University Press, 1966.

Mazo, Earl, *Richard Nixon: A Political and Personal Portrait*. New York: Harper & Row, 1959.

Miller, Francis Pickens, *Man from the Valley*. Chapel Hill: University of North Carolina Press, 1971.

Miller, Merle, *Plain Speaking*. New York: G. P. Putnam, 1974.

Millis, Walter and E. S. Duffield (eds.), *The Forrestal Diaries*. New York: Viking Press, 1951.

Moscow, Warren, *The Last of the Big-Time Bosses*. New York: Stein and Day, 1971.

————, *Politics in the Empire State*. New York: Knopf, 1948.

Moynihan, Daniel P., *Maximum Feasible Misunderstanding*. New York: The Free Press, 1969.

National Advisory Commission on Civil Disorders, *Report*. New York: E. P. Dutton, 1968.

National Commission on the Causes and Prevention of Violence, *Rights in Conflict*. New York: E. P. Dutton, 1968.

Navasky, Victor S., *Kennedy Justice*. New York: Atheneum, 1971.

Nevins, Allan, *Herbert H. Lehman and His Era*. New York: Scribner's, 1963.

Newfield, Jack, *Robert Kennedy, a Memoir*. New York: E. P. Dutton, 1969.

Novak, Michael, *Choosing Our King*. New York: Macmillan, 1974.

————, *The Rise of the Unmeltable Ethnics*. New York: Macmillan, 1971.

O'Brien, Lawrence F., *No Final Victories*. Garden City, N.Y.: Doubleday, 1974.

O'Neill, James M., *Catholicism and American Freedom*. New York: Harper & Row, 1952.

Ottenberg, James S., *The Lexington Democratic Club Story*. New York: Lexington Democratic Club, 1959.

Parmet, Herbert S., *Eisenhower and the American Crusades*. New York: Macmillan, 1972.

Parmet, Herbert S. and Marie B. Hecht, *Never Again: A President Runs for a Third Term*. New York: Macmillan, 1968.

Paterson, Thomas G. (ed.), *Cold War Critics*. Chicago: Quadrangle, 1971.

Patterson, James T., *Congressional Conservatism and the New Deal*. Lexington: University of Kentucky Press, 1967.

————, *Mr. Republican: A Biography of Robert A. Taft*. Boston: Houghton Mifflin, 1972.

Peirce, Neal R., *The Deep South States of America*. New York: Norton, 1974.

————, *The Megastates of America*. New York: Norton, 1972.

————, *The Pacific States of America*. New York: Norton, 1972.

Phillips, Cabell, *The Truman Presidency*. New York: Macmillan, 1966.

Phillips, Kevin, *The Emerging Republican Majority*. New Rochelle, N.Y.: Arlington House, 1969.

Redding, Jack, *Inside the Democratic Party*. Indianapolis and New York: Bobbs-Merrill, 1958.

Rischin, Moses, *"Our Own Kind": Voting by Race, Creed, or National Origin*. Santa Barbara, Calif.: Center for the Study of Democratic Institutions, 1960.

Ross, Irwin, *The Loneliest Campaign: The Truman Victory of 1948*. New York: New American Library, 1968.

Royko, Mike, *Boss: Richard J. Daley of Chicago*. New York: E. P. Dutton, 1971.

Ryskind, Allan H., *Hubert: An Unauthorized Biography of the Vice President*. New Rochelle, N.Y.: Arlington House, 1968.

Scammon, Richard M. and Ben J. Wattenberg, *The Real Majority*. New York: Coward-McCann, 1970.

Schlesinger, Arthur, Jr., *Kennedy or Nixon: Does It Make Any Difference?* New York: Macmillan, 1960.

——, *A Thousand Days*. Boston: Houghton Mifflin, 1965.

Schlesinger, Arthur, Jr. and Fred L. Israel, *History of American Presidential Elections, 1789–1968*. 4 vols.; New York: Chelsea House, 1971.

Shannon, William V., *The American Irish*. New York: Macmillan, 1966.

Sherrill, Robert, *The Accidental President*. New York: Pyramid Books, 1968.

——, *Gothic Politics in the Deep South*. New York: Grossman, 1968.

Sherrill, Robert and Harry W. Ernst, *The Drugstore Liberal: Hubert H. Humphrey in Politics*. New York: Grossman, 1968.

Shields, Currin V., *Democracy and Catholicism in America*. New York: McGraw-Hill, 1958.

Sidey, Hugh, *A Very Personal Presidency: Lyndon Johnson in the White House*. New York: Atheneum, 1968.

Sindler, Allan P. (ed.), *Change in the Contemporary South*. Durham, N.C.: Duke University Press, 1963.

Smith, Frank, *Congressman from Mississippi*. New York: Pantheon Books, 1964.

Sorensen, Theodore C., *Kennedy*. New York: Harper & Row, 1965.

Starobin, Joseph R., *American Communism in Crisis, 1943–1957*. Cambridge, Mass.: Harvard University Press, 1972.

Steinberg, Alfred, *Sam Johnson's Boy*. New York: Macmillan, 1968.

——, *Sam Rayburn: A Biography*. New York: Hawthorne Books, 1975.

Stevenson, Adlai E., *Major Campaign Speeches*. New York: Random House, 1953.

——, *The New America*. New York: Harper & Row, 1957.

Stewart, John G., *One Last Chance*. New York: Praeger, 1974.

Sundquist, James L., *Dynamics of the Party System: Alignment and Re-*

alignment of Political Parties in the United States. Washington, D.C.: The Brookings Institution, 1973.

———, *Politics and Policy: The Eisenhower, Kennedy, and Johnson Years*. Washington, D.C.: The Brookings Institution, 1968.

Theoharis, Athan, *The Yalta Myths*. Columbia: University of Missouri Press, 1970.

Theoharis, Athan and Robert Griffith, *The Specter: Original Essays on the Cold War and the Origins of McCarthyism*. New York: New Viewpoints, 1974.

Thompson, Hunter S., *Fear and Loathing on the Campaign Trail '72*. San Francisco: Straight Arrow Books, 1972.

Thomson, C. A. H. and F. M. Shattuck, *The 1956 Presidential Campaign*. Washington, D.C.: The Brookings Institution, 1960.

Tindall, George Brown, *The Disruption of the Solid South*. Athens: University of Georgia Press, 1972.

Truman, Harry S., *Memoirs*. 2 vols.; Garden City, N.Y.: Doubleday, 1955–1956.

Tull, Charles J., *Father Coughlin and the New Deal*. Syracuse, N.Y.: Syracuse University Press, 1965.

Underwood, Kenneth Wilson, *Protestant and Catholic*. Boston: Beacon Press, 1957.

Unger, Irwin, *The Movement: A History of the American New Left, 1959–1972*. New York: Dodd, Mead, 1974.

Vadney, Thomas E., *The Wayward Liberal: A Political Biography of Donald Richberg*. Lexington: University Press of Kentucky, 1970.

Vandenberg, Arthur H., Jr., *The Private Papers of Senator Vandenberg*. Boston: Houghton Mifflin, 1952.

Walton, Richard J., *Cold War and Counterrevolution*. New York: Viking Press, 1972.

Watters, Pat, *The South and the Nation*. New York: Pantheon, 1970.

Watters, Pat and Reece Cleghorn, *Climbing Jacob's Ladder: The Arrival of Negroes in Southern Politics*. New York: Harcourt, Brace & World, 1967.

Weil, Gordon L., *The Long Shot: George McGovern Runs for President*. New York: Norton, 1973.

Westerfield, H. Bradford, *Foreign Policy and Party Politics: Pearl Harbor to Korea*. New Haven: Yale University Press, 1955.

White, Theodore H., *The Making of the President 1960*. New York: Atheneum, 1961.

———, *The Making of the President 1964*. New York: Atheneum, 1965.

———, *The Making of the President 1968*. New York: Atheneum, 1969.

———, *The Making of the President 1972*. New York: Atheneum, 1973.

Wicker, Tom, *JFK and LBJ: The Influence of Personality upon Politics*. New York: Morrow, 1968.

———, *Kennedy without Tears*. New York: Morrow, 1964.

Wilkinson, J. Harvie III, *Harry F. Byrd and the Changing Face of Virginia Politics, 1945–1966.* Charlottesville: University Press of Virginia, 1968.

Yarnell, Allan, *Democrats and Progressives: The 1948 Presidential Election as a Test of Postwar Liberalism.* Berkeley and Los Angeles: University of California Press, 1974.

Young, Roland, *Congressional Politics in the Second World War.* New York: Columbia University Press, 1956.

Index